THE
HOUSES
THAT
JAMES BUILT

and

Other Literary Studies

R. W. STALLMAN

Ohio University Press
Athens, Ohio

Copyright © 1961 by R. W. Stallman
Library of Congress Catalog Card Number 60-53548
Manufactured in the United States of America
ISBN 0-8214-0362-1 cloth
0-8214-0363-x paper

Originally published by
Michigan State University Press in 1961;
Reprinted in 1977 by
Ohio University Press

TO THORNTON WILDER

In token appreciation for his sponsorship
of an apprentice poet and critic: 1934-1935

*We go to gain a little patch of ground
That hath in it no profit but the name.*

—HAMLET: IV, iv, 18-19

BY R. W. STALLMAN

CRITIQUES AND ESSAYS IN CRITICISM: 1920-48 (1949)

THE ART OF MODERN FICTION, co-edited (1949, 1956)

THE CRITIC'S NOTEBOOK (1950-1977)

"INTRODUCTION," THE RED BADGE OF COURAGE (1951, 1956)

STEPHEN CRANE: AN OMNIBUS (1952, 1954)

THE CREATIVE READER, co-edited (1954-1962)

STEPHEN CRANE: STORIES AND TALES (1955)

THE ART OF JOSEPH CONRAD: A CRITICAL SYMPOSIUM (1960)

STEPHEN CRANE: LETTERS, co-edited (1960)

THE HOUSES THAT JAMES BUILT (1961, 1977)

AMERICAN LITERATURE: READINGS AND CRITIQUES, co-edited (1961)

THE WAR DISPATCHES OF STEPHEN CRANE, co-edited (1964)

THE NEW YORK CITY SKETCHES OF STEPHEN CRANE, co-edited (1966)

STEPHEN CRANE: A BIOGRAPHY (1968; revised edition 1973)

THE SULLIVAN COUNTY TALES AND SKETCHES OF STEPHEN CRANE (1968: paperback edition 1969)

THE STEPHEN CRANE READER (1972)

STEPHEN CRANE: A CRITICAL BIBLIOGRAPHY (1972)

"STEPHEN CRANE," ENCYCLOPEDIA BRITANNICA (1974)

THE FIGUREHEAD AND OTHER POEMS (1977)

FOREWORD

THERE ARE TWO THINGS THAT I AM CONFIDENT I CAN DO VERY WELL (to quote Dr. Samuel Johnson): *"One is the introduction to any literary work, stating what it is to contain, and how it should be executed in the most perfect manner."* True, it is not difficult to write the introduction to any literary work other than my own, but to introduce my own work is—I find it—very difficult other than to state what it is to contain: see the Table of Contents! *"The other is a conclusion shewing from various causes why the execution has not been equal to what the author promised to himself and to the publick."* What I promised myself at the start was simply a collection of essays. What I've ended with is a collection of essays having interrelationship one to the other. Although I've worked at this book for more than a decade (and so have my students year by year), I'm not yet satisfied with its execution. My difficulties with certain essays remind me of Ryder's remark about a painting he had worked at for a decade: "The sky begins to look interesting."

All in all, I feel rather like Huck Finn: "pretty comfortable all down one side and pretty uncomfortable all up the other."

Selected from a much larger body of my publications in criticism during the past fifteen years (with about half of them published during the last five years), these studies of modern fiction by being juxtaposed gain an added richness. What's gained are the points of kinship established here from one novel to another: kinships in themes, literary parallelisms in techniques, etc. The leitmotif of crossed or confused identity, for example, extends from Crane's *Maggie* and James's *The Portrait of a Lady* and *The Ambassadors* to Conrad's *The Secret Agent;* it becomes brilliantly exploited by Fitzgerald in *The Great Gatsby* and *Tender Is the Night* and by Hemingway in *The Sun Also Rises.* What's discovered here is that Hemingway's *The Sun Also Rises* is built upon the same blueprint Fitzgerald devised for his *Great Gatsby* and that Fitzgerald used it again in his *Tender Is the Night.* By progressing from one work to another in analyses of what's what, by studying these related works, which at the start were seemingly unrelated, what's discovered is their linked analogies—kinships not apparent on first readings.

The novel as poem, the art-novel, becomes a different novel on each subsequent reading. When finally the critic issues his interpretation, the result of years of familiarity with the given work, his interpretation (as Albert J. Guerard remarks) frequently strikes the casual reader as "irresponsible," whereas what's irresponsible is in fact the casual reader. The richer works by virtue of their complexity and inclusiveness resist a final or exhaustive reading. They elicit diverse critical response; no one interpretation satisfies as *the* answer. "In a complete and successful work there are hidden masses of implications, a veritable world which reveals itself to those whom it may concern: to those who deserve it" (Le Corbusier). E. A. Robinson once asked Thornton Wilder whether he had ever read *Macbeth;* Wilder replied that he had—of course. "No," said Robinson; "I mean, have you ever *really* read *Macbeth?*"

"Deeply interested in your finding all that half-buried schematization in *The Great Gatsby,*" Thornton Wilder wrote me some years ago (9 September 1956). "As a 5,000 hour student of *Finnegan's Wake,* of Eliot and Pound, I'm ready to say that such schematization is one of the sole ways left to make the novel valid. I'll reread *Gatsby* before long. Many thanks for your searching paper."

"And you're working in James too. It seems clearer to me all the time that James 'kept himself interested' by writing cryptographically. Read *The Golden Bowl* one way and Maggie and her father were 'in the right'— read it another and they're 'life-denying.' *This quasinarcissistic secret talk goes far back in American literature*—Poe, E. Dickinson, and especially Melville. It's—in part—'contempt for the audience.' "[1]

Cryptographic works ask for and reward the analytic critic. To resolve ambiguities is the critic's function. It is Creative Criticism that I should like to think *The Houses That James Built* achieves.

It's not that these studies of modern fiction intend to compete with the original creations, but rather that they aim to send the reader back to the works which they analyze. Failing in this, they fail to attain their main purpose, which is mainly to illuminate the given work's hidden world, the substructure of multiple interrelationships of images and leit-motifs cryptographically cross-referenced and thus concealed.

Some of these readings require the same apt perception that the given literary work imposes on the casual reader, the wary reader, even the critical reader. They challenge the surface reader to look at the work anew. Attend the text! Like harpooners, critics keep an eye on the text, which is the word. "Pious harpooners never make good voyagers—it takes the shark out of 'em; no harpooner is worth a straw who ain't pretty sharkish" (*Moby Dick,* XVIII).

The past decade has witnessed a shift of critical concern from the analysis of poetry to the analysis of fiction. A decade ago Criticism of Fiction critics were rather scarce. Here, then, is the New Criticism— analytical studies—applied to modern fiction. In the field of modern fiction I believe that *The Houses That James Built* is the first.

If not the first, neither will it be the last; for art "lives upon discussion, upon experiment, upon curiosity, upon variety of attempt, upon the exchange of views and the comparison of standpoints" (Henry James). As for my method of harpooning, I have applied to modern fiction the critical method of the G. Wilson Knight of *The Wheel of Fire* (1930) and *The Imperial Theme* (1931). Knight's Shakespearian studies methodize all

[1] Quoted with the permission of T. N. Wilder.

thematically related images or actions; they catalogue related images by theme or anti-theme and explicate them individually and in interrelationship. All Things in an Interrelationship—the Jamesian canon—informs the works scrutinized in *The Houses That James Built*. While my critical principles and approach derive from Henry James, T. S. Eliot, and the Southern Critics, my debt is to no one critic or school.

These essays interpret anew representative works of fiction by Henry James, Thomas Hardy, Stephen Crane, Joseph Conrad, F. Scott Fitzgerald, Ernest Hemingway, and William Faulkner. That much fashions Part One. Part Two presents "The New Critics," a synthesis of British and American criticism of poetry, and "Fiction and Its Critics," an attack on the Marxian concept of the novel. My argument is for the infusion of the poetic use of language in prose fiction. This controversial issue (not yet resolved) is, I think, the most important critical problem today in the field of fiction criticism.

Published here for the first time are five essays—including "Crane's *Maggie* in Review," which draws upon more than two dozen contemporary reviews of *Maggie* (1896) not known to exist and published here for the first time since their original publication (1896).

As for the title of this book, Henry James discusses the architectonics of his novel as though he were an architect constructing it like a building (fiction is The House of Fiction) and he employs metaphoric use of houses in *The Portrait of a Lady*. My title essay scrutinizes the blueprint of that stately structure. What my punning title—*The Houses That James Built*—intends is that James, both by his canon of art and by his example in fiction, influenced subsequent architects of modern fiction and built thus many more houses than his own.

ACKNOWLEDGEMENTS

TO J. M. Dent and Sons Ltd. for use of quotations from Joseph Conrad's *The Secret Agent.*

TO Alfred A. Knopf, Inc. for reprint of some of my Introductions to my *Stephen Crane: An Omnibus* (Knopf, 1952; Heinemann Ltd., 1954).

TO New American Library for portions of my "Note on the Text of *The Ambassadors,*" reprinted from my edition of *The Ambassadors* (New American Library, 1960).

TO Random House, Inc. for permission to reprint from my Introduction to the Modern Library edition of *The Red Badge of Courage* my "Notes Toward an Analysis of *The Red Badge of Courage*" (copyright 1951 by Random House, Inc.). Also to Random House, Inc. for quotations from William Faulkner's *As I Lay Dying.*

TO the Ronald Press Company for reprint of "The New Critics" from my *Critiques and Essays in Criticism: 1920-1948* (Ronald Press, 1949), which essay was first published in *A Southern Vanguard,* edited by Allen Tate (Prentice-Hall, 1947).

TO Charles Scribner's Sons for quotations drawn from F. Scott Fitzgerald's *The Great Gatsby* (copyright 1925 Charles Scribner's Sons; renewal copyright 1953 Frances Scott Fitzgerald Lanahan) and *Tender Is the Night* (copyright 1934 Charles Scribner's Sons), and also for quotations drawn from Ernest Hemingway's "The Snows of Kilimanjaro" (copyright 1936 Ernest Hemingway) and *The Sun Also Rises* (copyright 1926 Charles Scribner's Sons; renewal copyright 1954 Ernest Hemingway).

TO the Editors of the journals in which some of these essays were first published: *Texas Quarterly, Modern Fiction Studies, Sewanee Review, New Republic, Twentieth Century Literature, Texas Studies in Literature and Language, Kenyon Review.* In particular I wish to thank the Purdue Research Foundation and Maurice Beebe, Editor of *Modern Fiction Studies,* James Colvert and Frederick Eckmann of *Texas Quarterly's* Board of Editors.

TO Mr. Roland Baughman, Head of Special Collections at Butler Library, Columbia University, for permission to publish here for the first time reviews of Stephen Crane's *Maggie* (1896), not reprinted since their original newspaper or magazine appearance (1896).

TO the American Philosophical Society for grant in aid of research on Stephen Crane.

TO my University of Connecticut undergraduate students in American fiction (277, 278) and my graduate students in modern fiction (380), who during each semester since 1949 have disputed, corrected, or approved these interpretations of works scrutinized in this volume, I remain most grateful. In particular Sy Kahn, Herbert Martey, Morton Winston, Margaret Ofslager, and Gerald Guidera.

TO Professor Arthur Waldhorn for reading most of these essays and advising on them; to Professor John Malcolm Brinnin for a footnote item, an identification or source note; to Mrs. Rufus Blanshard for proofreading the final manuscript; and for typing it I thank Mrs. D. O. Hammerberg and Miss Harriet Babcock, English Department Secretaries, and also my wife Virginia.

R. W. Stallman
September 27, 1960   *University of Connecticut*

CONTENTS

Part One

Part Two

PART ONE

HENRY JAMES

The Houses That James Built—*The Portrait of a Lady*

"You'll be my friend till you find a better use for your friendship."
—Madame Merle to Isabel Archer

Many friends, many gloves—for fear of the itch.—Baudelaire

(1)

WHAT HAS NOT BEEN NOTICED about the structure of James's greatest novel is the simple fact that the scene at the opera house which opens Book II of *The Portrait of a Lady* initiates a decline in the heroine's subsequent destiny, a falling away from the romantic arch of her soaring aspirations culminating in the final scene of Book I at Saint Peter's Cathedral. The cathedral and opera house scenes—located at the very center of the novel—are juxtaposed thus to design a reversal of situation, the reversal of Miss Archer's intentions being pivotal to James's ironic rendering of his heroine's romantic and self-deluded quest.

They are the pivotal scenes in the novel's structure: the cathedral, emblematic of the spiritual, and the opera house, emblematic of the mundane; truth in the one, falsity in the other. They are conjoined to elicit the hidden contradiction in Isabel Archer's character and the change in her personality, a change foretold in the decline from cathedral to opera house. Conjoined, they signify the changed heroine: " 'I had treated myself to a charming vision of your future,' Ralph observed. . . . 'I had amused myself with planning out a high destiny for you. There was to be nothing of this sort in it. You were not to come down so easily or so soon' " (Book II, 69).[1] Her coming down is what the opera house scene foretells, while the promise of her high destiny culminates at Saint Peter's. It epitomizes her "desire for unlimited expansion." In the great spaces of the cathedral, strolling across its tessellated acres, where she found herself "beneath the far-arching dome and saw the light drizzle down through the air thickened with incense and with the reflections of marble and gilt, of mosaic and bronze, her conception of greatness rose and steadily rose. After this it never lacked space to soar" (I, 424). After this, on the contrary, her large way of looking at life contracted. "What had become of all her ardours, her aspirations, her theories, her high estimate of her independence and her incipient conviction that she should never marry?" (II, 82). The Isabel Archer of Book I is not the same person as the Isabel Archer of Book II. What accounts for the changed heroine is Gilbert Osmond.

Osmond "has very large ideas" (II, 218), and so has Isabel; but as Ralph Touchett sees him, he is narrow, selfish, and "small" (II, 70). When Osmond told her, after their marriage, that she had too many ideas and that she must get rid of them, "It had been like the bell that was to

3

ring up the curtain upon the real drama of their life." He had told her that before their marriage, but then she had not noticed it. He meant it now—"he would havé liked her to have nothing of her own but her pretty appearance" (II, 194-95). This motif of meretricious appearance is initiated in the scene at the opera, where it seems to Lord Warburton "that Miss Archer had, in operatic conditions, a radiance, even a slight exaltation. . . . Her voice had tricks of sweetness, but why play them on *him*?" (II, 3). Isabel's falsity has its parallel in the meretricious opera: "The opera's very bad; the women look like laundresses and sing like peacocks." In Book II Isabel's tendency to deceive, beginning with the changed heroine of the opera scene, becomes increasingly overt and pronounced. Mask and duplicity dominate the second half of the novel.

"Spread your wings; rise above the ground" (I, 319). So Ralph advised her at San Remo, before she knew Italy's Florence and Rome and Osmond. But even at that time "images of energy"—personified by the exuberant Lord Warburton and the dynamic Caspar Goodwood—"had fallen into the background of our young lady's life" (I, 322). Energy is not manifested in Isabel, except in her "ridiculously active" imagination. Even this fags after she marries the indolent Osmond, that "sterile dilettante"—so the invalid Ralph calls him (II, 71). Ralph and Osmond and Isabel are devoid of energy. Isabel admits "I'm horrid when I'm tired" (II, 17). As though in quest of Energy, Isabel when waiting for Osmond at the Hôtel de Paris indolently browses through a volume of A. M. Ampère having to do presumably with electric current. Osmond prefers her without electric current: "I should like to see you when you're tired and satiated. . . . I shall prefer you in that state" (II, 14). She tires notably *after* her round-the-globe tour with the energetic Madame Merle and her subsequent marriage to a man who rests "on vague laurels" (II, 12). "Your husband's awfully cold-blooded," says Ned Rosier to Isabel during his courtship of Pansy, Osmond's diminutive daughter (II, 122). Cold-blooded also is Isabel, though in a different sense; she is lacking sexual vitality. The tired heroine is frightened again and again by the brash appearance of Caspar Goodwood, Vitality Personified. He expressed for her "an energy—and she had already felt it as a power—that was of his very nature" (I, 162). His eyes—the clear-burning eyes of "some watcher at a window"—attack the frigid Isabel: "they seemed to shine through the vizard of a helmet" (I, 219). If Huntress Archer figures as Diana, goddess of the moon and of chastity, Caspar Goodwood figures as Mars—"he was naturally plated and steeled, armed essentially for aggression" (I, 220). (Caspar *as* Mars explains why Isabel Archer rejects him: "The idea of a diminished liberty was particularly disagreeable to her at present" (I, 162). As Osmond remarks, Caspar Goodwood is "the most modern man we know!" (II, 309). On his visit to Rome, "He looked bigger and more overtopping than of old, and in those days he certainly reached high enough." Not without irony, Osmond expresses surprise that his wife had not married this energetic suitor: "It would have been an excellent thing, like living under some tall belfry which would strike all the hours and make a queer vibration in the upper air. He declared he liked to talk with the great Goodwood: it wasn't easy at first, you had to climb up to the top of the tower; but when you got there you had a big view and felt a little fresh breeze" (II, 288, 293).

Largeness characterizes Caspar; the three men who love her most share the attributes of great spaces, regions of the upper air. It is when she is with Caspar or Lord Warburton or Ralph that the world seems spacious. Grandly she airs her theory to the "perpendicular Bostonian": "The world —with all these places so arranged and so touching each other—comes to strike one as rather small." "It's a sight too big for *me!*" Caspar exclaims (I, 227). Again at the very end, when he pleads with her on the lawn at Gardencourt not to return to Osmond, he argues that "The world's all before us—and the world's very big. I know something about that." She concedes he is right, but utters just the opposite of what she means: " 'The world's very small.' . . . The world, in truth, had never seemed so large; it seemed to open out, all round her, to take the form of a mighty sea, where she floated in fathomless waters" (II, 435). Confusion and incertitude associate in Isabel's mind with images of great space, and when Caspar kisses her she thinks of voyagers shipwrecked "and under water following a train of images before they sink" (II, 436). Her imagination when Osmond proposes to her "hung back: there was a last vague space it couldn't cross—a dusky, uncertain tract which looked ambiguous and even slightly treacherous, like a moorland seen in the winter twilight" (II, 22). And yet her quest has been for life at its most spacious: for infinite vistas, for those soaring conceptions of greatness that she experienced in the far-arching dome of Saint Peter's. After she has "ranged through space" (II, 32), however, she entraps herself in Osmond's small world. During the year of his courtship, "She had effaced herself when he first knew her; she had made herself small, pretending there was less of her than there really was" (II, 191). Then the "gulf had opened between them," and then "she had suddenly found the infinite vista of a multiplied life to be a dark, narrow alley with a dead wall at the end. Instead of leading to the high places of happiness, from which the world would seem to lie below one, so that one could look down with a sense of exaltation and advantage, and judge and choose and pity, it led rather downward and earthward, into realms of restriction and depression where the sound of other lives, easier and freer, was heard as from above, and where it served to deepen the feeling of failure" (II, 189). Here, in sum, is the turnabout, the reversal of situation which the pivotal scenes of the book initiate. What "the sounds of other lives" recalls is the boisterous noise of children in the Dutch schoolhouse across the street from her grandmother's Albany house; there too her life was secluded.

The great space of Saint Peter's brings Osmond to say: "It's too large; it makes one feel like an atom." Its spaciousness contradicts his ego, making him feel small and unimportant. " 'Isn't that the right way to feel in the greatest of human temples?' she asked with rather a liking for her phrase. 'I suppose it's the right way to feel everywhere, when one *is* nobody. But I like it in a church as little as anywhere else.' 'You ought indeed to be a Pope!' Isabel exclaimed, remembering something he had referred to in Florence" (I, 427). Whereas at the start Isabel seemed to Ralph finer "than a Gothic cathedral" (I, 86), she ends, as it were, rather like the "mouldy church" she visits in Rome—"she could almost smile at it and think of its smallness" (II, 327). It is Ralph who makes her feel what her life might have been; the mere fact of his being in Rome "made the blasted circle round which she walked more spacious" (II, 203). On his deathbed at Gardencourt, "when he opened his eyes to greet her it was as if she were looking into immeasurable space" (II, 411). Immeasurable space is the attribute of Lord Warburton, whom she rejects for Osmond's way of life, which she mistook then as "so large, so enlightened. . . . Hadn't he all the appearance of a man living in the open air of the world, indifferent to small considerations . . . ?" It isn't until he has led her "into the mansion of his own habitation, then, *then* she has seen where she really was" (II, 196). She knows then that she has thrown her life away, she whom Ralph thought would be the last person he'd see caught. On hearing of her engagement he warns her ". . . you're going to be put into a cage" (II, 65).

Whereas at Saint Peter's she is still free to move through great spaces and in light (it is the only edifice in Book I that is lighted), at the opera house she is boxed-in. It is a *secondary* theatre, a "large, bare, ill-lighted house," and Isabel and her friends sit in one of the largest boxes. The Verdi opera, "the bare, familiar, trivial opera," is not identified except that it contains a ballet, and of Verdi operas with ballet and bearing in their title a suggestive note having relevance to our heroine's history *Un Ballo in Maschera* and *La Forza del Destino* present likely correlatives. Of these *A Masked Ball* seems more especially suitable in view of the mask-motif which the present scene evokes. Isabel watches the stage "screened by the curtain of the box," in a gloomy corner of which Lord Warburton is symbolically located at the rear, while Gilbert Osmond—just behind Isabel in the large darkened box—remains in front and leans forward. At Saint Peter's, on the contrary, Lord Warburton is at her side; he is the first person she encounters upon passing beneath the huge leathern curtain that strains and bangs at the entrance (I, 424). The reversed position of Lord Warburton in the cathedral and opera scenes has its significance. He is alone with her in making the circuit of the cathedral up to the Pope's choir. She peers into the interior "beyond the dense group in front of her" and sees "the afternoon light, silvered by clouds of incense that seemed to mingle with the splendid chant, slope through the embossed recesses of high windows. After a while the singing stopped"—and now, precisely at this moment when the singing has stopped, she confronts her destiny, Gilbert Osmond. They change places as Lord Warburton recedes; now at her side *is*, so to speak, the Pope himself. "He now approached with all the forms—he appeared to have multiplied them on this occasion to suit the place" (I, 425).

What transpires inside the church contradicts the sanctity of the place.[2] Isabel's friends, after the singing stops, express interest not in the vesper service, but solely in the appearance of Gilbert Osmond as a new admirer of their beloved Isabel, while Henrietta Stackpole declares to Mr. Bantling that Saint Peter's dome is inferior to the dome at Washington. The first of these dissonances is struck when Osmond enters, the secular and the mundane replacing the spiritual.

(2)

In his preface to *The Portrait of a Lady* Henry James discusses his novel as though it were a stately edifice—"It came to be a square and spacious house"—with nothing out of line, scale or perspective in his construction of it. Caspar Goodwood, as we have seen, is rendered as a belfry tower; Isabel, in Ralph's metaphoric view of her, figures as a house: "He surveyed the edifice from the outside and admired it greatly; he looked in at the windows and received an impression of proportions equally fair." This appraisal applies not only to Isabel, but also to *The Portrait of a Lady*. What follows applies not only to Ralph's relationship to Isabel, but also to the reader's relationship to her; she bewilders us, too: "But he felt that he saw it only by glimpses and that he had not yet stood under the roof." In his addiction to metaphors of houses James had, as it were, an edifice complex. The following pre-Freudian image is unwittingly witty: For Ralph "The door was fastened, and though he had keys in his pocket he had a conviction that none of them would fit" (I, 87). Henry James defines the art of fiction as "the house of fiction" and, in retracing his process of composition, he speaks of the artist as though he were the architect and builder of a literary edifice. His own magnificent structure was begun with a single corner-stone—"the conception of a certain young woman affronting her destiny"—and erected brick by brick until the finished whole measured up to the blueprint. After submitting the first three installments for serial publication in *Macmillan's Magazine* (1880), he proceeded to complete the novel *during* its serial publication; what remained to complete the whole permitted no deviations from what had already seen print. He tempted fate and nursed his luck; mind you, no revisions![3] Considering the hazard, one marvels quite as much at *how* he brought *The Portrait of a Lady* to perfection as *at* the achieved masterpiece itself. Second to *Moby Dick*, *The Portrait of a Lady* strikes me as the richest perfection in American literature.

Like the Pyncheon house in Hawthorne's *House of the Seven Gables*, the houses in *The Portrait of a Lady* serve to interpret their inhabitants metaphorically. As artist, James was addicted to the symbolic significance of *things*: a cracked tea-cup, a golden bowl, works of sculpture or painting or music, tapestries, ancient coins. By such minute particulars James renders symbolically the nature and plight of his fictional characters—in *The Portrait of a Lady* notably by the metaphors of gardens and houses. Technically, the gap between James's first and second novels is immense, and it is James's study of Hawthorne that accounts for the difference. James, as every student of Hawthorne recognizes, refined upon Hawthorne's symbolic devices. Midway through *Roderick Hudson* (1874, published 1876) James deposited his hero in the Villa Pandolfini. It is the same villa that Gilbert Osmond inhabits in *The Portrait* (1881); in point of fact, it is the Villa Mercede on the Piazza Bellosguardo (we had an apartment in the Villa Mercede in 1954) and James visited here in 1869 (cf. *Letters*, I, 23). From the formal gardens of the Villa Mercede can be seen "the crenclated tower of a neighboring villa," as James mentions in *Roderick Hudson*. This is Villa Montauto, where Hawthorne once lived. It figures as the crenelated tower that Kenyon visits in Chapter XXIV of *The Marble Faun*. James was especially fond of Hawthorne's Roman allegory, but *Roderick Hudson* is proof enough that at the time of its composition he had not yet read *The Marble Faun*. He had read it, however, by the time he wrote his second novel, *The American* (1877). Here he employs the same symbolic devices as in *The Portrait*, whereas his first novel is devoid of symbolism.

The Villa Mercede (then known as the Villa Castellani) has a lovely *cortile*, reputed to be among the best preserved in Florence, with an ancient well and a private chapel. In *Roderick Hudson* it is described as "a great cool *cortile*, graced round about with light arches and heavily-corniced doors of majestic altitude and furnished on one side with a grand old archaic well." *The Portrait*, employing Hawthorne's chiaroscuro style, presents it as a "high court, where a clear shadow rested below and a pair of light-arched galleries, facing each other above, caught the upper sunshine upon their slim columns and the flowering plants in which they were dressed" (I, 364). It is here that Isabel first visits Osmond, and the setting as rendered with its shadow-sunlight attributes is therefore appropriate symbolically. Roderick Hudson's villa, on the contrary, has no metaphoric import; it is simply a villa—that and nothing more. In *Roderick Hudson* the ample front of the villa ("pierced with windows of various sizes, no one of which, save those on the ground floor, was of the same level as the other"), and the *cortile*, and the rare elevation and great view from the hilltop *piazzetta*,[4] sloping straight up from the Porta Romana—all these things remain unused, symbolically, and merely picturesque. Mary Garland feels merely "the sovereign charm of the place. . . . She fell in love on the spot with Florence, and used to look down wistfully at the towered city from their terraced garden." In *The Portrait* nothing is merely picturesque. Here realism is extended into symbolism by metaphors of designed purpose.

Dark houses metaphorically render Isabel's history. Disillusioned after her marriage to Osmond, she regards her marriage as "the house of darkness, the house of dumbness, the house of suffocation. Osmond's beautiful mind gave it neither light nor air; Osmond's beautiful mind indeed seemed to peep down from a small high window and mock at her" (II, 96). It is from Isabel's point of view that Osmond is associated with "a small high window," whereas in fact Osmond presents to the world quite a different front as we know by the metaphoric Palazzo Roccanera in Rome, the house of the Osmonds. Here, as also at Osmond's Florence villa where he courted Isabel, "the proportions of the windows and even the details of the cornice had quite the grand air." Seen by Edward Rosier when he first courts Pansy, Osmond's daughter, the palace seems like a fortress imprisoning his lady-love. It also imprisons Isabel; but is it not she herself, rather than Osmond, who has imprisoned Isabel Archer? Their Roman palace duplicates the imprisoning house at Albany where Isabel's history began; it is the Albany house all over again, done on the grand style. Beginning with the Albany house and concluding with the Palazzo Roccanera, Isabel ends her quest where she began it—in a house of darkness.

As Ned Rosier rescues Pansy from the Palazzo Roccanera at the end of the novel, so at the start Mrs. Daniel Touchett, like the fairy godmother come to rescue the princess from her dungeon, gives our heroine her freedom from "a kind of domestic fortress." As Mrs. Touchett sees the Albany house, "It's a very bad house"; the parallel is Ned Rosier's view of the Palazzo Roccanera:

> It seemed to him of evil omen that the young lady he wished to marry, and whose fastidious father he doubted of his ability to conciliate, should be immured in a kind of domestic fortress, a pile which bore a stern old Roman name, which smelt of historic deeds, of crime and craft and violence, which was mentioned in "Murray" and visited by tourists who looked, on a vague survey, disappointed and depressed, and which had frescoes by Caravaggio in the *piano nobile* and a row of mutilated statues and dusty urns in the wide, nobly-arched loggia overhanging the damp court where a fountain gushed out of a mossy niche (II, 100).

As for the identity of the Palazzo Roccanera, James tells us only that it is "a high house in the very heart of Rome; a dark and massive structure overlooking a sunny *piazzetta* in the neighborhood of the Farnese Palace." It is the Palazzo Antici Mattei on the Via Michelangelo Caetani; it is a stately and somber structure and, furthermore, it is picturesque. James describes the palace exactly as it is, omitting to mention only the Cortona frescoes in the library. (The Caravaggio painting is *Saint Peter and Saint Paul.*) While it is less ostentatious than either the Palazzo Farnese or the Palazzo Barberini, it is more impressive architecturally than many other palaces in Rome, including the Palazzo Caetani adjoining it. It is for these reasons that James selected this palace and not another, because it suited admirably Osmond's character and Isabel's (particularly her predilection for the picturesque). The palace is in the measure of Osmond's social ambitions; Isabel claims that she "and her husband had chosen this habitation for the love of local colour." Osmond's motive, however, "was as vulgar as the art was great. To surround his interior with a sort of invidious sanctity, to tantalize society with a sense of exclusion, to make people believe his house was different from every other, to impart to the face that he presented to the world a cold originality—this was the ingenious effort of the personage to whom Isabel had attributed a superior morality" (II, 144).

James drew upon actualities for the germinal seeds of his invented, consciously schematized, and frequently cryptographic compositions. The illuminating point is how he fashioned the given situation, person, thing, or house into a designed whole: how he converted the literal to the symbolic. Without mentioning Osmond, James creates a sense of his presence while describing the Osmond villa in Florence: its windows are of "noble proportions, extremely architectural; but their function seemed less to offer communication with the world than to defy the world to look in. They were massively cross-barred, and placed at such a height that curiosity, even on tiptoe, expired before it reached them" (I, 326). That is exactly the Villa Mercede, here converted to a metaphor signifying Osmond. The villa's "antique, solid, weather-worn, yet imposing front had a somewhat incommunicative character." The villa's front is "pierced with a few windows in irregular relations," suggestive of Osmond's own irregular relations (*i.e.*, with Madame Merle). Furthermore, the piazza is "of crooked shape." It is small and "empty."

When Isabel promises to return to the villa another time, she is cornered by Osmond at "one of the angles of the terrace." Angles, crooked piazza, and irregular windows—all hint at Osmond's moral obliquity. Osmond's massive and forbidding villa foretells the domestic fortress of their Roman palace and harks back to the gloomy Albany house. What James says of Osmond's villa also describes Osmond's palace: "There was something grave and strong in the place; it looked somehow as if, once you were in, you would need an act of energy to get out. For Isabel, however, there was of course as yet no thought of getting out, but only of advancing" (I, 364). Advancing not at all, she ends in a house that duplicates the houses of her courtship days, namely Osmond's Florence villa and Mrs. Touchett's Palazzo Crescentini. James's characters in *The Portrait* are analogous one to one another, and so too are their houses. Book I foretells the heroine's career by the houses James built there.

Mrs. Touchett's Palazzo Crescentini, in its antiquity and architectural richness, bears relevant kinship with Osmond's villa and again with his Roman palace. The first edifice faces a narrow street (Mrs. Touchett is morally pinched and decidedly narrow-minded), the second confronts a small and empty piazza, and the third looks down upon a piazzetta adjoining an alley. All three are ancient buildings, and all three give the appearance of history at its most sinister. In the Palazzo Crescentini, as Aunt Lydia tells Isabel during her visit at the Albany house, "three people have been murdered; three that were known and I don't know how many

more besides." The Albany house is "very bourgeois," but Isabel regards it
as romantic. "A great many people have died here; the place has been full
of life." "Is that what you call being full of life?" (I, 34-35). What this
tells us—right at the start of the novel—is that as the Albany house is
empty of life, though not devoid of experience ("people's feelings and
sorrows"), so too will be her final house. At the start when Mr. Touchett
jokingly remarks that Lord Warburton's Lockleigh is a wretched old bar-
rack in comparison with Gardencourt, Isabel confesses: "I don't know—
I can't judge" (I, 22). That she cannot judge houses indicates why she
misjudges both Lord Warburton, for one reason, and Osmond for another. As the terrace front of Osmond's villa has "jealous apertures," so
the rooms likewise signify Osmond: "beautiful empty, dusky rooms . . .
and here and there, through an easy crevice, the splendid summer day
peeped in, lighting a gleam of faded colour or tarnished gilt in the rich
gloom" (II, 26). As though speaking of her brother, Osmond's sister
warns Isabel: ". . . don't sit there; that chair's not what it looks. There
are some very good seats here, but there are also some horrors" (I, 366).
Enchanted both by Osmond and by his villa, Isabel detects no horrors:
"Everything seems to me beautiful and precious."

All the houses Isabel inhabits or visits—including the hotels and the
churches and the opera house—are dimly-lit interiors precisely like the
Albany house of picturesque gloom. Dark and cold is the Palazzo Roccanera, the same as Osmond's villa in Florence, whereby her future is foretold. The cold bedroom of Osmond's palace recalls the cold antechamber
of Osmond's villa, which "was cold even in the month of May" (I, 364).
The rich gloom of his hilltop villa recalls "the dim chambers of Gardencourt where the dark ivy would cluster round the edges of the glimmering
window" (II, 296). But Gardencourt's deepest shadows are not so dark as
the Palazzo Roccanera's nor so chill. The image of Rome chills her, "and
she drew back into the deepest shade of Gardencourt" (II, 421). The par-
lor of the Roman convent is "a vast, cold apartment," and—reminding us
of Pansy herself—there is "a collection of wax flowers under glass" (II,
375). The convent, however, is the only building in Book II that has light.
Nevertheless, the convent is as much of a penal establishment as the
Palazzo Roccanera: "All these departments were solid and bare, light
and clean; so, thought Isabel, are the great penal establishments" (II,
381). The convent's long staircase and enclosed garden provide connection with Mrs. Touchett's Florentine palace, where a great staircase rises
from the court. At Gardencourt likewise the wide-armed staircase is one
of Gardencourt's most striking features. That staircase and the generous
lawn seem emblematic of the friendly and generous nature of the Touchett
family. The enclosed garden at Palazzo Crescentini is a sunny garden
"where nature itself looked as archaic as the rugged architecture of the
palace. . . . To live in such a place was, for Isabel, to hold to her ear all day
a shell of the sea of the past" (I, 355).

A shell of the sea of the past defines Gilbert Osmond, and it's here that she first meets him—at the Palazzo Crescentini. Mrs. Touchett is herself a shell of the sea of the past: An old Florentine, "She's a contemporary of the Medici; she must have been present at the burning of Savonarola, and I'm not sure [says the Countess Gemini] she didn't throw a handful of chips into the flame. Her face is very much like some faces in the early pictures; little, dry, definite faces that must have had a good deal of expression, but almost always the same one." Is not Mrs. Touchett thus an elderly version of Isabel Archer? "Mr. Touchett used to think that she reminded him of his wife when his wife was in her teens" (I, 74).

Isabel wondered "if her aunt repented of having taken her own way so much," and the parallel to this is Isabel's having so much her own way. Again her aunt has "a little moral account-book," and so does Isabel Archer. As characters the difference between Mrs. Touchett and her niece is that Isabel wants everyone to like her, whereas her aunt doesn't care "whether one does or not" (I, 63).[5] If Mrs. Touchett is something out of Ghirlandaio, Isabel—pale and grave during her mourning for Daniel Touchett's death—is represented in Mrs. Touchett's comparison as a solemn Cimabue Madonna (I, 300). Pansy, "as if she were praying to the Madonna," implores Isabel to aid her in Rosier's courtship difficulties, to which prayer Isabel replies as "the Madonna with unusual frigidity" (II, 256). As Pansy so regards Isabel, so too does Henrietta. Henrietta's favorite painting in the Uffizi is the Correggio of the Tribune: the Virgin kneeling before the sacred infant. The implied comparison is Isabel as the Correggio Virgin (II, 237). Osmond owns some Correggios and in marrying Isabel he'll be adding this one to his collections. " 'That's a very pleasant life,' she said, 'to renounce everything but Correggio!' " (I, 383). In the Palazzo Crescentini garden Ralph sits "in the clear gloom, at the base of a statue of Terpsichore—a dancing nymph with taper figures and inflated draperies in the manner of Bernini" (II, 63). Here the implied comparison is Isabel as the Muse of Dancing, but her dancing days are over now that she is engaged to Osmond. After her marriage she admits: "I'm a wall-flower" (II, 210). He had told her before their marriage "that one ought to make one's life a work of art" (II, 15), whereas Ralph at the start saw her as "a real little passionate force" and rejected the thought of comparing her with the finest works of art (I, 86). They have much in common, however. "Ralph had something of this same quality, this appearance of thinking that life was a matter of connoisseurship; but in Ralph it was an anomaly, a kind of humorous excrescence, whereas in Mr. Osmond it was the keynote, and everything was in harmony with it" (I, 377). Isabel seemed to him in harmony with his fine taste; for instance, at the Capitoline Museum in Rome when, just after Lord Warburton has bid her goodbye at the statue of the Dying Gaul, Osmond rejoins her at the statue of Antinous and the Faun, to which she refers as well as to Osmond in remarking that now she's in the best company (II, 6, 9). Very early in Book I James casts his heroine in the simile of "a goddess in an epic," and Osmond, as the Countess Gemini declares, "has always appeared to believe that he's descended from the gods" (I, 391). To Isabel as Diana, Madame Merle figures as Juno or Niobe (I, 249); superior to Diana is Juno, queen of goddesses.

Ralph thinks his cousin "better worth looking at than most works of art," and presumably Isabel, who strikes Ralph as rather presumptuous, thinks the same thing. The irony of Isabel's figuring as a work of art—or finer than "a Greek bas-relief, than a great Titian, than a Gothic cathedral"—is that she is as blind to self-knowledge as she is to art. "I'm absorbed in myself," she confesses to Ralph. "I try to care more about the world than about myself—but I always come back to myself. It's because I'm afraid" (I, 319, 520). What she is afraid of are the very things she professes to believe to be the supreme good fortune, independence and freedom, "the essence of the aristocratic situation," which enable one to be in a better position than others are "for appreciating you." She likes, as she tells Mr. Goodwood, " 'my liberty too much. If there's a thing in the world I'm fond of,' she went on with a slight recurrence of grandeur, 'it's my personal independence' " (I, 228). That she ends trapped in a cage results from her ignorant sensibility. She thinks she knows a great deal about the world, as her Aunt Lydia reports it; "like most American girls; but like most American girls she's ridiculously mistaken" (I, 56). Whereas in fact she reads only the pictured frontispieces of books, not in the library but rather in the so-called office beyond the library in her grandmother's Albany house, "Her reputation of reading a great deal hung about her like the cloudy envelope of *a goddess in an epic.* . . . The poor girl liked to be thought clever, but she hated to be thought bookish. . . . She had a great desire for knowledge, but she really preferred almost any source of information to the printed page" (I, 45). Much later we notice the same criticism: "With all her love of knowledge she had a natural shrinking from raising curtains and looking into *unlighted* corners" (I, 284).

As Caspar Goodwood represents the antithesis of darkness and frigidity, he stands "near the lamp"—at the Albany house where he first courts Isabel (I, 47). Caspar pursues her to London, and "in the dim illumination of Pratt's Hotel," where she tries to lose herself in a book, she turns away from Caspar to look out the window "into the dusky void of the street, where a turbid gaslight alone represented social animation" (I, 225). Except for this dim radiance her apartment is in darkness. But isn't Caspar the lamp for her darkness? As Ralph might have been had she heeded his light: ". . . his face was like a lighted lantern patched with paper and unsteadily held" (II, 58). " 'Ralph will light my candle,' Isabel gaily engaged. 'I'll light your candle; do let me light your candle, Miss Archer!' Lord Warburton exclaimed" (I, 92). After her marriage "the shadows had begun to gather; it was as if Osmond deliberately, almost malignantly, had put the lights out one by one. . . . there were certain corners of her prospect that were impenetrably black" (II, 190). Osmond remarks about his marriage: "We're as united, you know, as the candlestick and the snuffers" (II, 309). Distrust of him, "this was what darkened the world" (II, 189). But Isabel is always seeing herself as the bright thing darkened by others: "These shadows were not an emanation from her own mind: she was sure of that. . . ." She makes the same condemnation of Caspar: "He had come to her with his unhappiness when her own bliss was so perfect; he had done his best to darken the brightness of those pure rays" (II, 279). At the scene of the Roman Forum, in whose excavations Isabel has no real interest despite her professed fondness for history, she retreats from these diggings into the past and, sitting amidst a row of cracked slabs on a prostrate Roman column, she contemplates her future. It is just then that Lord Warburton, who personifies her true future, enters the ruins—"a shadow was thrown across her line of vision" (I, 415). But the fact is that she has no vision, no insight, and that it is she herself who darkens her own light. Her idea of happiness? It is the picture of a carriage in flight, empty of any lover, and rushing over unknown roads in darkness. "Do you know where you're drifting?" Henrietta asks. "No, I haven't the least idea, and I find it very pleasant not to know. A swift carriage, of a dark night, rattling with four horses over roads that one can't see—that's my idea of happiness." " 'Mr. Goodwood certainly didn't teach you to say such things as that—like the heroine of an immoral novel,' said Miss Stackpole. 'You're drifting to some great mistake.' " (I, 235). The "immoral novel" (to identify it) is Flaubert's *Madame Bovary*, from which James has recast Isabel's image of happiness.[6]

Miss Archer, in common with the archeress Diana, has kinship with that artificially-lighted satellite, the dark cold moon. She is a creature of darkness, and the light she needs—the insight—is proffered her in vain by her friends and lovers. As Ralph had held a candlestick while showing her his art collection in the imperfect light of Gardencourt, so Osmond, like the cicerone of a museum, guides her about his art treasures in the imperfect light of his dusky Florentine villa: "Let me take down that picture; you want more light" (I, 375). It is fitting that her courtship with Osmond begins in a palace named after the *crescent* moon, the Palazzo *Crescentini* with its dark front. Don't marry Osmond, Ralph advises her—like Henrietta, he knows she is in the dark. "Wait a little longer"— wait "for a little more light." To which counsel she pertly asks: "Where should my light have come from? From you?" Ralph's reply is: "I might have struck a spark or two" (II, 67). A powerful spark is struck by Caspar Goodwood when he kisses her on the dark lawn of Gardencourt: "His kiss was like white lightning," whereupon she darts from the spot. "But when darkness returned she was free" (II, 436). Her history begins and ends in darkness. So at the Albany house, restless and agitated, she had wandered "from one room to another, preferring the places where the lamplight expired" (I, 41). She rejects Lord Warburton because he is like the sun. Perhaps she recognizes him as such when he returns from the East: "He was splendidly sunburnt; even his multitudinous beard had been burnished by the fire of Asia" (I, 417). Where should her light have come from but from Lord Warburton! Of "bronze complexion, fresh beneath its seasoning," he is "an explorer; he was such a representative of the British race as need not in any clime have been disavowed by those who have a kindness for it" (I, 417). A radiant personality in the zenith of his manhood, a territorial magnate, Lord Warburton "loomed up before her, largely and brightly, as a collection of attributes and powers which were not to be measured by this simple rule [*i.e.*, measuring individual eminence by the simple rule of moral images, "whether they pleased her sublime soul"], but which demanded a different sort of appreciation that the girl, with her habit of judging quickly and freely, felt she lacked patience to bestow. He appeared to demand of her something that no one else, as it were, had presumed to do." Isabel regards him as having "conceived the design of drawing her into the system in which he rather invidiously lived and moved." She resists him because "virtually she had a system and *an orbit of her own*" (I, 143-44). He offers her any place on the globe: "You can pick out your climate, the whole world over" (I, 152). But even this "splendid security so offered her was *not* the greatest she could conceive" —was there ever a more presumptuous heroine! Of "her opportunity she managed to move back *into the deepest shade of it,* even as some wild, caught creature in a vast cage." Isabel as moon resists change and light.

If Henrietta Stackpole, newspaper correspondent for the *Interviewer,* was influenced by her friend's lunar attributes into writing her masterpiece of reporting entitled "Moors and Moonlight" (II, 138), Isabel in turn has been influenced in her predilection for darkness by Madame Merle, who confides "my darkest sides are my tamest. Isabel rose eagerly to the sense of her shades. . . ." "But when I've to come out and into a strong light—then, my dear, I'm a horror!" (I, 278, 275). Once she has detected Merle's mask she knows that Merle is "the product of a different moral or social clime from her own, that she had grown up under other stars" (II, 39). Perhaps because Gemini is a star, the Countess Gemini "was never herself till midnight" (II, 316). After Isabel has rejected Lord Warburton, she figures no longer as moon but rather as a star. Caspar sees her "whirled away into circles from which he was inexorably excluded" (I, 227); and Ralph sums up the changed Isabel Archer in the image of a heavenly body fallen earthward: "You seemed to me to be soaring far up in the blue—to be sailing in the bright light, over the heads of men. Suddenly some one tosses up a faded rosebud—a missile that should never have reached you—and straight you drop to the ground" (II, 70). Once she is married to Gilbert Osmond she is never described by any celestial imagery. One notices that as Isabel's course descends Osmond's rises; *here too is a reversal of situation—now it is Osmond who figures as the moon.* Whereas before her marriage "she had seen only half his nature then, as one saw the disk of the moon when it was partly masked by the shadow of the earth. She saw the full moon now—she saw the whole man" (II, 191).

(3)

All the crucial events in our heroine's career occur in houses—not in gardens.[7] When Lord Warburton proposes to her on the sunlit lawns of Gardencourt, what's in her mind is Caspar's courtship as announced in the letter she has just then finished reading; and when years later Caspar comes to rescue her from her husband, what is in her mind is the visit that Lord Warburton had made but a few minutes ago to bid her goodbye. Just as on that former occasion six years ago when Lord Warburton proposed and she had felt frightened, turning "quickly back to the house," so now again when Caspar—to her terror—kisses her, she takes flight back to a dimly-lit house. She finds sanctuary in dark houses. In gardens she defers "the need of really facing her crisis" (I, 153).

She confronts crises in houses because houses represent the accumulated refinement and corruption of civilization, our tragic history echoing throughout the House of Experience. " 'Who are you—what are you?' Isabel murmured. 'What have you to do with my husband?' " (II, 326). It is inside her own house that she discovers the treachery of Madame Merle. Her first intimation of it occurs on her returning to the Palazzo Roccanera after gathering flowers on the Campagna, a scene of Eden-innocence, whereupon she finds her husband in a compromising situation; he is sitting while Madame Merle stands. "Their relative positions, their absorbed mutual gaze, struck her as something detected" (II, 164). Their conspiracy against Isabel is plotted not in a garden, but in a house—in the Countess Gemini's apartment. Here Osmond sits "half-behind, half-beside Madame Merle's chair" (I, 410), by which situation we know that it is Madame Merle who instigates the plot and who dominates Osmond. She instructs him to proceed to Rome in pursuit of the woman she has chosen for him. His courtship continues at Saint Peter's Cathedral and then at the opera house (the pivotal scenes of the book), and next we find Osmond proposing to Isabel in the Hôtel de Paris in Rome.

Courtships occur both in gardens and in houses, but the proposals resulting in marriage—Osmond's at the hotel and Ned Rosier's in the yellow room of the Osmond palace—occur in houses. Osmond courts Isabel first at Casa Touchett in Florence, then at his own villa and in its garden, and next at the Palazzo Crescentini again. When she returns from the East she lives for three weeks in Madame Merle's Rome apartment, and here in the house of his former mistress Osmond courts Miss Archer. Whereas it is on the sunny lawns of Gardencourt that Lord Warburton proposes to her, it is inside the house—in the art gallery—that she discloses her reasons for rejecting him. Here, as in the previous scene in Gardencourt's art gallery, Isabel reveals again her lack of insight—amidst works of art of which she is ignorant.

Our heroine's destiny is plotted between two deaths. They chart her progress from concealed ignorance to revealed truth. When Ralph is on his deathbed, Isabel unmasks: "She had lost all her shame, all wish to hide things" (II, 414). It takes his dying to bring her round to reveal now the truth of her plight, whereas before this crisis Ralph Touchett, as he had surmised, "should learn nothing; for him she would always wear a mask" (II, 141). At the first death in Gardencourt, while old Mr. Touchett is dying, she meets Madame Merle. She is mistaken about Madame Merle at the start: she supposes her a French lady—in that light she seems to Isabel all the more romantic. Like Emma Bovary, Isabel is possessed of the romantic malady. Gardencourt, Lockleigh, the Casa Touchett, even Osmond's Roman palace, as well as his Florentine villa and Osmond himself—everything strikes Isabel as romantic. She expresses the same illusion about the second-rate Verdi opera as previously she had attached to her grandmother's ugly house in Albany: everything seems to her picturesque. She is impressed by Madame Merle's piano-playing, but what she fails to notice is that it is indiscreet of Madame Merle to be playing the piano while she is a guest in the house of her dying host. As her sincerity is here impugned, so is Osmond's when he proposes to Isabel at the Hôtel de Paris. He proposes in a setting of gaudy décor not appropriate for the declared sincerity of his professed love. Osmond himself recognizes the disparity. His declared sincerity is commented on, as it were, by the mawkishly decorated room of vaulted ceilings "painted over with naked muses and cherubs. For Osmond the place was ugly to distress; the false colours, the sham splendour were like vulgar, bragging, *lying talk*" (II, 13). His declaration of love affects her with the sharp pang that suggests "the slipping of a fine bolt—backward, forward, she couldn't have said which" (II, 18). The answer is backward; for the slipping of the bolt has to do with the bolted door of the unused and condemned half of the Albany house, to which the bolted door was nevertheless the proper entrance. The bolted door signifies her sexual frigidity (even after her marriage, as we know by her cold yellow bedroom, she remains essentially virginal); it signifies also her propensity for sanctuary from life and the proprieties of protective conventions. "You were not to be trapped by the conventional," Ralph moans; Osmond represents Convention personified. The reader is likely to be trapped into accepting Ralph's remark, not noticing that Osmond at the start declared: " 'You say you don't know me, but when you do you'll discover what a worship I have for propriety.' 'You're not conventional?' Isabel gravely asked. 'I like the way you utter that word! No, I'm not conventional: I'm convention itself' " (II, 21). Well, then, she knew what she was marrying; Osmond did not deceive her—she deceived herself. "I'm not in the least stupidly conventional. I'm just the contrary," Isabel told her uncle (I, 78). She ends "stupidly conventional," trapped not by Osmond but by Isabel herself.

"If one's two-sided it's enough," Isabel remarks at Ralph's claim that she is many-sided (I, 213). Her two sides are represented by the house-garden and the dark-light ambivalence of her double consciousness. Her doubleness is represented by the Albany house—it is a double house. The green paper sidelights at the door beguile Miss Archer with unwary optimism. They suggest the Eve-like innocence of one whose nature has about it a "garden-like quality, a suggestion of perfume and murmuring boughs, of shady bowers and lengthening vistas" (I, 72). At the Albany house all of Isabel's visits "had the flavour of peaches" (I, 29). Gardencourt, where "the wide carpet of turf that covered the level hill-top seemed but the extension of a luxurious interior," duplicates the Albany house; for here too nature is at one with the house itself. Gardencourt also has its doubleness. Its true front is not the side facing the river, where life seems in flux; its true front "was quite in another quarter" (I, 3). Both houses deny contact with the outer world. Henrietta Stackpole would like Gardencourt "a great deal better if it were a boarding-house" (I, 133); the Albany house offers "the appearance of a bustling provincial inn kept by a gentle old landlady who sighed a great deal and never presented a bill. Isabel of course knew nothing about bills; but even as a child she thought her grandmother's home romantic" (I, 28). Gardencourt strikes her as romantic, because she cannot judge houses, but it is rather "a dreadfully dull house" (I, 201). To get impressions of *real* life for the *Interviewer,* Henrietta leaves Gardencourt for London. By their incommunicative fronts the Osmond villa and palace link with the deceptive front of the Albany house. It was said of that side of his villa facing the crooked *piazzetta* and commerce with the Florentine world, *"It was the mask,* not the face of the house" (I, 325).

Like Pansy in Rome, Isabel at the Albany house "had no wish to look out, for this would have interfered with her theory that there was a strange, unseen place on the other side—a place which became to the child's imagination, according to its different moods, a region of delight or of terror" (I, 30). Isabel had never opened that bolted door, nor removed that green paper to look into the vulgar street filled with the noisy hum of schoolchildren from the Dutch house opposite her sanctuary. Outside are cosmic treacheries of which Isabel as yet knows nothing, but which overtake her in the end. "A cruel, cold rain fell heavily. . . . Isabel, however, gave as little heed as possible to cosmic treacheries; she kept her eyes on her book and tried to fix her mind." But her mind, like the bolted door, is already fixed. Osmond's proposal disconcerts her because she has a dread of surprises that force her to choose and decide (II, 16). "I don't like such surprises," she tells Caspar when he appears unannounced at the Hotel Pratt apartment (I, 216). Ralph, on the contrary, is "extremely fond of the unexpected" and counts upon Isabel's giving some grand example of it. The grand example is Caspar Goodwood ("I've no plans" [I, 315]). Mrs. Touchett thinks the Unpredictable can't touch her; that is *her* illusion. "You know that as a general thing I don't expect" (I, 295). Expectations, great plans and theories epitomize our heroine, and it is her predilection for fixed ideas that trap her.

Illusions versus realities, theories and fixed ideas punctured by reality, inform the substance of the novel. While James focuses his theme of

Illusions or Appearances versus Reality in his heroine, he exempts none of his personages from the affliction that Isabel suffers from. Even Madame Merle has her illusions, although unlike Isabel she had never had "any illusions of *intelligence*. She hopes she may marry a great man; that has always been her idea. She has waited and watched and plotted and prayed; but she has never succeeded. I don't call Madame Merle a success, you know," says the Countess Gemini. ". . . Her great idea has been to be the incarnation of propriety. She has always worshipped that god. There should be no scandal about Caesar's wife, you know; and, as I say, she has always hoped to marry Caesar" (II, 369, 370). Osmond is no Caesar; that is one reason she would not marry him. Accomplished in the fine arts, as well as in the fine art of manipulating her friends, Madame Merle replaces Henrietta Stackpole as Isabel's ideal. She rejects the artless Henrietta (Caspar and Lord Warburton are in the same category) for the artful Madame Merle, who acts "as if the art of life were some clever trick she had guessed." Although later, when it is too late, she loses "the desire to know this lady's clever trick," at the start she "would have given anything for lessons in this art" (II, 155). Seemingly "imperturbable, inscrutable, impenetrable" (II, 313), Miss Archer conceals because, like the moon, she has no light of her own to offer. "You conceal everything; I haven't really come near you," Caspar complains (II, 318). Though she seems to her friends unpredictable, both in her rejection of Lord Warburton and in her engagement to Osmond, Isabel is as predictable as the moon itself. We know her various phases from the start; one phase is her quest for enlightenment, another is her quest for darkness.

The Portrait of a Lady begins at Gardencourt *and,* by a cutback, at the Albany house (III); it ends with the juxtaposition of Palazzo Roccanera and Gardencourt. In the first set of counterpointed houses Isabel is rescued from imprisonment; in the final set she returns to imprisonment. Our heroine belongs to gardens, places of greenness and innocence with prospects of unknown horizons, release, and freedom, with an amplitude of space for aspirations to soar. That is why James begins the novel on the great lawns of Gardencourt. Her quest for knowledge is figured in a house-image: she seeks to know the innermost rooms, the skeletons in the closets, the ghost at Gardencourt. Ralph keeps "a band of music" in his ante-room; the phonograph "keeps the sounds of the world from reaching the private apartments, and it makes the world think that dancing is going on within" (I, 82). It is the same at the palace in Rome as at Gardencourt; Osmond, like Ralph, conceals from the world his innermost apartment and camouflages the ante-room. So, too, does Isabel. She protests against "this perpetual fiddling; she would have liked to pass through the ante-room, as her cousin called it, and enter the private apartments." But this professed quest to know the inmost rooms is but a passing conceit; she is not an analyst of human personality, and she knows her best friends only superficially.

She is educated by what happens in houses, yet of their significance she is ignorant. "Nothing that belongs to me is any measure of me," she argues, "neither my clothes nor house."

> "I don't care anything about his house," said Isabel.
> "That's very crude of you. When you've lived as long as I you'll see that every human being has his shell and that you must take the shell into account. By the shell I mean the whole envelope of circumstances. There's no such thing as an isolated man or woman; we're each of us made up of some cluster of appurtenances. . . . I've a great respect for *things!* One's self—for other people—is one's expression of one's self; and one's house, one's furniture, one's garments, the books one reads, the company one keeps—these things are all expressive" (I, 287-88).

Madame Merle's bold analysis of human personality echoes the Jamesian theme: we exist only through our relationships with others, living and dead. Ralph Touchett speaks for Henry James, whom he in many ways resembles, in his criticism of Gilbert Osmond: "Yes, but everything is relative; one ought to feel one's relation to things—to others. I don't think Mr. Osmond does that" (II, 71). Neither does Isabel, whereas Madame Merle "existed only in her relations, direct or indirect, with her fellow mortals" (I, 274). She seeks "a large acquaintance with life" (II, 329); Osmond remarks, "I never knew a person whose life touched so many other lives" (I, 341); and Ralph says of her, "she's the great round world itself" (I, 362). These observations by Madame Merle and Ralph define, in fact, the Jamesian canon: All Things in Relationship. "A novel is a living thing, all one and continuous, like any other organism, and in proportion as it lives will it be found, I think, that in each of the parts there is something of each of the other parts" ("The Art of Fiction").

In *The Portrait* every person reflects characteristics of another. Pansy is Isabel in diminutive form. Lord Warburton courts Pansy because she reminds him of Isabel. At the convent Isabel and Pansy embrace "like two sisters" (II, 386); Pansy "looked to Isabel like a childish martyr decked out for the sacrifice" (II, 254). Other martyrs are Isabel herself and Ralph and Lord Warburton. " 'Ah, Lord Warburton couldn't be a martyr even if he wished!' Isabel sighed. 'That's a very poor position.' 'He'll never be a martyr unless you make him one,' said the old man" (I, 130). What Isabel says to Ralph—"I suspect you're a great humbug" (I, 83)—might have been said by Ralph of Osmond, while also it applies to Isabel. "Isabel has a great deal of imagination," Ralph remarks to Mrs. Touchett; "So have you, my son" (I, 261). Mrs. Touchett is as cool as her high cool rooms in the Palazzo Crescentini, and Madame Merle's "own coolness is fabulous. You're a strange woman," says the Countess (I, 390). Serenity characterizes every person in the novel, excepting Caspar and Henrietta and Isabel; it is notably the marked characteristic of Serena Merle and Mr. Daniel Touchett, mellow as "unthumbed fruit" (I, 57). As Pansy and Isabel provide a parallel, so too do Ralph and

Osmond pair off, and Caspar and Henrietta. What Ralph says of Henrietta —"Oh, I understand Henrietta as well as if I had made her!"—defines also Ralph's relationship to Isabel, who as Miranda was created by Ralph as Prospero (I, 169). He figures also as Iago: "I should like to put money in her purse" (I, 260). Iago-Ralph echoes Osmond as villain: "He tried and tried again to make her betray Osmond; he felt cold-blooded, cruel, dishonourable almost, in doing so" (II, 252). "I believe I ruined you," he confesses at the end (II, 414); but Isabel's ruin comes from within herself. "You won't confess that you've made a mistake," Henrietta reproves Isabel (II, 284); whereas Ralph confesses that his life has been a failure, while Madame Merle, like Caspar Goodwood, confesses as much by the fact of her returning to America in defeat. Henrietta, who gives up America to settle in England with Mr. Bantling, provides the novel with its only example of success. In a turnabout of expectations, in contradiction of her professed bias against Englishmen, she marries an Englishman. Isabel disapproves of their levity and marries Osmond, who takes himself seriously; rather than Lord Warburton, who, like Ralph, presents a more frivolous front. Isabel estimates people by appearances. Lacking insight because she has not yet suffered, she naïvely accepts people and things at their declared face-value, or else she stupidly rejects them without making any effort to understand them. She likes façades that favorably embellish her own, façades that somehow make her own appear superior. In this addiction to appearances Isabel is at one with Osmond and Madame Merle, rather than with her friends who see things as they are. Our heroine progresses from bewilderment to insight, earned by suffering; James's theme is Hawthorne's theme.

She succumbs to Osmond's calculated advances because she has had no training in life's realities. She has a fund of preconceived notions, but all her fixed ideas get punctured by the unexpected. *Her quest is for knowledge, but her capacity is for ignorance.* Her creator credits her solely with high spirits: "Isabel Archer was a young person of many theories; her imagination was remarkably active." But what follows undercuts Isabel's meretricious appearance, her gift for appearing as more—or on occasion as less—than she actually is. "It had been her fortune to possess a finer mind than most of the persons among whom her lot was cast; to have a larger perception of surrounding facts and to care for knowledge that was tinged with the unfamiliar." But in fact Isabel is Ignorance Personified. Among the persons who glorify Isabel as an intellectual is Mrs. Varian, her paternal aunt, whose "acquaintance with literature was confined to *The New York Interviewer;* as she very justly said, after you had read the *Interviewer* you had lost all faith in culture. Her tendency, with this, was rather to keep the *Interviewer* out of the way of her daughters; she was determined to bring them up properly, *and they read nothing at all"* (I, 67). Neither does Isabel.

We readers of Isabel Archer's career incline to fashion our portrait of Isabel according to the way it's painted for us by Isabel's friends: Mrs.

Varian, Ralph, Henrietta. We tend on a first reading to ignore the Jamesian criticism of our heroine; our bias is theirs. But notice how James injects the truth: "She only had a general idea that people were right when they treated her as if she were rather superior. Whether or not she were superior, people were right in admiring her if they thought her so; for it seemed to her often that her mind moved more quickly than theirs, and this encouraged an impatience that might easily be confounded with superiority." We readers attribute to Isabel a superiority she does not deserve, and this is because we are persuaded by her friends into acknowledging unearned attributes. We are tricked by their persuasive bias, ignoring meanwhile the author's critical corrective. His voice damns his heroine thus: "It may be affirmed without delay that Isabel was probably very liable to the sin of self-esteem; she often surveyed with complacency the field of her own nature; she was in the habit of taking for granted, on scanty evidence, that she was right; she treated herself to occasions of homage. Meanwhile her errors and delusions were frequently such as a biographer interested in preserving the dignity of his subject must shrink from specifying" (VI, 67). Her biographer *does* specify her errors and delusions, but what deludes us as beginner readers is that they are glossed over by the portraits of Isabel rendered from the multiple viewpoints of her imperceptive, duped friends. James's creation of Isabel Archer amounts to another Flaubertian critique of romantic inspiration.

"Of course the danger of a high spirit was the danger of inconsistency—the danger of keeping up the flag after the place has surrendered; a sort of behaviour so crooked as to be almost a dishonour to the flag. But Isabel . . . flattered herself that such contradictions would never be noted in her own conduct" (I, 69). Our heroine,. however, is riddled by self-contradictions. She "wished Lord Warburton to triumph before her husband, and at the same time she wished her husband to be very superior before Lord Warburton" (II, 268). Caspar, knight-at-arms, comes to rescue her: "She had wanted help, and here was help"—whereupon she rejects him (II, 435). "Her consciousness was so mixed that she scarcely knew where the different parts of it would lead her, and she went about in a repressed ecstasy of contemplation, seeing often in the things she looked at a great deal more than was there, and yet not seeing many of the items enumerated in her Murray" (I, 413-14). Fond of history, she turns her back upon the excavations into the Roman past at the Forum. Seemingly warm and attractive, she is in fact "cold and dry," devoid of sensuality. She wonders "if she were not a cold, hard, priggish person" (I, 157). She strikes even Ralph as rather presumptuous (I, 64), and as Lord Warburton says: "You can't improve your mind, Miss Archer . . . It's already a most formidable instrument. It looks down on us all; it despises us" (I, 111). "Do you think Lord Warburton could make me any better than I am?" she asks Henrietta (I, 194). Aloof, dissociated from others, possessed by a false notion of superiority, she prides herself on the idea of shaping her own destiny, and that is what traps her. "What are my illusions?" she asks Henrietta. "I try so hard not to have any." Addicted to speculations and theories, she lives in a world of her own: "The peril for you is that you live too much in the world of your own dreams. You're not enough in contact with reality—with the toiling, striving, suffering, I may even say sinning, world that surrounds you. You're too fastidious; you've too many illusions" (I, 310). She doesn't want to touch the cup of experience, so she tells Ralph; yet her professed excuse for not marrying Lord Warburton is that in marrying him she'd escape experience. " 'It's a poisoned drink! I only want to see for myself.' 'You want to see, but not to feel,' Ralph remarked" (I, 213). Instincts she possesses not at all; she prides herself on logic (I, 228), but her logic consists of thinking in self-contradictions: "I've heard you take such opposite views," her uncle opines. "I'm on the side of both. I guess I'm a little on the side of everything" (I, 100). That explains the ambivalence of her double consciousness and her characteristic insincerity: "she felt as if her face were hideously insincere" (II, 257).

The naïve Isabel Archer ends inscrutably masked. "You're perfectly inscrutable, and that's what makes me think you've something to hide," so Caspar declares (II, 318). By her promise to him that she'd "probably never marry" and by her saying it "with such a manner that I pretty well believed it" (II, 50), she deceives Caspar *Goodwood*. (As his name implies, he's a plank of American timber, not planed to any smooth finish. So too is Miss Stack*pole*.) By her saying nothing about her engagement to Osmond when writing Ralph, she deceives him: "your silence put me off guard" (II, 65). When Ralph dies at Gardencourt, the doctor looks at Isabel "very hard," as though what killed Ralph was Isabel herself (II, 419). The name of the doctor is presumably "Dr. Despair," as the former doctor whom Ralph discharged is named Dr. Hope! Cruel to Ralph, she has been cruel also to Lord Warburton, as Osmond himself observes (II, 9); her cruelty to honest Caspar needs no comment. She dupes not only Ralph and Caspar and Mrs. Touchett, but also her own sister, concealing from her the affair with Lord Warburton (II, 34). She deceives above all herself: *"I never was what I should be"* (II, 414). At the start, on the contrary, her aspired ideal of selfhood is that "she would be what she appeared, and she would appear what she was" (I, 69). But even at the start (even on this same page), she is characterized by "her inflated ideals, her confidence at once innocent and dogmatic, her temper at once exacting and indulgent, her mixture of curiosity and fastidiousness" (I, 69). That she marries Osmond, whose combination of curiosity and fastidiousness provides a match to her own, is prepared for at the start. *A pretentious and shallow creature duped by her own presumptuous ideas, Isabel is not the person we have been persuaded—all through Book I— to think that she is.* "A part of Isabel's fatigue came from the effort to appear as intelligent as she believed Madame Merle has described her," and her mask is kept up out of fear of exposing her "grossness of perception" (I, 379). Thus, in effect, *she dupes even Osmond.* Her cheek burns in recognition of the fact that "she had really married on a factitious theory" (II, 193), the romantic theory of bestowing her wealth upon a charity case.

So presumptuous is our heroine that her author intrudes to apologize for *his* deception: "if there was a great deal of folly in her wisdom those who judge her severely may have the satisfaction of finding that, later, she became consistently wise only at the cost of an amount of folly which will constitute almost a direct appeal to charity" (I, 145). If the unwary reader—nudged by the author's appeal to charity—exempts Mrs. Osmond from condemnation, it is owing to the point of view by which we are biased—she is rendered mainly from the window of her own consciousness. Other windows—Ralph and Caspar and Henrietta and Mrs. Touchett—reflect light upon her, but even when criticizing their heroine they express sympathetic accord with her plight. Isabel sees her way of life only from her own point of view (I, 167); she resists seeing it from the point of view of her friends. She has the theory that her point of view is strictly American; but as Mrs. Touchett remarks, that is a shockingly narrow outlook. " 'My dear young lady,' said Mrs. Touchett, 'there are as many points of view in the world as there are people of sense to take them.' " "If she had listened to me," says the Countess Gemini about Isabel's marriage to her brother, "she'd have got rid of him" (II, 234). As Ferner Nuhn remarks: Isabel is a victim of innocence, rather than of injustice (*The Wind Blew from the East*, p. 113). What she is innocent of, to define it, is insight. That explains why she marries Osmond and rejects Lord Warburton, resisting the opposition of her friends to her rash engagement. Who plotted it all but Madame Merle! That *she* was deeply false had been discovered long before by Aunt Lydia, "but Isabel had flattered herself at this time that she had a much richer view of things, especially of the spontaneity of her own career and the nobleness of her own interpretations, than poor stiffly-reasoning Mrs. Touchett" (II, 329). "You must be our crazy Aunt Lydia!" exclaimed this brash young thing when first she encountered her benefactor. Brash she is, and short-sighted: "the opposite shore seemed still a part of the foreground of the landscape" (I, 87-88).

In gardens neither crises nor revelations occur, whereas in houses occur *all* the revelations. In Osmond's house his sister discloses to Isabel Osmond's past and the identity of Pansy ("My first sister-in-law had no children"); inside Gardencourt the marriage of Lord Warburton is announced (II, 407); here also Madame Merle unmasks herself: "I'm very ambitious." Inside the convent Madame Merle discloses to Mrs. Osmond that it was Ralph Touchett who made her a rich woman. They confront each other at a window overlooking the convent garden, and it is significant that Isabel, although looking at the garden, does not see it. She has become wholly given over to houses. As she looks out the window her back is turned toward Madame Merle; whereas when she first met Madame Merle at Gardencourt it was the back of this woman who was to become her arch-enemy that presented itself to the imperceptive heroine.

Their positions are also reversed by the fact that Madame Merle, in recognition of being unmasked, "seated herself with a movement which was in itself a confession of helplessness" (II, 379). In this convent scene Isabel stands above her false friend and with her back to her. It was in the Touchett mansion that Madame Merle made known the existence of Gilbert Osmond, whereas it was outside on Gardencourt's lawns that Isabel first met Ralph and Lord Warburton. They represent those attributes of her garden-nature which she, in self-contradiction, rejects.

Mrs. Osmond, on our first view of her *after* marriage, wears a black velvet dress (I, 105), and black was the color of her gown when on the lawns of Gardencourt she first met Ralph Touchett and Lord Warburton (I, 21). The black gown accentuates her dark hair, "dark even to blackness," and her white neck and white hands. "Your sisters, in America, wished to know how you dress. . . . they seemed to have the right idea: that you never wear anything less than black brocade," so Mrs. Touchett reports (II, 406). Her propensity for darkness is manifested even in the gowns she wears. When at the Hotel Pratt she quarrels with Caspar, she wears brown holland (I, 232), but presumably her favorite color is black. When she quarrels with Osmond, who accuses her of deceiving him about Lord Warburton's suit for Pansy's hand, it is presumably a black dress she wears under the white cloak in which she figures as "the angel of disdain, first cousin to that of pity" (II, 276). Those whom she disdained now pity her. That white cloak, worn when Lord Warburton's image is in her mind, associates with the only occasion in her history when she wears white—when Lord Warburton proposed to her she wore a white gown at sunlit Gardencourt. It was "ornamented with black ribbons" (I, 139). After her rejection of Lord Warburton she never again wears a white gown.

Isabel's plight is staged by the alternation of scenes of dark houses and sunlit gardens—when she's in gardens it never rains. Houses, not gardens, dominate the settings of the narrative (by about three to one). James constructs his characters by antitheses and, similarly, their settings—houses and gardens, darkness and great open sunlit spaces. The novelist, as James remarks in one of his Prefaces, is riddled by the Law of Antithesis. It is significant that at Gardencourt, which seems to Isabel "a picture made real," the generous rooms correlate with the generous open lawns whose "deep greenness outside . . . seemed always peeping in" (I, 73). It was the same at the Albany house with its green sidelights, whereas she ends her life in a house without a garden because she has lost that Eve-like innocence which greenness signifies. All houses have gardens except the Palazzo Roccanera, for here she is isolated from her garden-like nature. She returns to it immediately after the shock she receives from Madame Merle's disclosure at the convent; then she visits the Campagna with Pansy to pluck flowers. The only other garden-scene subsequent to her marriage occurs on Gardencourt's darkened lawns. Caspar, proprietor of cotton-mills, regards nature as something to be put to good use; he kisses Isabel in an attempt to win her over to his practical policy. Nature at *Gardencourt,* as the name suggests, combines nature and civilization in a harmonious relationship. This combination is represented by Lord Warburton. But when he proposes to her she feels frightened and turns "quickly back to the house." So again, six years later while sitting on the same bench at Gardencourt's lawn, she takes flight from garden to house—Caspar, to her terror, kisses her. What guides her back to the darkened house is a light—a moral illumination—gleaming from the Gardencourt window down the straight, narrow path. All's dark, but darkness is not without its lights; and, obversely, light is stained by darkness. The light of Madame Merle's eyes "seemed only a darkness" (II, 327). Obversely, dark things flash upon Isabel's mind "with a sudden light" (II, 375). As darkness has its lights, so too have sunlit perspectives—Isabel's bright prospects are darkened by hints of shaded gardens.

Her perverse theory that by marrying Lord Warburton she would exempt herself from life contradicts her nature, for Isabel, as garden, should naturally be conjoined with Lord Warburton, as sun. She cannot be happy, she tells him, by separating herself. "By separating yourself from what?" "From life. From the usual chances and dangers, from what most people know and suffer" (I, 187). "I wish to choose my fate," she remarks with unwitting irony, "and know something of human affairs beyond what other people think it compatible with propriety to tell me" (I, 22). In marrying Gilbert Osmond she weds life at its most artificial, for Osmond's ideal is to live as though life itself were a work of art: "Don't you remember my telling you that one ought to make one's life a work of art? You looked rather shocked at first; but then I told you that it was exactly what you seemed to be trying to do with your own" (II, 15). In Pansy, Osmond accomplishes his ideal: life reduced to a work of art. Looking like "an Infanta of Velasquez," she is all style. Ned Rosier, an art collector like Osmond, regards Pansy as "a Dresden-china shepherdess" (II, 90). Like Isabel, Osmond's artificial daughter is afraid of the sun; only when the sun has moved to the opposite side of the terrace does she enter the garden at their Florence villa. Not to get scorched by the sun, not to face into life, *that* is Isabel's addiction, while her professed philosophy is the obverse of her addiction: "She couldn't marry Lord Warburton; the idea failed to support any enlightened prejudice in favor of the free exploration of life that she had hitherto entertained or was now capable of entertaining" (I, 155). She is afraid of life, and that is the true reason that she rejects Lord Warburton, who is Life Personified; whereas she rationalizes by the romantic notion that "I can't escape unhappiness. . . . In marrying you I shall be trying to" (I, 186). That she ends as she began is signified by the black gown worn subsequent to her engagement to Osmond and by the darkened houses wherein she seeks sanctuary. Even when in gardens she keeps out of the sun. "You're like the stricken deer," Henrietta admonishes her, "seeking the innermost shade" (II, 303).

"You *have* changed, in spite of the impossibility," Henrietta accuses

Isabel (II, 285), and the changed Isabel is signified by the colors she is associated with—from green to red. She begins in the greenness of Albany and Gardencourt; when Osmond proposes to her, however, it is in the rosiness of the pink lamp with its "drooping veil of pink tissue-paper" diffusing "a strange pale rosiness over the scene" (II, 14). To Isabel it is strange because she is familiar only with green and yellow. Red are the damasks that cover the walls in the first room of the Palazzo Roccanera, where Osmond imprisons his bride. Damasks (presumably red) hang also in Madame Merle's apartment in the sunny Pincian. Isabel's yellow bedroom in the Palazzo Roccanera recalls the yellowish-white walls of the Albany house and links thus the end of her history with its beginnings, whereby we know that one strand in her double nature has remained unchanged.

(4)

"But I have the imagination of disaster," Henry James wrote A. C. Benson, "and see life as indeed ferocious and sinister." Osmond is similarly the realist, not given to optimism and lofty ideals. As his name suggests, he is *the world*—and he incorporates its corrupted past. But *is* Osmond the villain of *The Portrait of a Lady?*—*that* is my question. "Osmond is a kind of neurotic aesthete, self-centered, unscrupulous within the limits of safety, and thoroughly unpleasant, *but* the species of terror which Isabel comes to feel in regard to him is absolutely unexplained by any of his actions or by any characteristic described." (I quote here Yvor Winters from his *In Defense of Reason*, p. 332.) True, "He betrayed Isabel in regard to his marriage with her, *but* this betrayal is scarcely a motive for the particular feeling which Isabel comes to experience." Is Osmond—"the terrible Osmond," as F. W. Dupee calls him—the monster that he's made out to be by James's critics? No, I reply; they misread him. I agree—at least on this occasion—with Winters.

As for Osmond's "contempt for his fellow humans, his vanity, his snobbery, his arrogance," what is *evil* about that? True (as Edel says), Osmond "is the acquisitive and predatory individual wholly passive and parasitical," but what is *evil* about that? Is it Evil to marry a woman because she is an heiress? The morally ambiguous person in *The Portrait of a Lady* is rather Madame Merle. Osmond, it is true, is cold and selfish, but so too is Isabel. Frigid, "cold and dry" (I, 71), selfish ("I'm absorbed in myself"), she is given to smugness and a presumptuous superiority (*viz.*, I, 193, 223). As against the notion of Osmond's "thoroughly evil nature," Isabel herself does not accuse him of having done any misdeed or wrong, other than that of having married her for her wealth: "he was not violent, he was not cruel; she simply believed he hated her. That was all she accused him of, and the miserable part of it was precisely that it was not a crime, for against a crime she might have found redress" (II, 190). True, "we detest him thoroughly" (to quote Edel), but that is because he is rendered mainly from the points of view of Isabel, of her friends, and of his enemies; we sympathize with their bias against him at the risk of misinterpreting both Osmond and Isabel. *That* is, by my reading, what the critics of *The Portrait* have done. They damn Osmond while exempting Isabel, whereas in fact she shares with Osmond the same egotism, arrogance, and self-esteem.

"Yes, she had been hypocritical" (II, 195); whereas Osmond was sincere and unpretentious, not pretending to like something he didn't like. "He had succeeded because he had been sincere; it never occurred to her now to deny that" (II, 191). It is Isabel, our deceptive heroine, who is pretentious and insincere. "There were times when she almost pitied him; for if she had not deceived him in intention she understood how completely she must have done so in fact" (II, 191). *The deceiver is, then, the heroine herself, as well as the so-called villain she marries.* If Osmond has been hypocritical, so too has Isabel. Ralph sees him as a hypocrite, but then that is Ralph's point of view, his theory; and Ralph "was very skilful in fitting the facts to his theory" (II, 145). His theory of Osmond?

> Everything he did was a *pose*—*pose* so subtly considered that if one were not on the lookout one mistook it for impulse. Ralph had never met a man who lived so much in the land of consideration. His tastes, his studies, his accomplishments, his collections, were all for a purpose. His life on his hill-top at Florence had been the conscious attitude of years. His solitude, his ennui, his love for his daughter, his good manners, his bad manners, were so many features of a mental image constantly present to him as a model of impertinence and mystification. His ambition was not to please the world, but to please himself by exciting the world's curiosity and then declining to satisfy it. It had made him feel great, ever, to play the world a trick (II, 145).

All that this tells us is that Osmond succeeds admirably in the attainment of making his life a work of art; he appeals only to those who subscribe to the same theory—Isabel Archer, for one. She too is given to *pose*. When Osmond tricked Isabel into marriage (to quote Ralph's metaphor), he tricked the world; for "the gullible world was in a manner embodied in poor Isabel" (II, 146). Osmond, representing the world with its corrupted past, and Isabel, representing the gullible world, fashion thus the two sides of the coin. As neither side is exempted from pose or mask, they share identities. Osmond's other self—the true Gemini—is not his sister, the Countess Gemini; it is rather his wife. They represent opposite faces of the moon, a dead planet devoid of energy.

Osmond suggests, "fine gold coin that he was, no stamp nor emblem of the common vintage that provides for general circulation; he was the elegant complicated medal struck off for a special occasion" (I, 329). Osmond as gold coin possesses integrity. Although he traps Isabel Archer into a false marriage and masks the truth, he remains always true to himself, not pretending to be otherwise. He appears as not the person he is; he schemes to impress the gullible world, and he succeeds—Isabel is victimized by Osmond's mask. But Isabel wears a mask of her own; hers is the mask of innocence. Even Osmond is duped. "He had discovered that she was so different, that she was not what he had believed she would prove to be" (II, 190). Osmond stands exempt from Isabel's brand of hypocrisy: violence in her impulses, crudity; "it seemed to him that she even spoke faster, moved faster, breathed faster, than before her marriage. Certainly she had fallen into exaggerations—she who used to care so much for pure truth" (II, 143). As she admits, "the sole source of her mistake had been within herself. There had been no plot, no snare; she had looked and considered and chosen" (II, 160). But even in this she is mistaken, for Madame Merle had plotted Isabel's destiny. Ensnared by her conspiracy with Osmond, Isabel is ensnared also by her own gullibility.

She is duped by her mistaken conception of Osmond, as also she is duped by her preconceived and mistaken idea of Madame Merle. It was Isabel who disguised herself, rather than Osmond. It is Isabel who expects great things of her husband. Madame Merle had the same aspirations, but when Osmond showed her his sketch of the Venetian Alps (emblematic of the great heights they once had aspired to), she ridicules his watercolor sketch as though to say that his prospects strike her as insignificant, a falling-off from the scope of her ambitions. "The desire to have something or other to show for his 'parts'—to show somehow or other—had been the dream of his youth; but as the years went on the conditions attached to any marked proof of rarity had affected him more and more as gross and detestable" (II, 12). Although Osmond looks like a prince in disguise, he's a prince "who has abdicated in a fit of fastidiousness and has been in a state of disgust ever since," so Ralph pictures him to his cousin. "He has a great dread of vulgarity; that's his special line; he hasn't any other that I know of" (I, 358). In his conceptions of the aristocratic life, "it was altogether a thing of forms, a conscious, calculated attitude" (II, 198). Isabel thought of him as "the first gentleman in Europe," and that indeed "was the reason she had married him. But when she began to see what it implied she drew back; there was more in the bond than she had meant to put her name to. It implied a sovereign contempt for every one but some three or four exalted people whom he envied, and for everything in the world but half a dozen ideas of his own" (II, 197). She comes to believe that "he despised her; she had no traditions and the moral horizon of a Unitarian minister" (II, 201). "The real offence, as she ultimately perceived, was her having a mind of her own at all. Her mind was to be his—attached to his own like a small garden-plot to a deer-park" (II, 200). In that garden-plot Osmond's "egotism lay hidden like a serpent in a bank of flowers" (II, 196), but the Eve we sympathize with is not without egotism herself, nor without deceptions; "she had deceived him at the first" (II, 202). "A mind more ingenious, more pliant, more cultivated, more trained to admirable exercises, she had not encountered; and it was this exquisite instrument that she had now to reckon with" (II, 194).

What she must reckon with is a person quite different from what she had imagined him to be, the difference being Isabel's full view of him at last. Her view of him changes, whereas Osmond remains the same now as when first she fell under his spell. No, he "was not changed; *he had not disguised himself, during his year of courtship, any more than she*" (II, 191).

Osmond is a realist; he is the realist undermining the presumptuous fixed ideas of our romantic heroine. That is the designed purpose of our so-called villain. He opens her eyes to the realities: "he pointed out to her so much of the baseness and shabbiness of life, opened her eyes so wide to the stupidity, the depravity, the ignorance of mankind, that she had been properly impressed with the infinite vulgarity of things and of the virtue of keeping one's self unspotted by it." He trains her to share his dread of vulgarity, his worship of traditions and the forms they consecrate; she assents to this and marches to his tune—"she who of old had been so free of step, so desultory, so devious, so much the reverse of processional" (II, 197, 199). The paradox in Osmond is that the base, ignoble world he scorns is what he nevertheless lives for: "one was to keep it forever in one's eye, in order not to enlighten or convert or redeem it, but to extract from it some recognition of one's superiority" (II, 197). Under "the guise of caring for intrinsic values Osmond lived exclusively for the world." After Osmond has awakened her to the realities, including the truth about herself, she no longer regards her husband as clever: "He has a genius for upholstery." The Osmonds were strangely married; "it was a horrible life."

Contra Edel ("The only truly hateful character in the story is Gilbert Osmond"), far more villainous and hateful is the contemptible Madame Merle. It is she who initiates and directs the plot to have her former lover marry the American heiress so that their illegitimate daughter Pansy may attain thereby the proper conditions for courtship and marriage according to their social ambitions. It is Madame Merle who manipulates both Osmond and Isabel. While Osmond cannot be exonerated from the charge of an adulterous affair, the burden of duplicity rests mainly with Madame Merle. She cuckolded her Swiss husband and, during her adulterous liaison with Osmond, she encouraged Ralph Touchett into a brief infatuation for her, an affair which Osmond knew nothing about. Added to this duplicity is her characteristic insincerity in establishing friendships solely for what use she can put them to for her own purposes. When she first proposes that Osmond court Miss Archer, what he remarks in hesitation at her plot echoes what Ralph himself later says: " 'Isn't she meant for something better than that?' 'I don't pretend to know what people are meant for,' said Madame Merle. 'I only know what I can do with them' " (I, 345).

The final point to be made in defense of Gilbert Osmond is that only two persons in the entire novel speak well of him: Isabel before her marriage, seeing him as "a very good and very honourable man," and Caspar Goodwood, who after her marriage thought Osmond "very well-informed *and obliging and more than he had supposed like the person whom Isabel*

Archer would naturally marry" (II, 310). Except for Caspar, Osmond's only friend, everyone speaks ill of Osmond—especially his own sister. Of course he's a gentleman; the Countess can't deny that much, but she damns him for his unfounded pretentions: "What has he ever done? . . . nothing, nothing, nothing" (I, 391). " 'I'm sure then he has been odious!' the Countess cried. 'Did he say he was glad poor Mr. Touchett's dying?' " (II, 359). What Osmond said is simply that he forbade Isabel to go to England to visit Ralph on his death-bed, but the malicious slander sticks in the reader's mind. Osmond wasn't odious, except from Isabel's point of view; from Osmond's it is improper for his wife to make such a trip: "I dislike, from the bottom of my soul, what you intend to do. It's dishonourable; it's indelicate: it's indecent. . . . I've an ideal of what my wife should do and should not do. She should not travel across Europe alone, in defiance of my deepest desire, to sit at the bedside of other men." His opposition is for decorum's sake, whereas to Isabel it's "calculated. It's malignant." But we forget that Osmond does not know that it was Ralph who bestowed upon Isabel her fortune; that's why he insists—not knowing that Ralph was her benefactor—that her cousin is nothing to him; "he's nothing to us. You smile most expressively when I talk about *us*, but I assure you that *we, we*, Mrs. Osmond, is all I know. I take our marriage seriously; you appear to have found a way of not doing so. I'm not aware that we're divorced or separated; for me we're indissolubly united" (II, 355-56). He speaks sincerely, without sarcasm, "in the name of something sacred and precious—the observance of a magnificent form." Isabel suspects him of "blasphemous sophistry," but finally concedes that "in his wish to preserve appearances he was after all sincere, and that this, as far as it went, was a merit" (II, 356-57).

So then Osmond, *contra* his many critics, does have his merits. When Ned Rosier exclaims to Isabel, "Ah, what a monster you make him out!" we tend to ignore the point of view here expressed: "you" should be in italics. At the very end Isabel repudiates not Osmond, but rather Caspar: " 'You can't deceive me any more; for God's sake be honest with a man who's so honest with you. You're the most unhappy of women, and your husband's the deadliest of fiends.' She turned on him as if he had struck her. 'Are you mad?' she cried" (II, 432). Notice how in saying this she but echoes her husband, uttering the same words to Caspar as Osmond rebuked her with when their relationship reached its crisis: " 'I suppose that if I go you'll not expect me to come back,' said Isabel. He looked at her a little, and then, 'Are you out of your mind?' he enquired" (II, 357-58). That she echoes him in rebuking Caspar, whom she rejects for Osmond, signifies her final identity with what Osmond represents—the social code of appearances, conformity, resignation. That she returns to Osmond, after going to Gardencourt in defiance of his appeal, confirms the fact of her recognition, during the crisis-scene back in the Roman palace, that her husband's standards—exemplifying the straight and narrow path— represent that rightness to which she must herself subscribe. "Why should you go back—why should you go through that ghastly form?" Caspar demands; to which Isabel cruelly responds: "To get away from you" (II, 433).

Osmond shakes hands with his left hand, and Madame Merle "draws her handsome mouth up to the left" (II, 92); *sinister* they are. Osmond's affair with Madame Merle and his mercenary marriage to Isabel impugn his integrity; granted. But nevertheless Osmond is not devoid of honor and honesty; they are the pride of his code of selfhood. Critical of others, he is equally critical of himself: "I'm sick of my adorable taste," he admits to Madame Merle, and to Isabel when courting her he admits that Italy makes one "idle and dilettantish and second rate . . . , and I'm perfectly aware that I myself am as rusty as a key that has no lock to fit it" (I, 371). But the crucial test of Osmond's honesty occurs in his relationship with Caspar Goodwood: "To be as honest as that made a man very different from most people; one had to be almost equally honest with *him*" (II, 293).

Why Mrs. Osmond returns to her husband instead of fulfilling her original quest for freedom puzzles any number of Jamesian critics. "To our amazement," says Michael Swan, "she affronts her destiny and returns to her husband" (in *Henry James*, 1952, p. 50). Another superficial reader of *The Portrait* is Pelham Edgar, for whom the ending is inartistic. To contend that the ending of *The Portrait* is inartistic, or that Isabel's destiny (as Swan misreads it) ought to terminate in New England as a rejection of the European life that brought her such bitter experiences, casts doubts on James's critics as readers of *The Portrait*. The ending of the novel is determined by its beginnings. Isabel's destiny is toolmarked from the start by the houses James built for his pretentious, imperceptive, and self-deluded heroine. That Isabel must return to the Palazzo Roccanera is a foregone conclusion. What forecasts where she ends is the house where her history begins. She is trapped from the start. Her ironically rendered plight is rendered inevitable through the designed sequence of houses in terms of which our heroine progresses,—ending ironically where she began. Advancing from house to house, Isabel, seemingly progressing, ends trapped as tragic heroine. Her progress towards happiness has been illusory, for each subsequent house bears—though not explicitly so—kinship with the former one. It's this concatenation of houses Isabel visits or inhabits that establishes the ending of *The Portrait* as inevitable.   (1956, 1960)

NOTES

1. Page references are to the Modern Library edition.
2. In Boccaccio's *Decameron*, similarly, the sanctimony of the church is contradicted by what transpires therein, by the ribald tales narrated by the group of story-tellers.
3. James later extensively revised the novel; his revisions are traced in "The Painter's Sponge and Varnish Bottle," in *Henry James: The Major Phase*, by F. O. Matthiessen (1946).

4. A plaque on the Piazza Bellosguardo commemorates the famous persons who once lived in one or another of the villas there: Clara Schumann, Elizabeth and Robert Browning, Hans von Bülow, Nathaniel Hawthorne, James Fenimore Cooper, Henry James, and Galileo.

The Villa Mercede (named after Mercedes Huntington) is now a school for American girls. The school catalogue provides a copy of the original architect's perspective of the villa, a drawing of 1553 of which the original is in the Uffizi. The villa was then known as Belvedere al Saracino. Nearby is the Torre de Bellosguardo. "Its central tower is one of the landmarks of Florence and was built in the 13th century by Dante's friend, Guido Cavalcanti. The villa itself was built two centuries later and commands a magnificent, panoramic view of the 'old city.'" The Villa Mercede catalogue (1959) mentions that the Villa Mercede is described in Henry James's *Portrait of a Lady.*

5. Where did James get the original for Mrs. Touchett? The Countess Gemini provides the clue: "Indeed I can show you her portrait in a fresco of Ghirlandaio's" (I, 372). In *The Birth of John the Baptist,* one of the celebrated Ghirlandaio frescoes in the Church of Santa Maria Novella, on which piazza Henry James lived during his 1874 visit to Florence, several of the women Ghirlandaio depicts bear resemblance to James's portrait of Mrs. Touchett by their "little, dry, definite faces." Of these one conjectures that the mother of Saint John the Baptist might be the original for Mrs. Touchett, mother of Ralph the Martyr.

6. Emma Bovary "thought, sometimes, that, after all, this was the happiest time of her life—the honeymoon, as people called it. To taste the full sweetness of it, it would have been necessary doubtless to fly to those lands with sonorous names where the days after marriage are full of laziness most suave. In post-chaises behind blue silken curtains to ride slowly up steep roads, listening to the song of the postilion re-echoed by the mountains, along with the bells of goats and the muffled sound of a waterfall; at sunset on the shores of gulfs to breathe in the perfume of lemon-trees; then in the evening on the villa-terraces above, hand in hand to look at the stars; making plans for the future." (Ch. VII, p. 46 in Modern Library edition.)

7. My study of *The Portrait of a Lady* had its beginnings several years ago as a refutation of William Troy's reading of the house-garden symbolism (in his "The Altar of Henry James," reprinted in *The Question of Henry James,* 1945): "Is it merely an accident, for example, that in an early work like *The Portrait of a Lady* all the great climaxes in Isabel Archer's career—from her refusal of the English lord to her final flight from Caspar Goodwood—are made to occur in a garden? If an accident, it was a fortunate one, for the garden-symbol provides a wonderful point of concentration for the widest number of associations—the recollection especially of the famous garden in which one of Isabel's ancestresses was also confronted with the fruit of the tree of the knowledge of good and evil." On the contrary, I find that in gardens Isabel defers "the need of really facing her crisis" (Book I, p. 153).

Richard Chase in his *American Novel and Its Tradition* (1957) discusses the house-garden symbolism in his treatment of *The Portrait* as a romance; he makes no reference to Troy's essay. Chase's study seemingly anticipates some insights of my own. The explanation is that my essay was written and accepted for publication in 1956, the editors of *Botteghe Oscure* assuring me of its publication as late as 1958. Having kidnapped it for eighteen months, they finally returned it.

"The Houses That James Built" was read in shortened form on the Critics' Program at the University of Texas in October 1957.

"The Sacred Rage": The Time-Theme in *The Ambassadors*

Look, he's winding up the watch of his wit.
By and by it will strike.
—THE TEMPEST: II, 1, 12-13

(1)

The Ambassadors begins on a question: The beginning phrase of the novel is a question, "Strether's first question," and that first question starts off the sequence of questions and answers or theories that comprise the nimble-minded substance of the narrative. It initiates the recurrent motif of Strether's üncertainties, misgivings, doubts: "I'm always considering something else; something else, I mean, than the thing of the moment. The obsession of the other thing is the terror" (ch. I).[1] He prejudges events by theorizing about them. His characteristic utterance is the question-mark. Little Bilham's answer is: "Don't put any question; wait, rather—it will be much more fun—to judge for yourself" (X). Maria Gostrey gives him the same advice: "Don't make up your mind" (IX). She teaches him the message of Europe: How to Live. "You must take things as they come" (XII). And then some months later, in Gloriani's garden, Strether—like a schoolboy echoing his teachers—instructs Bilham that here in Europe "people can be in general pretty well trusted, of course—with the clock of their freedom ticking as loud as it seems to do here—to keep an eye on the fleeting hour" (XI). It is ironical that Strether, who has missed out on life by not letting himself go, should deliver to Bilham, who has lived his youth up to the hilt, the Jamesian burden: "Live all you can; it's a mistake not to" (XI).

Life for James is at its richest in the perception and enjoyment of things or persons as they are in the Moment Now. ("*Ennui* is at the end of everything that [does] not multiply our relations with life.") To miss out on life is to miss everything. Missing it is what "The Altar of the Dead" and "The Beast in the Jungle" are all about. Strether, unlike Marcher, scrutinizes himself in self-recognition of his plight, "his usual case: he was forever missing things through his general genius for missing them, while others were forever picking them up through a contrary bent" (XXVI). In the final scene of *The Ambassadors,* in the last pose we get of Strether, he's leaning back in his chair, but with his eyes on a small ripe round melon" —not leaning forward now, but passively reflecting on life in all its minute particulars, taking things as they come, his curiosity mixed with indifference. To sit there in the garden retreat of Miss Gostrey's house was "to see life reflected for the time in ideally kept pewter; which was somehow becoming, improving to life, so that one's eyes were held and comforted." Though the melon suggests Strether himself, "ripe" and "charming," he nevertheless senses that however ripe and charming he may be he's not

34

in real harmony with what surrounds him. "You *are*," he tells Miss Gostrey. "I take it too hard. You *don't*. It makes—that's what it comes to in the end—a fool of me." Even when he lets himself go in moods of negative capability for perceiving things rather than reflecting on them, as now in his observation of the melon, even then while momentarily he succeeds at enjoyment of things he fails; for what intrudes always is the opposite pole of his consciousness.

Timing the return of Chad Newsome, that is Strether's mission. He must bring Chad back from Paris to Woollett *on time*: "He can come into the business now—he can't come later" (IV). It's a manufacturing business; but what the Newsomes manufacture in Woollett, Strether never discloses —"It's vulgar." "Unmentionable?" "Oh no, we constantly talk of it; we are quite familar and brazen about it" (IV). At the theater with Miss Gostrey (IV) what blocks Strether's enjoyment of the play is the recollected image of the Newsome factory; it overlays the stage precisely when Miss Gostrey reverts to that key topic, the Woollett Question: "And what is the article produced?" Strether procrastinates: "I'll tell you next time." As at the beginning of the novel, so at the very end Miss Gostrey reminds him "of his having never yet named to her the article produced at Woollett. 'Do you remember our talking of it in London—that night at the play?' " What follows immediately this Woollett Riddle is the image of a clock:

> He found on the spot the image of his recent history; he was like one of the figures of the old clock at Berne. They came out, on one side, at their hour, jigged their little course in the public eye, and went in on the other side. He too had jigged his little course—him too a modest retreat awaited (XXXVI).[2]

As his enjoyment of the play was blocked by the image of Newsome's roaring factory, the "hum of vain things" drowning Miss Gostrey's question about the Woollett product, so in the final scene his enjoyment of the melon is blocked by the image of the old Berne clock: "the charming melon, which she liberally cut for him, and it was only after this that he met her question"—the Woollett Question. Strether in the image of the old Berne clock identifies himself with time, and by implication the Woollett product is also identified with time. For immediately following the identification of Strether with the clock comes Strether's offer "to name the great product of Woollett. *It would be a great commentary on everything.*"

Time is the great commentary on everything; what we constantly talk about is time; *The Ambassadors* talks about it on almost every other page. Time is the mainspring theme of *The Ambassadors*—How to Live It.

> The affair—I mean the affair of life—couldn't, no doubt, have been different for me; for it's, at the best, a tin mould, either fluted or em-

bossed, with ornamental excrescences, or else smooth, and dreadfully plain, into which, a helpless jelly, one's consciousness is poured—so that one 'takes' the form, as the great cook says, and is more or less compactly held by it; one lives, in fine, as one can (XI).

Life fixed in "a tin mould"—*that* sums up Strether's life, at least up to his encountering Miss Gostrey. At the same time that he meets her he encounters also an anonymous lady in a glass cage; she dispatches Waymarsh's telegram. Life fixed is what the lady in the glass cage symbolizes. She personifies Mrs. Newsome. Woollett and its products—Mrs. Newsome, the Pococks, and Strether—they are all encased each in a hard shell. The shell or tin mould is their obsession to fit things into a theory.

Woollett's fixed ideas preclude the possibility of the incalculable; consequently, the unpredictable upsets Woollett's previsions and theories and untimely formulas; consequently, Strether—the Ambassador of the Woollett Idea—finds himself again and again duped by the unpredictable, the unexpected event. The unpredictable is "the fate that waits for one, the dark doom that rides. What I mean is that with such elements one can't count" (IX). Paris contradicts Woollett because life—in Europe—isn't fixed; it's fluid and unpredictable.

Woollett "isn't sure it ought to enjoy," and neither is Strether; Miss Gostrey shows him how: "You see what I am," she tells him. "I'm a general guide—to 'Europe,' don't you know?" She is his Baedeker, the guidebook to new vistas; she releases Strether from his fixed self. She is the agent of "illuminations," and that is why Strether admits "I'm afraid of you." He's afraid of life, which is what Miss Gostrey represents. (The parallel is Mme. de Vionnet with her capacity for "revelations.") In opposition is Mrs. Newsome: "I was booked by her vision," but her vision or program is upset by what Strether experiences of Paris; it doesn't at all "suit her book" (XXIX).

Strether's way of keeping an eye on the hour is by keeping an eye on the clock, and that is why the fleeting hour escapes him:

> I see it now. I haven't done so enough before—and I'm old; too old at any rate for what I see. Oh, I *do see*, at least; and more than you'd believe or I can express. It's too late. And it's as if the train had fairly waited at the station for me without my having had the gumption to know it was there. Now I hear its faint, receding whistle miles and miles down the line (XI).

Strether is addicted to watching the clock lest he miss the train, and that's why he misses it. Reluctant to live time except by the clock, he's always trying to regain time because he has lost so much of it in an "empty present." Time is what Strether cannot help thinking about because he comes from Woollett, though his experience of Europe constitutes for clock-timed Strether a lesson in How Not To Think About It.

In Strether's sensibility James projected his own: "I have only to let myself *go!* So I have said to myself all my life—so I said to myself in the far-off days of my fermenting and passionate youth. Yet I have never fully done it" (*Notebooks*). Neither had William Dean Howells, and it was Howells' admonishment Not To Miss Life that provided his friend the germinal situation of *The Ambassadors*. Strether's mistake is James's mistake; it's Howells' mistake; it's everyone's mistake. It's the mistake of not letting yourself go; don't let life clock you. It's Woollett's mistake; it's Woollett's "sacred rage" (as Strether calls it). It's Strether's terrifying obsession, and it's the obsession of us all; namely to look at the hour without enjoying its values, without experiencing time in its point-present nowness. In Europe life cannot be clocked, whereas at Woollett (Worcester or Waltham, Massachusetts? Or Hartford, Connecticut?) the fleeting hour is clockwise fixed.

I rejoiced, says James in his Preface to *The Ambassadors,* in the prospect of creating a hero so mature, a man of imagination. Strether is brother to Isabel Archer of *The Portrait of a Lady* in that he shares her "ridiculously active imagination." But Strether has a questioning mind. No sooner is one question settled than another query and theory about it come to the front—"thanks to his constant habit of shaking the bottle in which life handed him the wine of experience, he presently found the taste of the lees rising, as usual, into his draught" (IX). Everything he wanted was comprised moreover in a single boon—"the common, unattainable art of taking things as they came" (V). Though time dominates Strether's imagination, the clocks of Woollett ticking off his fleeting hours, there are intervals when, as it were, the clock stops and the pendulum of his mind halts for moments of enjoyment amidst its routine swing back to Woollett and Mrs. Newsome. These intervals, moments of passive perception, constitute for Strether his happiest occasions.

One of these occasions occurs in the final scene of the book. *The Ambassadors*, ending where it began, circles back to England; once more Strether is with Miss Gostrey. There's been the breach with Mrs. Newsome in the interim, and there's been a change in Strether: "I *have* no ideas. I'm afraid of them. I've done with them" (XXXVI). His tin-moulded ideas have made a fool of him: namely Mrs. Newsome's ideas, her program. Mrs. Newsome embodies the Law of the Calculable. What upsets the calculable is the incalculable: " 'Call it then life'—he puzzled it out— 'call it poor dear old life simply that springs the surprise.' " The surprise when it springs is for Strether "paralyzing, or at any rate engrossing. . . ." (IX). The shock of recognition—at its most intense—occurs in the scenes of Strether's excursion to the countryside, which he had hitherto looked at "only through the little oblong window of the picture-frame."[8] His intent is simply to enjoy new vistas and experience firsthand a spot of French ruralism, but even in doing so Strether cannot refrain from fashioning his experience of nature into a pretty picture; he looks at the Parisian countryside as though it were a painting by Lambinet. Memories of Boston thus impinge upon his vision of the Parisian countryside and frame its impressions as within a gilt frame: "The oblong gilt frame disposed its enclosing lines; the poplars and willows, the reeds and river—a river of which he didn't know, and didn't want to know, the name—fell into a composition, full of felicity, within them. . . ." He began his journey with "His theory of his excursion," and now happily "not a single one of his observations but somehow fell into a place with it"; everything seemingly fits into the frame of his theory. But, obversely, Strether is framed. What frames him is his Fixed Idea. It's the idea that Chad's affair with Mme. de Vionnet is, after all, an innocent relationship untainted by sensual and moral corruption. It's a pretty picture, as Strether views it, until the Unpredictable upsets it. What upsets it is the intrusion of some figures in a boat rounding the bend of the river: "a young man in shirt sleeves" and "a young woman easy and fair." The river, to name it, is Reality (Strether did not want to know its name); and the boat-figures are Mme. de Vionnet and Chad. They've come by water; Strether by land. The lovers signify by their river-journey their identification with unclocked life. The unnamed river is time, the flux of things, the unpredictable which cannot be clocked.

The coincidence of Strether's meeting the lovers explodes Strether's fine theory. Strether naively rationalizes, when he first sights the lovers coming round the bend in the river, that Chad and Mme. de Vionnet are out simply for a day in the country, same as himself. The shock of recognition begins from the point of view of the lovers: their boat drifts wide, and their course wavers once they spot Strether. The truth of their affair is about to be unmasked—even their boat is, as it were, embarrassed. Their excursion, in contrast to Strether's, involved no plan, no preconceptions about it. And that is what life is: it's not what it seems to be by your prevision, but rather it's what it unexpectedly *is*. Mme. de Vionnet —like life itself—"was an obscure person, a muffled person one day; and a showy person, an uncovered person the next." She is unpredictable. "He thought of Mme. de Vionnet to-night as showy and uncovered, though he felt the roughness of the formula, because, by one of the short-cuts of genius, *she had taken all his categories by surprise*" (XV).

(2)

As Strether cannot bring himself—except momentarily—to *face into* life, to come to terms with the fleeting hour, so neither can he bring himself (until at the very end) to name the mysterious Woollett product. That James planned the Woollett article to be a "distinctly vulgar article of domestic use (to be duly specified)" we know from the scenario preserved in *The Notebooks*; but James changed his mind and in the novel he intrudes to declare his intentions at the start not to disclose its identity: "It may even now frankly be mentioned that he [Strether], in the sequel, never was to tell her" (IV). Miss Gostrey guesses it's "Clothespins? Saleratus? Shoe-polish?" No, says Strether. "No, you don't even 'burn.' I don't think, you know, you'll guess it" (IV). Mr. E. M. Forster, in *Aspects of the Novel*, put forth the whimsical notion of its being button-hooks! Forster ribs James for not telling us what the article is, and he injects a criticism of the Jamesian novel: "For James to indicate how his characters made their pile—it would not do." Like Miss Gostrey, Mr. Forster doesn't even "burn." It is not because the unnamed article is vulgar that James decided not to name it. In *The American*, to cite one example to the contrary, James is not squeamish about disclosing even such a vulgar object as bathtubs—on bathtubs and copper Christopher Newman made his pile.

Although James never identifies the unnamed article, a clock or watch —as I have elsewhere argued it[4]—is logically the answer to the never-answered riddle about the mysterious object Woollett produces. It fits all of Strether's specifications and not only is it literally the one possible article of appropriate fitness, but furthermore it elicits symbolically the time-theme of the whole book. In James nothing is without interrelationship, all things in relationship being the keystone of the Jamesian canon.

Ambiguity is the Jamesian aesthetic, and to resolve ambiguities is the critic's function. James was given to playing tricks on his readers and critics, notably in *The Turn of the Screw:* "a piece of ingenuity pure and simple, of cold artistic calculation, an *amusette* to catch those not easily caught." He delighted in the cryptic, in planting buried meanings, figures-in-the-carpet, designs and traps that elude the unwary reader. But, as in *The Portrait of a Lady*, he misleads us for a purpose; not merely as a trick. It is unthinkable to suppose that James—addicted to the Significance of the Thing, addicted to the symbolic import of minute particulars—conceived the unnamed Woollett object as a thing of no symbolic or thematic import. That time is manifested in what Woollett manufactures (clocks or watches), it seems logical to infer from the fact that the Woollett Riddle opens and closes the narrative the time-span of the narrative being spaced by Miss Gostrey's initial question in the opening chapter of Part Second and by its sequel occurring in the final scene of the book. The gap between these two occasions spaces the narrative— exclusive of the first three chapters which constitute its Prologue. The Woollett Question remains unanswered for the reason that to name it would consitute a spoiling of the riddle motif. I suppose there are other reasons as well, including the law of the artist "which somehow always makes the minimum of valid suggestion serve the man of imagination better than the maximum" (Preface to *The Aspern Papers*).

If the article were something unimportant, such as button-hooks, there wouldn't be any purpose in having Strether so reluctant to name it. Why, then, does James make such a mystery about it? His deliberate intention not to name it was, as I see it, solely for artistic purposes. That he uses it as a riddle, *that* in itself hints at its importance, its thematic impor-tance. The identity of "the little nameless object" informs the meaning of the whole novel—it correlates with the dominant time-theme, promotes it, manifests it.

The Prologue to the narrative (chs. I-III) concludes with Lawyer Waymarsh rushing into a jeweller's shop to purchase an unnamed article. "Then how will that jeweller help him?" Miss Gostrey speculates. "Strether seemed to make it out, from their standpoint, *between the interstices of arrayed watches* [italics mine], of close-hung dangling gewgaws." "You'll see!" (III). Waymarsh is late in keeping his appointment with Strether because—I presume—he lacks a timepiece. How will the jeweller help him? Well, by providing him with a timepiece. *The Ambassadors* ends with a disengagement and begins with a misengagement: Waymarsh late at the appointed hour, Strether on time. The parallel situation is Chad's being late in meeting the Pococks at Havre (they've come over to retrieve Strether). It is ironical that the Pococks representing New England moral rigidity should seem to Strether "a quantity as yet unmeasured," representing thus the unpredictable. That Strether is "now expert enough to recognize his uncertainty, in the premises," indicates that by now he's become wary of the unpredictable.

At the start Strether meets Miss Gostrey—instead of Waymarsh—and strolls with her through Chester and its countryside. But while Strether delights in new impressions, mixed with his delight is his sense of guilt at not sharing it with Waymarsh; he feels as if she were "taking from him something that was his due." Miss Gostrey senses that something is amiss, for Strether keeps looking at his watch. It signalizes his misgivings about what he later calls the clock of freedom, his misgivings about Europe's way of taking in the fleeting hour. "You're doing something that you think not right." What's not right for Strether is to be strolling with his new acquaintance; what's not right for Miss Gostrey is that Strether keeps looking at his watch. She educates Strether's time-troubled conscience anew. Consequently, when once more Strether takes out his watch to check on the time, he does so not earnestly but mechanically out of habit, unconsciously: "He looked at the hour without seeing it"—as though indifferent now to clock-time though nevertheless possessed by what the watch-face says.[5]

It is the image of Mrs. Newsome ("the ghost of the lady of Woollett") that obstructs his pleasure in the fleeting hour—she hovers over every scene. Here at the end of his journey it is the same as at the beginning, when, in the Paris springtime, he roamed the garden of the Tuileries; even here the compulsion of the clock impinges upon his consciousness: "He watched little brisk figures, figures whose movement was as the tick of the great Paris clock, take their smooth diagonal from point to point. . . ." (V). In the image of himself as the old Berne clock Strether, so to speak, winds up where he began: it's "as if his last days were copying his first" (XXXV).

There are two ways of keeping "an eye on the fleeting hour": Strether's way—keeping your eye on the clock while simultaneously considering something else *than* "the thing of the moment." And Chad's way: enjoying the fleeting hour—*as* it comes, *as* it goes, in the Now, unclocked. Chad Newsome and his mistress, Mme. de Vionnet, and Maria Gostrey represent the Sense of the Present (they are Paris personified); as such, they bring Strether round to the recognition of what it means to be alive in Time Now—how to take things as they come. Poor Strether—booked by Mrs. Newsome's "vision"—comes round to the recognition that life is richer when lived unbooked. To be booked by Mrs. Newsome is to be held back by a Sense of the Past.

That is why Mrs. Newsome is an invalid. It is ironical, then, that she embodies the Law of the Calculable. Strether—unlike Mrs. Newsome—possesses imagination enough to embrace contraries—to see things from opposite sides or contrary points of view. Making comparisons defines Strether's habit of mind. What distinguishes Strether is his Double Vision. As ambassador of Mrs. Newsome's program to retrieve her son from wicked Paris, Strether feels duty-bound to the Newsome Idea (with the prospect of marriage to Mrs. Newsome as his promised reward), but his sense of commitment traps him. It provokes him into jumping to conclusions and, as it were, jumping the clock. In his first encounter with Chad it strikes Strether as imperative for the success of his mission not to dawdle, "not to lose another hour, nor a fraction of one"; his notion is to attack at once, "to advance, to overwhelm, with a rush" (VII). His time-sense is at odds with the Keatsian Moment Now; for either it lags behind the event, the flux of things, or on the contrary it anticipates the issue of the moment. His usual habit is to temporize. When he first meets Miss Gostrey, he stops on the grass before reaching her and goes "through the form of feeling for something, possibly forgotten, in the light overcoat he carried on his arms; yet the essence of the act was no more than the impulse to gain time" (I). Whereas Chad had "no delays," Strether procrastinates; lighting a cigarette "gave him more time. But it was already sharp for him that there was no use in time" (XII). Although he is always on time, he is always too late. As Mamie Pocock is too late for Chad, so in another sense Strether is too late for Maria Gostrey. "I'll tell you next time," Strether promises when Miss Gostrey queries him about the Woollett product; but the next time doesn't occur until the very end of the novel; and then when Strether offers to name the thing, Miss Gostrey changes places with him in not wanting to know: "At this she stopped him off; she not only had no wish to know, but she wouldn't know for the world" (XXXVI).

Perhaps Miss Gostrey has finally guessed what in fact the Woollett article is: "She had done with the products of Woollett—for all the good she had got from them." Its identity is hinted at in the fact of Miss Gostrey's revulsion against the products of Woollett; her revulsion is understandable since her interest to free Strether from his obsession with time has not met with any triumphant success. Time has cheated her of Strether, as time has cheated Mme. de Vionnet of Chad. When Strether takes final leave of Mme. de Vionnet, having decided that he's "done with her," he thinks of the passion she represented—"and the possibilities she betrayed. She was older for him to-night, visibly less exempt from the touch of time. . . ." (XXXIII). She had been to him another Cleopatra, exempt from time, "like Cleopatra in the play, indeed various and multifold" (XV). She has lost her youth; Strether momentarily regains his. At the start it was Miss Gostrey who reinstated his youth: "I began to be young the moment I met you at Chester" (XVIII).

The conjectured Woollett article—clock or watch—seems to me manifested in Strether's *clocked* consciousness. "Strether had read somewhere in Théophile Gautier of a Latin motto, a description of the hours, observed on a clock by a traveller in Spain; and he had been led to apply it in short to Chad's number one, number two, number three—through numbers indeed as to which it might be a question whether those of mere modest clock-faces wouldn't be exceeded" (V). Again: Strether "never found himself wishing that *the wheel of time* would turn it [the Lambinet painting] up again. . . ." (XXX). Strether identifies Chad with the clock in linking Chad's love affairs ("number one, number two, number three") with the Latin motto on the Spanish clock: *"Omnes vulnerant, ultima necat*—they had all morally wounded, the last had morally killed." When Chad cables home that he declines to return, Strether claims: "I've stopped him" (XVIII). Strether stops Chad's "pendulum" swinging homeward. It's a "multitudinous image in which he [Strether] took comfort. He took comfort, by the same stroke, in the swing of Chad's pendulum back from that other swing, the sharp jerk towards Woollett so stayed by his own hand. He had the entertainment of thinking that if he had for that moment *stopped the clock* . . ." (XIX). That clocks are what Woollett produces seems evidenced in the double identification of Strether and Chad with clocks, and furthermore by the fact that Woollett "was essentially a society of women" (XIX) and women are constantly imaged by the attributes of water—time itself. It is appropriate, then, that Mrs. Pocock's salon in Paris is a gilded room all mirrors and "clocks" (XXI).

Mrs. Newsome also is identified with time, and the time-theme is frequently evoked by water imagery—water frozen or fluid. That Mrs. Newsome constitutes for Strether his "whole moral and intellectual being or block," as Miss Gostrey sees it, brings out in Strether's imagination the apt image of Mrs. Newsome as "some particularly large iceberg in a cool blue northern sea" (XXIX). Women elicit river and water imagery throughout *The Ambassadors.*[6] Sarah Pocock, Mrs. Newsome's daughter, is a chip off the old iceberg: " 'packed so tight she can't move. She's in splendid isolation'—Miss Barrace embroidered the theme" (XXVI). She is "buried alive!" "She *is* free from her chin up," Miss Barrace concedes; but the rest of her is sunken ice, only "She can breathe." As Mrs. Newsome "knows everything," so Mamie Pocock boasts: "Oh, yes, I know everything." As for Sarah—"she's all *cold* thought" (XXIX). It's Woollett's moral pressure that blocks Strether's sensibility.

Mrs. Newsome also is identified with space: "Her tact had to reckon with the Atlantic Ocean, the General Post Office and the extravagant curve of the globe" (IX). She is identified with time by the fact that her cabled ultimatum is weighted down by Strether's watch. When he receives her "blue paper," Strether in order to keep it from blowing out the open window keeps it "from blowing away by the superincumbent weight of his watch" (XVII). The fact that Strether weights down Mrs. Newsome's Blue Message *with his watch* rather than with any other object establishes the identity of Mrs. Newsome with clock-time, establishes the identity of Woollett with clocked morality, establishes the identity of the very object manufactured by the Newsome factory: watches or clocks. Commanding Strether from across the Atlantic Ocean, her blue cablegram imposes Woollett's clocked morality—Live By the Law of the Clock —upon Strether's clocked consciousness. Henry James manipulates his criticism of New England moral rigidity by the metaphor of submission to the clock.

Woollett's compulsion to live by the Law of the Clock, by the law of the calculable, manifests Moral Pressure. The New Englander Strether disengages himself momentarily from his watch (in weighting down the Blue Message with his watch); *that* is at the literal level. At the symbolic, he disengages himself momentarily from clock-time—and from Mrs. Newsome. Thus Mrs. Newsome is equated with clock-time; what article other than clocks *could* her factory issue? Momentarily, Strether, having disengaged himself from his watch (emblem of the temporal *and* moral burdens impinging upon Strether's double consciousness), has disengaged himself from his habitual addiction to watching the clock, from his addiction to clocking the fleeting hour instead of enjoying it. To Mrs. Newsome, who equates with conventional time *and* conventional morality, Strether responds like a pendulum. His double consciousness pulls him back from enjoying simple perceptions to theorizing about life, from sensations to thoughts; or obversely from calculations about things back to simple observations of them.

Again and again Strether finds himself "thrown back on a felt need to remodel somehow his plan" (IX). It is his sensibility, compounded of curiosity and indifference, that conditions him to adjust himself to the unpredictable, the surprise awaiting every conceived plan. He was supposed to find Chad gone to the bad and his wicked woman "horrible," since Mrs. Newsome figured that's what she must be; but instead he finds Chad made over, improved, distinguished—and the woman delightful. Mrs. Newsome imagined stupidly; as Miss Gostrey puts it: "She imagined meanly" (XXIX). Although Chad has been transformed by Europe, the transformation strikes Sarah Pocock as an unfortunate development ("I call it hideous"); and she is shocked furthermore by Strether's adoration of the charming Mme. de Vionnet. She seems to him "a real revelation," whereas to Sarah she represents an affront to decency— what is she but a divorced woman leading poor Chad astray? A revelation! Sarah springs at Strether; do you think "I've come to such a woman for a revelation? You talk to me about 'distinction'—you, you who've had your privilege?—when the most distinguished woman we shall either of us have seen in this world sits there insulted in her loneliness, by your incredible comparison!" (XXVI).

That is Sarah's fixed idea. What infuriates her is that Strether has apparently gone over to the other side, betrayed his allegiance to Mrs. Newsome. But what her theory leaves out of account is the unmeasured quantity of happenings which have brought Strether round. Strether refutes her theory that he had calculated the whole affair:

> "I don't think there's anything I've done in any such calculated way as you describe. Everything has come as a sort of indistinguishable part of everything else. Your coming out belonged closely to my having come before you, and my having come was a result of our general state of mind. Our general state of mind had proceeded, on its side, from our queer ignorance, or queer misconceptions and confusions— from which, since then, an inexorable tide of light seems to have floated us into our perhaps queerer knowledge" (XXVI).

Strether confirms Miss Gostrey's theory (everyone has theories, and everyone's theories get upset by the unexpected), admitting that Mrs. Newsome "was essentially all moral pressure" (XXVI). When Strether dines with Mme. de Vionnet, her posture at the table—"graceful with her elbows on the table"—summons to his mind the moral image of Mrs. Newsome (XVI). "It was a posture unknown to Mrs. Newsome, but it was easy for a *femme du monde*. 'Yes—I am "now"!' " Mrs. Newsome dominates the globe, in the style of Queen Elizabeth. As Mrs. Newsome reminds Strether of Queen Elizabeth, so Maria Gostrey reminds him of Mary Stuart (Miss Gostrey knowing no law but the law of the incalculable); and Mme. de Vionnet invokes comparison with the still more passionate Cleopatra. Strether owes more to women, as Miss Gostrey remarks, "than any man I ever saw. We do seem to keep you going" (XXIII). Mrs. Newsome takes "great views" of everything; though she has ideas about everything, her great views turn out to be altogether too much for her. "Everything's too much for her." Her incapacity for meeting life is signalized by her plight: she is an invalid. Also, "She's just a *moral* swell."

(3)

Europe upsets everyone's theory, plan, or schedule, because here the Clock of Freedom ticks, not the Clock of Woollett; it's as though here everyone lives exempt from the touch of time. The Ambassadors signify those who would draw us away from Living in the Now. When Strether calls on Chad to deliver Mrs. Newsome's ultimatum that he return to Woollett, Chad's not at home, and Strether finds comfort in an image of a clock: "He took comfort, by the same stroke, in the swing of Chad's pendulum back from that other swing, the sharp jerk towards Woollett, so stayed by his own hand. He had the entertainment of thinking that if he had for that moment stopped the clock, it was to promote, the next minute, this still livelier motion" (XIX). Strether's own "pendulum" swings likewise away from Woollett, halts as if time has had its stop, or swings towards Paris with livelier motion; what promotes its livelier motion is finally Mme. de Vionnet, Chad's mistress. But then back it swings to Woollett again and again. In the interim come the pauses: "Poor Strether had at this very moment to recognize the truth that, whenever one paused in Paris, the imagination, before one could stop it, reacted. This perpetual reaction put a price, if one would, on pauses. . . ." (V). In the pauses Strether lives in the Moment Now, and that much defines one pole of his double consciousness; the opposite pole, in conflict and in reaction, finds the pendulum of his imagination magnetized by Mrs. Newsome and swinging back to Woollett. In the Luxembourg gardens, instead of enjoying them, Strether reads letters from Mrs. Newsome: "It filled for him, this tone of hers, all the air; yet it struck him at the same time as the hum of vain things" (V).

The Hum of Vain Things, the roaring trade of the Newsome factory, signifies the Idea of Time, which (like the unnamable Woollett product) "may well be on the way to become a monopoly" (IV). Chadwick Newsome declares, in his final interview with Strether, his intention of returning to Woollett and entering the advertising end of the roaring trade: "The right man must take hold. With the right man to work it *c'est un monde*." Chad knows the world, knows how to live time's fleeting hour; don't tamper with the clock, but rather advertise it. Having clocks in mind, Chad concludes: "*To wind up* where we began. My interest's purely platonic" (XXXV). In "our roaring age," Strether admits, "Advertising is clearly, at this time of day, the secret of trade."

Trading with time, that's what the novel is all about.

> "It's the sacred rage," Strether had had further time to say; and this sacred rage was to become, between them, for convenient comprehension, the description of one of his periodical necessities. It was Strether who eventually contended that it did make him [namely, Waymarsh] better than they. But by that time Miss Gostrey was convinced she didn't want to be better than Strether (II).

The Sacred Rage means, for one thing, the rage for life moulded into the ordered forms of conventional morality and conventional time. It's the rage for what's fixed and scheduled and calculable. It's another name for the Conscience of Woollett, Milrose, and Boston, where time and morality—boxed in by puritanical conceptions—are regulated according to fixed ideas for controlling them. Woollett, that "prison house" of tradition, exhibits a monopoly on how everything must be run: on time. Milrose, represented by the lawyer Waymarsh, takes a stiff view of things and fixes life by some grim theory about it. In the main, it's Mrs. New-some's theory, Waymarsh being in occult relation with her. "He thinks us sophisticated, he thinks us worldly, he thinks us wicked, he thinks us all sorts of queer things," says Strether in summing up his friend to Miss Gostrey (II). Boston, represented by the Pococks, is obsessed by "the theory of the horrible." Mamie Pocock (Sarah's sister-in-law), whom Chad was booked to marry, "came over with ideas. Those she got at home. . . . She was to *save* our friend" (XXV). But by the time she gets there Chad's already saved; Paris has not demoralized him, rather it has transformed him into something rich and strange. Mrs. Newsome has miscalculated. The wicked woman—Mme. de Vionnet being Paris per-sonified—has "saved" Chad, and with Chad saved it leaves poor Mamie with nothing to reconstruct. "Not even to love him?" asks Strether of Bil-ham; to which he replies with a turn-of-the-screw: "She would have loved him better as she originally believed him." "She's too late. Too late for the miracle" (XXV).

What Chad loses in renouncing Paris and Mme. de Vionnet for Wool-lett is what Strether, addressing Mme. de Vionnet, sums up as "the most precious present I've ever seen made. . . ." (XXXIII). Strether appreciates her out of his past experience of life and its "movements" he was always too late for. He's always waited too long, delaying (ironically) so as to gain time; it's his lag in his time-sense that retards him from experience of things in their point-present Keatsian Nowness: "there were sequences he had missed and great gaps in the procession: he might have been watch-ing it all recede in a golden cloud of dust" (V). "The fact that he had failed, as he considered, in everything, in each relation and in half a dozen trades. . . . might have made, might still make for an empty present; but it stood solidly for a crowded past." The empty present is what Strether has such a damnable time trying to fill. "I'm a perfectly equipped failure," he confesses to Miss Gostrey, who—being herself a failure—echoes his cry: "Thank goodness, you're a failure—it's why I so dis-tinguish you!" "Look at me," she sighs—"the dreams of my youth! But our realities are what has brought us together. We're beaten brothers in arms" (III). It's Strether's capacity for seeing Woollett from the point-of-view of Europe that accounts for Strether's great success (by the standards of Woollett) *at* being a failure.

So every person in *The Ambassadors* shares identity or plight with that of another. In Gloriani's garden (XI) Strether mistakes Mme. de Vionnet's daughter for Chad's beloved, a misidentification by which Mme. de Vionnet's relationship with Chad is saved as innocent—from Strether's duped point of view. Simultaneously, Strether self-consciously sees himself as bracketed with Miss Gostrey and wonders "what account Chad would have given of their acquaintance" (XI). So, every character in *The Am-bassadors* becomes the symbol of another character, one person substitut-ing for another. Thus, Little Bilham—in the first balcony scene—is mis-identified by Strether for Chad; symbolically thus they change places.

Strether, studying the balcony above him and looking at his watch, wonders who is up there smoking sparks. The balcony "didn't somehow show as a convenience easy to surrender" (V). (Little Bilham, as his name suggests, represents Chad's other self in diminutive form.) By their mixed identity the attributes of Chad transfer to his counterpart. James repeats his trick in the second balcony scene (XXIV), where Mamie mistakes Strether for Little Bilham. The tardy Bilham is late in keeping his tryst with Mamie Pocock; the time-conscious Strether is on time. Their mixed identity establishes a kinship between Young Bilham and Old Strether, between Youth and Age. "Oh, I thought you were Mr. Bilham!" Mamie, momentarily, confuses the two. Again, in the final balcony scene, Strether's kinship with Chad gets reinforced by Strether's being brought together with him on the balcony of Chad's apartment in Paris: a high place representing "some moral elevation from which they could look down on their recent past" (XXXV). The figure on the balcony, leaning on the rail and looking down at him, is Chad's; but Strether recalls in Chad's pose Bilham's pose when first Strether visited Chad's apartment on the Boulevard Malesherbes (V). Another balcony scene occurs in Chapter XXVIII; it is third in the sequence of four balcony scenes binding the narrative. "He spent a long time on the balcony; he hung over it as he had seen little Bilham hang the day of his first approach, as he had seen Mamie hang over her own the day little Bilham himself might have seen her from below. . . ." Here Strether on Chad's balcony awaits Chad while reading a "lemon-coloured" novel. It is no doubt a "bad" novel inasmuch as yellow connotes "bad" in the image of the London actress: "a bad woman in a yellow frock, who made a pleasant, weak, good-looking young man in perpetual evening dress do the most dreadful things" (IV).

The change in Strether, from his enslavement to "the long Woollett years" to his enjoyment of the precious Paris hours, is so pronounced— in Jim Pocock's simple view—that he becomes identified with the youthful Chad. As Strether remarks, Jim "understands, you see, that Chad and I have above all wanted to have a good time, and his view is simple and sharp. Nothing will persuade him—in the light, that is, of my behavior— that I really didn't, quite as much as Chad, come over to have one before it was too late. He wouldn't have expected it of me; but men of my age, at Woollett—and especially the least likely ones—have been noted as liable to strange outbreaks, belated, uncanny clutches at the unusual, the ideal" (XXIII). The claim of the Ideal, to define it, is the impulse to renounce conformity and escape the conventions by which our lives are moulded; it's "the impulse to let things be, to give them time to justify themselves or at least to pass" (XVI).

The Sacred Rage is thus as two-fold as Strether's double consciousness. It embraces both the rage for freedom from fixed temporal and moral impingements and—just the opposite—the rage for commitments to the fixed order of things, the obsession of life ordered by the law of the calculable. The progress of the novel consists of alternations between these two poles of Strether's consciousness, the pendulum of his imagination swinging from Paris and the precious moment back to Woollett and the sacred rage for the future (for Sarah Pocock "there's only tomorrow") or for the past. He felt "at that moment, that he was launched in something of which the sense would be quite disconnected from the sense of his past, and which was literally beginning there and then" (I). *The Ambassadors* builds on contraries, contradictions, ambivalences arising from poles of opposition. Consequently, identities and scenes overlap, one image or vision impinging upon another. Thus we are never in Paris but what simultaneously we are also in Woollett. It is a device of juxtaposition which James may very well have derived from *Antony and Cleopatra*, for in Shakespeare's play likewise Rome impinges upon Egypt and Egypt upon Rome. Strether's double vision embraces dual concepts of morality and time; the lag in his time-sense retards him from making the most of an otherwise empty present. When Strether makes his last call at Chad's apartment, he "felt, strangely, as sad as if he had come for some wrong, and yet as excited as if he had come for some freedom. But the freedom was what was most in the place and the hour; it was the freedom that most brought him round again to the youth of his own that he had long ago missed" (XXVIII).

Whereas Europe brings out in Strether a renewal of youth, Europe underscores for Mamie Pocock her lack of it. Old before her time, she reminds Strether of his own lost youth and invokes "his sense of the flight of time" (XXIV). Chad's freedom from the clock ends, ironically, in his submission to it; but he can afford to submit to Woollett and the clocked way of life because he has had his fling. Strether regains his youth, and Chad foresakes his. This turnabout in their relationship forms (as E. M. Forster was first to point out) the hour-glass structure of the book. Strether and Chad change places, "and it is the realization of this that makes the book so satisfying at the close." The change for Chad is absolute, a complete break with his European past; whereas for Strether it's what he has been that keeps constantly catching up with him in his periodic attempts to capture the moment now and free himself from Woollett and the clock.

Mamie is too upholstered to experience contact with life; she misuses her precious Paris hours by shopping for clothes, "voluminous clothes," and her shopping excursions cause eternal delays. "What Mamie was like was the happy bride, the bride after the church and just before going away" (XX). Not even her wardrobe is timely, and "the complexities of her hair missed moreover also the looseness of youth. . . ." (XXIV). The truth of Chad's affair with Mme. de Vionnet is exposed (in the Recognition Scene) by the fact that the woman in the embarrassed boat lacks even a shawl. The moral fibre *and* the time-sense of the women in *The Ambassadors* are rendered symbolically by their clothing. The gown Miss Gostrey wears is " 'cut down,' as he believed the term to be, in respect to shoulders and bosom, in a manner quite other than Mrs. Newsome's and who wore round her throat a broad red velvet band with an antique jewel—he was rather complacently sure it was antique—attached to it in front. Mrs. Newsome's dress was never in any degree 'cut down,' and she never wore round her throat a broad red velvet band. . . ." (IV). Mme. de Vionnet also wears a low-cut gown, "and round her neck she wore a collar of large old emeralds. . . . Her head, extremely fair and exquisitely festal, was like a happy fancy, a notion of the antique, on an old, precious medal, some silver coin of the Renaissance. . . ." (XV). Thus Mme. de Vionnet and Maria Gostrey share each other's attributes. "Antique" and jewels manifest their crossed identities. That they personify the amoral world of Paris is established by the image of Paris as "a jewel brilliant and hard. . . . It twinkled and trembled and melted together; and what seemed all surface one moment seemed all depth the next" (V). Like Cleopatra, Mme. de Vionnet is extraordinarily charming. Miss Barrace admits: "She's various. She's fifty women" (XIV). Miss Barrace, who smokes cigarettes, strikes Strether as "both *antique* and modern" (XIV), whereby Miss Barrace is linked with Miss Gostrey and Mme. de Vionnet.

Although Strether is not convinced that he can "save" the bad Chad from the toils of a wicked woman, he can perhaps save Waymarsh meanwhile; the way to save "the pilgrim from Milrose" is to establish him in a relationship with Miss Barrace. "And mightn't the sacred rage, at any rate, be kept in abeyance by creating for *his* comrade's mind . . . the possibility of a relation?" Turn Waymarsh *from* his sacred rage against Europe to its opposite, the sacred rage against Milrose, Woollett, Boston. He'll be freed from the former once he falls in love with Miss Barrace. Henry James imparts to Strether his own double vision and ironic viewpoint. To be freed from the sacred rage is "to be whirled away"—Strether himself "had never been whirled away. . . ." (IX). Well, Waymarsh *is* whirled away. He strikes now for a different kind of "freedom."

At the start, however, Lawyer Waymarsh was in a sacred rage to escape the Claim of the Ideal. Hating Europe ("he can't stand it") because everything here swims in uncertainties, ambivalences, delays and leisurely postponements, Waymarsh makes a "sudden grim dash" into the jeweller's shop to make "some extraordinary purchase." Strether has a theory as to what he purchases: it is an article purchased "For nobody. For nothing. For freedom" (III). Whereas Strether welcomes freedom from Woollett and questions Woollett's standards, Waymarsh welcomes freedom from Europe and questions Europe's standards (or lack of them). Waymarsh at the start sought freedom not from the clock but from the unclocked world of Paris. The tardy Waymarsh presumably purchased a watch because he can't stand anything at loose ends and, being a lawyer, he's addicted to the Law of the Calculable. It's in this sense that "He has struck for freedom"—freedom from the Claim of the Ideal. Henry James thus fashions two brands of freedom, which, like the double versions of The Sacred Rage, stand in contradiction each to its opposite. Lawyer Waymarsh, exemplar of the Calculable, ends—in the company of Miss Barrace—whirled away. Waymarsh thus changes places with Chad, exemplar of the Incalculable.

Although Miss Barrace won't accept anything but "innocent flowers," Waymarsh purchases for her expensive gifts. He's buying his "freedom" now. Freedom from the Clock, whereas from Europe's point of view he could have had that kind of freedom at no cost. Flowers would suffice and they don't last long, and that fits Miss Barrace's time-sense—her appreciation for things of the moment now. But Waymarsh, by his American standards, is willing to pay dearly for being "whirled away," and for this rebellion against the American brand of the Sacred Rage, Strether admires him. Now, truly, his friend has "struck for freedom." Now his friend, "the pilgrim from Milrose," belongs at last to "the real tradition," the European tradition, and for this triumph Strether rejoices. What a change; what a turnabout! "What a rage it is! . . . It's an opposition" (XIV). It's an opposition against the American version of the Sacred Rage—the rage for order. Waymarsh, like Chad and Strether, has had his fling.   (1957, 1960)

NOTES

1. Text references are to the New American Library edition (1960).

2. Illustrations of the Berne clock are given in Alfred Chapuis's *Les automates, figures artificielles d'hommes et d'animaux* (Neuchâtel: Editions du Griffon, 1949).

3. In Chapters XXX and—the Recognition Scene—XXXI. The location of the spot is probably Arguientveil, where the French impressionist painters frequented. Possibly it is the same village inn and river view Renoir depicts in his *Luncheon by the River.*

Strether's excursion epitomizes Strether's education and progress from innocence to insight and experience, and the stages of his progress are marked by recurrent balcony and garden scenes, of which the countryside inn represents a fusion of both balcony and garden. The garden scenes occur at the hotel in Chester (I), in the Tuileries and Luxembourg gardens (V), in Gloriani's garden (X and XI), where Strether first meets the Countess de Vionnet, in the garden of a village inn overlooking the river (XXX and XXXI), and finally in Miss Gostrey's "scrap of old garden" (XXXVI). William Troy observed that garden scenes in James's novels—I would say notably in *The Ambassadors*—suggest the Garden of Eden. The four major garden scenes, as William Gibson reports in "Metaphor in the Plot of 'The Ambassadors,'" constitute "crucial stages in Strether's eating of the fruit of the tree . . ." (*New England Quarterly:* September 1951).

4. In "Time and the Unnamed Article in *The Ambassadors*," *Modern Language Notes,* LXXII (January 1957), pp. 27-32.

In his Preface to *The Ambassadors* James discusses the function and technical virtues of the scene at the London theater (Part Second, ch. IV); he sums it up by reference to a clock: The scene is compressed and yet comprehensive —"with its office as definite as that of the hammer on the gong of the clock, the office of expressing all that is in the hour." It's a curious coincidence that James should define this scene by the image of a clock, for it is in this theater scene that the question is first raised as to what the Newsomes manufacture. Strether thinks the article "vulgar," but on the other hand he thinks the London theater "grand"; whereas for Miss Gostrey the theater is dreadful. "This dreadful London theater? .It's impossible, if you really want to know!" But Strether does not want to know, any more than he cares to disclose the identity of the Woollett article. That the article is compared with the theater, where time is suspended, suggests its identity as having to do with time.

5. Cf. *Portrait of a Lady*, I, p. 320: "Put your watch back," Ralph Touchett admonishes Isabel Archer. Like Strether, Isabel Archer is afraid of her freedom.

6. Over the river, *that* is where—on the left bank in Paris—Mme. de Vionnet lives (XII). It's at her apartment, along "the shining, barge-burdened Seine," that Strether felt "for an hour, in the matter of letting himself go, of diving deep"; "Strether was to feel that he had touched bottom" (XVI). Maria Gostrey is imaged as, alas, but a pail of water: "the time seemed already far off when he had held out his small thirsty cup to the spout of her pail. Her pail was scarce touched now, and other fountains flowed for him; she fell into her place as but one of his tributaries. . . ." (XVIII). At the start, Strether felt "washed up on the sunny strand, thankful for breathing time, stiffening himself while he gasped, by the waves of a single day" (V). He has survived drowning, drowning in Mrs. Newsome's terrifying sea. He's afraid of women, afraid of life, afraid of water; consequently he hesitates to know better his new acquaintance, Miss Gostrey, as he approaches her on the lawn "in the watery English sunshine. . . ." (I). He's afraid that she's *"launching"* him; wasn't it that "a woman of fashion was *floating* him into society, and that an old friend, deserted on the brink, was watching the force of the current?" (III). "Women were thus endlessly absorbent, and to deal with them was *to walk on water*" (XXXIII). Even Waymarsh is "drawn into the eddy" and like Strether is temporarily swallowed down; "and there were days when Strether seemed to bump against him as a sinking swimmer might brush a submarine object. The fathomless medium held them—Chad's manner was the fathomless medium; and our friend felt as if they passed each other, in their deep immersion, with the round, impersonal eye of silent fish" (IX). As for Mme. de Vionnet, Strether compares her "to a goddess still partly engaged in a morning cloud or *a sea-nymph waist-high in the summer surge*" (XV). Marie as water-nymph is identified with life: "She may be charming—his life!" (IV). Chad is Antony to Mme. de Vionnet as Cleopatra, goddess of the Nile.

A Note on the Text of *The Ambassadors*

The Ambassadors was published in book form first in England in September, 1903, by Methuen & Co., and in America by Harper & Brothers in November, 1903, having first seen print here in serial form in the *North American Review* from January to December, 1903. Henry James, restoring portions omitted in the abridged *North American Review* draft and expunging other portions from that draft, extensively revised the serial form of the novel for the First English Edition, but he saw only this edition through the press.

Not in the *North American Review* first-draft, for instance, is the image of Paris: "It hung before him this morning, the vast bright Babylon, like some huge iridescent object, a jewel brilliant and hard, in which parts were not to be discriminated nor differences comfortably marked. It twinkled and trembled and melted together; and what seemed all surface one moment seemed all depth the next" (V). This added image of Paris as jewel serves a double purpose: it identifies Miss Gostrey with Paris as jewel as she "wore round her throat a broad red velvet band with an antique jewel" (IV).

A most curious error has plagued the publication of *The Ambassadors*. For the First American Edition, James sent to Harper & Brothers two chapters that did not appear in the *North American Review*, namely Chapter XXVIII ("He went late that evening") and Chapter XXXV ("He was to delay no longer"); but the editor, in the process of inserting the new material, reversed Chapters XXVIII and XXIX. Until recently all subsequent editions, including the New York Edition (published 1907-1909 by Charles Scribner's Sons and, in London, by Macmillan & Co., 1908-1909), reprinted the defective Harper 1903 text. In November, 1957, Harper issued a "corrected" text. Yet even in this "corrected" edition, Chapters XXVIII and XXIX are still incorrectly placed. Chapter XXVIII erroneously opens Part Eleventh, whereas by the Methuen text it should conclude Part Tenth. Also Chapter XIX ("He rambled largely") is misplaced in Part Eighth—it belongs as the second chapter. Similar errors plagued English editions. In the Everyman 1948 and 1957 editions, Chapter XXVIII incorrectly figures as the second chapter of Book Eleventh, whereas it belongs as the fourth chapter of Book Tenth; the chapters are in reversed order. This error has now been corrected in the Everyman 1959 edition (J. M. Dent & Sons, Ltd.), for which edition I provided the Note; but the Everyman text does not reproduce the Methuen 1903 text.

Neither do two recent paperback editions: one issued by Bergen Evans (Premier World Classic, February 1960), which duplicates the Harper 1957 text and its errors; and the other issued by F. W. Dupee (Rinehart, March 1960), which, while correcting the switched Chapters XXVIII and XXIX—therein called Chapter I and II of Book Eleventh—and reproducing the text of the New York Edition, differs from the Methuen text.

James himself never discovered the error of the transposed chapters. It was first discovered by Robert E. Young, an undergraduate student at Stanford, and independently by Susan Humphreys; but neither Mr. Young nor Miss Humphreys examined the Methuen 1903 text, as Leon Edel subsequently pointed out.

In my Introduction to the Doubleday Anchor Book edition of *The Ambassadors* (1958), I claimed: "The present Anchor edition is a faithful copy of the text of the Methuen first edition"—only to discover, when the book was published and by then already distributed, that the Methuen text had *not* been used, and once again the two ill-fated chapters were produced in reverse sequence. The Doubleday editor, ignoring the claim of my Note, had used the *corrected* Harper 1957 edition and switched back the ill-fated chapters to the reversed sequence that has cursed all editions here and abroad since the Harper 1903 incorrect edition. As tragic-comic coda to the history of errors in editions of *The Ambassadors*, Harper Books and Authors, the news bulletin of Harper & Brothers, blithely announced in April 1955: "Transposed Chapters in James' *The Ambassadors* Set Aright in New Printing," but by another Harper House error the 1955 Harper "corrected" edition duplicated the 1903 error of the transposed chapters.

The Methuen 1903 edition is scarce and difficult to obtain in this country. It is available in the rare-book collections of only four libraries here. However, by an amazing coincidence, John Seelye, a student from Claremont Graduate School, offered me *his* battered copy, along with collations, and it is from these that the New American Library text is set. By the device of brackets, my Methuen text indicates the most significant passages, or phrases, or words, that do not appear in any of the other editions. On occasion, footnotes provide samples of other variants in the text—variants from all other than the Methuen edition.

(1959, 1960)

THOMAS HARDY

Hardy's Hour-Glass Novel

I[n] the commonwealth I would by contraries
Execute all things.
—THE TEMPEST: II, 1, 147-148

THE GROUND-PLAN OF *The Return of the Native*, the only novel in which Hardy consciously attempted to observe the Unities (*Later Years*, p. 235), is contrived with the symmetry of an architect's blueprint. Its geography reads like a surveyor's map. Its chronology seems plotted by an almanac-maker. Its architectonics of Time, Space, and Action are diagrammatic. The narrative, running the cycle of a year and a day, is spaced by the two signal fires of November fifth, 1842 and 1843; these are its poles of Time and Action. The axis of Space is Rainbarrow, for within the immediate radii of Rainbarrow all action is located. The plot is a piece of geometry. The key to it is a geometric pattern. My critical interest is this structural interest: to discover the geometric pattern and to diagram the structure of the novel.

The geometric pattern is the figure of an hour-glass.

The structure of Hardy's hour-glass novel can be summed up in this one diagrammatic symbol. *Thaïs* by Anatole France and *The Ambassadors* by Henry James suggest structural affinities. In Mr. E. M. Forster's analysis (*Aspects of the Novel*, pp. 214, 219), the shape of *Thaïs* is an hour-glass. Both plot and pattern are framed by the converging lines of Paphnuce the ascetic and Thaïs the courtesan: "In the central scene of the book they approach, he succeeds; she goes into a monastery and gains salvation, because she has met him; but he, because he has met her, is damned. The two characters converge, cross, and recede with mathematical precision, and part of the pleasure we get from the book is due to this." For pattern, as distinguished from plot (the logical chain of events which appeals to our intelligence), "appeals to our aesthetic sense, it causes us to see the book as a whole." In *The Ambassadors,* likewise, the hour-glass pattern is complete: "Strether and Chad, like Paphnuce and Thaïs, change places, and it is the realization of this that makes the book so satisfying at the close." A similiar pleasure derives from *The Return of the Native.* The difference is a structural one. In *Thaïs* and *The Ambassadors* a single hour-glass pattern frames a single hour-glass plot. Similarly, *To the Lighthouse,* by Virginia Woolf. In *The Return of the Native* the hour-glass pattern is repeated in a concatenation of inversions over and over again.

In Hardy's design, furthermore, the structural symbol is represented in an actual hour-glass, the hour-glass of Eustacia Vye. She discovers it the first time we meet her, where she stands fixed "as the pivot of this circle of the heath-country" beside a fire of illuminating coals. What those coals revealed, you recall, was "a small object, *which turned out to be an hour-glass, though she wore a watch.* She blew long enough to show that the sand had all slipped through." Why does Eustacia, you ask, require an hour-glass *and* a watch? Is it not that Eustacia with her watch *tells* Time and with her hour-glass *perceives* Time? That she requires both hour-glass and watch is indicative not only of her own philosophical mind but also of her creator's. Hardy is making a double use, a structural and a philosophical use, of Eustacia's hour-glass. Even as her telescope is the symbol of Space, so her hour-glass is the symbol of Time, of Hardy's time-consciousness and of his concern with the time-motif. But the hour-glass itself is also the emblem—the aesthetic pattern—of Time's turnabout of events.[1]

Let us begin with Hardy's philosophical use of the symbol (the hour-glass as the symbol of Time). Eustacia in her slow walks to recover from depression of spirits "carried her grandfather's telescope and her grandmother's hour-glass—the latter because of *a peculiar pleasure she derived from watching a material representation of time's gradual glide away.*" The sands that clock the Moment Now are the "material representation" of Time, of "real-time" in the Bergsonian sense. In her hypnotic gazing upon the sands of Time, Eustacia seeks to penetrate beyond mere "clock-time" into the secret of "real-time." Like the author of *Tess,* Eustacia is intensely conscious of "the flux and reflux, the rhythm of change [that] alternate and persist in everything under the sky." Her time-sense is telescoped. Hence "To dance with a man is to concentrate a twelve-month's regulation fire upon him in the fragment of an hour." Her point-present awareness is intensified: "The actual moment of a thing is soon gone," she remarks. And the Past, apart from its possible consequences upon the Present, is dead, is unreal.

> "Wait, let it go—see how our time is slipping, slipping, slipping!" She pointed towards the half-eclipsed moon.
> "You are too mournful."
> "No. *Only I dread to think of anything beyond the present*. What is [the Present], we know. We are together now, and it is unknown how long we shall be so . . ." (III, iii).

Since real existence for Eustacia is in the Present, the only "real-time" for her is Now; hence her rapt attention to Time's hurried flight, and her despairing attempts to check it. "The sand has nearly slipped away, I see, and the eclipse is creeping on more and more. Don't go yet! Stop till the hour has run itself out." Eustacia's time-sense of "real-time" is to be contrasted with Thomasin's time-sense of "clock-time." Eustacia in her point-present time-sense, in her pained awareness of this transistory Moment Now, is the opposite of Thomasin, who "is impressed with a sense of the intolerable slowness of time" and who braids her hair "according to a calendric system."

Eustacia's questioning delight in peering into hour-glass Time and tele-scopic Space identifies her with her creator—with Hardy's own probing into these two basic forms of philosophic thought. Witness his use of Time as an instrument of Fate (as in *Far from the Madding Crowd:* "the moment was the turning-point of a career"), his ironic commentaries on Time in the Wessex world (as in *Tess of the D'Urbervilles:* "The man to love rarely coincides with the hour of loving"), and his repetitious personi-fication of the time-motif now as "dicing Time," now as "Time's Laugh-ingstocks," again as "Father Time," or again as "Time the archsatirist." Witness his frontispiece to the Wessex Poems: a sketch of an hour-glass drawn in Hardy's own hand.

Time in Hardy's philosophy is a piecing together of a series of moments. Incidents, accidental happenings in "The Inevitable Movement Onward," are linked in an iron chain of cause and effect. Each incident in the chain, while seemingly but wanton Chance or "Crass Casuality," is actually, when seen in a backward view, the instrument of Fate. These chance col-lidings of willful and indifferent forces, as Mr. Jacques Barzun asserts, are without purpose or adequate cause; no cause is adequate to the tragic suffer-ing they bring about. In this hour-glass world of accident, though the Casuality of Time and Chance still prevail—they are the fundamentals of Hardy's ironics—an inexorable determinism rules. Coincidences in *The Return of the Native* have become integral to the mechanics. Episodic strings of chance and mischance (for example: Wildeve's bizarre dice-game and his surprising legacy, or Clym's blindness and his miscarried letter) doom Eustacia from the start. An apparatus of concurring coincidences produces (as one critic phrases it) the ironic and tragic resultant on which Hardy has calculated.

The basis of his predilection for contrivances of uncommon events—"strange conjunctions of circumstance"—is his conviction that

> A story must be exceptional enough to justify its telling. We tale-tellers are all Ancient Mariners, and none of us is warranted in stopping Wedding Guests . . . unless he has something more unusual to relate than the ordinary experience of every average man and woman.
> The whole secret of fiction and the drama—in the constructional part—lies in the adjustment of things unusual to things external and universal. The writer who knows exactly how exceptional, and how nonexceptional, his events should be made, possesses the key to the art (*Later Years*, pp. 15-16).

This is his conviction and this is his principle: "The uncommonness must be in the events, not in the characters; and the writer's art lies in shaping that uncommonness while disguising its unlikelihood, if it be unlikely" (*Early Life*, p. 194). This doctrine of the exceptional is the directing force in the artifice of Hardy's mechanics. Unexpected turns are his *dei ex machina*, Mr. Barzun points out. And his coincidences invariably turn out unlucky. As Mr. Ernest Baker notes: "a stroke of good fortune never occurs but it is instantly reversed in a stroke of savage derision."

I suppose an uncommon event is at its most exceptional, contrived in its most geometric form, when initial circumstances are ironically reversed. What is unique about *The Return of the Native* is its schematic figuring of reversed events whereby the fortunes of the lovers are again and again turned upside down. The human pair, fixed in Time like glass, are simultaneously turned contrariwise, their crisscross fortunes inverted with each shift of the hour-glass sands. From start to finish, Fate or Chance or Coincidence or Time keep tumbling the hour-glass over and over.

The Return of the Native resolves structurally into a mechanical concatenation of seven hour-glass plots. The species of diagram for this geometric counter-turning is a sequence of seven crisscross designs: The first two hour-glass reversals are caused by a single chance happening; a single fateful incident causes the third and fourth; initial circumstances of the third are determined by the issue of the second; the last two turnabouts are determined by the issue of the fifth, which has been prepared for by the ill-falling out of preceding events. Each reversed situation is thus logically located in a rigid system of causation. Double turnabouts (occurring in 1 and 4, 2 and 5, 3 and 6) contrive three full revolutions of the glass. Irony upon irony, Hardy's deterministic machinery grinds on to its appointed end.

The first reversal turns upon the accidental hitch in the marriage of Thomasin and Wildeve: their marriage license is made out for the wrong place. Wildeve, by taking advantage of this slip, reverses his position both to Thomasin and to her aunt. *Where earlier Mrs. Yeobright by forbidding the banns had Wildeve in her power, Wildeve by evading the marriage has Mrs. Yeobright at last in his.*

> "As a matter of justice it is almost due to me," said Wildeve. "Think what I have gone through to win her consent, the insult that it is to any man to have the banns forbidden. . . . I can never forget those banns. A harsher man would rejoice now *in the power I have of turning upon your aunt* by going no further in the business" (I, v).

It is Thomasin who suffers the double irony of this one fateful incident. To spare her aunt the wounds of disgrace, she is forced to beg Wildeve to carry out the marriage:

> "Here am I asking you to marry me; when by rights you ought to be on your knees imploring me, your cruel mistress, not to refuse you, and saying it would break your heart if I did. I used to think it would be pretty and sweet like that, but how different!"
> "Yes, real life is never at all like that" (I, v).

(That trick—that point—by which Hardy implies "I present only *real*, not fictitious, *life*" is cleverly turned.)

The reversal of initial positions resulting from this chance miscalculation in their marriage-license constitutes the second hour-glass plot. *Thomasin, who was once the pursued and who is now the pursuer, is given over by Wildeve for Eustacia, who before had been given over for Thomasin.* It is because of Eustacia that Wildeve goes "further in the business"; their relationship forms the third turnabout.

The hour-glass of this third turnabout is weighed first against Eustacia, then against Wildeve. She has drawn the still unmated moth to her signal fire:

> "I determined you should come; and you have come! *I have shown my power.* A mile and half hither, and a mile and half back again to your home—three miles in the dark for me. *Have I not shown my power?*" (I, vi).

But Eustacia—an irony again—counts upon a power she does not now possess. By the scant facts that Chance has provided her (by the highway encounter of Diggory Venn and Captain Vye), she misinterprets Wildeve's motives. Chance, not love for Eustacia, brings Wildeve to her yet unwed. Even now, like Thomasin, she is his pursuer. The choice is his: "The scales are balanced so nicely," Wildeve observes, "that a feather would turn them." "Wildeve's backward and forward play," as Diggory Venn calls it, only increases his attraction and intensifies her desire; now that another favors him, Eustacia desires him most. For Wildeve, conversely, Eustacia's preciousness increases "in geometrical progression" with each advance in another's desire for her. This device of injecting situations with a drop of irony ("Often a drop of irony into an indifferent situation," Hardy remarks, "renders the whole piquant") is a fundamental in Hardy's artistic code. The intervention of the reddleman forces Wildeve to make his choice. And this shifts the hour-glass sands and shapes the third reversal: *Eustacia, who before pursued Wildeve, is now pursued by him.*

> "You come to get me because you cannot get her. This is certainly a new position altogether. I am to be a stopgap" (I, xi).

"Not desiring the undesired of others," Eustacia, far from standing in the way of Thomasin's marriage to Wildeve, now is glad to promote it. For the providential return of the Native puts Eustacia on the side of the Yeobrights and reduces her former lover to a superfluity.

> "O that she [Thomasin] had been married to Damon before this!" she said. "And she would if it hadn't been for me! If I had only known —if I had only known!" (II, vi).

"Then we are both of one mind at last," she remarks to Venn as he pockets her letter of rejection.

Diggory Venn's proposal to Thomasin is the stick by which Mrs. Yeobright beats Wildeve into marriage with her niece. And thus the fourth hour-glass situation results: *Whereas Mrs. Yeobright,* without this weapon of Venn's proposal, *had been in Wildeve's power, she now in turn has him in her power.* One full revolution of the glass is charted by this double reversal in their relationship.

> Wildeve in the power of Mrs. Yeobright;
> Mrs. Yeobright in the power of Wildeve.
>
> Mrs. Yeobright in the power of Wildeve;
> Wildeve in the power of Mrs. Yeobright.

Again, as the third consequence of the reddleman's proposal, the fifth turnabout is framed: *The jilted suitor is forced to pursue the woman who before pursued him.* For to lose both women "was too ironical an issue to be endured. He could only decently save himself by Thomasin." Once more the hour-glass has been turned full cycle:

> Wildeve in the power of Thomasin;
> Thomasin in the power of Wildeve.
>
> Thomasin in the power of Wildeve;
> Wildeve in the power of Thomasin.

That Wildeve's bride should be given away by her former rival is a final ironic climax.

By the causal confluence of untoward events, from Wildeve's fantastic dice-game and its issue in Eustacia's quarrel with Mrs. Yeobright to the fateful incident of the closed door and the resulting divorce between

Eustacia and Clym, once more Eustacia is forced to pursue Wildeve. This situation shapes the sixth hour-glass: *Wildeve, who before pursued Eustacia, is now pursued by her.* The hour-glass of their courtship has been turned completely upside down. For in the situation which shaped the third reversal, Eustacia, who before pursued Wildeve, was in turn pursued by him. This double reversal is the third and final full revolution of the glass:

> Eustacia in the power of Wildeve;
> Wildeve in the power of Eustacia.
>
> Wildeve in the power of Eustacia;
> Eustacia in the power of Wildeve.

Coalescing with this sixth turnabout is the inverted relationship between Eustacia and Clym. *In the beginning Eustacia,* while Wildeve pursued her, *was the pursuer of Clym.* Yet *in the end,* when the deterministic interlocking of coincidences that first brought them together finally thrusts them apart, *Clym is the pursuer of Eustacia.* In this reversal, the seventh in Hardy's chain of inverted plots, the sands of Fate (Time and Chance) are against Clym. Time, in Clym's undelivered letter, and Chance, in Eustacia's mishap at Shadwater Weir, hasten on the last pyramiding of the hour-glass sands. No wonder Eustacia has dreaded "to think of anything beyond the present," when everything in her future has been so tool-marked and pinned down upon this blueprint of her hour-glass world.

This analysis reduces *The Return of the Native* to seven structural hour-glass plots. But extra-structural hour-glass patterns recur throughout the book. The "ru-um-tum-tum" turnabout in the relationship between Wildeve and Diggory Venn suggests that pattern. On reading Eustacia's letter of rejection, Wildeve asks:

> "Do you know what is in this letter?"
> The reddleman hummed a tune.
> "Can't you answer me?" asked Wildeve warmly.
> *"Ru-um-tum-tum," sang the reddleman.*
>
> .   .   .   .
>
> "But of all the odd things that ever I knew, the oddest is that you should so run counter to your own interests as to bring this to me."
> "My interests?"
> "Certainly. 'Twas your interest not to do anything which would send me courting Thomasin again, now she has accepted you—or something like it. Mrs. Yeobright says you are to marry her. 'Tisn't true, then?"
> "Good Lord! I heard of this before, but didn't believe it. When did she say so?"
> Wildeve began humming as the reddleman had done.
> "I don't believe it now," cried Venn.
> *"Ru-um-tum-tum," sang Wildeve.*

A second extra-structural hour-glass pattern is framed by the two dice-games between Wildeve and Christian Cantle and between Wildeve and Diggory Venn, in which by chance counterturns Mrs. Yeobright is outwitted by Wildeve, who in turn is outwitted by Venn. Mrs. Yeobright, at an ill-timed moment that seems most timely, sends the village idiot to Mistover with money to be divided between Clym and Thomasin. On the way, elated with his success in winning a raffle (the prize of a "gown-piece" going to "the man no woman will marry"), Christian gambles and loses to Wildeve both his own and Mrs. Yeobright's money. At this point Wildeve has the better of Mrs. Yeobright. But Chance lets the reddleman win back all of Wildeve's winnings; Wildeve's luck is turned abruptly upside down.

On the framework of this "dicing Time" reversal Hardy arranges the final chain of coincidences that link on to the inevitable catastrophe. The reddleman's "providential countermove," as Mrs. Yeobright misinterprets it, turns out to be only another of those "cruel satires that Fate loves to indulge in." The sum of guineas, which Venn through a chance remark of Wildeve misplaces in Thomasin's hands, is divided, but only after Eustacia and Mrs. Yeobright have quarreled; it is then too late. Christian's mishap causes Mrs. Yeobright to suspect Eustacia of receiving a dishonorable gift from Wildeve. The widened breach between them leads to Eustacia's neglect to open the door when Mrs. Yeobright calls for a reconciliation with her son. It is by chance that Wildeve visits Eustacia on the very afternoon when Mrs. Yeobright comes. Eustacia by chance thinks that Clym has opened the door, when actually he is asleep; he dreams that he is knocking at his mother's door and cannot get in. Mrs. Yeobright's chance recognition of her son upon his entering the house and of Eustacia upon her looking though the window causes the broken-hearted woman to depart. By chance she is killed by an adder's bite. Her chance remark to Johnny Nunsuch leads to the rift between Clym and Eustacia, which in turn leads to the tragedy at Shadwater Weir.

It is the cumulation of these conjunctive coincidences that is fatalistic. I repeat: what seems to be by chance is systematically beaded upon a deterministic string. The union of Eustacia and Clym was ill-fated from the start; but then, any love she might win was destined, as Eustacia surmised, to "sink simultaneously with the sand in the glass." For the missed opportunities involved in the counter-journeys across the heath by Mrs. Yeobright and by her son, Eustacia is at fault; yet instead of blaming herself she blames some "colossal Prince of the World, who had framed her situation and ruled her lot." Framed by an inexorable opposition of chance circumstances, she cannot escape:

"How I have tried and tried to be a splendid woman, and how destiny has been against me! . . . I do not deserve my lot!" she cried in a frenzy of bitter revolt. "O, the cruelty of putting me into this ill-conceived world! I was capable of much; but I have been injured and blighted and crushed by things beyond my control! O, how hard it is of Heaven to devise such tortures for me, who have done no harm to Heaven at all!" (V, vii).

The infernal malice of that "ingenious machinery contrived by the gods for reducing human possibilities of amelioration to a minimum," which *The Mayor of Casterbridge* expresses, has doomed her to the wrong place and to the wrong man. "Take all the varying hates felt by Eustacia Vye toward the heath, and translate them into loves, and you have the heart of Clym." Or diagram this symmetrical antithesis by an hour-glass pattern: Eustacia's hatred of the heath simultaneously shifts to love of Paris as Clym's hatred of Paris shifts to love of the heath. The disparity of opposing tensions between them increases as their schematic lines converge and their ill-conceived desires crisscross. Again, equally diagrammatic is the extra-structural hour-glass pattern of those crisscross-journeys over the heath—Clym going off towards his mother's house for the same purpose for which she has just come to his. The heath is at the center of the hour-glass of *The Return of the Native*, precisely as Paris is at the center of the hour-glass of *The Ambassadors*.

"It required an artist," Hardy wrote to a discriminating reviewer of *Jude the Obscure*, "to see that the plot is almost geometrically constructed" (*Later Years*, p. 40). Indeed, geometry is the primary specification in the layout of almost all of his structures. At each turning point in the intrigue of *The Return of the Native*, M. Pierre d'Exideuil observes, "we are conscious of the interplay and reactions of these warring forces [the quadrilaterals of tensions between Wildeve and Clym and Eustacia and Thomasin], the antagonisms of which could be transcribed as upon a working plan." The diagram of this working plan, I submit, is the shape of an hour-glass—discovered in the actual hour-glass of Eustacia. This geometric pattern is tool-marked upon each causal link in the chain of reversed situations. There are seven links to the chain, seven hour-glass plots. Here, then, is the blueprint of the book.

But it is this very structural blueprint on which Hardy plumed himself that advanced technique and criticism have scrapped as all too rigid and schematic, too obviously Daedalian. For critics like Mr. Forster and Mr. Frank Chapman, the construction of *The Return of the Native* is too rigid and mathematical: the characters are ordered to square with the requirements of its plan. Yet most of the characters, in spite of the geometry of their specifications, subsist not merely as calculated mathematical abstractions, but as beings with a life of their own. For Mr. Herbert Muller (his essay, and also Mr. Barzun's, is included in the famous Hardy Memorial number of *The Southern Review*), few important novelists have contrived their scaffoldings so cunningly or worked their characters so hard—"made them sweat through so many theatrical situations." Mr. Muller thinks that "even the magnificent architectural structure of *The Return of the Native* may now seem too artificial, and his most powerful scenes melodramatic." I argue for the contrary: "the magnificent architectural structure," in spite of its artificiality, places this novel highest among the Wessex group. Take apart Hardy's scaffolding, and there still remains, transcending his machinery of tragic accident and parallel recurrences (above and not wholly dependent upon it), what Mr. William R. Rutland defines as "his sense of the tragic fact." What you feel as you read is that "the tragedy of the book is essentially true [not true to Life, but true to the specifications of life within the framework of the book]; and the clumsiness of the machinery detracts little from it." What you object to as critic is "the clumsiness of the machinery"—its Elizabethan contrivances of mistaken identities, untold secrets, miscarried letters, crossed fidelities, chains of improbable coincidences. "It is to his artistry, the inventions themselves," that Mr. Muller and other Hardy critics object. The worst fault of *The Return of the Native*, Mr. Rutland asserts, "is an excessive and illegitimate use of coincidence." (A third critic is Eustacia Vye: "O, the cruelty of putting me into this ill-conceived world!") But coincidence figures in the blueprint of Eustacia's hour-glass world, each according to pattern. If one contrivance fails to work, another will. They are integral to the mechanics, their cumulation is fundamental to the structural design. My point is that the single coincidence, *because it has been prepared for,* is neither illegitimate nor incredible. Critical scrutiny should focus, not upon the single incredible coincidence, but upon the entire incredible machine. I conclude that what is incredible about that machine is the fact that its resultant tragedy becomes so wholly credible.

The whole secret of the novelist's craft, Hardy revealed, is in his "adjustment of things unusual to things external and universal." The value of Hardy's novels as art, Mr. Rutland judges, "depends, indeed, largely upon their power to convey this sense ['of the tragic fact'] irrespective of fortuitous outward events. And in this respect *The Return of the Native* is supreme." Its mechanics are integral to the total aesthetic effect, even as its coincidence is integral to the mechanics. In the very novel which most consistently geometrizes its mechanics the triumph over mere mechanics is at its greatest. In this triumph of total aesthetic effect lies the wonder of Hardy's art.   (1947)

NOTES

1. In "Hardy's Double-Visioned Universe" (*Essays in Criticism:* October 1957), M. A. Goldberg writes: "Hardy's double-visioned universe emerges from a reconciliation of two major Victorian concepts—the Darwinian world of mechanical science and natural law, and Arnold's world of culture and poetry—both of which Hardy admits with a kind of dialectical tension throughout the novel. Though for the main part critics have concerned themselves with Hardy's mechanism, they have almost invariably failed to identify this with nineteenth-century scientific currents, or to relate it with the cultural tradition in which he wrote. Thus, Lascelles Abercrombie (*Thomas Hardy*, 1912, pp. 111-112) points to the 'critical algebra' and 'mathematical abstraction'

which in Hardy reduce character to formula and life to a series of fortuitous accidents. Similarly, Robert W. Stallman's analysis of the novel ('Hardy's Hour-Glass Novel,' *Sewanee Review*, LV, 1947) contends that it 'resolves structually into a mechanical concatenation of seven hour-glass plots,' incidents being linked together in an iron chain of cause-and-effect and revealing an inexorable determinism ruling the universe. The same formula is repeated in the full-length studies by Lionel Johnson, Samuel Chew, Joseph Warren Beach and Harvey C. Webster. It has, in effect, become the *sine qua non* of Hardy criticism."

STEPHEN CRANE

He who wakes us always wounds us.—Nietzsche.

Crane's *Maggie* in Review[1]

APPEARING SIX YEARS before Norris' *McTeague, Maggie: A Girl of the Streets* was the first social exposé in fiction to render truthfully How the Other Half Lives—the title of Jacob Riis's sociological study of New York City tenement-life. *Godey's Magazine* of October 1895 reviewed the 1893 edition of *Maggie* along with Edward Waterman Townsend's *Jimmie Fadden* ("a household familiar . . . whose vivid language has infected the nation"), the book by which the Bowery was then best known. *Maggie*, it granted, was probably the strongest piece of slum writing we have; in keenness of wit, minuteness of observation, and bitterness of cynicism, *Maggie* compares with Arthur Morrison's *Tales of Mean Streets* (London, 1895). Crane renders the "foredoomed fall of a well-meaning girl reared in an environment of drunkenness and grime," and his plainness of speech may "give a shock to spasmic prudishness, but there is nothing to harm a healthy mind, and they [*i.e.*, the novels here under review] all should have the effect of creating a better understanding and a wiser, more active sympathy for the unfortunates who must fill the cellar of the tenement we call life. To do this," the reviewer (Rupert Hughes) concluded, "is far better even than to be artistic."

Maggie "is a powerful sermon on the need of missionary work among the heathen in the tenements of our big cities, and it cannot fail to open the eyes of many who have only taken a sentimental interest in a class that seems to be no nearer to them than the natives of the Congo" (San Francisco *Chronicle*: August 9, 1896). *Maggie*, said the London *Academy* (January 16, 1897), "is one of the most downright earnestly-written books ever published. The gruesome tragedy of environment, with all its sordidness of detail, is hammered in with brief, pitiless sentences. Mr. Crane's command of language is remarkable: he does not spare his readers one jot or tittle of the horror of New York slum life." Crane's heroine is doomed from the start—by her environment. "From the first, Maggie was forced to bear heavy burdens which should have been carried by the older and stronger members of her family. Then, too, heredity and environment, the two bugbears of to-day, are strong factors to contend with and when, as in this case, their chief elements are drunkenness and even worse vices, the end is not hard to foresee" (Denver *Republican:* July 26, 1896).

"I recall no tale that approaches 'Maggie' in the illustration of drunkenness, promiscuous pugilism, joyless and repellent dialogue, and noise. Of course," says this reviewer, "I like it. Mr. Howells has educated me in realism, and I hope I know a good thing in that line when I see it" (New York *Town Topics:* June 25, 1896). In the 1896 Heinemann edition with revised title *Maggie: A Child of the Streets,* Howells in his Foreword remarked against "the many foolish people who cannot discriminate between the material and the treatment in art, and think that beauty is inseparable from daintiness and prettiness." (An unidentified London journal commented on the Heinemann edition: "Mr. Heinemann has given to Mr. Stephen Crane's 'Maggie' something of the appearance of an old-fashioned Sunday school prize-book.") It is a terrible satire, said the New York *Mail & Express* (November 6, 1896), "but the writer has stopped short of cynicism—not far enough, however, to make 'Maggie' palatable to the lovers of only pleasant things." Howells, in the New York *Press* of April 15, 1894 (remarking on the 1893 *Maggie*), had admitted: "There is so much realism of a certain kind in it that unfits it for the general reading, but once in a while it will do to tell the truth as completely as Maggie does." In announcing the forthcoming Appleton edition *The Critic* (February 22, 1896) summed up briefly the history of *Maggie* since its first appearance in paper-bound mustard-yellow covers with a pen-name for the author and with no name at all for the publisher: " 'Maggie' was not an immoral story, as many persons imagined from its title; it was coarse in the way that 'Chimmie Fadden' is coarse; but there was more objection to bad language from the mouth of a girl-tough than from a boy." Bowery slang, "of which other writers have given us a taste, reaches its perfect flower in Mr. Crane's chronicle," the Indianapolis *News* conceded (August 14, 1896). Crane "has gone to the lowest depths of degradation for material, and he does not spare the reader in telling of his observations." The *News* concluded: "This is by no means a cheerful tale. There is something inexorable in the movement of the incidents of the girl's life. It is all very pitiful, and it is told with power. There is no halfway in Mr. Crane's realism." The *News* added, however: "The great question is not of veracity, but is as to the right of an author to use an undeniable power in presenting a tale of unrelieved misery, despair and sin. It is to be hoped that Mr. Crane will turn his talents to the writing of some less wretched tale." The same squeamish note appeared the next day in the Nashville *Banner.* Like the Indianapolis *News,* the *Banner* recognized *Maggie's* realism; "it is a magnificent piece of realism, which loses its artistic value because its shadows are too deep and its lights too faint and evasive, missing, indeed, the highest aim of literature, which is to give some small degree of pleasure, at least, to the world, and to prove itself not a clog, but an inspiration in the uplifting of humanity's heart."

The obsession with the idea that art aims to inspire, please, and enlighten by tender and uplifting sentiments was the aesthetic malady that afflicted the 1890's; in poetry and criticism this misconception of art prevailed until T. S. Eliot. *Maggie,* said the *Banner,* is not an immoral book; it's rather "a strong sermon urging the need of greater charity of sentiment, as well as of gold for the poverty-hardened people of the slums." But in spite of its strength, it is a failure. Why? Because "It is too hopeless, too full of misery, degradation and dirt. The reader flounders in a mire of pessimism, never once receiving from the author the offer of a helping hand or a word of encouragement, and the memory of the book is a nightmare, and the thought of it inexpressibly hopeless and depressing." The *Banner* reviewer wanted it both ways: realism minus the degradation and dirt, and realism touched up with noble sentiments. Neither way is it then Realism.

What offended the squeamish morality of the Gilded Age was the then seamy realism of Crane's exposé. They didn't want the truth exposed, but in Crane's *Maggie* they got just that. Even William Dean Howells, the leading crusader for Realism, thought *Maggie* too realistic—it wasn't the kind of realism he had asked for, and he advised the young author to remove the profanities which he thought would shock the public. (Crane applied for copyright on *Maggie* in 1893, and according to the New York *Times* on May 31, 1896, he took out a new copyright in 1896; that much indicates revisions.)[2] *Maggie,* said the New York *Advertiser,* "is as realistic as anything that Emile Zola has ever written. Though some of its chapters are enough to give one the 'creeps,' none can deny that the characters which he draws with such a master hand are absolutely true to life." Echoing Howells, the New York *Advertiser* (June 1, 1896) praised Crane's artistry: *Maggie* "is free of maudlin sentiment." The *Advertiser* scored an important insight: "No missionary ever ventures near 'Rum Alley.' Its denizens are left to their own resources, and they simmer in them." As the San Francisco *Chronicle* observed: "There is no attempt, as in Ned Townsend's latest story, to idealize the characters. The coarseness, the sordidness of life in these overcrowded buildings of New York is something which affects one like the reek of the Mulberry Bend gutters on a hot August night. The genius of the writer is revealed in the simplicity of his means of producing powerful effects." One of the best English reviews is unfortunately unidentified; it is worth quoting in full here:

It is surely a fine tribute to the art in a book that the reviewer should be compelled to praise it against his will. And this tribute must certainly be given to Mr. Stephen Crane's latest story. 'Maggie' is a study of life in the slums of New York, and of the hopeless struggle of a girl against the horrible conditions of her environment; and so bitter is the struggle, so black the environment, so inevitable is the end, that the reader feels a chill at his heart, and dislikes the book even while he admires it.

Maggie, in sum, is thwarted by her environment, but what gives the book its artistry is Crane's realism:

> Mr. Crane's realism is merciless and unsparing; in these chapters are set before us in cold blood hideous phases of misery, brutality, drunkenness, vice; while oaths and blasphemies form the habitual speech of the men and women who live and move in this atmosphere of vileness. Yet every scene is alive and has the unmistakable stamp of truth upon it. The reader does not feel that he is reading abqut these horrors; he feels as if the outer walls of some tenement houses in the slums had been taken away and he could see—and see with comprehension— the doings of the teeming inmates. Over the whole grimly powerful tragedy is the redeeming grace of the author's implied compassion; but he never mars the effect of the story by speaking this compassion or by pointing a moral. He has drawn a vivid picture of life at its lowest and worst; he has shown us the characters as they would be, with no false glamour of an impossible romance about them; and the moral may confidently be left to look after itself, since it stares from every page. Maggie herself is a wonderfully well-drawn character, and the book, repellent though it is, is in its way a triumph.

In January 1896 Crane, writing John Northern Hilliard, expressed the same dictum as the anonymous reviewer of the 1896 Heinemann edition of *Maggie:* "Preaching is fatal to art in literature. I try to give to readers a slice out of life; and if there is any moral or lesson in it, I do not try to point it out. I let the reader find it for himself. The result is more satisfactory to both the reader and myself. As Emerson said, 'There should be a long logic beneath the story, but it should be kept carefully out of sight.' "[3] We know that Crane was pleased with the reception in England of *The Red Badge of Courage* and that he agreed with the London *Academy's* claim: "Like so many Americans, he owes his success to British enthusiasm. It was not until *The Red Badge of Courage* was brought out in this country, in the autumn of 1895, that America 'found' its author. Mr. Crane would be the first to acknowledge his indebtedness to the English critics and the English public, who, with one accord, forced his name into well-deserved prominence." As for the American reception of *Maggie,* as the *Academy* explained in reference to the failure of the 1893 edition: *"Maggie* is not a pleasant book, and in those days the public was not ripe for the reception of instantaneous literary photographs of slum life. . . . But we have changed all that," boasted the *Academy.* As a matter of fact, however, *Maggie* received a considerable number of very favorable American reviews. The San Francisco *Argonaut* of August 31, 1896, after reviewing *Maggie* on July 13, introduced excerpts from the novel with the explanation that "its popularity has grown to such an extent that we have decided to put before our readers a few of the more striking scenes. . . ." The New York *Times* (May 31, 1896) praised Crane as artist in rendering his pictures "with such vivid and terrible accuracy as to make one believe they are photographic. Mr. Crane cannot have seen all that he describes, and yet the reader feels that he must have seen it all. This, perhaps, is the highest praise one can give the book."

Other reviewers went *"Maggie*-mad," but not in the way Crane hoped for. "This unpleasant story," said the Pittsburgh *Bulletin* (August 8, 1896), "will make Stephen Crane's admirers wish they had stopped at his 'Red Badge of Courage.' Its heavy vulgarity leads nowhere and effects nothing." A certain English critic was similarly offended, and the Boston *Globe* (November 5, 1896) quoted him: "The fame of Stephen Crane has spread abroad in the wild way in which it has here, and a London critic writes in this wise of the young and glowing colorist: 'Mr. Crane always shouts in his writings; in fact he positively blares, with never a pause. To read his latest book, "Maggie," is to put one's ears into the bell of a cornet blown by giant lungs. It leaves one limp, exhausted, mistreated. The book is like a lump of red, raw beef. It is food for tigers, not for women and men. Mr. Crane may be as clever as Mr. Howells makes him out to be, but he is abusing his talents. Even supposing he does split our ear drums with his loud bass what shall it profit him or us?' " I think the answer is that a review is not a review when it is not a critical discussion of the book reviewed.

These *Maggie* reviews document the literary and moral barometer of the 1890's, the impact of Crane's sociological iconoclasm upon the Gilded Age, and the contemporary reputation of a very young American writer destined to survive all his anonymous reviewers. He survived also his reputation in Port Jervis. So shocked were the ladies of Port Jervis after the 1896 publication of *Maggie* that several of them consulted his brother "as to the propriety of receiving Stephen Crane in their homes. . . ." (Thomas Beer in the Appendix to his *Stephen Crane,* 1923). They probably took their stance from the *Home Journal* of July 8, 1896: "One of our most noted contemporary literary critics, preëminent for his good taste, fairness, and discrimination, has sharply castigated this book. But whatever may be the general trend of the notices it has received, it is inconceivable that any reader, even with moral tone not above the average, could go over these pages without a shock to his sensibilities, and the pressure of the old question, 'Qui bono?' No good at all, must be the answer that springs to the lips of every right-thinking man or woman that turns over the leaves of Mr. Crane's 'Maggie.' Reeking with profanity, blasphemy, the low, brutal dialect of the slums, etc., how could such a book "find acceptance among the better and purer classes of the reading world?" It didn't. But it found acceptance among those who recognized the importance of its "aggressive and pitiless realism" and felt that this picture of tenement-house life "in its sordidness and pathos amounts to a positive revelation" (Boston *Beacon:* June 27, 1896). As the Boston *Times* (July 12, 1896) pointed out: "The pitiful tragedy of the plot is being enacted over and over again all about us. It tells of a girl whose dormant soul was never kindled, who was ruined by the overwhelming forces of heredity and environment." After concluding that "Despite the sadness of her death one does not wish that she might have lived longer," the *Times* added: "There is not a gleam of sunshine in the whole book, but in Mr. Crane's hands this simple, ordinary story is so horribly real that it makes an indelible appeal to the fortunate portion of mankind, to right the wrongs which are making such hideous mischief all about us." As for the better and purer classes of the reading world, Crane didn't give a damn; the difference defines his lasting merit.

In "New York Low Life in Fiction," appearing in the New York *World* of July 26, 1896 (reissued in the 1896 Heinemann edition of *Maggie* as "An Appreciation"), Howells said: "I think that what strikes me most in the story of 'Maggie' is that quality of fatal necessity which dominated Greek tragedy." Chelifer (Rupert Hughes, a fraternity brother of Crane) echoed Howells in *Godey's Magazine* of September, 1896: "It has the inevitableness of a Greek tragedy, and the reader that grants to the fate of Euripides's fanciful 'Medea' an import and significance he refuses to see in the predestined ugliness of the end of this well-meaning 'Maggie,' has an outlook in life that is too literary to be true. Indeed he has misread his classics, if the woes of their creatures leave him uneducated into sympathy with the miseries of the miserables of his own town." John D. Barry made a similar reading of Crane's *George's Mother* (Edward Arnold, 1896) in *The Daily Tatler* of November 12, 1896:

> This is the book that raised a howl of rage and disgust from earnest reviewers who are supposed to encourage literature.[4] For many reasons I feel profoundly grateful for it—not to the author, however, for a more *impersonal* story has never existed; if you think of him at all, it is only as the agent through which tremendous forces in nature have been marshaled and expressed. One of these reasons is that it has formulated to myself the justification of the use in literature of utterly squalid material. I can imagine Mr. Crane's theme treated in a way that would make it the really debasing thing the reviewers have called *George's Mother.* But Mr. Crane's book is its own justification; it teaches us what the lesson of the life it depicts would teach us if we were to know it at firsthand, the dreadful pity of it. I don't see how any one could resent or blame the characters in *George's Mother;* given the conditions surrounding them, and they had to be what they were. In this lies the whole pathos of all human life!

Whereas Barry found Crane not a realist in *George's Mother* ("The little mother is real, but the son stands for a class, not an individual"), Jeannette L. Gilder in the New York *World* thought the scenes "had been sketched from life and the conversation taken down in shorthand. In 'Chimmie Fadden' we have the romance of the slums. In 'George's Mother' we get their hard and stern reality" (May 31, 1896).

Many readers will find it impossible to become interested in *Maggie: A Girl of the Streets*, remarked the Richmond *Times* (July 26, 1896), "because, as they will tell you, 'it deals with such low people.' These will belong to the class who consign Mr. Dickens to the back shelves, or tolerate him coldly, as a person who devoted great talents to a low use. Mr. Crane can afford to dispense with their admiration. As a matter of fact, in the ghastly story of this girl of the streets, he has revealed the tragedy in the degradation of the lowest ten thousand with the pen of a master." *Maggie,* said Hamlin Garland in his June 1893 *Arena* review of the 1893 edition, "deals with poverty and vice and crime also, but it does so, not out of curiosity, not out of salaciousness, but because of a distinct art impulse, the desire to utter in truthful phrase a certain rebellious cry. It is the voice of the slums."

Frank Norris, on the contrary, thought Crane concerned himself too much with style at the expense of truth-to-life; and in one sense he was right, namely the fact that Crane is more stylist than realist. (Realism is copyistic of reality, aiming at photographic verisimilitude. Realism and Naturalism get confounded in the critical discourse and in the historical discourse of critics and historians of literature. Literary naturalism defines the philosophical outlook stemming from the given literary work. Dreiser's *American Tragedy* is the example. Realism, however, clashes with Naturalism in Dreiser's rendering of *American Tragedy*. It is the same in Norris's *McTeague*. Portions of both works contradict both the Realism they aim at and the philosophical naturalism they supposedly exemplify.)

Reviewing *Maggie* in the San Francisco *Wave*, Frank Norris complained that Crane's characters seemed deficient in psychological realism. "It is as if Mr. Crane had merely used the 'machinery' and 'business' of slum life to develop certain traits or to portray certain emotions and passions that *might happen anywhere*." Norris was right, but for the wrong reasons. He was mistaken in wanting *Maggie* to be otherwise than it is. Psychological realism belongs not here, but rather in *The Red Badge*. In both novels the realism is an invented, imagined realism; not studied from life but created—created in such a way as to render an illusion of reality. The reader, Frank Norris opined, "is apt to feel that the author is writing, as it were, from the outside. There is a certain lack of sympathy apparent. Mr. Crane does not seem to *know* his people. You are tempted to wonder if he has ever studied them as closely as he might have done. He does not seem to me to have gotten *into* their life and to have written from what he saw around him" (*Wave:* July 4, 1896). The Boston *Ideas* that same day expressed just the opposite viewpoint: "The writer must have absorbed the meaning of the life here described deeply into his consciousness; it must have lingered there, to enable him to so accurately depict characters and scenes of which the average intelligent reading public catches but incidental outward glimpses without sympathetically understanding their causes and interludes." This reviewer noted the inevitableness of Maggie's end ("Circumstances are too strong for her") and, as though replying to Frank Norris, he pointed out that *Maggie* necessarily is quite different from *The Red Badge of Courage.*

Other reviewers (as we have seen) considered *Maggie* too realistic, too vulgar in its realism. In the Gilded Age it was castigated as "wicked"; "but that charge is absurd. A more convincing picture of the utter horror, despair, and squalor of vice could not well be made" (New York *Press:* July 12, 1896). "The story of darkest America has been told in the most realistic way by Stephen Crane. In all the work he has ventured upon, he has rendered the seamy side of modern existence, the real life of the slums, with a force and actuality of description that has not been equalled by any depiction of low life" (Boston *Courier:* June 28, 1896). As for "the realistic picture which Mr. Crane portrays," said the New York *Press* on October 17, 1896: "And Mr. Crane is nothing if he is not realistic. There is realism in every chapter of 'Maggie'—it is the realism of every day life. Mr. Crane wields a trenchant pen, and there has not been published a sterner picture of life in the slums of New York than is here presented." Said the San Francisco *Argonaut* in commenting on selected excerpts from the novel: "All this is very horrible, but it is also very powerful. Mr. Crane presents the squalid and abject lives *with the vividness of life itself,* and one can not but admire his skill. But at the same time one feels that he could find better subjects for his unquestionable talent." The Boston *Times* (July 12, 1896) praised *Maggie* for its "fidelity to life . . . the dialect is as gross and realistic as decency will permit." With Crane, said Frank Norris, "it is the broader, vaguer, human interest that is the main thing, not the smaller details of a particular phase of life." The Brooklyn *Life* (August 22, 1896), as though in refutation of Norris, singled out from *Maggie* such minute particulars in Crane's Bowery landscape as this one: " 'Over on the island,' he says in painting the outlook from the tenement-house window, 'a worm of yellow convicts came from the shadow of a gray ominous building and crawled slowly along the river's bank.' " This image, to inject a pertinent note here, defines the limitations of Maggie's world: it consists of the Bowery, with its perspective of the convict island and the river. It opens out not at all upon any other possible world; the novel confines its heroine to an imprisoned realm and thereby dooms her from the start. For Maggie to escape from her author's given environment would surely be—of all endings indeed—the most contrary and inartistic conceivable.

The publisher's blurb for the Appleton 1896 edition of *Maggie* (priced at 74 cents, whereas the unsaleable 1893 edition was priced at 50 cents) proclaimed it "a real and strenuous tale"—and strenuous it was; but as the *Literary Digest* said, it is more "impressionistic" than "real," and "true to the impressionistic practice, alike in paint and in letters, the essential figure is the least delineated. Maggie is far less important to the canvas than her brother Jimmie, or her sottish mother, or the coarse and tawdry Bowery bartender who is the villain of the piece, and her destroyer" (August 8, 1896). But Maggie is of course just as important as the other characters who comprise her enforced destiny; to distinguish the latter as dominant because delineated with more detail is to blur the relationship of the one to the other. They represent her environment: "None of the dirt of Rum Alley seemed to be in her veins." Of course, people in fiction are composed of words, not of flesh and blood, and to identify them with reality is absurd. Though the characters in *Maggie* are not individuals but types, individualized characters are no more true to life than "mere types"; their anonymity reflects Crane's intention.[5]

"Every sentence bristles with the steely sinews of the Nemesis that lays its heavy burden upon the dwarfish development of these poor, puny lives. Every phrase is a noteworthy one, a revelation of a people waiting for a savior." The reviewer for the Boston *Courier* was very perceptive. So too was the reviewer of the Springfield, Ohio, *Womankind* (August 1896). *Maggie* "is not the story of 'A Girl of the Streets'—rather a record of her evolution, how she unwittingly and unwillingly became the thing she despised." He points out: "In a line or two—without saying anything about them, himself, at all, Mr. Crane shows the utter futility of the ordinary 'mission' methods for reaching such people as Maggie and her brothers; again in a line he reveals the contemptible Pharisaical spirit of certain of the clergy; and in the brutal laugh and jest that greet the successive appearances of the old drunken mother in the police court, he hints at the wickedness and folly of our present methods of dealing with such pitiable creatures." The Boston *Saturday Evening Gazette* (June 20, 1896) saw *Maggie*, similarly, as having perhaps some sociological effect: "In the hands of an artist like Mr. Crane the simple story becomes an awful arraignment of our humanity. Such books are needed to impress upon the fortunate portion of mankind the truth that their fair cities bear ulcerous spots which threaten hideous mischief." *The Daily Tatler* in its first review of the book (November 11, 1896) remarked on the *Literary World's* comment that "there is nothing pleasing or pretty about Mr. Crane's work; but it has its place undoubtedly"—what the *Literary World* means, said the *Tatler*, is that "the complacent among christians need the lesson conveyed by Maggie's wicked life and consequently untimely death." The highest office of the writer, so Chelifer thought in *Godey's Magazine* (October, 1895) is the education of human sympathy. "Literature is the greatest of all democratizing forces." One gets more into sympathy with *Maggie* than with *George's Mother*, the New York *Press* opined (July 12, 1896): "It is assured from the beginning that in the ordinary course of events she will go to the bad. Mr. Crane makes one feel the morally downward pull of her surroundings with a power all the greater because he skillfully avoids all hint of sermonizing and almost all comment of any sort."

Crane's contemporary reviewers substantiate my 1952 reading of *Maggie:* "Innocence thwarted and betrayed by environment is the sum of *Maggie*. Innocence debased and deluded is *George's Mother*" (*Omnibus*, p. 9).

Crane's writings fill twelve volumes—eighty-six sketches and tales, five brief novels, three volumes of verse, and a mass of journalistic stuff. The greater part of all this work is second-rate. The artist had succumbed to the journalist (for example: *Active Service, The O'Ruddy, Great Battles of the World*), though some of the pure Crane shone even at the end of his comet-like career. Notably "The Upturned Face." As Edward Garnett complained in 1921, "If America has forgotten or neglects Crane's achievements, above all in 'Maggie' and 'The Open Boat,' she does not yet deserve to produce artists of rank."   (1959)

NOTES

1. This article presents hitherto unpublished material: contemporary reviews of *Maggie* here quoted for the first time. Their significance in the literary history of the Nineties and the literary naturalistic movement is that they give us a much fuller idea than we have ever had of what the public reception of *Maggie* actually was.

These reviews form a collection belonging to the Butler Library Crane Collection at Columbia University and are here used by the kind permission of Mr. Roland Baughman, Head of the Manuscript Division of Butler Library. I also wish to thank Professor Daniel G. Hoffman for permission to use this material. And the American Philosophical Society for a grant in aid of research on Stephen Crane.

2. For a collation of the 1893 and 1896 editions see my "Stephen Crane's Revisions of *Maggie: A Girl of the Streets,*" *American Literature,* XXVI (January 1955), pp. 528-536.

3. In my *Stephen Crane: An Omnibus* (1952), Part VII Letters, p. 673.

As the original of this Crane to Hilliard letter has now come to light, the correct date for it is January 2, 1896. See *Stephen Crane: Letters,* edited by R. W. Stallman and Lillian Gilkes, with an Introduction by R. W. Stallman (New York University Press, 1960).

4. The reviewer in *The Bookman,* for example, who begged to suggest "that an author who within a single year has forced critics to compare his work with that of the greatest living realists, ought not, as a mere matter of self-respect, to take over his literary ash-barrel and ask us to accept his old bones and junk as virgin gold." (Reviewed in *Bookman* of July 1896 by Harry Thurston Peck, who had reviewed favorably Crane's *The Black Riders.*)

5. This point is made by Henry Hazlitt in his Introduction to the Knopf 1923 edition of *Maggie:* Crane's "generalized characters are not the result of an inability on Crane's part to create sharp individual portraits; they reflect his intention."

Crane's *Maggie:* A Reassessment

"WHAT, AFTER ALL, is it that keeps alive with such savage force a period-piece like *Maggie,* though as a social study it is hilariously out-dated?", Alfred Kazin asks in the New York *Times Book Review* for September 30, 1952.[1] *The answer is the art by which it is constructed.* As the New

York *Press* for July 12, 1896, observed, "One part of the art is in the omission of all that is unnecessary—all that detracts from the main idea that is to be expressed." Frank Norris, himself no stylist, conceded the charm of Crane's style and defined it as "aptitude for making phrases— sparks that cast a momentary gleam of light on whole phases of life." Reviewing Crane's *Active Service* in *Criterion* for January 6, 1900, Rupert Hughes wrote: "A most notable feature of Mr. Crane's style is the hunt for the one fit word. Always with him it is the unexpected, the unusual, the vivid epithet." A tone-painting, rather than a realistic photograph, *Maggie* is the painter's novel, the poet's novel—the art-novel.

Crane and, more importantly, Henry James gave modern American fiction its beginnings. In the viewpoint of our literary historians, however, Norris and Dreiser outstripped Crane in importance because of their influence in the subsequent history of literary ideas and trends, namely literary naturalism. One wonders how Dreiser, whose prose seems to me a model of How Not to Write could possibly influence any artist except for the worse. Crane is the superior artist, but Dreiser is more important because "he reveals the very nerves of American society." Marxian and sociological critics judge literary works on much the same grounds as the academic literary historian. In the Nineties, similarly, Howells and Garland advocated that literature deal with the fundamental realities of American life. Crane, however, transcended the theory he subscribed to.

Crane once defined a novel as "a succession of sharply outlined pictures, which pass before the reader like a panorama, leaving each its definite impression." *Maggie,* divided into nineteen chapters or episodes is a panorama of impressionistic vignettes, disconnected scenes that reel off with much the same jerky, nervous effect that early motion-pictures convey. Not logic but mood defines the relationship between images and episodes. Moods of romantic sentiment, illusion, or hope collapse in contradictory moods of futility, disillusionment, or despair.

> She envied elegance and soft palms. She craved those adornments of person which she saw every day on the street, conceiving them to be allies of vast importance to women. Studying faces, she thought many of the women and girls she chanced to meet smiled with serenity as though for ever cherished and watched over by those they loved.

What immediately follows, however, contradicts this mood of romantic delusion, the mood of envy and illusion being undercut by the contradictory mood evoked by harsh reality:

> The air in the collar-and-cuff establishment strangled her. She knew she was gradually and surely shrivelling in the hot, stuffy room (Section VIII).[2]

Double Mood, the contrast of contradictory moods, or bathos pattern the novel. Maggie "blossomed in a mud-puddle." The bathos of "blossomed" / "in a mud puddle" has kinship with Jimmie's saying "wonderingly and quite reverently, 'Deh moon looks like hell, don't it?'" Or again in Jimmie's becoming "so sharp that he believed in nothing." He has "the chronic sneer of an ideal manhood." Pete, Maggie's lover, "brought forth all his elegance and all his knowledge of high-class customs for her benefit." "He displayed the consideration of a cultured gentleman who knew what was due. 'Say, what's eatin' yeh? Bring d'lady a big glass. What use is dat pony?'" As a villain Pete is pretty slick: his hair is curled down in an oiled bang, and his patent-leather shoes shine "like weapons." Pete is a Bowery version of fashion plate social decorum; his "aristocratic person looked as if it might soil."

> Maggie perceived that here was the ideal man. Her dim thoughts were often searching for far-away lands where the little hills sing together in the morning. Under the trees of her dream-gardens there had always walked a lover.

In juxtaposed contrast, ironically contradicting Maggie's illusion, is the bathetic image of Pete—"the ideal man."

> Pete took note of Maggie, "Say, Mag, I'm stuck on yer shape. It's outa sight," he said parenthetically, with an affable grin (V-VI).

Illusion versus Reality: "He was a knight," so Maggie pictures Pete; but returning to the sordidness of her home she encounters the grim reality:

> A clock, in a splintered and battered oblong box of varnished wood, she suddenly regarded as an abomination. She noted that it ticked raspingly. The almost vanished flowers in the carpet pattern, she conceived to be newly hideous. Some faint attempts which she had made with blue ribbon to freshen the appearance of a dingy curtain, she now saw to be piteous.
> She wondered what Pete dined on (VI).

The faded carpet-flowers define Maggie's own plight. As for the knots of blue ribbon on the dingy curtain, they "appeared like violated flowers" (VI); the epithet "violated" transfers to Maggie's plight. The sordid reality she seeks escape from is imaged in the clock that "ticked raspingly" in its battered box of *varnished* wood. But always Maggie seeks escape from reality in transcendent dreams: "She wondered what Pete dined on." Always with Emma Bovary, too, "disappointment quickly gave way to a new hope" (*Madame Bovary* III, VI).

Crane is a master of the mock-heroic, the satiric mode, the contradictory effect. At the bar-show in Section VII two girls, billed as "sisters," came forth and sang a duet which is heard occasionally at concerts given under church auspices. They supplemented it with a dance, which, of course can never be seen at concerts given under church auspices" (VII).

This scene—"a great green hued hall" with "an orchestra of yellow silk women and bald-headed men"—is identified by the reviewer, A. H. Lewis, for the New York *Journal* for March 8, 1896, as "a pretty good description of the Atlantic Garden on the Bowery." So, then, Crane studied the Bowery. *Maggie,* as Hamlin Garland said, is "the voice of the slums." "It is not written by a dilettante; it is written by one who has lived the life," said Garland in his 1893 *Arena* review. The fact is, however, that Crane did not know the Bowery intimately until after he had written one or two drafts of his novel. He composed the first draft at the Delta Upsilon house at Syracuse University during the spring of 1891. (The evidence, *contra* John Berryman's *Stephen Crane,* is documented in *Omnibus,* pp. 5-7.)[3] He invented the plot of *Maggie.* It was the same with *The Red Badge of Courage. Maggie,* said the New York *Journal,* "will not add to his reputation. He wrote it during the golden period of his youth which leads us to stray as far as possible from the path of conventional cleanliness in search of our subjects, and being young and inexperienced, he learned just enough of his theme to make him think that he had mastered it, and he painted all his characters and scenes in the dark colors that make themselves apparent to anybody who studies what is technically known as 'low life' through the car windows."

Well, then, where did Crane obtain the inspirational source for his invented novel? It is constructed like *Madame Bovary,* by alterations of contradictory moods—illusions and dreams shattered by realities. As Emma Bovary idolizes Léon, so Maggie idolizes Pete; and as Emma's plight is ignored by the priest (VI), so Maggie's plight is ignored by the minister she encounters on the street (Section XVI). As she "timidly accosted him he made a convulsive movement and saved his respectability by a vigorous side-step. He did not risk it to save a soul. For how was he to know that there was a soul before him that needed saving?" It is after the minister ignores her that Maggie changes to a hardened street-walker, a girl of "the painted cohorts of the city," "emerging from the places of forgetfulness" (XVII). Maggie is identified with her mother when a man bumps into Maggie and jokingly calls: "Hi, there, Mary, I beg your pardon! Brace up, old girl" (XVII). In *Madame Bovary* the priest by ignoring Emma's plight unwittingly prepares for her downfall, for her adulteries with Rodolphe and Léon. As with Flaubert, so with Crane—the institution of religion is the butt of their criticism.

At the opera Emma romantically identifies herself with the prima donna whose voice "seemed to her to be but echoes of her conscience, and this illusion that charmed her as some very thing of her own life. But no one on earth had loved her with such love" (II, XV). Emma next identifies herself with the black-cloaked lover in Spanish hat, "and, drawn towards this man by the illusion of the character, she tried to imagine to herself his life—that life resonant, extraordinary, splendid, and that might have been hers if fate had willed it. They would have known one another, loved one another." When Maggie is with Pete at the bar-show in the great green-hued hall, her cheeks blush with excitement and her eyes glisten. "She drew deep breaths of pleasure. No thoughts of the atmosphere of the collar-and-cuff factory came to her" (VII). Similarly, Emma Bovary is lost in dreams while at the opera and is oblivious of reality:

> She longed to run to his arms, to take refuge in his strength, as in the incarnation of love itself, and to say to him, to cry out, "Take me away! carry me with you! let us go! Thine, thine! all my ardour and all my dreams!"
> The curtain fell.

And with the fall of the curtain her dream-mood ends, and reality intrudes: "The smell of the gas mingled with that of the breaths, the waving of the fans, made the air more suffocating . . . and she fell back in her armchair with palpitations that choked her."

Crane's *Maggie* is a Bowery version of Flaubert's *Madame Bovary*. At the theatre "Maggie lost herself in sympathy with the wanderers swooning in snow storms beneath happy-hued church windows, while a choir within sang 'Joy to the World.' To Maggie and the rest of the audience this was transcendental realism. Joy always within, and they, like the actor, inevitably without. Viewing it, they hugged themselves in ecstatic pity of their imagined or real condition" (VIII). Emma Bovary engages likewise in self-pity while at the opera, and for her, as for Maggie, happiness is always at a distance. "The nearer things were, moreover, the more her thoughts turned away from them. All her immediate surroundings, the wearisome country, the middle-class imbeciles, the mediocrity of existence, seemed to her exceptional, a peculiar chance that had caught hold of her, while beyond stretched as far as eye could see an immense land of joys and passions" (IX). As for Maggie, "She imagined a future rose-tinted because of its distance from all that she had experienced before" (XII). Just before drowning herself, "Street-car bells jingled with a sound of merriment," as though in mockery of her plight. So in *Madame Bovary* the song of the blind man mocks Emma on her death-bed. For Maggie, instead of church-bells there are only street-car bells. "Afar off the lights of the avenues glittered as if from an impossible distance. . . . The varied sounds of life, made joyous by distance and seeming unapproachableness, came faintly and died away to a silence" (XVII).

Distance defines the location of places of happiness for Emma Bovary, for whom to taste the full sweetness of her honeymoon "it would have been necessary doubtless to fly to those lands with sonorous names where the days after marriage are full of laziness most suave." Compare the passage already quoted from *Maggie:* "Her dim thoughts were often searching for far-away lands where the little hills sing together in the morning." Now in *Madame Bovary* the same atmosphere of landscape singing accompanies Emma's dream of happiness: "the song of the postilion re-echoed by the mountains, along with the bells of goats and the muffled sound of a waterfall. . . ." For Maggie: "Under the trees of her dream-gardens there had always walked a lover" (V). For Emma: "Why could not she lean over balconies in Swiss châlets, or enshrine her melancholy in a Scotch cottage, with a husband dressed in a black velvet coat with long tails, and thin shoes, a pointed hat and frills?" (VII). As Maggie's dream-reverie collapses in the bathos of Pete's saying, "Say, Mag, I'm stuck on yer shape," so Emma's imaginary voyage to distant lands of happiness is cancelled out by the immediate image of her dull husband: "But as the intimacy of their life became deeper, the greater became the gulf that separated her from him."

Illusions *versus* Reality pattern both books.

> Love, she thought, must come suddenly, with great outbursts and lightnings,—a hurricane of the skies, which falls upon life, revolutionises it, roots up the will like a leaf, and sweeps the whole heart into the abyss.

Mood A is cancelled by Mood B, the contrasted reality:

> She did not know that on the terrace of houses it makes lakes when the pipes are choked, and she would thus have remained in her security when she suddenly discovered a rent in the wall of it (V).

In *Maggie,* similarly, *a mood of hope*—Maggie prepares for Pete's promised visit by making a lambrequin to decorate the stove in the kitchen—is counterpointed by *a mood of despair:* "On Sunday, night, however, Pete did not appear. . . . The fire in the stove had gone out. The displaced lids and open doors showed heaps of sullen grey ashes. Maggie's mother, stretched on the floor, blasphemed, and gave her daughter a bad name" (VI).

It is because *Maggie* is apparently no more than a sequence of tableaux that Crane's critics have claimed that *Maggie* lacks structural unity. Hamlin Garland in his *Arena* review for June 1893, said *Maggie* "fails of rounded completeness. It is only a fragment." And the 1896 reviews echoed him. The *Book Buyer* for July 1896, for example, said that *Maggie,* like *The Red Badge,* is not a sustained narrative, but only "a sequence of extraordinary tableaux." No critic has yet troubled to investigate how Crane's *Maggie* is in fact constructed. What has gone unnoticed by Crane's critics is the pattern and purpose of every episode in the novel, how every seemingly disconnected part is designed to form the meaning of the whole. Crane's logic is not at the surface.

Every scene is a scene of chaos, physical and mental or moral disorder. *Maggie* begins with Jimmie's defending the "honor" of Rum Alley against the gutter urchins of Devil's Row, but his delusions of grandeur suffer degradation when his drunken father drags him home. His deed of valor ends in confused reports, "distorted versions of the fight." These Bowery characters view reality by "distorted versions of the fight," the fight being their quarrel with themselves rather than with their environment. "Distorted versions" applies to every scene of the book. Formidable tenement women "with uncombed hair and disordered dress" scream in frantic quarrels. Maggie's mother turns the household into a battlefield; she smashes all the furniture and she and her son wrestle "like gladiators." As the *Literary Digest* for August 8, 1896, noticed: "The book is strong in fights. It begins with a fight, continues with fights, and culminates in a really considerable 'scrap' between Pete, the Bowery hero—who 'showed that he was a lion of lordly characteristics by the air with which he spat'—and Jimmie, and a 'pal.' " The justification for the patterned quarrel scenes in *Maggie* is that the novel is itself a quarrel with environment—*"unholy* atmospheres," as Crane called environment in "An Experiment in Misery."

Maggie's mother scraps with street-urchins and defies "the universe to appear and do battle." Jimmie challenges the "god-driver," imagining himself as a sun-charioteer, and Pete, a golden sun in Maggie's eyes, strides like a knight in armour. They challenge the universe, they disdain the reality of their environment under the delusion of being superior to it, they contend not against it but meanwhile against themselves, one against the other seeking release from their destiny in violence or, on the other hand, in illusions of happiness and grandeur. They escape reality in "places of forgetfulness," in saloons, hilarious halls "of *irregular* shape," where Pete drunkenly dispenses his wealth from an "irregular shaped pocket," in opera and theatre and in mission-houses, where the preacher exhorts these sinners with sermons composed of "you's"—*"You* are damned." To which the ragged souls demand: "Where's our soup?" Bathos again!

The confused Maggie, like the confused Emma Bovary, confounds dream and reality. So do they all. Jimmie, the truck-driver, imagines himself a sun-charioteer and, seated on his throne, he challenges the "god-driver" who obstructs his path. He disdains the stars, but he exhibits respect for a passing fire-engine. At the mission-house his mind "confused the speaker with Christ," and Pete's "countenance shone with the true spirit of benevolence," while drunk at the saloon. "He was in the proper mood of missionaries" (XVIII). His drunken confusion imparts his moral confusion.

As the swaggering Pete, the betrayer of Maggie, is ironically confused with missionaries, so again he is identified as a priest when, "Overwhelmed by a spasm of drunken adoration, he drew two or three bills from his pocket and, with the trembling fingers of an offering priest, laid them on the table before the woman" (XVIII). The saloon is thus cross-identified as a church, and so is an apartment in the tenement-building where Mary Johnson lives: "In a room a woman sat at a table eating like a fat monk in a picture" (XIX). In a saloon on the occasion of the fight between Pete and Jimmie, Jimmie fights "with the face of a sacrificial priest" (XI). Jimmie and his mother fight "like gladiators"

(IX), and Jimmie is elsewhere identified with a "god-driver" of the sun-chariot (IV). Jimmie is cross-identified thus with Pete, whom Maggie compares with "a golden sun" (VIII). Confused identity is exemplified also in the missionary preacher's being mistaken for Christ (IV) and in Maggie's being identified as "Mary," *i.e.,* as Magdalene; etc. The Johnson household is cross-identified both with church and theatre, with mission-houses inasmuch as the Johnsons emit the mission-house brand of maudlin sentiment, and with theatre inasmuch as the apartment is rendered as though it were a stage: "Children ventured into the room and ogled her as if they formed the front row of a theatre" (XV). Mary's friend, the mourner whose strained voice sounds "like a dirge on some forlorn pipe," speaks for the whole Bowery world: "Her vocabulary was derived from mission churches" (XIX). Confused and mixed identity correlates in motif with the confusion between illusion and reality as exemplified by every person in the novel and as summarized in Crane's phrase "transcendental realism;" every one of these Bowery characters transcends reality in self-deluding dreams. The crossed identity of the characters and the evoked confusion of every scene in *Maggie* reflects the moral confusion of the Bowery world.

As I phrased it in *Omnibus* (1952, p. 9), "Innocence thwarted and betrayed by environment is the sum of *Maggie.*"[4] "None of the dirt of Rum Alley seemed to be in her veins" (V). But the mud-puddle in which she "blossomed" traps her. Maggie "did not feel like a bad woman. To her knowledge she had never seen any better" (XII). There is no other world for escape, as Crane has limited his world-view to that of the Bowery; no mention is made of the existence of any other possibility. The only exception is the island: "Over on the island a worm of yellow convicts came from the shadow of a grey ominous building and crawled slowly along the river's bank" (I). Crane's *Maggie* is par excellence the exemplar of literary naturalism. The paradox is that it is also a work of art.

"The true villain of this comic melodrama is Maggie's environment, including the persons and institutions composing it—notably the church." I quote here from my article on *Maggie* in *New Republic* (September 19, 1955). What Crane ridicules in *Maggie* is the cowardice of the Bowery world, on the one hand, and on the other the hypocrisy of the church and mission-house as a religious force in the nether-world of the city. Maggie is victimized not only by the collar-and-cuff factory, but also by the saloon and theatre sanctuaries, the places of escape from grim realities, where the same maudlin sentiment is emitted as at the mission-houses. Through "a mist of muddled sentiment" derived from the mission-house, the Bowery people view reality—through "blurred glass." Jimmie "walked to the window and began to look through blurred glass" (X). His sister is ruined, and he wonders "vaguely" whether some of the women of his acquaintance had brothers. It does not occur to him that he has despoiled the women of his acquaintance, even as

Pete has despoiled and betrayed his sister. Mary does not admit that she ruined her daughter, and Pete "did not consider that he had ruined Maggie" (XVI). Jimmie, the Bowery pimp, regards himself nevertheless as a virtuous fellow, and cannot forgive his sister for disgracing the family "honor"; Pete, the destroyer of Maggie's virtue, swaggers with an air of "respectability"—his eyes well into tears at the thought of the purity of his motives. And Maggie's mother, weeping over the corpse of the daughter she has brutalized and driven from home, weeps an orgy of self-pitying sentiment: "Oh, yes, I'll forgive her! I'll forgive her!" What Crane fashions in this final episode is a parody of pious sentiment. "The grotesque buffoonery of this mock lamentation is comic enough, but tragedy underlies it in the theme that all is shame, even between mother and daughter" (*Omnibus*, p. 18).

Maggie's downfall is assured from the start. Some months after she has turned prostitute she street-walks the Bowery in search of a customer; her appeal is ignored or rejected by the dozen men who pass her by. They represent, in sum, the environment which has rejected her. In a passage not reprinted in any text of *Maggie* subsequent to the 1893 edition, Maggie meets a grizzled fat man with bleared eyes and disordered teeth. He is her last chance, and he mocks her: "His whole body gently quivered and shook like that of a dead jelly fish. Chuckling and leering, he followed the girl of the crimson legions." Crane's intentions in *Maggie* was "to show that environment is a tremendous thing in the world and frequently shapes lives regardless" (*Omnibus*, p. 594). That is his theme, and he proves it by fashioning his "environment" to grow round his characters. By paired and contrasted images he reinforces his theme, and he quickens his characters into "life" by metaphor. His plot is less impressive than his theme, and the theme less impressive than style, the metaphoric language that shapes the whole book. His plot is a sentimental melodrama, like Norris' *McTeague*, but in style *Maggie* is not sentimentalized. The ironic viewpoint from which Crane designs his forthright moral and social intent makes the crucial difference. That difference is what saves *Maggie* from the dustbin of outdated sociological novels. Greatly admired by H. G. Wells, Edward Garnett, and T. E. Lawrence, *Maggie* remains today vigorously alive.   (1955, 1959)

NOTES

1. Kazin here echoes Herbert J. Muller's appraisal: "It is indeed an amateurish performance that today seems ludicrous in its self-conscious and almost gloating display of brutal detail. . . ." In Muller's *Modern Fiction* (1937), pp. 200-201. Marcus Cunliffe in *The Literature of the United States* (1954) also thinks that *Maggie* is dated. All Crane critics have slighted *Maggie* or underrated it.

2. In my *Stephen Crane: An Omnibus* (1952), pp. 68-69.

3. "Crane got his 'artistic education' (as he put it) on the Bowery. But at nineteen when he wrote this draft of what was to become *Maggie: A Girl of the Streets,* he knew very little about the Bowery, slum life, and prostitutes."

(*Omnibus,* p. 5). His fraternity brothers testify that he wrote *Maggie* in the Delta Upsilon house in the spring of 1891, and Willis Johnson of the *Tribune* on seeing the manuscript that summer was impressed by Crane's "mastery of the speech and manners of the denizens of the New York slums, *although he had spent little time in that city and had enjoyed little opportunity for observation of its ways*" (p. 7).

As Marcus Cunliffe in "Stephen Crane and the American Background of *Maggie*" (*American Quarterly,* VII, Spring 1955), points out, Maggie is a somewhat unreal creature whose life as a prostitute is handled by Crane with a marked lack of certainty; even less convincing is Nellie. "This is the writing of an inexperienced author who is guessing at his subject, which he only knows about from hearsay, or from his reading." His reading may have included Talmadge's sermons and lectures and Brace's study, *The Dangerous Classes of New York,* as Cunliffe suggests. He agrees that the resemblance to Zola's *L'Assommoir* is rather slight. I'm convinced that Crane studied Flaubert's *Madame Bovary* and learned from Flaubert the method of double mood (as I establish it later in this essay).

Further evidence that Crane wrote a first draft of *Maggie* in the spring of 1891 is supplied by Corwin Knapp Linson's *My Stephen Crane,* edited by Edwin H. Cady (Syracuse University Press, 1958). Cf. my review, "Friendly Reminiscence," New York *Times Book Review*: October 5, 1958.

4. In "New Testament Inversions in Crane's *Maggie,*" *Modern Language Notes* (April 1958), William Bysshe Stein opines: "It is not enough, for instance, to say that the novel is the sum of 'innocence thwarted and betrayed by environment.'" He then documents some New Testament inversions in *Maggie,* but these provide additional evidence of my *Omnibus* thesis that Maggie is trapped by her environment. Crane's Biblical inversions do not contradict that reading; on the contrary, they buttress it.

The Red Badge of Courage

(1)

IN *The Red Badge of Courage,* an impressionistic painting notable for its bold innovations in technique and style, and in "The Open Boat," which fuses the impressionistic realism of *Maggie: A Girl of The Streets* and the symbolic realism of *The Red Badge,* Crane established himself among the foremost engineers of the techniques of modern fiction. These two main technical movements of modern fiction—realism and symbolism —have their beginnings here in these achievements of Stephen Crane.

"The Open Boat," said H. G. Wells, is "beyond all question, the crown of all his work." Conrad deeply admired it: "the deep and simple humanity of its presentation seems somehow to illustrate the essentials of life itself, like a symbolic tale." Both Conrad and Crane showed themselves very early in their careers to be symbolic artists—Conrad in "The Lagoon," and Crane in one of his earliest stories, "The Men in the Storm." The greater number of Crane's stories, however, are nonsymbolic. All too often, when he does attempt symbolism, the potential symbols collapse. Crane's technique is at its best in *The Red Badge, Maggie* and "The Open Boat." The technical device, for instance, of a double vision is introduced in "The Open Boat." Things viewed by the men at sea are viewed *as though* the men were on land. Colors, used only as decorative pattern in "An Experiment in Misery," are symbolically employed in *The Red Badge.* Here the symbolic value of any given color varies according to its location in a specific context. Symbolic patterns of life and death are established, for instance, by the *same* color. The one is signified by the *yellow* of the sun, and the other by the *yellow* of the uniforms on dead soldiers.

Symbols are created by establishing correlations between the plight of the characters and their environment (for example, battlefield, forest, or sea). The mental state, feeling, or mood is transposed and objectified in things, in natural objects or in other persons whose plight parallels the central situation or stands in contrast to it. Thus in *The Red Badge* Henry's mental state is objectified in a single recurrent object, the flag, and the meaning of the whole book gradually accretes around this dominant or focal symbol. In "The Open Boat" the confused mental state of the men is identified with the confused and "broken sea," and it is obversely objectified in the contradictory gulls that hover "comfortably" over them, gruesome and ominous birds utterly indifferent to the plight of the men. The bird's "black eyes were *wistfully* fixed upon the captain's head." The unconcern of the universe is symbolized by the wind-tower as it appears to them when they head for the beach:

> This tower was a giant, standing with its back to the plight of the ants. It represented in a degree, to the correspondent, the serenity of nature amid the struggles of the individual—nature in the wind, and nature in the vision of the men. She did not seem cruel to him then, not beneficient, nor treacherous, nor wise. But she was indifferent, flatly indifferent.

Symbols are generated by parallelisms and repetitions. A symbolic detail at the very beginning of "The Open Boat" prepares for the final incident, the death of the oiler. He is represented by the oar he steers: "It was a thin little oar and it seemed often ready to snap." In *The Red Badge* the chattering fear of a frightened squirrel, fleeing when Henry Fleming throws a pine cone at him (ch. VII), parallels the plight of the hero under shellfire.

Symbols are at their most effective when they radiate multiple correspondences or different contexts at different times or at the same time.

Two recent critics contend that Crane borrowed nothing of his technique from paintings, but I do not think the influence of the studio on Crane can be denied. Corwin Knapp Linson, the artist who did illustrations for some of Crane's stories ("The Reluctant Voyagers," for one), wrote reminiscences of their bohemian days when Crane used to spend his time at Linson's studio (winter 1892-1893) "rummaging through old periodicals, poring over the Civil War articles."[1] His reminiscences, covering four important years—1893-1897—in Crane's brief life, appeared in expanded form as *My Stephen Crane* (1958). It was the painter's touch in Crane's prose-style that most impressed Linson. "The painter's color sense is born—so was his." Himself a painter, Linson confirms the fact that "Steve reveled in the use of words as a painter loves his color" and that Crane was a consciously symbolic artist: "As to color, it always stood in his mind for a symbol, and so apt was his use of color-words that ever after they would image the thing they defined."

Melville swallowed whole libraries to write *Moby Dick,* and Crane studied to write his *Red Badge.* But we are still left wondering where he learned *how* to write. The answer to that question is given, I believe, in Hemingway's remark: "I learned to write looking at paintings at the Luxembourg Museum in Paris." Crane knew Albert Pinkham Ryder personally; he knew not only Ryder's paintings but also some of Monet's, Winslow Homer's, and the apprenticeship paintings of Corwin Linson and of his fellow lodgers at the Art Students' League, where Crane lived during the period when he was composing his own impressionistic paintings: *Maggie* and *The Red Badge.* "Impressionism was his faith," says R. G. Vosburgh in his reminiscences of Crane (*Criterion:* February 1901). As H. G. Wells concluded, "there is Whistler even more than there is Tolstoy in *The Red Badge of Courage.*" (In *North American Review:* August 1900) The critically relevant point is that there is a close parallelism between Crane's impressionistic prose and impressionist paintings. This much can be established: Crane adumbrated the French post-impressionist painters.

Crane's style is prose pointillism. It is composed of disconnected images, which coalesce like the blobs of color in French impressionist paintings, every word-group having a cross-reference relationship, every seemingly disconnected detail having interrelationship to the configurated whole. The intensity of a Crane work is owing to this patterned coalescence of disconnected things, everything at once fluid and precise. A striking analogy is established between Crane's use of colors and the method employed by the impressionists and the neo-impressionists or divisionists, and it is as if he had known about their theory of contrasts and had composed his own prose paintings by the same principle. Their principle, as one writer defines it, is this: "Each plane of shade creates around itself a sort of aura of light, and each luminous plane creates around itself a zone of shade. In a similar way a coloured area communicates its 'complementary' to the neighbouring colour, or heightens it if it is 'complementary.' "[2] In almost every battle scene in *The Red Badge of Courage* the perspective is blurred by smoke or by the darkness of night. Here is one example of the former contrast: namely, dark masses circled by light; and of the latter contrast: namely a luminous spot circled by darkness. (The former contrast is created in the first sentence of Crane's description, and the latter contrast in the second.)

The clouds were tinged an earthlike yellow in the sunrays and in the shadow were a sorry blue. The flag was sometimes eaten and lost in this mass of vapor, but more often it projected, sun-touched, resplendent (ch. VI).

Crane's perspectives, almost without exception, are fashioned by contrasts—black masses juxtaposed against brightness, colored light set against gray mists. At dawn the army glows with a purple hue, and "In the eastern sky there was a yellow patch like a rug laid for the feet of the coming sun; and against it, *black and pattern-like,* loomed the gigantic figure of the colonel on a gigantic horse" (II). Black is juxtaposed against yellow (II) or against red (II, XIII). Smoke wreathes around a square of white light and a patch of yellow shade (I, XVIII). Smoke dimly outlines a distance filled with *blue* uniforms, a *green* sward, and a *sapphire* sky (XXIII). Further examples of color-contrast, particularly white versus black, occur throughout "The Open Boat," and blue is used symbolically in "The Blue Hotel." Crane had an extraordinary predilection for blue, which Hamlin Garland took to be the sign manual of the impressionists. It seems likely that Crane read Garland's *Crumbling Idols* (1894), but in any case he wrote a novel about an impressionistic painter —the hero of *The Third Violet.* And in one of his sketches he wrote:

The flash of the impression was like light, and for this instant it illumined all the dark recesses of one's remotest idea of sacrilege, ghastly and wanton. I bring this to you merely as an effect, *an effect of mental light and shade,* if you like; something done in thought *similar to that which the French impressionists do in colour*; something meaningless and at the same time overwhelming, crushing, monstrous (*Work,* IX, pp. 245-6).

Crane paints with words "exactly" as the French impressionists paint with pigments: both use pure colors and contrasts of colors. Black clouds or dark smoke or masses of mist and vapor are surrounded by a luminous zone; or, conversely, specks of prismatic color are enclosed by a zone of shade. Shifting gray mists open out before the splendor of the sunrays (XIV). Or, conversely, billowing smoke is "filled with horizontal flashes" (IV); "the mist of smoke [is] gashed by the little knives of fire" (XXIII). Inside the surrounding darkness the waters of the river appear wine-tinted, and campfires, "shining upon the moving masses of troops, brought forth here and there sudden gleams of silver and gold. Upon the other shore a dark and mysterious range of hills was curved against the sky" (III; the same scene is duplicated in XIII). Cleared atmospheres, unimpeded vision or perspective, are rarely delineated; and where they occur the precision of vision is equated, symbolically, with revelation or spiritual insight. Dark mists and vapors represent the haze of Henry's unenlightened mind ("He, the enlightened man who looks afar in the dark, had fled because of his superior perceptions and knowledge"). Darkness and smoke serve as symbols of concealment and deception, vapors masking the light of truth. Sunlight and changing colors signify spiritual insight and rebirth. Henry is a color-bearer, but it is not until he recognizes the truth in his self-deception that the youth keeps "the bright colors to the front." In the celebrated impression of the red sun "pasted in the sky like a wafer" Crane is at once an impressionist painter and a symbolic artist.

Theme and style in *The Red Badge of Courage* are organically conceived, the theme of change conjoined with the fluid style by which it is evoked. The style, calculated to create impressions of confused motion and change, is deliberately disconnected and apparently disordered. Fluidity and change characterize the whole book. Crane interjects disjointed details, one non-sequitur melting into another. Scenes and objects are felt as blurred; they appear under a haze or vapor or cloud. Yet everything has relationship and is manipulated into contrapuntal patterns of color and cross-references of meaning.

"The interesting thing," Crane said to a fellow war-correspondent above the din of riflefire in Cuba, "is the mental attitude of the men." And on an earlier occasion when discussing war memoirs with Corwin Linson, he said: "I wonder that some of these fellows don't tell how they *felt* in those scraps. They spout enough of what they *did*, but they're as emotionless as rocks." It is the same in *The Red Badge*, seeing the imagined battlefield from the angle of psychological insight, and it is this psychological realism that separates Crane from the realism of Zola, Tolstoy, and Barbusse. His technique—his word-painting—differentiates him from all other "realists."

(2)

The Red Badge of Courage is a literary exercise in language, in the patterning of words and the counterpointing of themes and tropes and colors. It was realism that Crane himself aimed at, a photographic copy of reality, and his *Red Badge* has always been read as just that and nothing more. Shakespeare's play *I Henry IV* appears to be no more than a history play, a realistic reproduction of life; *Huckleberry Finn* is simply the biography of a boy, a record of his adventures. Beneath their surface drama, however, lies a concealed meaning. No work of art is what it appears to be.[3] Crane's *Red Badge* is far more than a fictional account of the Civil War.

The Red Badge is realistic enough, said the New York *World*, "to set the blood tingling in the veins of a veteran." "This young man," said Bierce, "has the power to feel. He knows nothing of war, yet he is drenched in blood. Most beginners who deal with this subject spatter themselves merely with ink." A British general, praising the book in the *Illustrated London News* for 1896 as "quite the finest thing in that line that has even been done," shrewdly observed that "the intuitions of the boy who has never seen war are worth far more than the experiences of any writer . . . even though he may have been in the thick of the fiercest battle." Bierce, the experienced soldier, would have agreed. It is ironical that Bierce, who was wounded in battle, used his war experience only for imaginative constructs and sardonic fantasies of it, whereas Crane, without any experience of war, created a much greater illusion of reality. So great was the illusion that the *Saturday Review* and other British periodicals took it for granted that the author of *The Red Badge* had seen actual warfare. "Certainly, if his book were altogether a work of imagination unbased on personal experience, his realism would be nothing short of a miracle." The blood of angry veterans tingled, but it was for quite different reasons. Crane's book was an insult to his country's honor, said General A. C. McClurg. It's "a vicious satire upon American soldiers. The hero is without a spark of soldierly ambition. No thrill of patriotic devotion ever moves his breast. There is no evidence of drill, none of discipline." In copies returned to Brentano's bookshop (according to Beer) other veterans scribbled such marginal notes of indignation as "insulting," "unpatriotic," and "damned nonsense."

Neither the question of personal experience nor the test of realism is relevant to any critical judgment of *The Red Badge of Courage*. (Verifying Crane's picture of warfare as the real thing can be done only by those who have experienced warfare, and trenches are not very handy for the critic.) Fidelity to life does not establish any work *as* a work of art; to equate life with art is to confuse their absolute boundaries. Truth in art consists not in the artist's fidelity to the observed facts of the actual world; it consists rather in the artist's fidelity to the *felt* truth of his vision. It is *there,* as Conrad intimated, that the honor of the artist lies—in fidelity to every part of the patterned whole. "The Open Boat" is a work of art not because it is a slice out of life, which explains only its source and its verisimilitude, but because it is an imaginative re-creation of life possessing a pattern of significance. Henry Fleming is composed not of flesh and blood, much as he may seem so to some readers; he is, of course, composed of words—solely of words patterened to evoke an *illusion* of reality.

Yet what Crane wrote still passes—even for Hemingway—as "real war literature." Modern realism, according to all the critics, was initiated by Stephen Crane. That is approximately true enough, but, like every other pronouncement about him, not quite accurate. To say that Crane "anticipated" modern realism "by thirty or forty years" is to ignore De Forest, whose work appeared more than a quarter of a century before *The Red Badge*. The fact of this matter is that neither Crane nor Bierce rendered the actualities of recruits under fire with anything like the graphic realism of De Forest. Crane did not write our first realistic war novel— our literary historians are mistaken. Nor did Crane write, as some critics have said, our first ironic novel. Neither *Maggie* nor *The Red Badge,* but Mark Twain's *Huckleberry Finn,* deserves that claim. Beer makes no mention of De Forest and he is mistaken about the Civil War's leaving "almost nothing printed that the literate peasants and clerks who fought would recognize as the truth of their acts." That is precisely what they got in *Miss Ravenel's Conversion* in 1867, or again in Colonel Wilbur F. Hinman's *Corporal Si Klegg and His "Pard"* twenty years later—and eight years before *The Red Badge*. De Forest's realism, though William Dean Howells spread the word, remained unnoticed for over fifty years. Crane captured the field, and the banner Realism has floated above him ever since.

"Most of my prose writings have been toward the goal partially described by that misunderstood and abused word, realism." Yet Crane is, in essence, no realist.

If Crane is a realist, then what label is left for De Forest's *Conversion* or, among later war novels, Henri Barbusse's *Under Fire*? Besides De Forest's *Conversion* and Barbusse's *Under Fire*, Crane's imagined account of the battlefield appears somewhat synthetic and even theatrical.

> In the centre of this mass of suffering stood several operating tables, each burdened by a grievously wounded man and surrounded by surgeons and their assistants. Underneath were great pools of clotted blood, amidst which lay amputated fingers, hands, arms, feet and legs, only a little more ghastly in color than the faces of those who waited their turn on the table. The surgeons, who never ceased their awful labor, were daubed with blood to the elbows and a smell of blood drenched the stifling air, overpowering even the pungent odor of chloroform. The place resounded with groans, notwithstanding that most of the injured men who retained their senses exhibited the heroic endurance so common on the battle-field. One man, whose leg was amputated close to his body, uttered an inarticulate jabber of broken screams, and rolled, or rather bounced from side to side on a pile of loose cotton, with such violence that two hospital attendants were fully occupied in holding him. Another shot through the body, lay speechless and dying, but quivering from head to foot with a prolonged though probably unconscious agony. He continued to shudder thus for half an hour, when he gave one superhuman throe, and then lay quiet for ever.[4]

The photographic realism of De Forest, of Tolstoy in *Sebastopol* and Zola in *La Débâcle*, Crane can be said to have approached only in some few scattered passages of *The Red Badge*. Of the two most frequently quoted examples of Crane's realism, one is the detail of the dead soldier leaning against a tree with sodden eyes staring as from a dead fish. That looks merely realistic, but the dead man is a symbol. The other is this picture of a corpse encountered in battle:

> Once the line encountered the body of a dead soldier. He lay upon his back staring at the sky. He was dressed in an awkward suit of yellowish brown. . . . And it was as if fate had betrayed the soldier.

> The ranks opened covertly to avoid the corpse. The *invulnerable* dead man forced a way for himself. The youth looked keenly at the ashen face.

The first part of the image contributes themes of betrayal and death, and the final part contributes still another theme—the motif of change and mobility, which is one of the main recurrent themes of the whole book. Barbusse's *Under Fire* (1917), influenced by Crane, paints the very same picture. It is the same except for the immobility of the corpse:

> As soon as our pushing and jolted file emerges, two men close to me are hit . . . the one with a sharp cry, and the other silently, as a felled ox. Another disappears with the caper of a lunatic, as if he had been snatched away. Instinctively we close up as we hustle forward—always forward—and the wound in our line closes of its own accord. The adjutant stops, raises his sword, lets it fall, and drops to his knees. His kneeling body slopes backward in jerks, his helmet drops on his heels, and he remains there, bareheaded, face to the sky. Hurriedly the rush of the rank has split open to respect his immobility.[5]

But you have only to compare it with Crane's picture to see the difference. Barbusse's details convey neither theme, symbolic intent, nor painterly design. They are facts in black and white. He evokes emotions, but they are not the same emotions or effects a painter like Crane evokes. The difference is that Crane's realistic detail is used metaphorically.

That Crane is incapable of architectonics has been the critical consensus for over half a century: "his work is a mass of fragments"; "he can only string together a series of loosely cohering incidents"; *The Red Badge of Courage* is not constructed—it is "not a sustained narrative, but a sequence of extraordinary tableaux" (*Book Buyer*, July 1896). That Crane lacks the great artist's arrangement of complex effects, as Edward Garnett pointed out in his 1898 appraisal of Crane, is certainly true. We look to Conrad and Henry James for "exquisite grouping of devices"; Crane's figure in the carpet is a much simpler one. What it consists in is the very thing Garnett failed to detect—a schemework of striking contrasts, alternations of contradictory moods. Crane once defined a novel as a "succession of sharply-outlined pictures, which pass before the reader like a panorama, leaving each its definite impression." His own novel, nonetheless, is not simply a succession of pictures. It is a sustained structural whole. Every Crane critic concurs in this mistaken notion that *The Red Badge of Courage* is nothing more than "a series of episodic scenes," but not one critic has yet undertaken an analysis of Crane's work to see *how* the sequence of tableaux is constructed.

Crane in his best works is a symbolic artist. Joseph Hergesheimer, whose edition of *The Red Badge* appeared in 1925 as Volume I of the collected *Work*, recognized that for Crane it was not a story he had to tell, but rather a literary exercise of some sort. Hergesheimer did not go into the meaning of the book, but he saw what Crane was up to. Nowhere else in the whole body of Crane criticism is there a hint that Crane was writing with symbolic intention. The exceptions occur in one of Conrad's tributes to Crane, where he mentions the word *symbolism*, and in two or three contemporary reviews. The New York *Bookman* reduced *The Red Badge* to a mere allegory: "The young soldier, starting out to face his first trial by fire, may be either an individual or man universal; the battle may be either the Battle of the Wilderness or the Battle of Life." The *Bookman* did not like the book because it employed a double meaning—"always a dangerous and usually fatal method in literature." The *Critic* for November 1895 said that the book is a true book—true in two senses: "true to life, whether it be taken as a literal transcript of a soldier's experiences in his first battle, or (as some have fancied) a great parable of the inner battle which every man must fight." The *Critic* was not convinced about that fancied idea, but the London *Bookman* two months later said simply, without any misgivings: *"The youth's mind is a battleground too."* The *Spectator* for June 27, 1896 struck off a singularly penetrating observation in pointing out that Henry's encounter with the wounded soldiers is his salvation. "He got back with them to the body of the regiment, and the sight of his comrades, notably the heroic death of one of them, made a beginning of the end of his egoism." As the *Critic* keenly noted, Crane's metaphors and similes "are not strung on for effect, but living and actual as Homer's." What the perceptive *Critic* was first to detect has gone unnoticed for the past fifty-five years: namely, that Crane's metaphors are employed purposefully—for theme or for structural pattern.

(3)

NOTES TOWARD AN ANALYSIS OF

The Red Badge of Courage

Ernest Hemingway's remark that *The Red Badge of Courage* "is all as much one piece as a great poem is" is doubly revelatory because it defines not only Crane's novel but Hemingway's own *Farewell to Arms. A Farewell to Arms* is an inverted *Red Badge of Courage:* the one deals with disenchantment and withdrawal, the other with quest and triumph. Hemingway's novel starts, as it were, where Crane's left off: Frederic Henry, the already maimed hero, is the idealist Henry Fleming turned cynic. It is significant that both are without father and virtually nameless. Crane's hero is always just "the youth," and it is not until halfway through the book (on the last page of chapter xi) that the youth discloses what his name is, and then, ashamed because he has fled the battlefield, he utters his name only to himself. Hemingway's hero has for surname a given name. Both heroes undergo change and insight through wounds, but in opposite directions. Where Crane's Henry progesses upward toward "manhood" and "moral triumph," Hemingway's Henry descends toward moral and spiritual degeneration. In both novels the education of the hero ends as it began: in self-deception. Frederic Henry renounces war, society, and the "comforting stench" of comrades and makes a "separate peace." But his farewell to arms is as illusory as Henry Fleming's farewell to vain ideals and compromising illusions. Both heroes are deluded, the one believing he can turn his back upon the battle of life, the other believing that he has triumphed in facing up to it shorn of all romantic notions.

Both novels are ritualistic, mythic, symbolic. The dominant symbolism is religious. Henry Fleming's forest chapel transposes into the mountain sanctuary of the lovers in *A Farewell to Arms*. As in *The House of the Seven Gables* and *Huckleberry Finn*, the alternating episodes of *Farewell* and *The Red Badge* concern withdrawal and return, the quest for self-identity, and insight or recognition through wound or suffering. The central theme of *Farewell*—everyone has to "get down off the mountains"—harks back through *The Red Badge* to *Huckleberry Finn*. And Twain's "You Can't Pray a Lie," the leitmotiv of deception in *Huckleberry Finn*, vibrates through both *The Red Badge* and *A Farewell to Arms*.

Like Henry Fleming, Frederic Henry has romantic illusions about war. The opening scene of the novel delineates this "picturesque front." The army is on the move:

> Troops went by the house and down the road and the dust they raised powdered the leaves of the trees. The trunks of the trees too were dusty and the leaves fell early that year and we saw the troops marching along the road and the dust rising and leaves, stirred by the breeze, falling and the soldiers marching and afterward the road bare and white except for the leaves.

Hemingway begins his novel exactly as Crane begins his: the opening picture manifests motifs of change and deception.[6] On the first page of *The Red Badge of Courage* the army is about to move. The landscape changes "from brown to green," and the river—"swiftly moving" in Hemingway's scene—here is purling "at the army's feet." As the falling leaves in Hemingway's picture symbolize an event that has not yet occurred—the death of Catherine—so the "retiring fogs" in Crane's opening sentence anticipate Henry's mental awakening: "The cold passed reluctantly from the earth, and the retiring fogs revealed an army stretched out on the hills, resting." They are the fogs of Henry's own mind, and not until they are dispersed ("reluctantly") can Henry establish warm identity with life.

The Red Badge of Courage probes a state of mind under the incessant pinpricks and bombardments of life. The theme is that man's salvation lies in change, in spiritual growth. It is only by immersion in the flux of experience that man becomes disciplined and develops in character, conscience, or soul. Potentialities for change are at their greatest in battle —a battle represents life at its most intense flux. Crane's book is not about the combat of armies, it is about the self-combat of a youth who fears and stubbornly resists change, and the actual battle is symbolic of this spiritual warfare against change and growth. Henry Fleming recognizes the necessity for change and development, but wars against it. But man must lose his soul in order to save it. The youth develops into the veteran:

"So it came to pass . . . his soul changed." Significantly enough, in stating what the book is about Crane intones Biblical phrasing.

The book begins with the army immobilized—with restless men waiting for orders to move—and, because the army has done nothing, with Henry disillusioned by his first days as a recruit. In the first picture we get of Henry, he is lying on his army cot—resting on an idea. Or, rather, he is wrestling with the personal problem it poses. The idea is a third-hand rumor that tomorrow, at last, the army will go into action. When the tall soldier first announced it, he waved a shirt that he had just washed in a muddy brook, waved it in bannerlike fashion to summon the men around the flag of his colorful rumor. It was a call to the colors—he shook it out and spread it about for the men to admire. But Jim Conklin's prophecy of hope meets with disbelief. "It's a lie!" shouts the loud soldier. "I don't believe the derned old army's ever going to move." No disciples rally around the red and gold flag of the herald. The skeptical soldiers think the tall soldier is telling just a tall tale; a furious altercation ensues. Meanwhile Henry in his hut engages in a spiritual debate with himself; whether to believe or disbelieve the word of his friend, whom he has known since childhood. It is the gospel truth, but Henry is one of the doubting apostles.

The opening scene thus sets going the structural pattern of the whole book. Hope and faith (paragraphs 1-3) shift to despair or disbelief (4-7). The counter movement of opposition begins in paragraph 4, in the small detail of the Negro teamster who stops his dancing, when the men desert him to wrangle over Jim Conklin's rumor. "He sat mournfully down." This image of motion and change (the motion ceasing and the joy turning to gloom) presents the dominant leitmotiv and the form of the whole book in miniature. (Another striking instance of emblematic form occurs in Chapter vi, where Crane pictures a terror-striken lad who throws down his gun and runs: "A lad whose face had borne an expression of exalted courage, the majesty of ho [*sic*] who dares give his life, was, at an instant, smitten abject.") In Chapter i the opening prologue ends in a coda (paragraph 7) with theme and anti-theme interjoined. It is the picture of the corporal. His uncertainties (whether to repair his house) and his shifting attitudes of trust and distrust (whether the army is going to move) parallel the skeptical outlook of the wrangling men. The same anti-theme of distrust is dramatized in the episode that follows this coda, and every subsequent episode in the sequence is designed similarly by one contrast pattern or another.

Change and motion begin the book. The army, which lies resting on the hills, is first revealed to us by "the retiring fogs," and as the weather changes, the landscape changes, the brown hills turning to a new green. As nature stirs, the army stirs too. Nature and man are in psychic affinity; even the weather changes as though in sympathetic accord with man's plight. In the final scene it is raining, but the leaden rain clouds shine with "a golden ray" as though to reflect Henry's own bright serenity, his own tranquillity of mind. But now at the beginning, and throughout the book, Henry's mind is in a "tumult of agony and despair." This psychological tumult began when Henry heard the church bell announce that a great battle had been fought. Noise begins the whole mental melee. The clanging church bell and then the noise disorder his mind by stirring up legendary visions of heroic selfhood. The noisy world that first colored his mind with myths now clamors to Henry to become absorbed into the solidarity of self-forgetful comradeship, but Henry resists this challenge of the "mysterious fraternity born of the smoke and danger of death," and withdraws again and again from the din of the affray to indulge in self-contemplative moods and magic reveries. The walls of the forest insulate him from the noise of battle. In seeking retreat to absolve his shame and guilt, Henry, renouncing manhood, is "seeking dark and intricate places." It is as though he were seeking return to the womb. Nature, that "woman with a deep aversion to tragedy," is Mother Nature, and the human equation for the forest is of course Henry's own mother. Henry's flight from the forest sanctuary represents his momentary rejection of womblike innocence; periodically he rejects Mother Nature with her sheltering arms and her "religion of peace," and his flight from Mother Nature is symbolic of his initiation into the truth of the world he must measure up to. He is the deceived youth, for death lurks even in the forest sanctuary. In the pond a gleaming fish is killed by one of the forest creatures, and in the forest Henry meets a rotted corpse, a man whose eyes stare like a dead fish, with ants scurrying over the face. The treachery of this forest retreat, where nothing is as it seems, symbolizes the treachery of ideals —the illusions by which we are all betrayed.

Henry's mind is in constant flux. Henry's self-combat is symbolized by the conflict among the men and between the armies, their altercation being a duplication of his own. Like the regiment that marches and countermarches over the same ground, so Henry's mind traverses the same ideas over and over again. As the cheery-voiced soldier says about the battle, "It's th' most mixed up dern thing I ever see." Mental commotion, confusion, and change are externalized in the "mighty altercation" of men and guns and nature herself. Everything becomes activated, *even the dead*. That corpse Henry meets on the battlefield, "the *invulnerable* dead man," cannot stay still—he "*forced* a way for himself" through the ranks. And guns throb too, "restless guns." Back and forth the stage scenery shifts from dreams to "jolted dreams" and grim fact. Henry's illusions collapse, dreams pinpricked by reality.

Throughout the whole book *withdrawals* alternate with *engagements*, with scenes of entanglement and tumult, but the same nightmarish atmosphere of upheaval and disorder pervades both the inner and the outer realms. The paradox is that when Henry becomes activated in the "vast blue demonstration" and is thereby reduced to anonymity he is most a man, and, conversely, when he affects self-dramatizing picture-postcard poses of himself as hero he is least a man and not at all heroic.

He is then innocent as a child. When disengaged from the external tumult, Henry's mind recollects domestic scenes. Pictures of childhood and nursery imagery of babes recur at almost every interval of withdrawal. Childhood innocence and withdrawal are thus equated. The nursery limerick that the wounded soldiers sing as they retreat from the battlefront is at once a travesty of their own plight and a mockery of Henry's mythical innocence.

> *Sing a song 'a vic'try,*
> *A pocketful 'a bullets,*
> *Five an' twenty dead men*
> *Baked in a—pie.*

Everything goes awry; nothing turns out as Henry had expected. Battles turn out to be "an immense and terrible machine to him" (the awful machinery is also his own mind). At his battle task Henry, we are told, "was like a carpenter who has made many boxes, making still another box, only there was furious haste in his movements." Henry, "frustrated by hateful circumstances," pictures himself as boxed in by fate, by the regiment, and by the "iron laws of tradition and law on four sides. He was in a moving box." And furthermore there are those purely theoretical boxes by which he is shut in from reality—his romantic dreams, legendary visions of heroic selfhood, illusions that the vainglorious machinery of his own mind has manufactured.

The youth who had envisioned himself in Homeric poses, the legendary hero of a Greek-like struggle, has his pretty illusion shattered as soon as he announces his enlistment to his mother. "I've knet yeh eight pair of socks, Henry. . . ." His mother is busy peeling potatoes, and, madonna-like, she kneels among the parings. They are the scraps of his romantic dreams. The youthful private imagines armies to be monsters, "redoubtable dragons," but then he sees the real thing—the colonel who strokes his mustache and shouts over his shoulder: "Don't forget that box of cigars!"

Spiritual change is Henry Fleming's red badge. *His red badge is his conscience reborn and purified.* Whereas Jim Conklin's red badge of courage is the literal one, the wound of which he dies, Henry's is the psychological badge, the wound of conscience. Internal wounds are more painful than external ones. It is fitting that Henry should receive a head wound, a bump that jolts him with a severe headache. But what "salve" is there to ease the pain of his internal wound of dishonor? That is Henry's "headache"! It is the ache of his conscience that he has been honored by the regiment he has dishonored. Just as Jim runs into the fields to hide his true wound from Henry, so Henry runs into the fields to hide his false wound, his false badge of courage, from the tattered man who asks him where he is wounded. "It might be inside mostly, an' them plays thunder. Where is it located?" The men, so Henry feels, are perpetually probing his guilt-wound, "ever upraising the ghost of shame on the stick of their curiosity." The unmistakable implication here is of a flag, and the actual flag that Henry carries in battle is the symbol of his conscience. Conscience is also symbolized by the forest, the cathedral-forest where Henry retreats to nurse his guilt-wound and be consoled by the benedictions that nature sympathetically bestows upon him. Here in this forest chapel there is a churchlike silence as insects bow their beaks while Henry bows his head in shame; they make a "devotional pause" while the trees chant a soft hymn to comfort him. But Henry is troubled; he cannot "conciliate the forest." Nor can he conciliate the flag. The flag registers the commotion of his mind, and it registers the restless movements of the nervous regiment—it flutters when the men expect battle. And when the regiment runs from battle, the flag sinks down "as if dying. Its motion as it fell was a gesture of despair." Henry dishonors the flag not when he flees from battle but when he flees from himself, and he redeems it when he redeems his conscience.

Redemption begins in confession, in absolution—in a change of heart. Henry's plight is identical with the Reverend Mr. Dimmesdale's plight in Hawthorne's psychological novel *The Scarlet Letter*. The mythology of the scarlet letter is much the same as that of the red badge: each is the emblem of moral guilt and salvation. The red badge is the scarlet letter of dishonor transferred from the bosom of Hester, the social outcast, to the mind of Henry Fleming, the "mental outcast." Henry's wounded conscience is not healed until he confesses the truth to himself and opens his eyes to new ways; not until he strips his enemy heart of "the brass and bombast of his earlier gospels," the vainglorious illusions he had fabricated into a cloak of pride and self-vindication, not until he puts on new garments of humility and loving-kindness for his fellow men. Redemption begins in humility—Henry's example is the loud soldier who becomes the humble soldier. The loud soldier admits the folly of his former ways. Henry's spiritual change is a prolonged process, but it is signalized in moments when he loses his soul in the flux of things; then he courageously deserts himself instead of his fellow men; then, fearlessly plunging into battle, charging the enemy like "a pagan who defends his religion," he becomes swept up in a delirium of selflessness and feels himself "capable of profound sacrifices." The brave new Henry, "new bearer of the colors," triumphs over the former one. The enemy flag is wrenched from the hands of "the rival color bearer," the symbol of Henry's own other self, and as this rival color-bearer dies, Henry is "reborn."

Henry's regeneration is brought about by the death of Jim Conklin, his friend since childhood. He goes under various names. He is sometimes called the spectral soldier (his face is a pasty gray) and sometimes the tall soldier (he is taller than all the other men), but there are unmistakable hints—in such descriptive details about him as his wound in the side, his torn body and his gory hand, and even in the initials of his name, Jim Conklin—that he is intended to represent Jesus Christ. We are told that there is "a resemblance in him to a devotee of a mad religion," and among his followers the doomed man stirs up "thoughts of a solemn ceremony." When he dies, the heavens signify his death—the red sun bleeds with the passion of his wounds:

The red sun was pasted in the sky like a wafer.

This grotesque image, the most notorious metaphor in American literature, has been much debated and roundly damned by all Crane critics (excepting Conrad, Willa Cather, and Hergesheimer, who admired it, but failed to explain why), ridiculed as downright bad writing—a false, melodramatic nonfunctional figure. It is, in fact, the key to the symbolism of the whole novel, particularly the religious symbolism that radiates outwards from Jim Conklin. Like any image, it has to be related to the structure of meaning in which it functions; when lifted out of its context it is bound to seem artificial and irrelevant or, on the other hand, merely "a superb piece of imagery." I do not think it can be doubted that Crane intended to suggest here the sacrificial death celebrated in communion.

Henry and the tattered soldier consecrate the death of the spectral soldier in "a solemn ceremony." Henry partakes of the sacramental blood and body of Christ, and the process of his spiritual rebirth begins at the moment when the wafer-like sun appears in the sky. It is a symbol of salvation through death. Henry, we are made to feel, recognizes in the lifeless sun his own lifeless conscience, his dead and as yet unregenerated selfhood or conscience, and that is why he blasphemes against it. His moral salvation and triumph are prepared for by this ritual of purification and religious devotion and, at the very start of the book, by the ritual of absolution that Jim Conklin performs in the opening scene. It was the tall soldier who first "developed virtues" and showed the boys how to cleanse a flag. The way is to wash it in the muddy river. Only by experiencing life, the muddy river, can the soul be cleansed. In "The Open Boat" it is the black sea, and the whiteness of the waves as they pace to and fro in the moonlight signifies the spiritual purification that the men win from their contest against the terrible water. The ritual of domestic comforts bestowed upon the saved men by the people on the shore, "all the remedies sacred to their minds," is a shallow thing, devoid of spiritual value. The sea offers the only true remedy, though it costs a "terrible grace." The way—as Stein said in Conrad's *Lord Jim*—is to immerse oneself in the destructive element.

Kurtz, in Conrad's "Heart of Darkness," washed his soul in the Congo, and Marlow, because he had become a part of Kurtz, redeemed the heart of darkness by the same token. Conrad, like Crane, had himself experienced his own theme, but Crane was the first to produce a work based on it. Crane's influence on Conrad is apparent in *Lord Jim*. Both *Lord Jim* and *The Red Badge of Courage* variously exploit the same thematic contrast of ideals versus realities. In terms of religious symbolism they have further affinities. When Lord Jim goes to his death, there is an awful sunset. Conrad's enormous sun—"The sky over Patusan was blood-red, immense, streaming like an open vein"—recalls Crane's symbolic red sun "pasted in the sky like a wafer." (1951, 1952)

(4)

"Notes Toward an Analysis of *The Red Badge of Courage*," first published as the concluding portion of my Introduction to the Modern Library (1951) edition of *The Red Badge of Courage*, was included in my "Stephen Crane: A Revaluation," in *Critiques and Essays on Modern Fiction, 1920-1951*, edited by John W. Aldridge (1952). That essay was in the press prior to my receiving photocopy of the manuscripts of *The Red Badge*, the gift of Mr. C. W. Barrett (December 1951). "Notes Toward an Analysis of *The Red Badge of Courage*," which is here reprinted almost precisely as first published, next appeared in my *Stephen Crane: An Omnibus* (Knopf, 1952; Heinemann, 1954), again almost without alterations except that much new matter was added to my interpretation of Crane's war novel. Here—reprinted from *Omnibus* (pp. 217-224)—is my added commentary having to do with the Long Version Manuscript of *The Red Badge:*

It would take another Keats to describe my excitement on first looking into Crane's handwritten manuscripts of *The Red Badge*. The new planets that swam into my ken brightened up my theory of the whole symbolic system and (I think) reinforced the interpretation I had already made.[7]

Many of the passages that Crane expunged from the typescript or canceled in the manuscripts during the process of revision contribute additional symbolic overtones, reinforce the dominant patterns of imagery and meaning; they help toward illuminating what the book is really all about. Their omission is therefore a distinct loss not only to the imaginative scheme of relationships but also to the directional line of the author's concealed intention. A few of these expunged passages are furthermore a loss to the picturesqueness of the style. *The Red Badge*, according to my reading of it, is loaded with Biblical allusions and religious symbolism. In one of the passages appearing in the final handwritten manuscript but not in the printed version of Chapter i, Henry Fleming receives a Bible from his mother.

Don't fergit to send yer socks to me the minute they git holes in 'em, and *here's a little bible I want yeh to take along with yeh, Henry.* I don't presume yeh'll be a-setting reading it all day long, child, ner nothin' like that. Many a time, yeh'll fergit yeh got it, I don't doubt. But there'll be many a time, too, Henry, when yeh'll be wanting advice, boy, and all like that, and there'll be nobody round, perhaps, to tell yeh things. Then if yeh take it out, boy, yeh'll find wisdom in it— wisdom in it, Henry—with little or no searching.

Perhaps Crane felt that this passage revealed too much of his hidden ground plan to appear this early and deleted it for that reason from the typescript copy of the final handwritten manuscript. Crane's theory (misquoting Emerson) was that "There should be a long logic beneath the story, but it should be carefully kept out of sight."

The same tendency to keep things hidden, oblique, and enigmatic is disclosed in other canceled or excised passages. For example, the original title for the novel: *Private Fleming / His various battles,* not only names the hero but hints that his battles are psychological as well as physical ones. Crane's revised and final title is far more enigmatic: *The Red Badge of Courage / an Episode of the American Civil War.* This last part of the title is straightforward, matter-of-fact; but the first part indicates a symbol.

This final title was unquestionably an added second thought. (It is written in darker ink and with far more pressure on the pen than used in writing the original title *and* the opening pages of the manuscript, the first title and the first page being done at the same time.) Now, the source of the final title (as Mr. Winterich notices[8]) was a sentence that Crane struck off in Chapter ix: "He wished that he, too, had a wound, a little [warm *canceled*] red badge of courage." The first title is crossed out by wavy slanting pencil-lines, and across the left margin at the top of the page there is the word *Cap* appearing in pencil—and by another hand. Evidently it was written there by the typist or by the editor; printer's copy or typescript was made from this final handwritten draft.

Two further points relating to Crane's revision of the title are also characteristic of his process of revision. The hero's name is concealed not only in the final title but throughout Manuscript LV, from the first page of the final manuscript to the last (with but few exceptions). To cite one instance where the hero's name is not crossed out, "What's the matter, Flem?" appears in the printed version as "What's the matter, Henry?" Crane intended anonymity for his soldiers except on occasions when they are addressing one another. Secondly, the final title announces and initiates the motif of color, which is recurrent throughout the book. The *Spectator,* reviewing *The Red Badge of Courage* on June 27, 1896, said that the book carried "an infelicitous title by the way." And Ripley Hitchcock, editor at Appleton's, anticipated that criticism and asked Crane to shorten the title. And so Crane, writing to Hitchcock from New Orleans on March 8, 1895, suggested that the word *red* be cut from the title: "That would shorten it." But so concerned was Crane with color that in one instance in the manuscript he used the word *color*, absent-mindedly, in place of *collar!* (In the phrase "long troughs of liquid mud" appearing in the printed version of the opening page of the novel, the word *long*, in the manuscript, was originally followed by the word *red*.) The use of the word *Red* in the final title, as Frank Noxon reports, "was part of a program. After the book appeared he and I had somewhere a talk about color in literature. He told me that a passage in Goethe analyzed the effect which the several colors have upon the human mind. Upon Crane this had made a profound impression and he utilized the idea to produce his effects" (in *Step Ladder:* January 1928).

The most interesting discovery in Manuscript LV is that the ending of the novel underwent several changes. Crane first intended the novel to end with the words: "oaths and walking sticks," which are the last words in the paragraph beginning "It rained."

> It rained. The procession of weary soldiers became a bedraggled train, despondent and muttering, marching with churning effort in a trough of liquid brown mud under a low, wretched sky. Yet the youth smiled, for he saw that the world was a world for him, though many discovered it to be made of oaths and walking sticks.

The words "The End" are written after this paragraph. On second thought Crane added fifty-five words to the paragraph. He had crossed out the phrases "walking sticks" and "The End" and now wrote in this second ending:

> walking sticks. He had rid himself of the red sickness of battle. The sultry nightmare was in the past. He had been an animal blistered and sweating in the heat and pain of war. He turned now with a lover's thirst to images of tranquil skies, fresh meadows, cool brooks—an existence of soft and eternal peace.

That this ending represents a second intention and was added at some later time, not during the period of original composition, is evidenced by the use of a new pen for writing it. (Most of Crane's revisions in Manuscript LV were made after the whole draft had been finished, the evidence for this being the dark ink and the comparatively heavy pen pressure used when crossing out and writing in the first and second variant. Revisions made during original composition are quite infrequent.)

Compared with the first ending, this second one is the less effective of the two. Crane realized this himself and therefore added a third ending. It consists of a single image:

> Over the river a golden ray of sun came through the hosts of leaden rain clouds.

This third ending does not appear in the manuscript. The proof that it was Crane himself who inserted it in the typescript is that this final ending recapitulates one of the dominant contrast-patterns of the book: the despair-hope contrast mood initiated by the opening scene of Chapter i. The mood of hope and faith evoked by this opening scene (paragraphs 1-3) shifts to despair and disbelief (paragraphs 4-7), and this same alternation of mood patterns every tableau in the whole sequence and is epitomized in the final sun-through-rainclouds image. That fact alone suffices, I think, to discredit Winterich's supposition that this third ending "bears the unmistakable spoor of the editor—an editor not too happily inspired." Who but the artist himself could possibly possess the requisite insight for inventing this double-mood image by which the ending of the book reconstructs its very beginning? That Crane consciously designed the book with this device and burden is revealed in a passage canceled in Manuscript LV: "*Again* the youth was in despair." It would seem reasonable to assume then, since this final ending must have been the invention of the author, that most of the other alterations made in the typescript were similarly the rewrite work of the author, though it certainly was the editor who corrected Crane's innumerable errors in grammar, syntax, punctuation, and spelling."[9]

Winterich, in his Introduction to the Folio Society edition of *The Red Badge*, goes on to say that "The 'rain clouds' ending sounds like a concession to the send-the-audience-home-feeling-good school. But let us all feel good ourselves—there are not many novels in which the reader is offered a choice of three endings." But the reader is not offered any choice, and in fact no choice is possible. The final ending is built on the two preceding ones, and each of these prepares for the one that follows it. The "sun-through-rainclouds" image gives an ironic twist to the flat sentimental "images of tranquil skies, fresh meadows, cool brooks—an existence of eternal peace." Henry has not attained eternal peace, and though the sun shines, it pierces "hosts of leaden rain clouds." It is interesting to notice that Hemingway's hero in *A Farewell to Arms* also makes his "separate peace"—that too an illusion not unlike Henry Fleming's. From the start Henry Fleming recognizes the necessity for change of heart but wars against it, and at the end he is the same Henry Fleming. He has undergone no change, no real spiritual development.[10] In an excised passage appearing in Chapter xii of the Short Version Manuscript Crane's ironic method presents the mocked hero as "*a-blaze with desire to change*. He saw himself, a sun-lit figure upon a peak, pointing with true and *unchangeable* gesture. 'There!' And all men could see and no man would falter." His self-contradiction is summed up in this single turnabout.

It is certainly not by chance that this theme of change begins the book and ends it. The altered mood of the soldiers in the opening scene is accompanied by a change in the weather, and this initial image of the book is paralleled in the concluding images of Chapter xxiv. Both *The Red Badge of Courage* and *A Farewell to Arms* close with the same image that their opening scenes prepared for. In both it is an image of fog or rain. In *A Farewell* the terminal word of the book is *rain*, and throughout the story rain is associated with motifs of death and deception. In the paragraph that Crane first intended as the ending of *The Red Badge*, rain reappears. Rain associated with the despondent mood of the soldiers here returns us to the beginning image of Chapter i: "The cold passed . . . and the retiring fogs . . ." In both novels the weather and

the terrrain *act* as protagonists, and all weather and terrain images—
sun and rain or fog, river, and so on—carry symbolic significance.

In the ending Crane first intended for his novel the image of "oaths
and walking sticks" echoes an image canceled from Chapter xx in the
final handwritten draft. This is the canceled passage: "The youth noted
that the lieutenant held his sword in the manner of a walking-stick."
(Crane first wrote the word *cane* for *sword*.) The lieutenant leans on his
sword as though in need of a cane or walking-stick to support him. Henry,
at the end of the book, smiles *although* it is raining and the soldiers are
despondent. He smiles because the world, so he now thinks, was made
for him. He has no need for walking-sticks—that is, creeds—to support
him. "Yet the youth smiled, for he saw that the world was a world for
him, though many discovered it to be made of oaths and walking sticks."
In a passage expunged from the printed version this telltale image appears
in the manuscript: "The imperturbable sun shines on insult and worship."
Insult equates with *oaths,* and *worship* equates with *walking sticks.* Men
insult with oaths the very creed they worship; they curse their walking-
sticks—that which props them. Crane's example is Henry Fleming.

Fleming, when Jim Conklin dies, curses the red sun pasted in the sky
"like a wafer." Nature, we are told, "had given him a sign." Henry
blasphemes against this emblem of his faith, the wafer-like red sun. The
manuscripts provide two variants of this final image for Chapter ix. In
the earlier draft Crane wrote: "The fierce red sun was pasted in the sky
like a fierce wafer." The first *fierce* was then canceled, and in the final
handwritten draft the image remained thus: "The red sun was pasted in
the sky like a fierce wafer." The emphatic *fierce* personifies the sun as
the Divinity, a wrathful Jehovah. This central and crucial episode of the
story is echoed in the "oaths and walking sticks" image of that paragraph
which Crane first intended as the final one for Chapter xxiv, and again in
the already quoted excised image: "The imperturbable sun shines on
insult and worship." That the sun is indifferent to the blasphemy of the
youth is underscored in another image new to the printed text: "But the
sky would forget." In contrast with Henry's blasphemy against the sun,
there was a soldier who "swore *by* the sun"—in a passage canceled in the
manuscript. The wafer-like sun, the object of insult and worship, signifies
the sacrificial death of *the* Son.

Religious symbolism toolmarks the whole book. Corroborative evidence
for this interpretation is found in several passages canceled in the manuscripts or expunged from the printed version. In Chapter iv Henry Fleming
—in an excised passage—vaingloriously regards himself as "the chosen of
some gods. By fearful and wonderful roads he was to be led to a crown."
Henry, in the cant phrase for it, thinks he is a little tin Christ. In a passage
appearing only in the Short Version Manuscript, Crane wrote in mockery
of his hero: "He had a feeling that he was the coming prophet of a
world reconstruction." (Crane wrote first the word *social* and then canceled it and added the variant *world*.) Another image revelatory of the

author's scheme of Biblical "parallelisms" occurs in an excised passage in Manuscript LV: Henry in his blind egotism remembers the words of the "insane lieutenant," words that praised his battle grit, and he reflects: "It was a little coronation." It looks as though Henry had read the Bible his mother gave him!

The Red Badge of Courage begins with a metaphor (implied in the printed version, explicitly present in the original draft), strikes off near its center another metaphor ("The red sun was pasted in the sky like a fierce wafer"), and ends with a metaphor. There can be no question that this book was constructed by an artist.   (1952)

NOTES

1. In "Little Stories of 'Steve' Crane," *Saturday Evening Post:* April 11, 1903, pp. 19-20.
2. Cited in *Painting in France: 1895–1949,* by G. di San Lazzaro (1949), p. 28 n.
3. In agreement with this idea, I find now, is Edmund Burke's remark in *A Philosophical Inquiry Into the Origin of Our Ideas of the Sublime and Beautiful:* "no work of art can be great, but as it deceives" (II, x). Quoted in *Times Literary Supplement:* December 7, 1956.
4. *Miss Ravenel's Conversion from Secession to Loyalty,* edited by Gordon Haight (Harper & Brothers, 1939), p. 258.
5. *Under Fire* (E. P. Dutton & Co., 1917), p. 256.
6. My reading stands opposed to Frederick J. Hoffman's in *The Modern Novel in America* (1951), pp. 86 ff: "It is doing more than justice to Crane to compare the opening paragraph from *The Red Badge of Courage* with that of *A Farewell to Arms.*"
7. Attacks on my interpretation of *The Red Badge*—too numerous to enumerate here—include "Fiction and the Criticism of Fiction" by P. Rahv, to which I made reply in "Fiction and Its' Critics" (*Kenyon Review:* Spring 1957), an essay which is reprinted in the present volume. The latest attack is by S. B. Greenfield in *Publications of the Modern Language Association* (December 1958): "The Unmistakable Stephen Crane." "We are indebted to a great degree to Stallman for the revival of an interest in Crane. But his critical method and interpretation I find very disturbing." He is disturbed, for one thing, that my Modern Library Introduction (1951) "is now appearing in a Greek edition of the novel." (Translated into the Greek, my Introduction and *The Red Badge* saw print in Athens, 1956.) "And this perseverance of the same argument and method of criticism has led to converts." These "converts" include Isaac Rosenfeld (in *Kenyon Review:* Spring 1953), James T. Cox (in *Modern Fiction Studies:* Autumn 1959), James B. Colvert (in *Texas Studies in English:* 1958), and Daniel G. Hoffman in his Introduction to *The Red Badge of Courage and Other Stories* (Harper, 1957). Hoffman's essay buttresses and extends my Modern Library 1951 reading of *The Red Badge.* As Colvert puts it: "Not until after 1950, when a revival of interest in Crane began to place him in a new critical light, was the standard approach to his writing challenged. Robert W. Stallman, who has been largely responsible for this revival, has shifted the focus of attention away from Crane's Naturalism to his style, which this critic finds not at all extraneous to Crane's art, but on the contrary the most significant aspect of it. . . . To Stallman, clearly, Crane's stories are for the consideration of practical criticism, long prose-poems; in those very ele-

ments which the 'Naturalist' critics ignore or find unaccountable, he discovers new dimensions of meaning."

James T. Cox writes: "On the question of Crane's fictional method, Stallman is still significantly right in his recognition of the extent to which 'Crane puts language to poetic uses, which is to use it reflexively and symbolically.' And it is past time that this fundamental question be considered apart from any given interpretation, for a full understanding and appreciation of the better works of Stephen Crane are absolutely dependent upon an awareness of this method." In *Modern Fiction Studies:* Stephen Crane Special Number (Autumn 1959), an important collection of essays on Crane's fiction. My Modern Library 1951 reading of *The Red Badge* is reprinted in *The Red Badge of Courage: Text and Criticism,* edited by Richard Lettis and others (Harcourt, Brace, 1960), a casebook of critical studies.

8. John T. Winterich in his Introduction to the Folio Society edition of *The Red Badge of Courage* (London, 1951). This edition published the final handwritten manuscript of *The Red Badge* for the first time, but no portion of the earlier and shorter *Red Badge* manuscript was reproduced, nor was there any reference here to its existence. The Folio Society text of the final and long version manuscript (Manuscript LV) is an incomplete and erroneous copy. It is reprinted in *The Red Badge of Courage and Selected Prose and Poetry,* edited by William M. Gibson (New York: Rinehart, 1956). So, then, the only correct and complete manuscript text of *The Red Badge* is in my *Omnibus*—until the Signet Classic edition, which I edited for New American Library (1960). This Signet edition of *The Red Badge* is reprinted from *Omnibus,* but with new manuscript pages (Manuscript LV) brought together here for the first time. The text of this Signet edition stands now as the definitive edition of *The Red Badge of Courage*—Copyright 1952, by Alfred A. Knopf, Inc., © 1960 by R. W. Stallman.

9. Conrad designated the third from the last paragraph of the printed version as the ending of the actual *action* of the narrative: "He had been to touch the great death, and found that, after all, it was but the great death. He was a man."

10. In my "Stephen Crane: A Revaluation," in *Critiques and Essays on Modern Fiction* (1952), I said that Henry Fleming's "farewell to vain ideals and compromising illusions" is illusory—except from Henry's point of view. That Henry has "undergone no change, no real spiritual development," as I stated it in *Omnibus* (1952), squares with my Introduction to the Modern Library edition of *The Red Badge of Courage* (1951); that essay and the *Critiques* essay were written long before the manuscripts of *The Red Badge* were examined. "It is interesting to observe that Stallman, *after* examining the earlier manuscripts of *The Red Badge of Courage,* seems to have had a change of mind about Henry's 'salvation,' " so S. B. Greenfield unjustly opines (in *P.M.L.A.:* December 1958). On the contrary, the manuscripts—by my reading—confirmed my 1951 interpretation: "This sun-through-rain image, which epitomizes the double mood pattern dominating every tableau in the whole sequence, is a symbol of Henry Fleming's moral triumph *and is an ironic commentary* upon it. Crane is a master of the contradictory effect." (I quote here from the Modern Library 1951 edition, p. xxiv.)

Ironically enough, even Greenfield concedes that there "*is* irony in the end of the novel; in fact, if one examines the longer version in the earlier manuscript of *The Red Badge of Courage,* he can have no doubt that there is." Well, I said as much prior to seeing the manuscripts, prior to knowing of their existence. I find Mr. Greenfield's scholarship rather disturbing. His notion of "earlier manuscripts" and of "the longer version in the earlier manuscript" is mistaken. There are two manuscripts, of which the longer version is the final manuscript, designated in my *Omnibus* as MS LV. The earlier manuscript is the shorter version, designated as MS SV. Most recent Crane criticism has seen Crane "through a glass darkly," says Greenfield; but among such critics—I conclude—belongs Greenfield himself.

Crane's Short Stories

(1)

IT WAS Conrad who first identified similarities between Crane's artistic temperament and his own and who first identified *The Red Badge of Courage,* with its psychological inquiry into "the moral problem of conduct," with his own *Nigger of the "Narcissus."* (Crane's enthusiasm for this story led him to seek out Conrad in England and thereby become his friend and later his neighbor.) Conrad might have noted further similarities had he known Crane's "An Experiment in Misery" and *Maggie,* for the short story carries the Conradian theme of Solidarity (the theme also of "The Open Boat"), and *Maggie* the Conradian theme of Fidelity—*Maggie* being a study in infidelity or betrayal. Crane and Conrad are closely akin not only in temperament, but also in artistic code and in thematic range and ironic outlook or tone. Both treat the subject of heroism ironically and both contrive for their heroes, usually weak or defeated men, unequal contests against outside forces, pitting them against the sublime obstacles of hostile or indifferent nature. "The Open Boat" epitomizes this subject for Crane, "Typhoon" for Conrad.

The Red Badge of Courage is readily identifiable with *Lord Jim,* but their differences are, I think, more instructive. Whereas Lord Jim has an innate capacity for heroism, Henry Fleming has it thrust upon him by chance and at the wrong moment. For Crane, as "The End of the Battle" testifies, heroism is not a predictable possession, but an impersonal gift thrust upon man with ironic consequences. The whole intention of his fable "A Mystery of Heroism" is to explode the myth of heroism. The soldier Collins does a heroic deed, but, as in Kipling, it is "the heroism of moral fortitude on the edge of a nervous collapse." Collins runs under shellfire to get water at a well and once there he is a hero, "an intruder in the land of fine deeds," but once there the poor hero is cut off (both literally and symbolically) from his fellow men, and the emptiness of his vainglorious triumph is symbolized by the bucket from which the wasted water spills as he nervously makes his way back to the men. Crane's characters are always common, insignificant, and virtually nameless persons; no Crane character is heroic, none is a leader, none is an ideal. When compared with Conrad's, Crane's concept of man's nature seems shallow. It is neither penetrating nor magnanimous.

(2)

Crane stands in close kinship to Conrad and Henry James, the masters of the impressionist school. Edward Garnett, in 1898, hailed Crane as "the chief impressionist of the age," adding that "Mr. Crane's talent is unique." All three aimed to create (to use Henry James's phrase) "a direct impression of life." Their credo is voiced by Conrad in his celebrated Preface to the *Nigger of the "Narcissus"*—it is "by the power of the written word, to make you hear, to make you feel—it is, before all, to make you *see*." Their aim was to immerse the reader in the created experience so that its impact on him would occur simultaneously with the discovery of it by the characters themselves. Instead of panoramic views of a battlefield, Crane paints not the whole scene but disconnected segments of it, all that a participant in an action or a spectator of a scene can possibly take into his view at any one moment. Crane is a master at creating illusions of reality by means of a fixed point of vision, through a specifically located observer.

> From their position as they again faced toward the place of fighting, they could of course comprehend a greater amount of battle than when their visions had been blurred by the hurling smoke of the line. They could see dark stretches winding along the land, and on one cleared space there was a row of guns making gray clouds, which were filled with large flashes of orange-colored flame (*The Red Badge of Courage,* ch. xviii).

"None of them knew the colour of the sky"—that famous opening sentence of "The Open Boat" defines the restricted point of view of the four men in the wave-tossed dinghy, their line of vision being shut off by the menacing walls of angry water. Busy at the oars, they knew the color of the sky only by the color of the sea, and "they knew it was broad day because the colour of the sea changed from slate to emerald-green, streaked with amber lights, and the foam was like tumbling snow." It establishes also the despair-hope mood of the men, and the final scene repeats the same mood of contrast. The same device of double mood patterns *The Red Badge of Courage*. In theme, in patterns of imagery and leitmotif, and in form, *The Red Badge* and "The Open Boat" are identical.

In both novels everything is keyed in a state of tension; in "The Open Boat" even the speech of the shipwrecked men is abrupt and composed of "disjointed sentences." Crane's style is itself composed of disjointed sentences, disconnected sense-impressions, chromatic vignettes by which the reality of the experience is evoked in all its point-present immediacy.

Crane's style has been likened to a unique instrument that no one after his death has ever been able to play. *The Red Badge of Courage* seems unprecedented and incomparable. But Chekhov, who was almost of an age with Crane, and a little later Katherine Mansfield, who adopted the method of Chekhov, were both masters of the same instrument. In its episodic structure and impressionistic style Chekhov's *The Cherry Orchard* suggests a parallel to *The Red Badge of Courage.* All three artists had essentially the same literary aim and method: intensity of vision, objectivity in rendering it. All three aimed at a depersonalization of art: they aimed to get outside themselves completely in order "to find the greatest truth of the idea" and "see the thing as it really is"; to keep themselves aloof from their characters, not to become emotionally involved with their subjects, and to comment on them not by statement, but by evocation in picture and tone. "Sentiment is the devil," said Crane (and in this he echoed Flaubert).

Crane's language is the language of symbol and paradox: the wafer-like sun in *The Red Badge;* or in "The Open Boat" the paradox of "cold, comfortable sea-water," an image that calls to mind the poetry of Yeats, with its fusion of contradictory emotions. This single image evokes the sensation of the whole experience of the men in the dinghy, but it suggests furthermore another telltale significance, one applicable to Stephen Crane. What is readily recognizable in this paradox of "cold, comfortable sea-water" is that irony of opposites which constituted the personality of the man who wrote it. It is the subjective correlative of his own plight. The enigma of the man is signified by his enigmatic style.

Crane was intense, volatile, spontaneous. He wrote as he lived, and his life was shot through with ironies. Seeing life from a water-soaked dinghy, as it were, the sea tossing him about this way and that, he saw it as an angry or indifferent sea—"the grim waves menacing" and "most wrongfully and barbarously abrupt." If he won any "grace" from that cold voyage it was, I think, the artist's gift of ironic outlook, that grace of irony which is so central to his art. Irony is Crane's chief technical instrument. It is the key to our understanding of the man and of his works. He wrote with the intensity of a poet's emotion, the compressed emotion that bursts into symbol and paradox.

A great stylist, Crane puts language to poetic uses, which is to use it reflexively and symbolically. *The works that employ this reflexive and symbolic language constitute what is permanent of Crane.*

(3)

Crane is always dealing with the paradox of man. *That* defines what his stories are really all about. Paradox patterns all his best stories; it defines their kinship one to another. The reading of fear as the "theme" of everything he wrote ignores about as many of his stories as, superficially, it accounts for. The soldiers in "The End of the Battle" are as fearless as the sheriff in "The Bride Comes to Yellow Sky." *Maggie* and *George's Mother* have nothing to do with fear, and there is no trace of panic in "An Episode of War."

As "The Price of the Harness" repeats several episodes and images from *The Red Badge*, so "An Episode of War" harks back to the novel too, to the incident of the wounded lieutenant there (ch. iv). More important are the external kinships between Crane's stories—"A Mystery" and "An Episode"—and Hemingway's novels of the wounded hero or outcast. In *The Sun Also Rises* Hemingway employs the same symbolism of wound as Crane in "An Episode" and in *The Red Badge*. Hemingway's social outcasts stand in line of descent as much from Crane's mental outcasts—Henry Fleming and, in "A Mystery," Collins—as from Twain's Huck Finn.

"An Episode of War" is about the withdrawal of the wounded lieutenant from the real world into an imaginary world. Wounded, he was puzzled about what to do with his unsheathed sword: "this weapon had of a sudden become a strange thing to him. He looked at it in a kind of stupefaction, as if he had been endowed with a trident, a sceptre, or a spade." He has become another person, a king or mythical figure, and his wounded arm seems fabulous—"made of very brittle glass." The wound is the symbol of his change of vision, enabling him now "to see many things which as a participant in the fight were unknown to him." The wounded, "no longer having part in the battle, knew more of it than others." "A wound gives strange dignity to him who bears it. Well men shy from this new and terrible majesty." The real world seen from the point of view of the wounded spectator now seems unreal, more like something in "a historical painting," and the men who belong to it seem immobilized as they gaze "statue-like and silent." "An Episode" thus bears comparison with "The Upturned Face" and, in its theme of a change of vision, it links with "A Mystery of Heroism" and *The Red Badge of Courage*. In structure "An Episode" is exactly like *The Red Badge*. It is formed of alternations of moods: perspectives of motion and change shifting into picture-postcard impressions where everything is felt as fixed and static. Henry Fleming is duped by realities; Collins is likewise disillusioned; and the lieutenant is deceived. "I won't amputate it," says the surgeon when asked about the wounded arm. "Come along. Don't be a baby." Like *The Red Badge*, "A Mystery of Heroism" is a study of disillusionment. The mood of disillusionment is evoked in the final symbol of the story: "The bucket lay on the ground, empty."

Crane's best stories are all of a piece, similar in theme and design. What Carl Van Doren said about "A Mystery of Heroism"—"pure, concentrated Crane"—applies equally to "An Episode" and "The Upturned Face." The germinal situations of these two stories reappear in "The Price of the Harness," a story of the Spanish-American War published in 1898 and written before them. While "A Mystery of Heroism" was written before Crane had occasion to witness actual warfare, "An Episode of War" likewise portrays a war he never saw; and "The Upturned Face" deals with a war that never existed. But no matter; what counts is the created illusion of reality, and in any work of art fact cannot be divided from fiction.

"The Upturned Face," though wholly imaginary, was inspired by the Spanish-American War. Timothy Lean and the adjutant: they must bury their comrade amidst riflefire, and they are puzzled about how to perform this delicate task. The story opens and ends with a question. " 'What do we do now?' said the adjutant, troubled and excited. 'Bury him,' said Timothy Lean." That opening question evokes the mood of hesitation and doubt, and Lean's answer—"bury him"—intensifies the question and does not answer it. It is the question of how to come to terms with the real thing. Even after burying him they are still in doubt. It is as though their coming to terms with the actuality has exploded their theory about it. " 'Perhaps we have been wrong,' said the adjutant. His glance wavered *stupidly*. 'It might have been better if we hadn't buried him *just at this time*.' 'Damn you,' said Lean, 'shut your mouth!' He was not the senior officer." In cursing the adjutant, Lean was breaking code, and this has its parallel in the abstract code or ritual of burial, which is shattered by its impingement upon a point in time. The final question in the story is, as it were, the unspoken query of the corpse, "which from its chalkblue face looked keenly out from the grave."

The one moment *before* the first shovel-load of earth is emptied upon the corpse pinpoints the whole story. It is the moment *while* the shovel is "held poised above the corpse," fixed "for *a moment of inexplicable hesitation*. . . ." Keenly, "in curious *abstraction* they looked at the body." They cannot bring themselves to face up to the real thing—"Both were particular that their fingers should not feel the corpse." But the abstract code becomes far more terrifyingly real to them than the bullets spitting overhead, and, in a sense, more real than the corpse. Louder than any riflefire is the sound of the earth landing upon the upturned face—"plop!" How poignant the reality of life, all its values realized in that impact! It is this burden that fills the grave. (In Bierce's "An Occurrence at Owl Creek Bridge" the same theme is evoked, and the same structural conception underlies the story: illusion shattered by realities.) "And from Thy superb heights," says Lean, reading the burial service. But he can remember only two lines of it. All that now remains of this ritual is a fragment. " 'Oh, well,' he cried suddenly, 'let us—let us say something—while he can hear us.' " It is as though he were denying the fact; it is as though the dead man were *alive*. Then the first shovel is emptied "on—on the feet. Timothy Lean felt as if tons had been swiftly lifted from off his forehead." It is as though the living man had been thus *exhumed*. But the key paradox is that in honoring their beloved comrade they dishonor him and honor themselves. Their consecration is a desecration: the ritual consecrates him, but the act of the ritual desecrates him. "Always the earth made that sound—plop!" So all relationships, like this one, involve that shock of reality by which intentions are contradicted by the act.

All Crane stories end in irony. Some end on a minor note, like *Maggie* and *George's Mother*—"not with a bang but a whimper." Every Crane story worth mentioning is designed upon a single ironic incident, a crucial paradox or irony of opposites. All of them are built out of anecdotal material, and all are concerned with virtually the same problem—the moral problem of conduct. It is the same in Conrad. In method of construction, however, Crane's closer affinities are with Chekhov. They were among the first to eliminate plot. Crane constructs his stories, like Chekhov, by building up to a crucial moment of impasse and collapse. A Crane story consists of that moment when the characters confront the inescapable impasse of a situation by which they are boxed in, and then—the moment of spiritual collapse—"nothing happens," and they are left with a sense of loss or insignificance or defeat, futility or disillusionment.

"The Blue Hotel" was written in early 1898 and finished in February at Brede Place in England three years after Crane visited a desolate junction town in Nebraska (in February 1895) and saw there a hotel that was painted a light blue. "The Blue Hotel" happens to be Hemingway's favorite, and one Crane critic has rated it "one of the most vivid short stories ever written by an American." This story, said Mencken in 1927, "is superlative among short stories." Howells, however, thought "The Monster" "the greatest short story ever written by an American." John Berryman claims that "The Blue Hotel" forms with "The Open Boat" Crane's "masterwork." And "The Monster" is "The Blue Hotel" "in more terrible form." So one critic applauds the story because its values are to him social and political, and another because he too finds in it what he is looking for—psychological source-material. It is Crane's mind, not Crane's story, that concerns him. "The Blue Hotel" localizes Crane's own "thrust toward suicide." The Swede in the blizzard is Crane in the blizzard "hearing the *bugles* of the tempest; and he *likes* this weather, 'I like it. It suits me.' Crane was going to war again." By my reading of the story, however, the Swede is Crane's diametric opposite. The man who wrote *Maggie* believed that our environment shapes our life; yet he himself did nothing to shape his own. He shared with Conrad a fatalistic resignation to what happens. The Swede in "The Blue Hotel" distrusts life and runs to meet and shape his destiny.

But consider the story *critically,* and you see at once that Crane has here violated his own artistic canon. He intrudes to preach a deliberate moral. The story ends with the grotesque image of the murdered Swede whose eyes stare "upon a dreadful legend that dwelt atop of the cash-machine: 'This registers the amount of your purchase.'" This point marks the legitimate end of the story. Crane spoiled the whole thing by tacking on a moralizing appendix. The off-key tone is at odds with the tone of the preceding part, and the theme that his beginning prepared for stands at odds with the trumped-up theme announced in the totally irrelevant and non-ironic conclusion. In "The Upturned Face," a slight thing but a perfection, Crane's grotesquerie is integral to his theme. In "The Blue Hotel" it is there on the page and it is misspent.[1]

Ford Madox Ford said that "The Bride Comes to Yellow Sky" was the

story that had "influenced" him "more than anything else I ever read."
But then, elsewhere, he also said that it was Crane's "Five White Mice."
Ford was given to distortion of facts, misquotation, and faulty memory.
Of some dozen portraits he has sketched of Crane, this one, exaggerated
but in substance likely enough, puts us in mind of "The Bride," which
Crane wrote about this time. Ford says that Crane "in those days, and
for my benefit, was in the habit of posing as an almost fabulous Billy
the Kid." This Stephen Crane looks more like Scratchy Wilson himself:

> I can see him sitting in the singularly ugly drawing room of the
> singularly hideous villa he lived in for a time at Oxted. Then he wore
> —I dare say to shock me—cowboy breeches and no coat, and all the
> time he was talking he wagged in his hand an immense thing that
> he called a gun and that we should call a revolver. From time to
> time he would attempt to slay with the bead-sight of this Colt such
> flies as settled on the table, and a good deal of his conversation would
> be taken up with fantastic boasts about what can be done with these
> lethal instruments. I don't know that he celebrated his own prowess,
> but he boasted about what heroes in the Far West were capable of. I
> did not much believe him then and I believe him still less now. *I don't
> believe any one is capable of anything with a revolver.*[2]

But neither did Crane believe that; Ford has lifted his belief from
Crane's story of Jack Potter. Scratchy Wilson "is a wonder with a gun—
a perfect wonder," but the point of the story is that no man "is capable
of anything with a revolver."

The story turns on a single ironic moment. The sheriff, whose business
is gunfire, carries no gun; and Wilson, who always shoots, is disarmed
by no gun at all. Potter's weapon is a spiritual one.

> —I ain't got a gun because I've just come from San Anton' with my
> wife. I'm married—said Potter. . . .
> —Married?—said Scratchy. Seemingly for the first time, he saw the
> drooping, drowning woman at the other man's side.—No!—he said.
> He was like a creature allowed a glimpse of another world.

Potter has married, as it were, a vision, and it is this dream—"all the
glory of the marriage, the environment of the new estate"—that buoys
him up through the crisis. He is a new man now, and his new world
saves him. It is Wilson's getting a glimpse of it that saves him, too. When
the shock of recognition comes he feels ashamed. His abasement is
symbolized thus: "His feet made *funnel-shaped* tracks in the *heavy* sand."
The only code he has ever known, the frontier code that Potter no longer
lives by, seems for once to have failed him. Potter and Wilson represent
two opposite worlds or points of view: the idealistic world of spiritual
values whose force lies in its innocence, and the non-imaginative world of
crass realities. *This same conflict, the conflict between ideals and realities,*

ruled Crane's struggle as artist and gave his life and his art all their
bitter ironies.

"The Bride" is built on a paradoxical reversal of situation. Structurally it has close affinities, therefore, with Crane's "Mystery of Heroism," "The Upturned Face," and "An Episode of War." In all four stories, that which is predictable—a code, a theory, or an ideal—is discovered to be un-predictable when faced by the realities. Wilson's "theory" about the sheriff collapses; the trapped man is Wilson himself. It is the same with Henry Fleming. The trapped or "baited" man is the characteristic ingredient of a Crane tale. The corollary is an ironic turnabout, a reversal of situation. Crane's fiction at its best combines these two ironic ingredients. No reversal occurs in "The Blue Hotel," and there the baited character has set his own trap. Potter, unlike the Swede, accepts his moment of destiny. It has been shaped for him by a man who (allegorically speaking) is not "married." In that crucial moment of impending death Potter attains spiritual triumph. "The Bride Comes to Yellow Sky" thus anticipates in both its theme and its structure Hemingway's "Short Happy Life of Francis Macomber."   (1952)

NOTES

1. The double ending of "The Blue Hotel," as I first spelled it out in *Omnibus* (1952), pp. 482-483, has been subsequently disputed. For variant readings see James T. Cox: "Stephen Crane as Symbolic Naturalist: An Analysis of 'The Blue Hotel'," *Modern Fiction Studies*, III (Summer 1957); Joseph N. Satter-white: "Stephen Crane's 'The Blue Hotel': The Failure of Understanding," *Modern Fiction Studies*, II (Winter 1956-1957); Walter Sutton: "Pity and Fear in 'The Blue Hotel,'" *American Quarterly*, IV (Spring 1952); and most recently Hugh Maclean's "The Two Worlds of 'The Blue Hotel,'" *Modern Fiction Studies*, V (Autumn 1959).
2. "Stevie & Co.," New York *Times Book Review:* January 2, 1927, p. 1.

JOSEPH CONRAD

Time and *The Secret Agent*[1]

"I suppose you know that the world is selfish, I mean the majority of the people in it, often unconsciously I must admit, and especially people with a mission, with a fixed idea, with some fantastic object in view, or even with only some fantastic illusion."

—THE ARROW OF GOLD, II, 1

A man haunted by a fixed idea is insane. He is dangerous even if that idea is an idea of justice. . . .

—NOSTROMO, 369

(1)

THOUGH *The Secret Agent* is one of the most crytographic works in all British fiction, Conrad perversely appended to it the subtitle: "A Simple Tale." The only thing simple in it is the simpleton Stevie, and even he is rather a complicated character. Perhaps it's Conrad's bogus subtitle— A Simple Tale!—that has beguiled Conrad's critics and unwary readers into the trap of dismissing *The Secret Agent*—one of his richest works of art—as having no more claim to merit than as an excellent example of detective fiction (the critic is Ernest Baker), "a good Hitchcock thriller" (W. T. Webster), or as an example of the political fable (Irving Howe). A splendid book, one critic has conceded, but it is a book "in the same class as *Tono Bungay* and *The Old Wives' Tale*." F. R. Leavis has not so much as scratched the surface of this book, but he does recognize it as "indubitably a classic and a masterpiece, and it doesn't answer to the notion at all —which is perhaps why it appears to have had nothing like due recognition." How can it possibly earn due recognition as long as its hidden meaning passes unnoticed?

All's chaos and confusion; all's incongruous and irrational, but nevertheless logic designs the structure of *The Secret Agent*. One critic attributes "the horror of the tale" to the notion that ordinary reason cannot comprehend the dialectic of evil, and he concludes that "the whole chain of circumstances defies the logic of thought." (Paul L. Wiley, *Conrad's Measure of Man*, 1954, p. 109.) No work of art defies the logic of thought. A cryptographic work of art gets itself read only by the cryptographic reader. What Marlow says of Jim's plight in *Lord Jim* applies to *The Secret Agent:* "There is to my mind a sort of profound and terrifying logic to it."

As *The Secret Agent* is among Conrad's less well known works, though it is among his greatest, a brief summary may be useful to the reader. The story, to quote Miss Bradbrook's summary (*Joseph Conrad: Poland's English Genius*, 1941, p. 48),

111

has for its main event a "senseless outrage" staged by Verloc, the *agent provocateur,* which unexpectedly involves the death of his feeble-minded young brother-in-law. Mrs. Verloc, whose maternal passion for Stevie is the mainspring of her simple existence, and who has never suspected her husband's activities, kills Verloc, and then in blind terror puts herself into the hands of one of the revolutionary party [Comrade Ossipon], who leaves her stranded on the Calais steamer. She throws herself overboard in despair. Such is the story, but its melodramatic events are all told with a deliberate and consistent foreshortening. They are described purely and externally, and always with an ironic overtone.

The story had its inception in an incident reported to Conrad by Ford Madox Ford, an attempt to destroy Greenwich Observatory with a bomb. The bomb-thrower, who was half an idiot, succeeded only in blowing himself to pieces. His sister afterwards committed suicide. From this germinal seed Conrad constructed the sordid domestic world of the Verlocs, and it may be noted (to quote Oliver Warner's *Joseph Conrad,* 1951) that such a *milieu* is seldom met with elsewhere in Conrad. The whole book is conceived in an ironical temper, as Conrad defined it in a letter to R. B. Cunninghame Graham (October 7, 1907): "a sustained effort in ironical treatment of a melodramatic subject." While different from the majority of Conrad's works, the difference, as Douglas Hewitt observes, is on the surface: "it is a difference of presentation rather than of the preoccupations which lie at the back of it. There is no central character in whom the problems of value are worked out, no character who is the focal point of the moral issues involved. It is more nearly a comedy than any other novel of Conrad—a comedy which is intensely serious and in which the pity and scorn of which he speaks in the 'Author's Note' are most important." The element of brutal and sordid farce, which appears also in "Heart of Darkness" and in "Falk," is here dominant (*Conrad: A Reassessment,* 1952, p. 85). Recasting the novel, Conrad later succeeded in creating a remarkable play: *The Secret Agent—A Drama in Four Acts* (1923).

What has eluded Conrad's critics is the simple fact that all time—legal time, civil time, astronomical time, and Universal Time—emanates from Greenwich Observatory *and* that Verloc's mission, in the intended bombing of Greenwich Observatory, is to destroy Time-Now, Universal Time, or life itself. Conrad's cosmic irony is exemplified in Mr. Vladimir's theory that "the blowing up of the first meridian is bound to raise a howl of execration." It's no wonder that Mr. Verloc is unnerved by Mr. Vladimir's orders—"Go for the first meridian."[2] His mission is the destruction of space and time, as the great circle of Greenwich meridian is the zero from which space is measured and time is clocked. From Greenwich zero, terrestrial longitudes are reckoned, and what are these when mapped but concentric circles? Stevie, Winnie Verloc's brother, spends his time drawing "circles, circles, circles; innumerable circles, concentric, eccentric; a corruscating whirl of circles that by their tangled multitude of repeated curves, uniformity of form, and confusion of intersecting lines suggested a rendering of cosmic chaos, the symbol of a mad art attempting the inconceivable" (III). It is ironical that Stevie, the only artist in the world of *The Secret Agent,* is a half-wit.

Stevie's circles diagram the design of the book. First of all, every person in *The Secret Agent* is rendered as a circle of insularity, each insulated from another by his own self-love, by self-illusions and fixed ideas or theories, while like eccentric circles each selfhood impinges upon another by sharing some portion of its attributes, outlook, or theory. The novel presents an ironic concatenation of theories or illusions shocked to zero by the impingements of reality, by the impingements of the unexpected and the unpredictable.

Ex-convict Michaelis—"round like a tub," having been fattened during fifteen years in a damp and lightless prison at the expense of an outraged society—expounds in Adolf Verloc's shop certain theories constituting his apostolic credo; but when his tirade is cut short by a harsh laugh from Comrade Ossipon, Michaelis thereupon falls into silence—and Stevie into drawing circles. What they all have in common is an abhorrence of ideas which contradict and upset their own. Insularity characterizes everyone in the novel. "There was no young man of his age in London more willing and docile than Stephen, she affirmed; none more affectionate and ready to please, and even useful, as long as people did not upset his poor head." Theories excite the irrational Stevie; they make him mad! Michaelis talks to himself, only to himself, "indifferent to the sympathy or hostility of his hearers, indifferent indeed to their presence, from the habit he had acquired of thinking aloud hopefully in the solitude of the four whitewashed walls of his cell . . . sinister and ugly like a colossal mortuary for the socially drowned" (III). The mere fact of "hearing another voice" disconcerted Michaelis painfully; he was no good at discussion.

It was the theory of violence which Karl Yundt declared in refutation of Michaelis' optimism that excited Stevie into drawing circles, as though to erect order out of chaos. More theorist than terrorist, Yundt is optimistic in his pessimism: " 'I have always dreamed,' he mouthed fiercely,

'of a band of men absolute in their resolve to discard all scruples in the choice of means, strong enough to give themselves frankly the name of destroyers, and free from the taint of that resigned pessimism which rots the world. No pity for anything on earth, including themselves, and death enlisted for good and all in the service of humanity—that is what I would have liked to see' " (III).

Ironically, "The famous terrorist had never in his life raised personally as much as his little finger against the social edifice." Each revolutionist accuses the other of being pessimistic about the future, and each outdoes the other in optimistic theories aimed at the destruction of the world as it is. Michaelis' "optimism began to flow from his lips. He saw Capitalism doomed in its cradle, born with the poison of the principle of competition in its system. The great capitalists devouring the little capitalists . . . and in the madness of self-aggrandizement only preparing, organizing, enriching, making ready the lawful inheritance of the suffering proletariat" (III). As the toothless terrorist Yundt puts it, the nature of our present economic conditions is cannibalistic. Cannibalism and gluttony are evoked in the image of Adolf Verloc butchering some meat for his supper on the night of Stevie's slaughter: "The piece of roast beef, laid out in the likeness of funeral baked meats for Stevie's obsequies, offered itself largely to his notice. And Mr. Verloc again partook. He partook ravenously, without restraint and decency" (XI). Cannibalism is suggested by the butcher knife in the Verloc household. The knife-motif is recurrent throughout the novel and culminates in the murder scene—and again by "the knife of infuriated revolutionists," which is the knife that Verloc fears. After the explosion at Greenwich Park nothing is left of Stevie but a mound of rags "concealing what might have been an accumulation of raw material for a cannibal feast" (V).

Although the theories of the revolutionists amount to cannibalism, they profess confidence in the future of life on this globe. "The humanitarian hopes of the mild Michaelis tended not towards utter destruction, but merely towards the complete economic ruin of the system." The patroness of Michaelis supports him (in a cottage at Greenwich Park) and believes in his Theory of the Future. She fails to see that his theory has a hole in it. Universal ruin, as prophesied by Michaelis, "would leave the social values untouched. The disappearance of the last piece of money could not affect people of position. She could not conceive how it could affect her position, for instance" (VI). Mr. Verloc, who himself has no future, is Vice-President of the Future of the Proletariat—which likewise has no future. Nobody has any future because nobody shares life or time now; nobody enjoys life except the moron Ossipon, who regards himself as quite the lady-killer. Professor X scorns Michaelis, the visionary prophet of the future. " 'Prophecy! What's the good of thinking what will be.' He raised his glass. 'To the destruction of what is,' he said, calmly" (XII).[3] As Conrad remarks, "perverse unreason has its own logical processes"—a remark which is exemplified in the person of Professor X, who has a built-in bomb secured to his emaciated body, a sane man insanely equipped to blow himself instantaneously into eternity. The great word that Michaelis utters is *Patience,* and with that word we've epitomized the character of Professor X, for he exercises heroic patience in his lifelong quest to perfect the detonator—one which doesn't go off at the wrong time! Perverse unreason is exemplified also by Michaelis, the Apostle, who is—like Stevie—a harmless creature and "a little mad." His ideas are "inaccessible to reasoning."

"You wouldn't deceive an idiot," says Mr. Vladimir (First Secretary of the Russian Embassy) to Secret Agent Verloc, whereupon Verloc proceeds to deceive the idiot Stevie. Stevie is blown to shreds on the road to Greenwich Observatory while carrying a varnish-can containing a bomb prepared by Professor X, and at the sight of what's left of him an idiotic constable opines "with stolid simplicity: 'He's all there. Every bit of him . . .' " (V). Poor Stevie never was all there, but then neither is Professor X. It is he, rather than the idiot Stevie, who represents madness personified. "Lunatic!" he shouts at Michaelis, and lunatic is Verloc's label for his wife just before she murders him. Perverse unreason is exemplified by Winnie Verloc, when after the murder she "imagined her incoherence to be clearness itself" (XII). Or again by Mr. Vladimir, whose "wit consisted in discovering droll connections between incongruous ideas" (II). Like Professor X, Vladimir is obsessed by a theory of bomb-throwing—if only "one could throw a bomb into pure mathematics." Mr. Vladimir's theory is to attack *the* sacrosanct fetish of our society. It's not religion, not art, not royalty; it's science. Therefore have a go at astronomy! "Such an outrage combines the greatest possible regard for humanity with the most alarming display of ferocious imbecility."

In the final scene at the Silenus beer-hall the "incorruptible Professor" echoes the sham journalistic sentiment of the newspaper reporting the suicide of Winnie Verloc: "Madness and despair! Give me that for a lever, and I'll move the world" (XIII). He'll move it by blowing it up! Madness and despair sum up his plight as well as Winnie Verloc's, and Winnie in turn shares identity with the irrational Stevie. Just before plunging the carving knife into her husband's breast, "As if the homeless soul of Stevie had flown for shelter straight to the breast of his sister, guardian, and protector, the resemblance of her face with that of her brother grew at every step, even to the droop of the lower lip, even to the slight divergence of the eyes" (XI). Every person in *The Secret Agent* shares identity with another; each circled selfhood overlaps.

As the revolutionists depend upon conventions, so Chief Inspector Heat depends on life—whereas Professor X depends on death. "Like to like. The terrorists and the policeman both come from the same basket. Revolution, legality—countermoves in the same game" (IV). Policeman Heat and the revolutionists—they are products of the same machine ("one classed as useful and the other as noxious"). Heat "could understand the mind of a burglar, because, as a matter of fact, the mind and instincts of a burglar are of the same kind as the mind and instincts of a police officer. Both recognize the same conventions, and have a working knowledge of each other's methods and of the routine of their respective trades" (V). Law and Order versus Rebellion against Convention, these two worlds coalesce—like Stevie's eccentric circles, "repeated curves of form and confusion." This situation, the ironic center of the narrative, is expressed otherwise in the Professor's contempt: "You revolutionists . . . are the slaves of the social convention, which is afraid of you; slaves of it as much as the very police that stands up in defense of that convention. Clearly you are, since you want to revolutionize it" (IV). Thus identities overlap, one interfusing with another.

Indolence, immobility, and rotundity characterize Winnie's mother, the plump Winnie Verloc, fat and lazy Verloc, Comrade Ossipon, and Michaelis ("Round like a distended balloon"). Prison has fattened up Verloc and likewise Michaelis—"pathetic in his grotesque and incurable obesity." The swollen legs of Winnie's mother have rendered her inactive. Inactive also are the revolutionists—Yundt, Ossipon, Michaelis, and Verloc. Fat Inspector Heat has kinship with the fat revolutionists; while the Assistant Commissioner of Police—"tall and thin"—has kinship with the thin terrorists—Yundt, Professor X, and the innocent Stevie (each is afflicted with a deformity). The Professor's "stunted stature" has its parallel in the stunted mentality of Stevie—he can't remember even his own name and address! "An absurdity," as Razumov in *Under Western Eyes* reminds us, "may be the starting-point of the most dangerous complications" (III, I).

Everybody in *The Secret Agent* is a fragmented and frustrated anonymity. Nameless are Professor X, Winnie's former butcher lover, Winnie's unscrupulous and deformed mother, the clever and noncommittal Assistant Commissioner, and Secret Agent Δ (as the nameless Adolf Verloc is known in the files of the Russian Embassy). Verloc's *alias* is Prozor; and Alexander Ossipon, among women intimate with him, goes by the name of Tom; Michaelis is known as the Apostle; and the Home Secretary as Sir Ethelred, as the Presence, as the Personage, and also as The Chief. Even when Conrad's characters have names, their identity remains fragmented; Heat, Wurmt, Toodles, Lombroso—all of them lack first names. Without last names are the Patroness,[4] Sir Ethelred, Vladimir, and Stevie— named after Saint Stephen, the martyr. Everyone in *The Secret Agent* is a fragmented selfhood, anonymous or deformed. The purpose of these characteristics is to indicate their lack of vitality, their insulation from life, and their moral indolence. The insularity of Verloc's perverted and lifeless existence is signified by the triangle sign designating his nameless selfhood, and again by the triangle of the street in which his box of a house is located; by that sign of a triangle Verloc is reduced to an abstraction. "There was no sparkle of any kind on the lazy stream of his life" (XI). A lifeless automaton, Verloc has no more vitality than the poisoned atmosphere of the Russian Embassy, where nothing exists suggesting life or contact with it except a faintly buzzing housefly. "The useless fussing of that tiny, energetic organism affected unpleasantly this big man threatened in his indolence" (II).

Everything exists in contradiction of itself, and nothing is but what is not. Winnie Verloc, whom we recognize as personifying death, is also described as representing "the mystery of life." The mystery of life is, of course, simply its unpredictableness. *As the emblem of life,* Winnie Verloc is ironically handicapped by a half-wit brother, a crippled and deformed mother, an anonymous and morally perverted husband, and a lover—Comrade Ossipon—by whom she is betrayed. Life is represented in *The Secret Agent* as irrational (for example, Stevie and the Professor), unreal and devoid of vitality (Verloc), routine and dull (the

Assistant Commissioner), conventional (Winnie Verloc), deformed and prostituted (Winnie's mother). The life of Winnie's mother has consisted in running what Conrad politely calls "business houses" where "queer gentlemen" boarded. One conjectures that Winnie, being a dutiful daughter to her "impotent" mother, contributed certain accommodations to these queer gentlemen. While the change from her Belgravian house to Adolf's shop affected her legs adversely, the moral sensibility of Winnie's mother presumably was not exactly shocked when she found herself housed in Verloc's shop of pornographic wares, as by then this Madam of Business Houses was no doubt rather familiar with them. Of all the persons in *The Secret Agent* the only one spared and protected from the author's grotesque and cosmic ironies is Winnie's mother, and what protects her is the fact of her early removal to an almshouse.

Verloc's contact with life is through Winnie, and Stevie's future depends upon her protection. Every man is supported or protected by a woman· Yundt, nursed by the woman he betrayed; Michaelis, sustained by his patroness; and Comrade Ossipon, whose selfish ego finds satisfaction in women who "put some material means into his hands." It is ironical that the Assistant Commissioner of Police is ruled by a domineering wife, a cantankerous woman who has thwarted his prospects of a career in Europe; wherefore he has nothing to look forward to but evening games of whist at the Explorer's Club. At the crisis, after the bombing at Greenwich Observatory, it is Verloc's bond of respectability that traps him— the convention of a virtuous attachment. Verloc would leave the country at once, just as the police have urged him to do, " 'only he felt certain that his wife would not even hear of going abroad. Nothing could be more characteristic of the respectable bond than that,' went on, with a touch of grimness, the Assistant Commissioner, whose own wife, too, had refused to hear of going abroad . . . 'From a certain point of view we are here in the presence of a domestic drama' " (X). By playing whist at the Club, the Assistant Commissioner is protected from facing his own domestic drama—he and his card-table cronies approach the game "in the spirit of co-sufferers, as if it were indeed a drug against the secret ills of existence" (V).

Conradian irony has reduced a story about revolutionists to their domestic drama, a domestic drama which—whether located in the Verloc household or in the parlors of the Patroness—represents sanctuary from the secret ills of existence, sanctuary from life or time itself. Winnie Verloc's attempt to escape with Comrade Ossipon to the Continent, to find sanctuary there under the illusion that he is her savior and lover, is thwarted at the start—how escape an island? "The insular nature of Great Britain obtruded itself upon his notice is an odious form" (XII). Stevie's sanctuary from reality lies in the fact that his grasp of language is limited, for he knows only the names of things and ideas that are simple enough not to upset him. "Certain simple principles had been instilled into him so anxiously (on account of his 'queerness') that the mere names of certain transgressions filled him with horror" (VIII). Like Stevie, the Patroness, and Michaelis live outside of time or reality, of which they are as ignorant as is Sir Ethelred—he has no time for details. "Don't go into details. I have no time for that. . . . Spare me the details" (VII). But it is the details, concrete things and facts, that comprise the reality of life; all else is abstraction.

Ford Madox Ford speculates that the London of *The Secret Agent* is a city "rather of the human soul than any place in topography. Similarly the Anarchists of *The Secret Agent* are Anarchists of Nowhere: the Enemies of any society" (*Thus to Revisit,* 1921). On the contrary, Conrad has rooted his characters in a specific city (not just "A City"): the London he knew intimately, far more intimately than his friend Ford speculates; and furthermore he has utilized the actualities of London—its streets and houses—to provide his characters analogies of themselves or their plight. Verloc's house in Soho is located in a triangular well of "blind houses and unfeeling stones" (XII). That description defines Verloc himself, unfeeling and blind to the realities. "But Mr. Verloc was not in the least conscious of having got rusty" (II). He's as rusty as "the rusty London sunshine struggling clear of the London mist" to shed a lukewarm brightness into the First Secretary's Russian Embassy room, where Conrad deposits Verloc for Chapter II. At the outrageous hour of half-past ten in the morning—outrageous because Verloc, a night-prowler, is as unfamiliar with the sun as he is with life itself—Verloc departs from Soho for the Russian Embassy. He goes westward—not towards the sun. It's "a peculiarly London sun—against which nothing could be said except that it looked bloodshot . . . It hung at a moderate elevation above Hyde Park Corner with an air of punctual and benign vigilance. The very pavement under Mr. Verloc's feet had an old-gold tinge in that diffused light, in which neither wall, nor tree, nor beast, nor man cast a shadow. Mr. Verloc was going westward through a town without shadows in an atmosphere of powdered old gold" (II). The bloodshot and shadowless sun identifies itself with Verloc. Its coppery gleams fall on the broad back of his blue overcoat and produce "a dull effect of rustiness."

The coppery gleams and old-gold-tinged light befit Verloc's present mood of self-satisfaction. He's in a mood of opulence as he broods on his Theory of Protection: "All these people had to be protected. Protection is the first necessity of opulence and luxury." His theory is upset by the contrary theory of the Russian First Secretary, a theory having to do with destruction rather than protection. That Verloc, secret agent, casts no shadow befits his anonymity. It signifies also that he has no future.

Verloc casts no shadow, but he's had a shady past. It included five years of rigorous confinement in a fortress for divulging the design of a new British field gun, a woman having betrayed him. Verloc's shop— "a square box of a place"—is located in "a shady street . . . where the sun never shone." The insularity of Verloc's household is indicated also by the fact that news from the outside world seldom reaches Brett Street;

newsboys never invade it. Verloc's shop, behind which lives the Verloc household, is a front masking his activities as *agent provocateur*. It wasn't out of love for Winnie that he transported her and her impotent mother and imbecile brother from their Belgravian house to Soho, where he set up the shop with money supplied by Winnie. He gathered that trio and their furniture "to his broad, good-natured breast" so as to provide himself thereby a protective mask. It's a shock to Verloc to be told by Mr. Vladimir that anarchists don't marry and that he has discredited himself in his world by his marriage. "This is your virtuous attachment—eh? What with one sort of attachment and another you are doing away with your usefulness" (II).

The novel begins (in Chapter II) with Verloc, the domesticated *agent provocateur,* wrenched from his habitual routine—"Mr. Verloc, going out in the morning." Verloc seldom goes out in the daytime, whereas the Professor seldom goes out at night. Like Verloc, Ossipon "slept in the sunlight." Verloc nominally left his half-wit brother-in-law in charge of the shop during the day, and then—as there was practically no business—the shop door remained closed. At night "it stood discreetly but suspiciously ajar"—for the shady customers of the shady wares, the "queer gentlemen" who "dodged in sideways, one shoulder first, as if afraid to set the bell going. The bell, hung on the door by means of a curved ribbon of steel, was difficult to circumvent. It was hopelessly cracked; but of an evening, at the slightest provocation, it clattered behind the customer with impudent virulence" (I). The bell signifies life, the sound of life vibrating in the silence of Brett Street, where the sun never shines and "all the sounds of life seemed lost as if in a triangular well of asphalt and brick" (XII). And that is why the door stands ajar for the queer customers of pornographic wares; so that they can enter without ringing the virulent bell—life, hostile to their moral and sexual impotence. When Winnie Verloc tends the shop, customers "get suddenly disconcerted at having to deal with a woman" (I). The shop bell rings, and the solitary deadness of the silent place is disturbed, stirred into life. It has an "aggressive clatter"; it disturbs Stevie until it quiets down. It also unnerves Chief Inspector Heat, the clatter of the cracked bell causing him "to spin round on his heel" (IX). Again, its clatter associates with Verloc's mood of restlessness and Stevie's nervous shuffling of his feet (VIII). When its clattering ceases, the tenants of the shop sense a vacancy, a loss (VIII). "And when the cracked bell ceased to tremble on its curved ribbon of steel *nothing stirred* near Mrs. Verloc, as if her attitude had the looking power of a spell" (IX). After murdering Verloc, Winnie is stirred to life by her chance encounter with the unscrupulous Ossipon, whose only saving attribute is his passionate nature. (Winnie's other romance was with a butcher, whom she rejected for a gentleman—whom she, in turn, butchered.) Ossipon sets the bell clattering both on his entrance to and exit from the shop, and it frightens him so much that he pins his arms to his side in "a convulsive hug." "Comrade Ossipon had no settled conception now of what was happening to him" (XII). The bell shatters his stability and self-possession. Is it any wonder then that the "queer gentlemen" try to sidle past that symbolic bell?

That cracked bell associates with moods of bewilderment and confusion. At the Silenus beer-hall instead of a bell there is a mechanical piano, whose deafening din confounds the theories voiced by Ossipon and his beer-hall companion, the Professor. It's a slightly defective mechanical piano and "lonely"—executing airs unaccompanied, "a valse tune with aggressive virtuosity" (IV). Like the cracked bell with its "aggressive clatter," this "semi-grand piano" signifies life. What's life but the companion of death, each competing against the other! Death is represented by the lonely and mechanical Professor X, who is but the ghost of a human being ("I am deadly"), an automaton executing mad theories with aggressive virtuosity, eloquent but slightly cracked. So the piano plays distant airs in painfully detached notes, or else it clatters "through a mazurka in brazen impetuosity, as though a vulgar and imprudent ghost were showing off. The keys sank and rose mysteriously" (IV).

As Razumov in *Under Western Eyes* remarks: "There is nothing, no one, too insignificant, too absurd to be disregarded. . . ." It is the insignificant *things* in *The Secret Agent,* the minute particulars of life, that manifest reality; and the characteristic of these pieces of reality is their absurdity—the cracked bell, the forsaken wedding ring, the lonely mechanical piano, Verloc's round hat rocking on its crown, Stevie's coat label, the buzzing fly. All "mere trifles," but not one of these pieces of reality is too insignificant, too absurd to be disregarded. *They each signify the unpredictable,* the absurdly incongruous thing which disturbs routine existence by the sudden fact of its uncalled-for and unexpected intrusion. The nature of reality in *The Secret Agent* is irrational, incongruous, and incalculable. Take, for example, that section of London where the Russian Embassy is located—across from Chesham Square at Number 10:

> With a turn to the left Mr. Verloc pursued his way along a narrow street by the side of a yellow wall which, for some inscrutable reason, had No. 1 Chesham Square written on it in black letters. Chesham Square was at least sixty yards away, and Mr. Verloc, cosmopolitan enough not to be deceived by London's topographical mysteries, held on steadily, without a sign of surprise or indignation. At last, with business-like persistency, he reached the Square, and made diagonally for the number 10. This belonged to an opposing carriage gate in a high, clean wall between two houses, of which one *rationally enough* bore the number 9 and the other was numbered 37.

Number 37 is on Chesham Square, but actually it belongs to Porthill Street. Here, as throughout the novel, the expected does not occur. Rather, what occurs is the unexpected, the irrational. There is no logical sequence to these stray and misnumbered edifices: The fact that Number 37 "belonged to Porthill Street . . . was proclaimed by an inscription placed above the ground-floor windows by whatever highly efficient authority is charged with the duty of keeping track of London's strayed houses." Let these houses get up and rearrange themselves in logical order! "Why powers are not asked of Parliament . . . for compelling those edifices to return where they belong is one of the mysteries of municipal administration" (II).

(2)

"Conrad's secret theory examined," F. Scott Fitzgerald wrote in his Notebooks; and the secret of Conrad's scheme? Well, he wrote the truth—"adding confusion however to his structure." Adding confusion to his structure, Conrad has dislocated the chronology of narrated events so as to shape his narrative in circular form. The circular design of *The Secret Agent* manifests Conrad's commentary on human progress, and in this Conrad is at one with Hawthorne: Progress is but circular—a spiral of concentric circles.

The event which initiates all subsequent action—namely, the explosion at Greenwich—is first made known in Chapter IV. The first three chapters present preliminary matters and serve as Prologue to the drama. The event which concludes the drama—Winnie Verloc's death by drowning—is made known by Ossipon's report of it to the Professor in the Silenus Restaurant—through a newspaper now ten days old. Likewise in Chapter IV, Stevie's death by fireworks is rendered as a reported event, and again it is made known through the newspaper which Ossipon reads to the Professor in the Silenus Restaurant: a "rosy sheet, as if flushed by the warmth of its own convictions, which were optimistic." Its account of the Greenwich affair is incomplete, and the sentimentalized newspaper report of Winnie's suicide is likewise fragmentary. Of the three main events—the explosion, the murder, and the suicide—only the murder scene is presented as a point-present action, whereas the first and the final events are reported piecemeal through multiple points of view. As the drama ends where it began, the final scene duplicating in setting and in method of presentation the scene in Chapter IV which initiates the entire action, *The Secret Agent* is designed in circular form.

Each of the three main events occurs in a single location, without movement or transition to another place; hence each scene is an enclosed unit, boxed in or encircled. Other than these three enclosed actions in IV, XI, and XIII (the action in IV and ·in XIII is verbal), all the other scenes present an action or movement progressing from place to place, a journey which ends where it began and which therefore figures as circular. Chronologically, the narrative begins with Chapter II: Mr. Verloc leaves his shop and journeys to the Russian Embassy, and then after his interview with Mr. Vladimir he returns to the shop, where his arclike journey began. The opening phrase of the novel—"Mr. Verloc, *going out in the morning*"—is misleading, inasmuch as Mr. Verloc does not go out of the shop until the scene of Chapter II, all of Chapter I being a cutback taking us *inside* the shop. It's rather like a film run backwards; in effect, time stands still. The scene of Chapter III, Verloc's shop where the revolutionists expound their various theories, is a self-contained unit of verbal action, enclosed as in a circle. This scene occurs the night of Verloc's harrowing interview with Mr. Vladimir, and then a week elapses between Chapters III and VIII, which scene is wrenched from the chronology—in time-sequence VIII follows III. Here again the action is in circular form: from the shop Winnie's mother is taken in "the Cab of Death" to the almshouse, Winnie and Stevie returning then to the shop where their journey began. At the beginning of Chapter IX Verloc has returned from the Continent, and ten days have elapsed since the incident of the cabman and his mistreated horse, for whom Stevie has the bizarre and "symbolic longing" to make them happy by taking them both to bed with him! In IX Verloc takes an afternoon walk with Stevie, and the next morning they again leave the shop, Verloc returning this time alone. As we knew in Chapter IV, which in time-sequence occurs a few hours after the opening parts of IX, Stevie's been blown to bits—a revelation made to Winnie by Chief Inspector Heat through her identification of Stevie's coat label. Meanwhile Verloc, who has gone out with an unidentified foreigner (the Assistant Commissioner), returns from the Continental Hotel to the shop. Thus in IX three journeys take place (each figuring in circular form, A to B and back to A).

The theme of *The Secret Agent* has to do with time—the destruction and confusion of time itself; the confused chronology of narrated events, by their disarrangement from time, effects a structure which is at one with the theme. Relocated chronologically, subsequent to Chapter IX come chapters IV, V, VI, VII, and then X, which begins where VII ends. In each of these scenes a circular action is rendered. Stevie's circles, "repeated curves" suggesting "form and confusion," diagram the design of the whole novel.

The scene of the murder (XI), which is the climax of the whole domestic drama, occurs simultaneously with the scene which concludes Chapter X. Thus as identities overlap from character to character, so likewise scenes overlap in the time-sequence, and actions circle back to their beginnings. In Chapter XII Winnie leaves the shop (having murdered her husband) and, on encountering Ossipon, she persuades him to return to the shop. Everything circles back upon itself. Actions are thus enclosed in circle form. The scenes in IV and XIII, occurring in the Silenus Restaurant, and in III and XI, occurring in the Verloc shop, present verbal actions only, gestures and words without movement from place to place; these four scenes are self-enclosed. All four of these scenes have to do with violence, theories or acts of violence. That Conrad is tinkering with the clock is hinted at in the scene of the Cab of Death: "and time itself seemed to stand still" (VIII). By backtracking the narrative progression, time is rendered as if standing still, and the same effect is created where one scene overlaps another simultaneously. The calendric span of the narrative is one month, precisely thirty-one days; but while much time elapses on the author's clock, the fact is that all the events *enacted* take place within four days.[5] In the murder scene the clock of narrated events slows down, and momentarily time seems to stand still.

In his *Joseph Conrad* (1947) Mr. Albert Guerard, Jr. opined: "We would not begrudge a hundred slow-moving pages devoted to a study of Winnie Verloc's feelings, but twenty pages sacrificed to the largely physical approach to the murder of her husband seems excessive." But this misses the intent and the significance of the whole thing. There are in fact more than thirty pages devoted to the murder, of which the preliminaries— beginning with Verloc's irony: "You'll want all your wits about you after I am taken away" (p. 232)—consume twenty pages. It is 8:25 P.M. when Winnie, prevented by Verloc from leaving the house, feels trapped and entertains the notion of stabbing—"she wanted a knife" (256). It is ten minutes to nine when, just after planting the butcher knife in her husband's "broad, good-natured breast," Mrs. Verloc "raised her head slowly and looked at the clock with inquiring mistrust" (264). When next she looks up mechanically at the wooden clock, "She thought it must have stopped. She could not believe that only two minutess had passed since she had looked at it last. Of course not. It had been stopped all the time. . . . She seemed to have heard or read that clocks and watches always stopped at the moment of murder for the undoing of the murderer" (268-69). It's not only the wooden clock on the wall that has stopped, but also the author's clock—notably at the moment of the murder. What Marlow in *Lord Jim* explains—"All this happened in much less time than it takes to tell, since I am trying to interpret for you into *slow speech* the instantaneous effect of visual impressions"—describes precisely what Conrad creates in the slow prose of the murder scene—a sense of time suspended.[6]

At the signal from her recumbent spouse, "Come here" (a call "intimately known to Mrs. Verloc as the note of wooing"), "she started forward at once, as if she were still a loyal woman bound to that man by an unbroken contract." He has the fixed idea that she is still his devoted wife, and she is possessed by the "fixed idea" that he "had taken the 'poor boy' away from her in order to kill him . . . the man whom she had trusted, took the boy away to kill him!" The shock of Stevie's death has torn her personality "into two pieces, whose mental operations did not adjust themselves very well to each other." She had become cunning:

> Her right hand skimmed slightly the end of the table, and when she had passed on towards the sofa the carving knife had vanished without the slightest sound from the side of the dish. Mr. Verloc heard the creaky plank in the floor, and was content. He waited. Mrs. Verloc was coming.

But not to woo him!

As if the homeless soul of Stevie had flown for shelter straight to the breast of his sister, guardian, and protector, the resemblance of her face with that of her brother grew at every step, even to the droop of the lower lip, even to the slight divergence of the eyes. But Mr. Verloc did not see that. He was lying on his back and staring upwards.

Conrad has shifted his camera from Winnie's to Adolf Verloc's point-of-view, and the effect of slow speech is created both by this shift in point-of-view and by the repetition of a motif which impedes the temporal progression. Here is a prose representation of slow time:

> He saw partly on the ceiling and partly on the wall the moving shadow of an arm with a clenched hand holding a carving knife. It flickered up and down. Its movements were leisurely. *They were leisurely enough* for Mr. Verloc to recognize the limb and the weapon.
> *They were leisurely enough* for him to take in the full meaning of the portent, and to taste the flavour of death rising in his gorge. His wife had gone raving mad—murdering mad. *They were leisurely enough* for the first paralyzing effect of this discovery to pass away before a resolute determination to come out victorious from the ghastly struggle with that armed lunatic. *They were leisurely enough* for Mr. Verloc to elaborate a plan of defence involving a dash behind the table, and the felling of the woman to the ground with a heavy wooden chair. *But they were not leisurely enough* to allow Mr. Verloc the time to move either hand or foot. The knife was already planted in his breast. It met no resistance on its way. Hazard has such accuracies (262-63).

Mr. Verloc's time-sense lags, and his theory of the situation is shattered by the incalculable. Theory or Fixed Idea versus the Shock of the Unpredictable—*that* patterns everything in the book.

Mrs. Verloc, in turn, is likewise confounded by a fixed idea. It's the fixed idea that a murder stops the clock. Whereas it seems to her that much time has elapsed since the moment of the murder, "As a matter of fact, only three minutes had elapsed from the moment she had drawn the first deep, easy breath after the blow, to this moment when Mrs. Verloc formed the resolution to drown herself in the Thames. But Mrs. Verloc could not believe that" (269). The clock, *that too* has deceived her. A ticking sound breaks the silence of the room, but she cannot believe that it could possibly come from the clock on the wall because it doesn't fit her theory. Nevertheless,

> It grew upon her ear, while she remembered clearly that the clock on the wall was silent, had no audible tick. What did it mean by beginning to tick so loudly all of a sudden? . . . Mrs. Verloc cared nothing for time, and the ticking went on. She concluded it could not be the clock, and her sullen gaze moved along the walls, wavered, and became vague, while she strained her hearing to locate the sound. Tic, tic, tic.

Suddenly, what replaces the *ticking* of the seemingly stopped clock is the trickling of blood from Verloc's corpse, the drops falling "fast and furious like the pulse of an insane clock. At its highest speed this *ticking* changed into a continuous sound of trickling." The Conradian pun identifies clocks and blood, time and life.

As "Mr. Verloc was temperamentally no respecter of persons" (XI), neither was he a respecter of conventions, nor of time and reality. In his denial of Time-Now he shares with Winnie Verloc, who cared nothing for time, and with Professor X, whose lifetime project is the destruction of what *is*. And again, like Professor X, Verloc's resemblance "to a mechanical figure went so far that he had an automaton's absurd air of being aware of the machinery inside him" (IX). Verloc has no ideas, and his wife thinks only in images. So they are pretty much in accord, and especially so once Verloc is dead: "Except for the fact that Mrs. Verloc breathed these two would have been perfectly in accord: that accord of prudent reserve without superfluous words, and sparing of signs, which had been the foundation of their respectable home life" (XI). Their domestic existence for seven years has been "stagnant and deep like a placid pool." In mourning for Stevie, Mrs. Verloc dresses in black and masks her face with a black veil: "all black—black as commonplace death itself, crowned with a few cheap and pale flowers." She personifies death veiled as life. When Ossipon discovers the bloody truth that Mrs. Verloc is a murderess, he is terrified. "He saw the woman twined round him like a snake, not to be shaken off. She was not deadly. She was death itself— the companion of life." At the end, all that remains of Winnie is her wedding ring. That "gold circlet of the wedding ring on Mrs. Verloc's left hand [had] glittered exceedingly with the untarnished glory of a piece from some splendid treasure of jewels, dropped in a dust-bin."

When Winnie had fled the shop, what stopped her at the door was this memento of her late husband: "A round hat disclosed in the middle of the floor by the moving of the table rocked slightly on its crown in the wind of her flight" (XI). Unnerved by that hat, she fails to turn out the light and she leaves the door ajar. Bewilderment and confusion occur again when Comrade Ossipon first sees the hat on his returning to the shop to put out the light and close the door. Now

> the true sense of the scene he was beholding came to Ossipon through the contemplation of the hat. It seemed an extraordinary thing, an ominous object, a sign. Black, and rim upward, it lay on the floor before the couch as if prepared to receive the contributions of pence from people who would come presently to behold Mr. Verloc in the fullness of his domestic ease reposing on a sofa . . . Mr. Verloc did not seem so much asleep now as lying down with a bent head and looking insistently at his left breast. And when Comrade Ossipon had made out the handle of the knife he turned away from the glazed door, and retched violently (XII).

Ossipon "was not superstitious but there was too much blood on the floor; a beastly pool of it all round the hat." This blood-encircled hat upsets his theory that Verloc was the person who was blown to bits at Greenwich. Here's the hat, and there's Verloc sound asleep.

Even at dinner Verloc wore his round hat, and—hatted thus—he indicates his disrespect for conventions, social rituals, and the very feast of life. *That hat represents life misused or denied.* Thus Verloc disregarded "as usual the fate of his hat, which, as if accustomed to take care of itself, made for a safe shelter under the table" (XI). Having fished under the sofa for his *misplaced hat,* Verloc on finding it "held it *as if he did not know the use of a hat*" (IX). To Stevie, on the contrary, Verloc's hat was a sacred object because it belonged to his beloved mentor and savior. Stevie on one occasion pounced on that hat "and bore it off *reverently* into the kitchen." Whereupon Mrs. Verloc remarked: "You could do anything with that boy, Adolf . . . He would go through fire for you" (IX). And he does just that. From the fireworks of the exploded bomb the only thing left to identify the disintegrated victim is a rag of a velvet collar with an address label on it—Stevie's sister had sewn it there as a precaution lest poor Stevie forget his home address. It is this label that traps Verloc.

> That his wife should hit upon the precaution of sewing the boy's address inside his overcoat was the last thing Mr. Verloc would have thought of. One can't think of everything. That was what she meant when she said that he need not worry if he lost Stevie during their walks. She had assured him that the boy would turn up all right. Well, he had turned up with a vengeance! (XI).

Chief Inspector Heat is bewildered by this unaccountable evidence—"I don't account for it at all, sir. It's simply unaccountable. It can't be explained by what I know" (VI). What's to be explained about that triangular label is that it is at once the emblem of Verloc's betrayal of humanity *and* the emblem of Winnie's fidelity, devotion, and love for a human being. Verloc has sacrificed an idiot for an idea, a human being for a theory, the concrete thing for the abstraction. Abstractions earnea nothing but Conrad's scorn.

The triangle which identifies the anonymous Secret Agent Verloc— signifying both anonymity and insularity—links with the triangle of Brett Street where Verloc lives insulated from sunlight and from life itself. Triangles and circles in *The Secret Agent* have multiple significances. Now there is nothing unpredictable about Mr. Verloc, theoretically speaking from Chief Inspector Heat's point of view, and yet the triangular sign of Verloc's identity becomes—in the triangle of the coat label—*the emblem of the unpredictableness of things.* Again, betrayal and fidelity are written there—the whole moral meaning of the novel. Only Winnie would have thought of that label, out of love for her brother. And he alone, that half-wit, believed in Verloc—believed in man. How irrational can man get?

(3)

When Stevie is confused he draws circles, and when Winnie is confused she remembers Stevie drawing circles: "Mrs. Verloc was sitting in the place where poor Stevie usually established himself of an evening with paper and pencil for the pastime of drawing these coruscations of innumerable circles suggesting chaos and eternity" (XI). When Stevie drew circles it was while sitting beside a clock. By drawing circles Stevie found sanctuary from time and from the revolutionists' theories of violence against time. He found sanctuary against chaos and confusion in the form manifested by a circle. What Stevie designed, however, represents both form and its opposite, chaos and confusion: "a coruscating whirl of circles that by their tangled multitude of repeated curves, uniformity of form and confusion of intersecting lines suggested a rendering of cosmic chaos, the symbolism of a mad art attempting the inconceivable" (III). What is inconceivable is eternity. "But eternity," as Comrade Ossipon envisions it, "is a damned hole" (XIII). A circle, itself the sign of perfection of form, represents thus a hole in time's continuity—time confused and chaotic, disarranged, terminated (as signified by the blood-encircled hat), or suspended (as signified in the murder scene when clock-time seemingly stops). Circles and their emblematic objects associate with conditions or states of mental confusion because they represent the impingement of the unexpected thing, symbolizing Time the Unpredictable. That is what Time, as distinguished from calculable clock-time, *is*. It is a hole in time's continuity, the unpredictable event in routine clocked existence. Hence, a circle represents insularity from time or life itself. Conrad's example is Verloc's blood-encircled round hat. Eternity's a damned hole. What eternity lacks is precisely what characterizes life or time's continuity, namely the unpredictableness of things. As Razumov in *Under Western Eyes* leaves Haldin's rooms he becomes a figure in "eternity"—with his watch broken, time stands still. When Stevie draws circles, holes in time, he is "very good and quiet," and when Razumov attempts to define Eternity, the inconceivable, he defines it as "something dull and quiet. There would be nothing unexpected—don't you see? The element of time would be wanting" (I). Obsessed with his theories and fixed ideas, Chief Inspector Heat is not very wise, since true wisdom "is not certain of anything *in this world of contradictions* . . . His wisdom was of an official kind, or else he might have reflected upon a matter not of theory but of experience that in the close-woven stuff of relations between conspirator and police there occur unexpected solutions of continuity, *sudden holes in space and time*" (V).

The time bomb—comprised of Chemical X and concocted by Professor X—is unexpectedly exploded by *X*, the unknown and incalculable factor in Verloc's calculated plot, in Vladimir's theory of bomb-throwing, and in Chief Inspector Heat's fixed idea. "Impossible!" exclaims Heat on first learning of the explosion. What is deadly to fixed ideas is X, the unknown thing. The example is the root of a tree stump on which Stevie stumbled, blowing himself into eternity. In'that unexpected obstacle of a tree stump Nature asserts its supremacy against man's conspiracy to destroy what *is*. The attack on the first meridian represents anarchy against Time, blasphemy against God and Nature.

Whereas Vladimir's theory aims at the destruction of science, Professor X's theory aims at the destruction of conventions by which mankind is restrained. Exterminate the multitude—the weak, the flabby, the silly, the cowardly, the faint of heart, and the slavish of mind. "Theirs is the kingdom of the earth. Exterminate! Exterminate! That is the only way of progress . . . Every taint, every vice, every prejudice, every convention meets its doom" (XIII). "To destroy public faith in legality was the imperfect formula of his pedantic fanaticism . . . He was a moral agent —that was settled in his mind" (V). In fact, however, the only true moral agent is Time. The Patroness, on temperamental grounds, "defies time with a scornful disregard, as if it were a rather vulgar convention submitted to by the mass of inferior mankind." Chief Inspector Heat, contemplating the instantaneous death of the victim of the explosion, rises momentarily "above the vulgar conception of time." "Instantaneous! He remembered all he had ever read in popular publications of long and terrifying dreams dreamed in the instant of waking; of the whole of past life lived with frightful intensity by a drowning man as his doomed head bobs up . . . for the last time." Heat experiences an epiphany—he envisions ages of atrocious pain and mental torture as being contained "between two successive winks of an eye" (V). Verloc's eyes, because they are "not well adapted to winking," perceive nothing of life in the Moment-Now—Time-Now happens between two successive winks. The Privy Councillor of the Russian Embassy, Wurmt, is literally shortsighted, and in the second sense of the word the Revolutionists of the Future are also shortsighted.

It is not until Mrs. Verloc confronts the clock after the murder that, for the first occasion in her life, she is made aware of time. It is not until Verloc is dead that he is rendered as though he were alive, for then, as he lies murdered on the sofa and Ossipon leaves the shop, the cracked bell clatters "as if trying in vain to warn the reposing Mr. Verloc of the final departure of his wife—accompanied by his friend" (XII). To perfect a detonator adjustable "to all conditions of action, and even to unexpected changes of conditions," Professor X needs more time. Exterminate Universal Time: "what's wanted is a clean sweep and a clear start for a new conception of life." "But the time! the time! Give me time! Ah! that multitude too stupid to feel either pity or fear. Sometimes I think they have everything on their side. Everything—even death—my own weapon." Blow-me-to-bits Professor X (he is death "enlisted in the service of humanity") rebukes Chief Inspector Heat, who personifies the convention of life: "I am doing my work better than you're doing yours." Much better, no doubt of that, since Professor X is, to identify him, Death—the human representation of deadly time. Agent of Death, and therefore, "I shall never be arrested." He is a parody of Time the Unpredictable. Insofar as he is human he is also imperfect, for no man can convert himself into a perfect automaton no matter how much machinery he carries inside himself. In the explosion at Maze Hill Station an unpredicted event confounds the calculated one—Stevie is blown to bits, instead of the first meridian. The imperfect bomb detonates—symbolically—at the wall protecting Greenwich Observatory, appropriately at Maze Hill.

Theories—scientific, political, sociological, economic, psychological— all are reduced to zero by Conrad's diabolic irony. What protection against life that we devise consists of superstitions, myths, theories, conventional conceptions of reality, systems and creeds, codes of behavior by which society is manipulated and controlled; in sum, all that the muddling intellect contrives. The nihilism of *The Secret Agent* ends in a covert affirmation of the supremacy of life. Could we but manipulate reality so that what happens happens as predicted, but no! Time-Now is the Unpredictable, life in all its irrational particulars; including *X* the unknown event. Wherefore I conclude that it is Time the Unpredictable—agent of life and death—that Conrad's novel cryptographically intends as *the* Secret Agent.

(1957, 1959)

NOTES

1. Quotations from *The Secret Agent* derive from the Dent Collected Edition of Conrad's works.

2. The world "in *The Secret Agent* appears stricken with moral insanity which breaks out in the incomprehensible attack on the fifth [*sic*] meridian." Paul L. Wiley writes in *Conrad's Measure of Man*, p. 107. Perhaps it is because he has his meridians mixed that the attack seems to him incomprehensible.

3. In Robert Payne's *The Terrorists: The Story of the Forerunners of Stalin* (1957), Sergey Nachayev, one of the terrorists who flung bombs and wrote inflammatory pamphlets, who believed in science and little else, was consumed by "a pure thirst for destruction." His self-abnegation and monstrous insolence and arrogance remind us of Conrad's Professor X. "Our task," said Nachayev, "is total, terrible, universal and merciless destruction."

4. The fixed idea possessing me during the past decade of readings of *The Secret Agent* was that the lady patroness of Michaelis, who is in fact not named in the novel, bore the name of Lady Mabel. In proofreading "Time and *The Secret Agent*," my essay in *The Art of Joseph Conrad: A Critical Symposium* (1960), I discovered however that I had therein bestowed upon that nameless creature the title Lady Mabel. In *The Secret Agent* that title is unwarranted; she has no name. I append this note here to correct my error. Where did I get this fixed idea? Well, she *is* named Lady Mabel in Conrad's dramatized version of *The Secret Agent:* "The Secret Agent: A Drama in Four Acts" (in *Three Plays*, by Joseph Conrad. London: Methuen & Co., 1934). The present note corrects my *Texas Studies* essay.

5. One week elapses between Chapter III and the subsequent scene in VIII, ten days elapse between VIII and IX (Verloc disappears on a trip abroad), and ten days elapse between XI and the final scene in XIII. Chapter IX uses up two days; VIII one additional day; II and III comprise another additional day.

Everything *happens* within these four days, beginning with the events of II-III, then VIII, then IX.

6. In *The House of the Seven Gables* Hawthorne, in the famous death scene of Judge Pyncheon in Chapter XVIII, creates by a shift in the point-of-view the effect of a halted segment of time, a symbolic representation of a frozen moment. The parallel is Chapter XI of *The Secret Agent.* Judge Pyncheon "holds his watch in his left hand, but clutched in such a manner that you cannot see the dial plate." Time ticks on, but not Judge Pyncheon; and, as in *The Secret Agent,* the narrative progression comes to a standstill by the shift in the point-of-view. Hawthorne addresses the corpse: "Rise up, Judge Pyncheon!" A housefly alights. on the dead man's forehead, and then on his chin, "and now, Heaven help us! is creeping over the bridge of his nose, towards the would-be chief magistrate's wide open eyes!" "Canst thou not brush the fly away? Art thou too swiggish?"

Hawthorne's housefly resettles in the Russian Embassy of *The Secret Agent,* where Verloc hears it buzzing against the windowpane (II). Conrad has also lifted from *The House of the Seven Gables* the shop bell, which before and after the death-scene clatters to return us from that halted segment of time to the recognition of the Moment-Now—back to time rushing on with life. In *Macbeth* the time period of Duncan's murder is framed first by the bell that is rung to bring Macbeth his wine and finally by the bell that clatters to alarm the castle, and so perhaps both Conrad and Hawthorne lifted their bell from Shakespeare.

In both *Macbeth* and *The House of Seven Gables* the bell transports us from the framed segment of time terminated, a hole in time's continuity and in the progression of narrated events; transports us back from this segment of time fixed and dead to life and time's flux. Verloc's shop-bell has the same symbolic import, but its symbolic import is not confined solely to this one. In *The Secret Agent* the shop-bell rings both before and after the murder, but the interim consumes such a time-span that only the chronologist would notice this bell-enclosing device.

As for other points of comparison, both Hawthorne and Conrad render the dead man as alive, *and* render the living as more dead than alive (with the exception of Holgrave and the scissor-grinder and Ned Higgins and Venner, etc.); in *Macbeth* the resurrected Banquo contends against the living Macbeth, and this ghost destroys his enjoyment of point-present nowness. The Pyncheons are similarly haunted by Maul's curse. All three works dramatize the theme of time.

Both Hawthorne and Conrad evince a predilection for circles. Concentric circles diagram the seven generations of Pyncheons, and circular selfhoods—patented by Hawthorne—reappear conspicuously in *The Secret Agent.* Another point of parallelism is the circular form of both novels. Again, both novels open on a cutback in the time-sequence, the opening action in both novels beginning in Chapter II.

F. SCOTT FITZGERALD

Gatsby and The Hole in Time

Time—that is what a clock must face.
R.W.S. IN TIME'S TERMITES (1944)

(1)

In the meantime,
In between time—

WHAT CRITICAL READINGS Fitzgerald's greatest novel has so far received amount to interpretations suggested in the main by Mr. William Troy's essay of 1945 with its offhand hints that *The Great Gatsby* is a criticism of the American dream, that Gatsby is a symbol of America itself, that Gatsby is one of the few truly mythological creations in our recent literature, and that the novel "takes on the pattern and the meaning of a Grail-romance—or of the initiation ritual on which it is based." Mr. Marius Bewley's "Scott Fitzgerald's Criticism of America" (*Sewanee Review:* Spring 1954) is the latest example. Now of course the novel is not, as Fitzgerald's biographer labels it, a tragic pastoral of the Jazz Age, but rather a criticism of the American dream. But to label it thus is but another oversimplification, as though *The Great Gatsby* means only that and nothing more. What the novel means can be discovered only by analyzing it. Mr. Bewley's reading oversimplifies it. "It is hardly too much to say that the whole being of Gatsby exists only in relation to what the green light symbolizes." Now the truth is that Gatsby exists in relation to everything in the novel, not solely in relation to the green light, and nothing is in the novel that does not exist in relation to everything else. If we explore it as an integrated whole, a new interpretation rewards our scrutiny.

A year before *The Great Gatsby* saw print, Fitzgerald's best friend had written him off as an irresponsible artist incapable of knowing what to do with the rare jewels that somehow fell into his lap. "I want to write something new," Fitzgerald told Maxwell Perkins, "—something extraordinary and beautiful and simple and intricately patterned." And new and extraordinary and beautiful and simple it is. But what transforms the novel into greatness is its intricately patterned idea. It is the idea of a myth-hero—the hero as a modern Icarus—who impersonates an Epoch while belonging to Space and Time. Gatsby belongs not exclusively to one epoch of American civilization but rather to all history inasmuch as all history repeats in cycle form what Gatsby represents—America itself. Gatsby transcends reality and time. His confused time-world results from the confused morality of the epoch he inhabits, "The Age of Confusion." Fitzgerald read Oswald Spengler's *The Decline of the West* the same summer he was writing *The Great Gatsby,* and the influence of Spengler's mixed perspectives of history is manifested in Fitzgerald's conception of a hero who confuses the past with the present and whose time-world is wrenched from the logic of time.

A "son of God" born out of his own "Platonic conception of himself," Gatsby goes "about His Father's business, the service of vast, vulgar, and meretricious beauty." The incredible Gatsby!—"liable at the whim of an impersonal government to be blown anywhere about the world." Smiling at Nick Carraway, Gatsby's smile metaphysically embraces "the whole eternal world." He resides only particularly at West Egg, for he exists simultaneously on two planes: the mythic or the impersonal *and* the human, the immaterial *and* the real. Through Nick, the narrator, the Inconceivable Gatsby is seen from the human point of view, but his universal genius is also viewed astronomically as it were from Cosmic Eyes Above. The province of his history extends from fabulous San Francisco (the city of his professed beginnings), eastward from the Golden Gate to the "clam-flats" of Lake Superior, the shores of Michigan, the peninsula of Long Island Sound, and down to the West Indies and the Barbary Coast; in Europe it extends similarly from one seaboard to the other: from England and France eastward to little Montenegro on the Adriatic. The incredible Gatsby has been three times around the continent, and he has lived in all the capitals of Europe like a rajah—"a turbaned 'character' leaking sawdust at every pore as he pursued a tiger through the Bois de Boulogne." Gatsby's world begins in the "Age of Confusion" and, crossing seas of antiquity, it romps ("like the mind of God") from the Jazz Age to the Age of Reason through the Restoration to the Dark Ages of the Holy Grail and, finally back to the Roman realms of Petronius wherein Gatsby as Trimalchio ends his career. It is no accident that Gatsby fears time; for Trimalchio (his prototype in Petronius' *Satyricon*) kept a trumpeter to announce constantly how much of his lifetime was gone and ordered a broken urn to be carved with a horologe in its center "so that anyone looking to see the time must willy-nilly read my name."

The Unidentifiable "Mr. Nobody from Nowhere" drifts "coolly out of nowhere" to settle, across the bay from Daisy Buchanan, at West Egg, an unprecedented place which is "a world complete in itself . . . second to nothing because it had no consciousness of being so." A feudal mansion of towers and Gothic library and Marie Antoinette music-rooms and Restoration salons, with vast expanses of trimmed lawns bordering upon prehistoric marshes! Gatsby's enormous house epitomizes the incomparable space-time dimensions of Gatsby himself, and Nick Carraway— staring at it as though it were the temple of some god—is compelled to ponder on time: "so I stared at it, like Kant at his church steeple, for half an hour."

(2)

Reach me a rose, honey, and pour me a last drop into that there crystal glass.

While Gatsby woos Daisy, Ewing Klipspringer pounds out on the keyboard the popular hits entitled "The Love Nest" and "Ain't We Got Fun?" The whole novel gets its time-theme summed up in the words of the latter: "In the meantime / In between time——." What is defined here is a hole in time. It is this empty in-between time that Fitzgerald renders in *The Great Gatsby,* that void of the corrupted present canceled out by the corrupted past—America's as well as Gatsby's. Gatsby has violated time in corrupting that in-between time of his life since he violated Daisy; and in violating Daisy, who represents the time-theme *as day,* Gatsby violated time. His repudiation of time-*now* is his sin of omission. "Just tell him the truth—that you never loved him and it's all wiped out forever." Here then is the whole conception of the novel, the idea of mending the clock—tampering with time. " 'Can't repeat the past?' he cried incredulously. 'Why of course you can. . . . I'm going to fix everything just the way it was before,' he said, nodding determinedly. 'She'll see.' " What more colossal *hubris* can "a son of God" commit than to tinker with the temporal order of the universe! To fix time and reinstate thus the past in the present (as though the interim were unreckoned and life has passed unclocked), to wipe the slate clean and begin anew—*that* is Gatsby's illusion.

When Gatsby at Nick's house first encounters Daisy, he's leaning on the mantelpiece with his head resting "against the face of a defunct mantelpiece clock, and from this position his distraught eyes stared down at Daisy, who was sitting, frightened but graceful, on the edge of a stiff chair." They meet stiffly, nervously, on edge; he makes "an abortive attempt at a laugh. Luckily the clock took this moment to tilt dangerously at the pressure of his head, whereupon he turned and caught it with trembling fingers, and set it back in place." He apologizes: "I'm sorry about the clock," as though apologizing for arranging to meet Daisy again —an event which upsets the clock. " 'It's an old clock,' I told them idiotically. I think we all believed for a moment that it had smashed in pieces on the floor." Their meeting sets the clock back, as it were, to that time when Gatsby possessed Daisy five years ago; Gatsby leaning against the clock and tilting it identifies himself thus with time. It's as though their five-year old clock is smashed to pieces; it's as though momentarily time thus stood still. That it is a scene of confusion is indicated also by the rain: "While the rain continued it had seemed like the murmur of their voices, rising and swelling a little now and then with gusts of emotion." Their moral confusion is hinted at by the confused clock and by the rainfall that spoils the day. There is happiness, however, when the rain stops and "twinkle-bells of sunshine" enter the room, Gatsby smiling "like a weather man, like an ecstatic patron of recurrent light," and repeating "the news to Daisy. 'What do you think of that? It's stopped raining.' 'I'm glad, Jay.' Her throat, full of aching, grieving beauty, told only of her unexpected joy." Daisy, as the sun shines, shines likewise. And Gatsby, "ecstatic patron of recurrent light," rejoices that the sun shines—Daisy shines as the sun because she is Day.

The Gatsby world is wrenched into confusion and disorder by Gatsby's two-way dream—into the past and into the future. "In the meantime / In between time"—what remains is the hole in time. As Gatsby cannot tell past from future, the present is the same for him as one or the other—*now* being for him the tomorrow he hopes to possess or the yesterday he hopes to recapture. It is his moral disruption that accounts for the disruption of time in the Gatsby world. In *The Great Gatsby* moral ambivalence correlates with the confused time-theme of the novel and has its corollary in Fitzgerald's Conradian technique of symbolism that is itself ambivalent.[1] The parallel to the divided selfhood of Gatsby is provided by the narrator, by the divided selfhood of the morally ambivalent Nick. Gatsby cannot distinguish time now from time past and future, nor right from wrong, whereas Nick is morally ambivalent not because he does not know right from wrong but rather because he is false to himself, a hypocrite. The Middle West is shown up for what it is by the person who best represents it, Nick Carraway.

So here is Nick back where he began, out in the West writing his bitter indictment of the East, a perplexed narrator writing backwards a dislocated chronology, confused and embittered by his own failure. His professed reason for leaving the West was to escape being "rumored into marriage," but the truth is he left the West because the East glitters with the future. "Instead of being the warm centre of the world, the Middle West now seemed like the ragged edge of the universe—so I decided to go East and learn the bond business." As a student of myth—"the shining secrets that only Midas and Morgan and Maecenas knew"—Nick studies how to gold-plate the future under the shining motto In Midas We Trust. Nick is the window of our viewpoint of Gatsby's romantic dream, the romantic being placed thus within a framework of cynical realism. Nick's character is determined thus by his function in the novel. Fitzgerald's method is hinted at in Nick's remark that "life is much more successfully looked at from a single window, after all." But Fitzgerald has placed us before a very deceptive piece of glass, an almost opaque and certainly a very complicated frame of reference. The very events of that summer of Nick's initiation into Eastern life elude analysis because of Nick's deliberate omissions and ambiguities in rendering his account of it. His facts resist reduction to simple certitude. Whether Nick is engaged to the girl back in the West, for instance, or whether Nick possessed Jordan (as Gatsby possessed Daisy) are questions difficult to answer because the truth is camouflaged. That Nick did possess Jordan can only be inferred, but even Jordan's accusation is ambiguous in its inferences: "Nevertheless, *you did throw me over*. . . . I don't give a damn about you now, but it was a new experience for me, and I felt a little dizzy for a while."

In his affair with Jordan, Nick is (he admits) only "half in love with her." Gatsby tells Nick his life-history "at a time of confusion, when I had reached the point of believing everything and nothing about him." The ambivalence of Nick's divided selfhood arises from his fear of committing himself to life by more than halves, and consequently he is drawn simultaneously in two directions: towards the Jordan side of his nature and towards its opposite in Gatsby. In the scene at Myrtle's party (Chapter II) when Nick tries to leave the place and walk to the park he is drawn back every time he tries to escape; he is pulled in two directions. Looking out of the window, he sees himself as "within and without, simultaneously enchanted and repelled by the inexhaustible variety of life." The same contradiction characterizes his appraisal of Jordan, the Buchanans, Gatsby, and of the East and West worlds; each now repels and now attracts him.

(3)

"Sail to the West and the East will be found."—Commodore Perry to the Japanese Emperor.

It has been said that *The Great Gatsby* is a "kind of tragic pastoral, with the East the exemplar of urban sophistication and culture and corruption, and the West . . . the exemplar of simple virtue."[2] Mr. Mizener tells us that Fittzgerald thought of the West as the exemplar of simple virtue, but what Fitzgerald presumably thought differs considerably from what he renders *in* his novel. What he wrote into his novel was a criticism of the West, as well as a criticism of the East. Not only is Western morality criticized in *The Great Gatsby,* but Fitzgerald presents not a single character to exemplify it. Every one of his Middle Westerners is dishonest. The only true exemplar of Christian morality is the insignificant Greek, Michaelis, and he is an Easterner. The moral rectitude of Nick is but the mask of hypocrisy. As for the Middle West, it is as narrow in outlook as Nick with his "provincial squeamishness," and it is hardened furthermore by its medieval-like "interminable inquisitions," which spare only the children and the very old. The East is not the sole exemplar of sophistication; for out West we get the pseudo-sophisticated and snobbish cliques of college youths matching their social registers: "Are you going to the Ordays'? the Hersheys'? the Schultzes'?" Their holiday gayeties faintly echo the hollow celebrations of Gatsby. Nor is the West exempted from corruption. Gatsby's gangster business is carried on not only out East but also out West.

In the temporal sense as in the moral, the West is as dead as its Eastern analogy, the Eastern "wasteland" with its valley of ashes. Even the farmland characteristic by which the West is known transposes itself to the East with its valley of ashes: "a fantastic farm where ashes grow like wheat into ridges and hills and grotesque gardens; *where ashes take the form of houses* and chimneys and rising smoke and, finally, with a transcendent effort, of men who move dimly and already crumbling through the powdery air." In Gatsby's house, which vibrates only during his Neroesque parties, and in Nick Carraway's defunct castle Rackrent, West Egg is represented by dead houses—as though built by the ashes of that valley located half-way between New York City and West Egg, *where ashes take the form of houses.* But if West Egg represents the negation of life and East Egg, in the dynamic Buchanans and their equally dynamic house and lawn, represents the affirmation of vitality, distinctions between West and East Eggs become blurred on considering the fact that the East is inhabited by such lifeless characters as Wilson, Voltaire, Nick Carraway, and the lively Myrtle whose name, suggesting a graveyard vine, contradicts her presumed vitality. Like everything else in the novel, both eggs—West and East—are blunted at their contact end. They are defective, not complete wholes—"not perfect ovals—like the egg in the Columbus story, they are both crushed flat at the contact end—but their physical resemblance must be a source of perpetual wonder to the gulls that fly overhead." That's not only wit; it hints also at Fitzgerald's device of ambiguity in the presented point of view. These eggs, Nick tells us, are dissimilar in every particular except in shape and size; he does not define their dissimilarity. Now one difference between Nick's West Egg and Tom Buchanan's East Egg is indicated by the fact that what Tom deals in, financially, are stocks, whereas Nick of West Egg deals in bonds. Tom trades on stocks which fluctuate by the hour, and East Egg throbs with life—in the Buchanan house. West Egg, the deader egg comparatively, suggests the Middle West where the flux of time is defunct or fixed, not flowing in rain but frozen in snow. Mr. Gatz refuses to ship the body of his son back West because Gatsby "rose up to his position in the East." Nothing in the Golden West is golden except the coaches of the Chicago, Milwaukee & St. Paul railway, and they are a murky yellow. Nobody goes West except Nick. And even when he is in the East, the rising sun "threw my shadow westward." The West, as in classical literature, figures as the land of the unliving, and that is what Nick retreats to.

They are all of them confused Middle-Western-Easterners, and the story that Nick narrates of his summer of Eastern life is a nine-reel Eastern-Western love story documenting the Decline of the West. "I see now that this has been a story of the West, after all . . ." And isn't it also a story about Nick, after all? The Nick story is inseparable from the Gatsby story, the one twining around the other to provide parallelisms to it. His matriculating at the Probity Trust is (as he says) like graduating backward into a second prep-school, and so Nick is put backward in time while simultaneously going forward—as a bond salesman dealing in futures. Nick thus provides analogy with Gatsby who, in his futuristic dream to repeat the past, is similarly drawn simultaneously forward and backward in time. Clocktime jumps back momentarily when Daisy asks him how long ago it was that they last met and Gatsby—reckoning by the future—answers: " 'Five years *next* November.' The automatic quality of Gatsby's answer set us all back at least another minute." Gatsby has set back the clock five years in that imaginary minute, and it is this contingency that Gatsby recognizes when he admits to Nick that his scheme to meet Daisy again has been all "a terrible, terrible mistake." Gatsby's mind—"the pressure of his head"—almost upsets the temporal order of things when the "defunct mantelpiece clock" almost topples. He is again identified with time in the clock that mocks his romantic dream: "A universe of ineffable gaudiness spun itself out in his brain while the clock ticked on the wash-stand. . . ." (VI). Again: "he was running down like an overwound clock." His so-called ancestral home at West Egg is a confused mélange of contradictory cultures and epochs, and his personal failure is symbolized by this "huge incoherent failure of a house"—the failure of Gatsby's own confused and incoherent life since five years ago when his dream possessed him. This "unprecedented place" represents his own quest to fix time, and Daisy is appalled by it because of its incoherence. Here the impossible has been achieved—time rearranged, history fixed. So Gatsby took over the house of a man who was as crazy as Gatsby about reinstating the past, a man who went into immediate decline when his unretarded neighbors obstructed his antiquarian program to have their cottages thatched with straw. It was like turning the clock back.

Nick presents himself on the first page of his story in the figure of a defunct archpriest in the confessional-box, a prig with holier-than-thou airs who has rejected all further "riotous excursions with privileged glimpses into the human heart." His summer excursion into the riotous heart of the East he now repudiates, now that he has failed at facing into life, and nettled by it he lumps his own failure with that of all the others, rationalizing that as Middle Westerners "we possessed some deficiency in common which made us subtly unadaptable to Eastern life." His initiation has ended with his retreat back home, a retreat back to the clean, hard, limited world of the West where life is conveniently regulated by the moral straight-jacket of the Simple Virtues. "When I came back from the East last autumn I felt that I wanted the world to be in uniform and at a sort of moral attention forever." So Nick on the rebound proposes to save the world by regimenting it, by policing it morally. That Nick is to be seen as the moral center of the book, as one critic proposes, that his character "can be regarded as a kind of choric voice, a man who embodies the moral conscience of his race," is a notion possible only to the duped reader who has been beguiled by the deceptive flow of Nick's words to take them at their face-value. At the center of the book what is there but a moral and temporal hole? Not Nick, but Time is the true moralist. Fitzgerald has contrived that first page of The Great Gatsby as a front to the whole book. Here is Nick as archprig all dressed up in a morally hard-boiled starched shirt of provincial squeamishness and boasted tolerance, the hypocrite! His boasted tolerance, as we come to see through his protective mask, is in fact intolerance, and his rugged morality but polished manners. His proposal to regiment the world amounts to a negation of faith in humanity and of faith in life itself, and it masks his own spiritual bankruptcy. No moral vision can radiate from Nick's closed heart. The moral uniform he would clothe the world in smothers the riotous heart; it denies life and challenges it at its very godhead. And that is what Gatsby, after all, in-carnates—the life-giving force.

One thing betrays Nick, and that is his ragged lawn at Castle Rackrent; what his "irregular lawn" signifies is that Nick himself is not as morally regular as he pretends. He professes a detestation of anything messy or disorderly, yet his own lawn is never trimmed except when Gatsby has his gardener repair it. He detests careless people, yet he himself is care-less; he detests bad drivers, yet he himself is a bad driver—a bad sport. And Gatsby, because his life is confused and disordered, has the same pas-sion for order and restraint as Nick. When his parties get out of hand, Gatsby grows more correct as the hilarity mounts. Nick's morality amounts to the restraint of keeping up appearances; he is a stickler for the punc-tilios of correct form and decent conduct. Because "I wanted to leave things in order," Nick pays a courtesy call on Jordan before leaving for the West. His leaving things in order amounts to his shaking hands with her after having thrown her over, that being the decent thing to do!

As Myrtle is appropriately named to suit her special function on earth (*myrtle*—sacred to Venus among the ancients—is an evergreen shrub whose leaf yields spice), so too is Jordan Baker. For Jordan bears the name of the river that flows to the Dead Sea, a foul stream she is that runs be-tween poisonous banks in a barren valley—used in Biblical times only for the brass founderies established there by Solomon. Hebrew writers did not sing her praises, and neither does Nick. While she shares the sun-attributes of Daisy in her "golden shoulder" and "autumn-leaf yellow of her hair," she belongs to the dying day and the season of the declining sun. "So we drove on toward death through the cooling twilight." Sterility characterizes the soulless Jordan. As they go over the dark bridge Nick remarks of Jordan that "unlike Daisy" she is "too wise ever to carry well-forgotten dreams from age to age," but in saying this Nick is also speak-ing for himself inasmuch as he, like Jordan, has no illusions. The past, though it lingers on in Jordan's aunt, who is "about a thousand years old," is dead and cannot be retrieved. Only Gatsby believes in the Wedding of the Dream. Though Nick disbelieves in it, he nevertheless arranges for the reunion of the lovers whom time has divorced, and thereby he in-volves himself, Honest Nick, in the adulterous affair and shares re-sponsibility for its consequences.

Nick's duplicity is again evidenced in his half-romantic and half-cynical attachment to Jordan. He makes love to her *and* he criticizes her at the same time; indeed he is never more critical of Jordan than during his love-scenes with her. His portraits of her are unwittingly also portraits of himself, however. Her "bored haughty face" turns to the world "a cool, insolent smile" as to conceal something. Jordan is a dealer in subterfuge and "universal scepticism," and so too is Nick, though the true Nick is not to be readily guessed from the pretty portrait he paints for himself. The fact is that Nick is guilty of "basic insincerity, though it is Daisy he scores for it. Jordan provides one more example. The Moral Nick resembles the "hard-boiled painting" of his uncle, who started the Carraways in the hardware business out West. Brass runs in the family blood. The Carraways pride themselves on their moral hardware, and Nick inherits a set of hardfast interior rules (they furnish him with "brakes on my desires"), which places him at a heightened advantage over others whose backgrounds are not so well-stocked with the polished fixtures of common decency: "as my father snobbishly suggested, and as I snobbishly repeat, a sense of the fundamental decencies is parcelled out unequally at birth." What brass! It's the hard-boiled Jordan who calls his bluff:

> "You said a bad driver was only safe until she met another bad driver? Well, I met another bad driver, didn't I? I mean it was careless of me to make such a wrong guess. I thought you were rather an honest, straightforward person. I thought it was your secret pride."
> "I'm thirty," I said. "I'm five years too old to lie to myself and call it honor."

Thus Honest Nick is identified with Crooked Jordan. They are both what they both profess to detest: bad drivers—irresponsible, careless, bad moral risks.

The cardinal virtue Nick professes—"I am one of the few honest people I have ever known"—has been stripped bare by this dissection of Fitzgerald's masked narrator, and seeing him in this light returns us to the novel to read it anew. His ambiguous honesty winks at the incurable dishonesty of Jordan, and also at his courting of her while he is writing the girl out West letters "once a week and signing them: 'Love, Nick.' " Also, while falling in love with Jordan he engages in vicarious flirtations with women picked out from strolling crowds and into whose lives he enters surreptitiously—affairs of his imagination which "no one would ever know or approve." Also, there is the short affair he has with a New Jersey office-girl who works in the *accounting* department of the Probity Trust! —an affair that Nick discreetly breaks off when it is discovered by the girl's brother, made known and disapproved. As for Nick's rumored engagement to the girl out West, he is anxious to write it off as merely "a vague understanding that had to be tactfully broken off before I was free" (free, that is, before making an offer of engagement to Jordan), but the affair out West is not yet broken off in August when he is still busy "trotting around with Jordan and trying to ingratiate myself with her senile aunt," and what is to be noticed is that in the same breath that he speaks of his rumored engagement as but a vague understanding he slips into admitting it as "that tangle back home." The truth is that the elusive Nick cannot bring himself to keep any commitments to life, and above all not a romantic one. It is this spiritual deficiency that incapacitates him for living life and that, in sum, accounts for his retreat from the East back to the West and "the thrilling returning trains of my youth."

(4)

"The master's body!" roared the butler into the mouthpiece. "I'm sorry, madame, but we can't furnish it—it's far too hot to touch this noon!"

East is West, night is day, reality is unreality. Reality, substance without substance, is overwhelmed by dream and confounded by illusion. Nothing in the novel is not confused. Even geography is scrambled. The cagey Nick probes Gatsby as to what part of the West he comes from: " 'What part of the Middle West?' I inquired casually." And Gatsby just as casually replies: "San Francisco." The confused identity of West and East is epitomized in the figure of Dan Cody as "the pioneer debauchee, who . . . brought back to the Eastern seaboard the savage violence of the frontier brothel and saloon." Blurred or confused identity patterns everything in the book. McKee's over-enlarged portrait of Mrs. Wilson's dead mother hovers like an ectoplasm on the wall, looking like "a hen sitting on a blurred rock. Looked at from a distance, however, the hen resolved itself into a bonnet, and the countenance of a stout lady beamed down into the room."

Confused and divided selfhood, exemplified notably in Gatsby and Nick, has its counterpart motif in mistaken and crossed identity. Everyone's identity overlaps another's. Nick is misidentified as Gatsby, when Spangle mistakes him as Jay himself; Jordan is misidentified as Daisy by Myrtle; Wilson substitutes for Tom Buchanan as the murderer of Gatsby; and in the enigmatic book entitled "Simon Called Peter" self-identity is similarly repudiated. The unknown Gatsby, known only by his false name, confounds identity and, being mistaken for the "murderer" of Myrtle, he is murdered because of it. Crossed identities of persons have their parallel in the switched cars at the crack-up. The names of Gatsby's house-guests that Nick records on the margins of a defunct railroad-timetable furnish, as it were, a forest-preserve of crossed identities. With the clan of Black-*buck* (the Blackbucks flip up their noses like goats at whosoever approaches them) Cecil Roe*buck*—figuratively speaking—crossbreeds, and Roebuck shares what Francis Bull has in common with the *Horn*beams. Edgar Beaver with cotton-white hair suggests not beaver but rabbit, by whom Endive (Clarence Endive) is devoured, as it were, and Beaver is pursued by Rot-Gut Ferret—*ferret* being a weasel. Dr. Civet, the surgeon who is to operate on a star (the *star* is Miss Baedeker, named after the official Baedeker guidebook for travellers, travellers through space). suggests relationship with Catlip, as *civet* translates into cat; and Catlip in turn suggests kinship with Katspaugh, Gatsby's gangster-friend. Chester Becker has the same surname as one of the gangsters who murdered Rosy Rosenthal and got the Hot Seat. The gangster Becker (who got the Hot Seat),[3] suggests relationship thus with a man named Bunsen, inasmuch as Bunsen was the inventor of the Original Burner! Nick describes Bunsen simply as a man he knew at Yale, but the connection that I detect here is not as fanciful as it may seem, for everything in the novel is punned upon, jokingly counterpointed or burlesqued, jazzed up—like Tostoff's "Jazz History of the World." Nick's timetable—outdated, outmoded, useless now—reflects the flaw in Nick's own time-sense: "an old timetable now, disintegrating in its folds, and headed 'This schedule in effect July 5th, 1922.' " Neither the timetable nor Nick is "in effect"—In the meantime / In between time.

Nick's timetable is infested with violence and disruption: Beaver had his nose shot off in the war, Muldroon strangled his wife, the Quinns are now divorced, Civet was drowned, Endive boxed a man named Etty, an automobile ran over Snell's right hand, and Palmetto killed himself "by jumping in front of a subway train in Times Square." Cannibalism, name devouring name, and violence link with confused identities: "Benny Mc-Clenahan arrived always with four girls. They were never quite the same ones in physical person, but they were so identical one with another that it inevitably seemed they had been there before." In contrast are the innocent plant-life names of Lilly, Orchid, and Duckweed, and the Leeches, and bounding through the forest is Ewing Klipspringer, *klipspringer* being an antelope. Another daisy-chain of puns, this one not furnished by Nick's timetable, is formed by Gatsby's first name, Jay, in rime with the last names of the two women who betray him, Fay and Kaye. So too Goddard couples with Stoddard, the one interchangeable with the other.

"Almost any exhibition of complete self-sufficiency," as Nick remarks, "draws a stunned tribute from me." Nothing in the book has self-sufficiency, not even Gatsby. Every person, place or thing exists in partnership with its opposite or with its double. Everybody borrows attributes of another and/or connects with somebody else. Gatsby, the Buchanans, Klipspringer, and Nick's girl out West, and Jordan, the golf champion—they are all sportsmen, at cricket, tennis, or golf. They are all thus Dealers in Space.

The photographer McKee makes enlargements of things in space, Jordan jumps space by moving her golf-ball forward from a bad lie, and space is connoted by Miss Baedeker's name—the official guidebook for travelling about the globe. As Chester McKee fixes space, so Meyer Wolfsheim fixes time—he fixed the World Series! Fixing space and time provides thus analogy with the great Gatsby. Fitzgerald shows a marked predilection for doubling the identities of persons, places, and things; fashioning them by two or pairs. Gatsby has two fathers (Mr. Gatz and his Heavenly Father, Owl Eyes); his life divides into two parts; he is tricked by two women. Nick has two girls (one in the East and one in the West); Myrtle plans to go West with Tom, and her husband plans to go West with Myrtle. Like Miss This-or-That and the Three Mr. Mumbles, it is all rather confusing. There are two timetables, two eggs, two necklaces, and so on. Two shining eyes look blankly at McKee, Tom demanding "Two what?" McKee means his two photographs: "Two studies. One of them I call

Montauk Point—The Gulls, and the other I call *Montauk Point—The Sea.*" They have the same bewildering difference as, say, East and West Egg. Gatsby's medieval mansion is at once a houseboat and a roadhouse —"the World's Fair." "I'll be a man smoking two cigarettes," says Daisy. Jordan Baker mannishly "wore her evening-dress, all her dresses, like sports clothes" (which are worn properly only in the daytime). All's confounded by mixed identity. Nothing is complete and whole as a thing in itself; nothing therefore is without imperfection. Nick reminds Daisy of an "absolute rose," but as Nick himself admits "I am not even faintly like a rose." There are no absolutes in the book. Everything resides in what is outside itself. Epochs and places share the same fate as persons. Juxtaposed upon Versailles, scenes of which are tapestried in Myrtle's love-couch, there is a blood-spattered scandal sheet, "Town Tattle." The great Voltaire sinks into Willie Voltaire, and by the same bathos the North and the South collapse into Mrs. Ulysses (Grant) *Swett* and Stonewall Jackson *Abrams.*

Everybody is maimed, physically or spiritually. Not one woman is without some physical imperfection, not even Daisy is beautiful. The physically maimed include Daisy's butler whose nose was injured from polishing too much silverware; the motion-picture director with his "blue nose"; the Becker who had his nose shot off during the war; and Wolfsheim with his "tragic nose"—"a flat-nosed Jew whistling the Rosary."

Unfinished business and frustrated or muddled and broken-off relationships characterize the maimed action of the entire novel. Characters and scenes are undeveloped; nearly every scene is broken off—not finished but disrupted ("to be continued"). The moralist Fitzgerald strikes out against the fragmented morality of his age by rendering his world thus: confused and fragmentary. When Nick turns to Gatsby he finds that Gatsby has vanished, and midway in his speech Gatsby's elegant sentences halt unfinished; Wolfsheim fills in unspoken words by a wave of his hand; Daisy's voice breaks off; and Tom's gibberish ends on a dash. " 'But science—.' He paused. The immediate contingency overtook him, pulled him from the edge of the theoretical abyss."

(5)

The Crack-up

That theoretical abyss from which Tom is pulled back materializes, so to speak, into an actual abyss—the elevator shaft down which McKee and Nick almost plunge. Gatsby nearly topples down a flight of stairs; Daisy "tumbled short" of Gatsby's sun-soaring dream; at Gatsby's parties the falling girls, swooning back into young men's arms, emit a falling laughter: it "spilled with prodigality, tipped out at a cheerful word." Figuratively speaking, everyone tumbles from some heightened promise of life and, literally, almost everyone hovers on the edge of an abyss ready for a fall.

In the opening scene where life seems overcharged with confusion and like glass ready to shatter, two women float along the ceiling suspended in air on an enormous couch that bounces about in space in denial of the laws of gravity, "buoyed up as though upon an anchored balloon." Jordan, the Balancing Girl, balances on the tip of her chin an invisible object which is quite ready to fall. (This scene is repeated in Chapter VII with the two women doing their aerial stunt as stiff "silver idols" unable to move, paralyzed as before but not now "p-paralyzed with happiness"). Wrecked cars and wrecked lives, fallen noses and fallen names pattern the motif of the fall of man and the fall of civilization itself. "Civilization's going to pieces. . . . Have you read 'The Rise of the Colored Empires' by this man Goddard?" Disorder confounds the time-world of *The Great Gatsby,* and the very earth, wrenched from its natural course, is theoretically about to fall into the sun. "I read somewhere that *the sun's getting hotter every year . . . It seems that pretty soon the earth's going to fall into the sun—or wait a minute—it's just the opposite—the sun's getting colder every year."* What Tom Buchanan here prophesies—the end of the world—occurs that very day; Gatsby's world goes to pieces with the disintegration of Wilson's world the day of the crack-up when Myrtle is killed by Gatsby's car.

Tom's combustion image embodies the central theme of the book, the theme of time confused and disordered. This key image of the earth-sun holocaust has three corollary themes or motifs imaged as (1) flights and falls, (2) confusion and the heat of the sun, and (3) the opposition of day *versus* night. This last I shall explore in the final section of this analysis. There is a contradiction in Tom's theory, and a like contradiction is at the heart of every character in the book. The earth is getting hotter *and* the sun is getting colder. The earth is falling into the sun *and* it is not falling into the sun—it's just the opposite. The main patterns of the book are epitomized in this key image, Tom's contradictory theory transposing into the human predicament. He himself is pulled in two directions, towards Myrtle and towards Daisy; Nick likewise is pulled in two directions, towards Jordan and towards Gatsby; the same contradiction fashions Gatsby's two-way dream, into the past and into the future. This earth-sun image reiterates the earth-sun attributes of Gatsby's fantastic car and the night-day attributes of Gatsby himself. Gatsby's month of love with Daisy ended on a cold autumn day, and since then the course of his life has veered away from the sun—away from Daisy, the sun he worships. So for Gatsby the sun *is* getting colder every year! In the middle of June Daisy has gone off on her wedding trip and Gatsby, not finding her in Louisville, departs on a hot day-coach with "the pale magic of her face" caught up in his own: "The track curved and now it was going away from the sun. . . ."

As the second part of Tom's thermo-dynamics theory explains why it is so cold out in the Middle West, so the first part explains why it is so hot in the East. Summer heat and moods of confusion combine to create the dominant atmosphere of the entire book. No day in it (excepting the period subsequent to Gatsby's death-day) is without the warm sun. The day of the crack-up, though it is the last day of summer, is the hottest day of the year. The day of Gatsby's death witnesses a sharp change in the weather, night having altered the summer to autumn, and now we get the first cool day in the calendar of the novel. Gatsby resents change and he refuses to recognize it. He refuses to let the swimming-pool be drained, though autumn leaves already threaten it. Gatsby dreads autumn, the season of change and of the receding sun. That pool, unused all summer, represents the hole in time, the years unlived with Daisy—time unused. It is a pool of fixed time. "Anything I hate is to get my head stuck in a pool," says Miss Baedeker.

The Great Gatsby is clocked on fast time, and not only is time speeded up but also space. "It was nine o'clock—almost immediately afterward I looked at my watch and found it was ten." The fall of the earth into the sun is averted by Tom's injected "wait a minute," and that theoretical pause defines what is for him an impossibility, a contradiction of his dynamic forward nature. Gatsby, that "overwound clock," cannot wait even for Daisy: "I can't wait all day." No Wasting Time was one of his resolves when as a boy he plotted how to mend the clock to make the most of time, but his time-schedule ironically he recorded on the fly-leaf of *Hopalong Cassidy*! Time cannot stop Gatsby; he cannot be arrested, though a frantic policeman attempts to arrest him, only to apologize for not recognizing who the great Gatsby really is. "Excuse *me!*" The rushing-time flow of the narrative gets arrested only momentarily here and there, as when Myrtle peers out of her garage window and "one emotion after another crept into her face like objects in a slowly developing picture." And space (only in McKee's photographs is space fixed) leaps likewise its boundaries. "The lawn started at the beach and ran toward the front door for a quarter of a mile [as though the lawn were Tom himself as Yale football-end racing for the goal line], *jumping over sundials* and brick walls and burning gardens—finally when it reached the house drifting up the side in bright vines as though from the momentum of its run." So *fresh* is this grass that it climbs impertinently into Buchanan's house, and "just as things grow in fast movies," so the leaves burst hurriedly on the Buchanan trees. On the broiling afternoon of the crack-up the confused time witnesses a silver curve of moon hovering "already in the western sky." This breach in nature exemplifies the book's theme of the breach in time, and a parallel sign of nature's disorder is the premature moon shining in the afternoon sky at Gatsby's July party, a wafer of a moon. The sunset glows upon Buchanan's porch, but there are four prematurely lighted candles. " 'Why candles?' objected Daisy, frowning. She snapped them out with her fingers." Daisy thereby identifies herself with Day, in opposition to Night. "I always watch for the longest day of the year and then miss it." She misses it because one season overlaps with another; summer, advancing before its appointed time, is already here (two weeks before June 21st). It is as though the stage props for Act II prematurely appeared for Act I.

Except for Wilson, McKee, and Catherine (Myrtle's sister), they are all dynamic, restless, confused, and "*advanced* people." They are advanced in the same sense as Buchanan's lawn. Buchanan's cocktails (as if self-propelled) bounce into the room: "just *in* from the pantry." The very clothes Tom wears suggest mobility: they are "riding clothes." Fitzgerald poses his characters leaning backward or leaning forward. Gatsby vibrates like "one of those intricate machines that register earthquakes ten thousand miles away." His heart pounds "in constant, turbulent riot," and even when dead he seems to vibrate. His shocked eyes protest to Nick: "Look here, old sport, you've got to get somebody for me [to come to his funeral]. . . . I can't go through this alone." And Nick responds by addressing the dead Gatsby as if he were alive: "I'll get somebody for you, Gatsby. Don't worry."

Space and time—which formerly only the gods controlled—are conquered today by the tin chariots that hurl us at the rate of a century a minute towards the green light of the future. Our ailing machines pause in flight only long enough to get reconditioned—at garages to get repaired, at house-parties to get uplifted, or at drug-stores to get refueled: "You can buy anything at a drug-store nowadays." A garage is our temple of worship, our spiritual machines resting here for repair. Here to minister to our needs is the archpriest of commotion, an anonymity named George B. Wilson, and here—conferring in secret—is the priestess of power and pressure and combustion. She is the Jazz Age goddess not of fecundity but of dynamo-energy, a woman with "no facet or gleam of beauty," but of such panting vitality that she seems "as if the nerves of her body were continually smouldering." Out of the temple we race towards the green light, down the roadway which recedes year by year before us. It is Nick's birthday and also it is the last day of summer, this day of the crack-up. "I was thirty. Before me stretched the portentous, menacing road of a new decade."

Time as the roadway has its parallel symbol in time as the current: "So we beat on, boats against the current, borne back ceaselessly into the past." Time-in-flux figures as rain, and time-fixed is symbolized by pools. Goddard's scientific idea (as Tom reports it) is that the white race is going to be "utterly submerged." Destiny by water conditions Gatsby's life from beginning to end. He meets death while floating in a pool, the swimming pool not before used all summer; Daisy he meets as he steps from a pool of rainwater, and as it rains then so it rains at his funeral. At every landing point in his incredible history his life juts upon water. Even his house belongs to the sea, in the persistent rumor that he lives not in a house but in a boat, "a boat that looked like a house and was moved secretly up and down the Long Island shore." "Blessed are the dead that the rain falls on"—*blessed* because the mess and refuse of their lives is washed away.

That Gatsby has connections of a supernatural order is evidenced by the yellow car he drives, that Chariot of the Sun. Bright with nickel and many layers of glass surrounding "a sort of green conservatory," it is "terraced with a labyrinth of wind-shields that mirrored a dozen suns." Thus it resembles the sun. But also—being green and terraced—it resembles the earth. As it is "swollen here and there in its monstrous length with triumphant hat-boxes and supper-boxes and tool-boxes," it bulges out into space. As tricky a contraption as any Daedalus ever conceived! A rolling hot-house as it were, Gatsby's car serves as the conservatory for his dream-flower—Daisy. (Its three-noted horn links it also with Daisy, for she wears a three-cornered hat.) Green, the color of its upholstery, symbolizes the future (as in the green light that flickers on the Buchanan dock across the bay from Gatsby); but green is also the symbol of excitements, desires unfulfilled, expectations or hopes. Nick can kiss Daisy providing he shows her his green passport: "present a green card. I'm giving out green——." Green and its analogous color yellow are grouped as complementary symbols, as in the long green railroad tickets and the murky yellow railroad cars in the Christmas scene out West (Chapter IX). Sick with disillusionment and shock at his discovery of Myrtle's infidelity, Wilson's face is *green* as Tom pulls up at Wilson's garage in Gatsby's *yellow* car (Chapter VII). Yellow becomes confused with green when Michaelis, confused about the color of the yellow death-car, reports it was a light green color. These symbols green and yellow have their counterpart in the duality of Gatsby's night-day and moon-sun selfhood.

(6)

> *In the morning,*
> *In the evening,*
> *Ain't we got fun—*

"The Rise of the Colored Empires"—the threat of black supremacy—means metaphorically the Rise of the Night. Daisy whispers her rejoinder to Tom's outcry: "We've got to beat them down," and she winks "ferociously toward the fervent sun." As here she is allied with the sun, her identity is revealed again in the scene at Myrtle's place, when Tom smashes Myrtle's nose. It is revealed that night by Myrtle's hysterical scream of "*Dai*sy! *Dai*sy! . . . I'll say it whenever I want to! *Dai*sy! *Dai*——." Daisy as Day is threatened by the ever-rising Night. Gatsby dreads Night and loves Day. In darkness he prays with outstretched arms to the green light.

Night and day (darkness and sunlight) are juxtaposed in every section of the novel, almost in every episode excepting the terminal one which depicts sunless scenes of rain and snow and night; and as the novel ends in night, so it begins with night descending upon the setting sun. East and West, though Nick pretends to make discriminations, are alike in their dread of night. In the West an evening is "hurried from phase to phase toward its close, in a continually disappointed anticipation or else *in sheer nervous dread of the moment itself.*" Thus time now eludes them all, and night is denied.

Night is dispelled by Gatsby's day-in-night parties, artificial suns substituting for the real one. "The lights grow brighter as the earth lurches away from the sun"—the orchestra playing "yellow cocktail music," a hot jazz, hot enough to brighten up everybody amidst the darkness that everybody fears. The "spectroscopic gayety" of these fantastic parties burns up the gardens and keeps them aglow long after the immaterial guests have departed. With Gatsby's house lit up like the World's Fair, the whole corner of the peninsula seems on fire, but Gatsby has an insatiable hunger for light and proposes to Nick a visit to Coney Island, where also night is turned into day. Moonlight twines with revels and reveries, dreams that deny the logic of time—the clock on the washstand and the moon soaked with wet light his *tangled* clothes upon the floor." In that tangled time after Gatsby went away Daisy renounced the day, falling asleep at dawn to sleep all day in an evening-gown "*tangled* among dying orchids on the floor beside her bed." Gatsby's life, like Daisy's, had been "confused and disordered since then," and he longs to return to that starting place and *go over it all slowly* so as to recover "some idea of himself perhaps, that had gone into loving Daisy." But time since then has pounded on faster and faster until finally the clock he has raced against overtakes him. When the lights at his house fail to go on, the uncertain lights falling "unreal on the shrubbery" (like Gatsby's spectral dream), his house is winked into darkness and "as obscurely as it had begun, his career as Trimalchio was over."

Gatsby incarnates the power of dream and illusion, the recurrent cycles of youth's capacity for wonder by which new worlds have been conquered since the beginning of civilization—the dream of a conquest of space-and-time, the illusions which reality deflates, the power of youth and faith in hope. (As Fitzgerald puts it, there are the winged and the wingless.) Gatsby, winged upwards by his "heightened sensitivity to the promises of life," transcends "what foul dust floated in the wake of his dreams," and his sun-thoughts soar beyond the sun, beyond Daisy, "beyond everything. He had thrown himself into it with a creative passion, adding to it all the time, decking it out with every bright feather that drifted his way." Like Icarus, Gatsby soars against the tyranny of space-and-time by which we are imprisoned, only to be tragically destroyed by his own invention.

Day opposes night, and consequently throughout the novel white dominates its opposite. The futuristic green light that Gatsby prays to promises the day—Daisy. When Gatsby first knew her she drove a white roadster and wore a white dress; in the opening scene of the book she and Jordan wore white dresses; both Gatsby and Nick wear white flannels; Buchanan's red and white mansion stands amidst the white palaces of fashionable East

Egg; Nick's books on banking shine in red and gold over the "white chasms of Wall Street." Out in the Middle West everything is white. Here in their homeland night is camouflaged by Christmas lights and holiday gayeties, bright snow contradicting the darkness. Nick's Middle West is represented as a long frosty dark-winter, whitened not by the sun (Daisy is out East!) but rather by the snow that keeps time frozen in.

That wintry night-world of the West—Nick's West differs from Gatsby's—is what Nick retreats to after his experience of life out East, and what he retreats from is that El Greco night-world of the East. The night-vignette Nick paints of the East as a drunken woman carried on a stretcher is an image symbolic not only of the East but also of the West, for it signifies the plight of all these Middle Western Easterners (or Eastern Middle Westerners): their isolation, their loneliness, their anonymity. Four nameless men carry the nameless woman, her hand dangling over the stretcher and sparkling "cold with jewels." Gravely the men turn in at a house—the wrong house. "But no one knows the woman's name, and no one cares." Everyone's identity overlaps with another's because everyone is without identity, isolated and anonymous and alone. "I found myself," says Nick at the end, "on Gatsby's side, and alone."[4] Gatsby's loneliness is proverbial, and Nick diagnoses what ails everyone in his confessing to that "haunting loneliness" he feels in himself and in others.

On Nick's last night in the East the moonlight discloses an obscene word some boy has chalked on the white steps of Gatsby's house, and Nick erases it. Nick performs the same service for the romantic Gatsby as the youth in *Madame Bovary* performs for that self-deluded romanticist, Emma Bovary, over whose grave a young boy kneels as in a ritual of dedication.   (1955)

NOTES

1. The influence of Conrad on Fitzgerald and Hemingway is spelled out in "Conrad and *The Great Gatsby*," and in the essays on *Tender Is the Night*, and *The Sun Also Rises*.
2. Arthur Mizener in *F. Scott Fitzgerald: The Man and His Work*, edited by Alfred Kazin (1951), p. 36. My reading challenges Nick Carraway's moral seriousness, his integrity. "With R. W. Stallman, W. S. Frohock finds Nick 'short on moral perspective' and Fitzgerald's style catching the 'feeling of things' but combined with 'a romantic inability to interpret them.'" Thomas A. Hanzo in *Modern Fiction Studies*, II (Winter 1956-1957). Hanzo defends Mizener's reading. Frohock's essay, "Morals, Manners and Scott Fitzgerald," appeared in *Southwest Review*, XL (Summer 1955).
  In "Scott Fitzgerald's Fable of East and West" (*College English*: December 1956), Robert Ornstein stands essentially in agreement with my interpretation (1955). He writes: "But how is one to accept, even in fable a West characterized by the dull rectitude of Minnesota villages and an East epitomized by the sophisticated dissipation of Long Island society? The answer is perhaps that Fitzgerald's dichotomy of East and West has the poetic truth of [Henry] James's antithesis of provincial American virtue and refined European-sensibility. Like *The Portrait of a Lady* and *The Ambassadors*, *Gatsby* is a story of

'displaced persons' who have journeyed eastward in search of a larger experience of life. To James this reverse migration from the New to the Old World has in itself no special significance. To Fitzgerald, however, the lure of the East represents a profound displacement of the American dream, a turning back upon itself of the historic pilgrimage towards the frontier which had, in fact, created and sustained that dream."

3. Not before noticed is the fact that the reference here to the Becker who got the Hot Seat is Detective Charles Becker of the New York City Police Force at the time when Theodore Roosevelt was Commissioner of Police. Detective Becker threatened to arrest Stephen Crane when Crane protested the innocence of Miss Dora Clark, arrested for street-walking. Brought into court on the charge of soliciting, she was released on the testimony of Crane: "Stephen Crane as Brave as his Hero Showed the 'Badge of Courage' in a New York Police Court"—so ran the headline in the New York *Journal* for September 17, 1896.

It is Fitzgerald's "Becker" who as Lieutenant Becker was indicted in ·1912 for the murder of Herman Rosenthal, Rosenthal having been murdered in reprisal for squealing on police and gambling-house graft. Convicted twice for this murder (1912), he lost his final appeal to the higher courts and went to the electric chair in 1915. Becker was the first New York City policeman to be sentenced to death. The Becker-Rosenthal case—prolonged and sensational—swept the nation and brought about investigations into police department corruptions throughout the country.

4. Arguing that the novel can be known as an organic whole only from a perspective of its Form, Norman Friedman claims that *The Great Gatsby* has as its end "the achievement of some sort of change in the protagonist's fortune, his state of mind, or his moral character . . ." (in *Accent:* Autumn 1954). He claims that Gatsby makes a "tragic self-discovery—'he must have felt that he had lost the old warm world, paid a high price for living too long with a single dream.' . . ." Perhaps Gatsby did, but there is no proof of his disillusionment. What Friedman ignores is that Gatsby's so-called disillusionment is rendered from Nick's point-of-view. Nick's words cannot be taken at their face value. Friedman has lopped off Nick's expressed point-of-view. The passage he quotes begins in fact with Nick's admitted bias: "*I have an idea* that Gatsby himself didn't believe it would come [the telephone message from Daisy], and per*haps* he no longer cared. *If that was true* he must have felt that he had lost the old warm world, paid a high price for living too long with a dream." [Italics mine] It is rather Nick who is disillusioned by his experience in the East, not Gatsby.

In trying to mould the novel to a Fixed Idea of Form, Friedman misreads the substance of the hero's plight. His notion that Gatsby undergoes a change effected by the Climax of the Plot ("the disillusionment of Gatsby's faith in his ideal—a change in his state of mind") is contradicted by Gatsby's final words to Nick and his final words to the butler. To Nick he says, "I suppose Daisy'll call too," and to the butler his final words are to bring him notice if anyone telephones while he is at the swimming-pool. Nick had urged him to escape:

"Go away *now*, old sport?"
"Go to Atlantic City for a week, or up to Montreal."
He wouldn't consider it. He couldn't possibly leave Daisy until he knew what she was going to do. *He was clutching at some last hope* [italics mine] and I couldn't bear to shake him free (ch. VIII).

If shaken in his faith, Gatsby nevertheless remains hopeful to the last breath. Although he dies on a Tuesday, he dies at three o'clock; although he is not exactly a Christ figure, Gatsby—a "son of God"—was waiting for a message.

Our Aristotelian critic opines that Fitzgerald's problem "was to effect a final recognition of the utter valuelessness of his ideal *in the mind of*

Gatsby. . . ." But "in the mind of Gatsby" we never get, and even from Nick's point-of-view Gatsby as Ideal remains not devoid of merit. Not even Daisy's treachery destroys Gatsby's faith—the damned fool clings to the Dream to the very end. No, he was not disillusioned. Gatsby exemplifies an ideal and remains faithful to the dream, and that is why Nick in admiration exempts him from his general condemnation.   (1959)

Conrad and *The Great Gatsby*

Deep memories yield no epitaphs.

—MOBY DICK, XXIII

FITZGERALD'S LITERARY SOURCES include the conjectured influence of Thackeray ("so far as I am concerned," he wrote an inquirer, "you guessed right"). Another conjectured influence is that of Edith Wharton (through Henry James), which Gilbert Seldes pronounced in a *Dial* review in 1925. Seldes discussed the Wharton relationship with Fitzgerald, and so if we accept the author's own word for it he derives from Thackeray and Edith Wharton inasmuch as he himself admits the influence of these authors. These authorized influences strike me as peripheral because the central one, as I see it, is the obsessive hold of Conrad in shaping Fitzgerald's greatest novel. His biographer reports that Fitzgerald "was never very conscious of his literary debts," but so numerous are his debts to Conrad that it is (I think) misleading to swallow this false notion in good faith. In Mr. Arthur Mizener's version of him, Fitzgerald is an Original Genius—almost nobody at all influenced this Very Bright Boy. He tells us that Fitzgerald had an "intuitive way of working," and that the source of one of his symbols in *The Great Gatsby* was a dust-jacket picturing two enormous eyes which suggested "Daisy brooding over an amusement-park version of New York." This dust-jacket, as Mr. Mizener admits, "was not, of course, the real source of that symbol," but he insists that "it was the only source Fitzgerald consciously understood, and he was hardly more aware of his literary sources."[1]

Shortly after writing *The Beautiful and Damned* Fitzgerald listed for *The Chicago Tribune* the ten most important novels, and Conrad's *Nostromo* was the one he singled out as "the greatest novel since 'Vanity Fair' (possibly excluding 'Madame Bovary')."[2] He does not say what Conrad works he read other than the admitted *Nostromo*, but these must have included "Heart of Darkness" and *Lord Jim*. What he learned from Conrad includes not only the device of the perplexed narrator and turns of phrasing, but also themes and plot-situations, ambivalence of symbolism, etc.—in fact, the craft of the novel, including a theory of its construction. Fitzgerald, as he wrote in his notebooks, examined "Conrad's secret theory" and discovered the secret, that Conrad wrote the truth—"adding confusion however to his structure." How closely he studied Conrad is indicated also by what he says in this same note: "Nevertheless, there is in his scheme a desire to imitate life which is in all the big shots. Have I such an idea in the composition of this book?" And how much of Conrad he must have read is indicated by the very next note: "Conrad influenced by *Man Without a Country*." (In *The Crack-Up* by F. Scott Fitzgerald, 1945, p. 179.) The claim of his biographer that the extent of Conrad's influence on Fitzgerald is limited to his use of the Conradian narrator and "the constant and not always fortunate echoes of Conrad's phrasing" collapses, I think, in the face of the present analysis.

While writing *The Great Gatsby*, Fitzgerald read that same summer[3] Oswald Spengler's *The Decline of the West*, and the influence of Spengler's mixed perspectives of history is manifested in Fitzgerald's conception of a hero who confuses the past with the present and whose confused time-world embraces all history. "Spengler prophesied gang rule, 'young people hungry for spoil,' and more particularly 'the world as spoil' as an idea, a dominant, supersessive idea." (Fitzgerald to Maxwell Perkins, quoted in FSP, 336.) Gatsby as gangster represents this idea of the world as spoil. Now this idea of spiritual cannibalism which Fitzgerald met in Spengler he had already found in Conrad. The world as spoil is the dominant idea in "Heart of Darkness" and also in *Nostromo*. *The Great Gatsby* transposes Conrad's world-as-spoil idea into the contemporary idiom. Transported from the gang-ruled wilderness of Conrad's "Heart of Darkness," Fitzgerald's reformed cannibals, reoriented in the gang-ruled wasteland of *The Great Gatsby*, prosper now in the "Swastika Holding Company." Kurtz's enslaved blacks have escaped the wilderness to become now a threat to white supremacy. "Civilization's going to pieces. . . . Have you read 'The Rise of the Colored Empires' by this man Goddard?" (GG, 16). Kurtz's so-called humanitarianism—"Exterminate all the brutes"—is faintly echoed by Daisy Buchanan's mocking plea: "We've got to beat them down." Kurtz's wilderness rings with the voice of ivory, and Daisy's voice rings "full of money." Meyer Wolfsheim's barbaric cuff-buttons—"Finest specimens of human molars"—substitute for Kurtz's hoarded ivory.

Like Kurtz, Gatsby is unscrupulous and without restraint (as Marlow says of Kurtz), except for the restraint of keeping up appearances. Like Gatsby, Kurtz lacks "restraint in the gratification of his various lusts . . . there was something wanting in him. . . ." (HD, 573). Gatsby violates Daisy, taking "what he could get, ravenously and unscrupulously," and then at the end when time overtakes him Gatsby still has his future in front of him; and Kurtz at the end similarly stands "on the threshold of great things" when his life begins "ebbing out of his heart into the sea of inexorable time" (HD, 589). Both Gatsby and Kurtz violate time; they corrupt the point-present Now. Kurtz's name contradicts him, and Gatsby's name is false. "Mr. Nobody from Nowhere" (as Tom Buchanan calls him) is beguiled by a dream, and likewise Kurtz. Kurtz's "unlawful soul" is "beguiled . . . beyond the bounds of permitted aspirations" (HD, 586). What Marlow says of that "universal genius" defines also Gatsby's unlawful soul: "I had to deal with a being to whom I could not appeal in the name of anything high or low" (HD, 586). Born from "his Platonic conception of himself," "a Son of God," Gatsby is like Kurtz, a "universal genius"—"he was liable at the whim of an impersonal government to be blown anywhere about the world" (GG, 179). The godlike Gatsby has a metaphysical smile "of *eternal* reassurance in it. . . . It faced —or seemed to face—the whole eternal world for an instant, and then concentrated on *you* with an irresistible prejudice in your favor" (GG, 58). Kurtz does not smile, but his stare has the same metaphysical attribute—"wide enough to embrace the whole universe . . ." (HD, 592).

Both Kurtz and Gatsby are conceived in the mode of a deity, with the difference that Kurtz is idolized and Gatsby is not. No more than a voice he seems to Marlow: an anonymous, disembodied voice, "an eloquent phantom," a Shade unrooted in reality, an "initiated wraith from the back of Nowhere" honoring Marlow with "its amazing confidences before it vanished altogether" (HD, 560). "Mr. Nobody from Nowhere" unidentifiable and mysterious, unpredictable, inexplicable, anonymous, has his counterpart in Kurtz, for whom the parallel in Conrad's story is the fabulous Russian: "His very existence was improbable, inexplicable, and altogether bewildering. He was an insoluble problem" (HD, 568). Gatsby shares the same attributes, and he possesses also Kurtz's phenomenal capacity for vanishing from sight.

Kurtz's final cry—"The horror! the horror!"—testifies to the appalling truth that there is a hollowness inside all of us, a moral depravity from which no man is exempt, and also it is a testimony of Kurtz's personal greatness in facing up to that dark selfhood he has dared to probe. It is reckoned by Marlow as "an affirmation, a moral victory," and that is why Marlow remains loyal to Kurtz to the last. He remains loyal to Kurtz because he feels that Kurtz—"All Europe contributed to the making of Kurtz"—redeems mankind by his triumph over "victorious corruption," the powers of darkness that once claimed him for their own, and he triumphs because of the magnitude of his vision and because of his unflinching faith in that vision. The corrupted Kurtz and the corrupted Gatsby are, after all, incorruptible.

Though Gatsby trades on time and bargains with the clock, he never trades on the dream that possesses him. He remains loyal to his transcendent vision, and that is why Nick is moved to write the book which bears Gatsby's name. In "Heart of Darkness" Marlow saves Kurtz "out of an impulse of unconscious loyalty" (HD, 596). As Marlow remains loyal to Kurtz, so Nick remains loyal to Gatsby—in spite of his scorn for everything that Gatsby represents. Nick intuitively recognizes Gatsby's unique and heroic stature (Gatsby's greatness is, after all, impersonal), and he ends exempting Gatsby from his bitter—and Conradian—indictment of "the abortive sorrows and short-winded elations of men."

What redeems Gatsby is his fidelity to an idea, his faith in the power of dream, and what redeems Nick Carraway is his fidelity to Gatsby.

Fidelity is for Conrad the all-redeeming virtue; and Conrad's works are in the main variations on this theme. Betrayals condition Conrad's plots, and they shape Fitzgerald's plot in *The Great Gatsby*. Daisy is disloyal to her husband, and twice she is deceived by him; Jay Gatsby is tricked by two women, both having names that rime on his—Daisy Fay and Ella Kaye.[4] Nick cheats in his affairs with Jordan Baker and the unnamed girl out West; and Myrtle Wilson deceives her husband, Tom Buchanan cheating on George B. Wilson.

Nostromo is riddled with betrayals. Both Gatsby and Nostromo are self-deluded heroes, and both are doomed by the past. The theme of time in *Nostromo* is uttered by Mrs. Gould: "It had come into her mind that for life to be large and full, it must contain the care of the past and of the future in every passing moment of the present." (Modern Library edition, p. 582.) Conrad's time-theme is inverted in *The Great Gatsby:* the corrupted present violated by the corrupted past. As Mrs. Gould meditates on time, "a great wave of loneliness . . . swept over her head." Gatsby's loneliness is proverbial, and Nick shares it in admitting "a haunting loneliness" that he feels in himself and at times in others. Though he disapproves of him from beginning to end, Nick Carraway allies himself finally with Gatsby. The loneliness of Lord Jim adds somehow to his stature, and it moves Marlow to observe: "It is as if loneliness were a hard and absolute condition of existence . . ." (LJ, 180). The isolated hero is typical of Conrad's plots: Kurtz as Chief of the Inner Station, cut off from the outer world; Haldin (in *Under Western Eyes*) isolated by his betrayal of Razumov; the lonely Leggatt and the untried captain in "The Secret Sharer"; and in *Victory* Heyst on his island.

Nick knows his Conrad. As the final image of Conrad's "Heart of Darkness" returns us to the opening scene on board the *Nellie*, where the story about Kurtz began, so *The Great Gatsby* is shaped in the same circular form, ending so as to circle us back to the beginning. The story about Kurtz begins and ends with Marlow sitting on board the *Nellie* "in the pose of a meditating Buddha." And Nick at the conclusion of his story about Gatsby imitates—and not by chance!—Marlow's Buddha pose: "I sat there brooding on the old, unknown world . . ." Nick in beginning his story portrays himself on the first page of the book as a sort of college father-confessor to the "privy secret griefs of wild, unknown men." Nick is bored by their intimate revelations, and he resents his unsought role as priest. The Marlow of *Lord Jim* begs off the same assignment out of his sense of humility: "I am not particularly fit to be a receptacle of confessions." Marlow is unfit for this priestlike role because of his own dark sins, though what he feels guilty of we do not know. It makes him feel like an imposter—"as though—God help me!—I didn't have enough confidential information about myself to harrow my own soul till the end of my appointed time" (LJ, 34). Nick lacks Marlow's warm humanity, his compassion and humility. Nick's "morality" camouflages his hypocrisy. He masks his duplicity. Nobody wrings from him a confession, but everybody confesses to Nick: Gatsby lays bare his soul to Nick; Myrtle discloses to Nick her affair with Tom Buchanan; Jordan tells him of Daisy's past; and Catherine confides in him Myrtle's past as well as her own. Nick hears Gatsby's confession—"the strange story of my youth"—on the night before he is murdered. In *Lord Jim*, similarly, Jim tells his past to Marlow in darkness. (There is a distinction between what Gatsby reveals about himself in darkness and what he tells Nick in sunlight. What he tells Nick in sunlight is chiefly falsehood; the occasion—Chapter IV—is a Sunday in late July. In sunlight Gatsby fabricates.)

The Marlow of "Heart of Darkness" is burdened by his own dark past, and he declares himself on Kurtz's side out of sympathetic kinship with Kurtz for that reason. "It is strange how I accepted this unforeseen partnership, this choice of nightmares forced upon me in the tenebrous land invaded by these mean and greedy phantoms" (HD, 589). Nick's ambiguous honesty—"I am one of the few honest people that I have ever known"—suggests comparison with Marlow's pride in the same cardinal virtue: "You know I hate, detest, and can't bear a lie, not because I am straighter than the rest of us, but simply because it appals me. There is a taint of death, a flavor of mortality in lies. . . ." (HD, 526). Yet at the end, in masking the truth from Kurtz's intended so as to save Kurtz by a lie, Marlow perjures himself in ironic contradiction of his adamant scruple not to lie. As Marlow lies to save Kurtz, so in *Nostromo* Mrs. Gould lies to save Nostromo.

The Great Gatsby refashions in contemporary idiom what was for Conrad "the moral problem of conduct,"[5] the problem which Conrad explored notably in the *Nigger of the "Narcissus"* and in *Lord Jim*. Jim is admonished by his dad *not* to "judge men harshly or hastily," and Nick gets the same advice from his dad: "Reserving judgments is a matter of infinite hope." Gatsby and his neglected dad (Gatsby denies his parents) have their parallel in Jim and his neglected dad (Jim without a clean slate cannot go home). Fitzgerald's conception of the cosmic Gatsby —"a son of God" going about "his Father's business"—returns us to Jim and his Heavenly Father—Jim's dad. Conrad defines Jim's dad with cosmic wit: "the finest man that ever had been worried by the cares of a large family since the beginning of the world" (LJ, 79).

When the rajah asks Jim to repair his clock ("a nickel clock of New England make"), Jim refuses to tinker with it and drops the thing "like a hot potato." His refusal to tamper with time is what Jim later on regrets; he longs to be back there in prison, "back there again, mending the clock. Mending the clock—that was the idea" (LJ, 254). Mending the clock—that is the idea not only of *Lord Jim* but also of *The Great Gatsby*. To reinstate the past, that is Gatsby's illusion; to obliterate the past, that is Jim's illusion. Jim's faith is that life can be begun anew, with the past wiped off the slate. "A clean slate, did he say? As if the initial word of each our destiny were not graven in imperishable characters upon the face of a rock" (LJ, 186). Gatsby's faith is that life can be begun anew, with the past reinstated; his way of wiping the slate clean is "to fix everything just the way it was before." Time, that is what Gatsby cannot repair nor Jim escape. Jim turns his back on the past, and the past catches up with him. What he escapes from overtakes and destroys him, his past which confronts him in the person of Brown. Marlow describes Jim as standing "on the brink of a vast obscurity, like a lonely figure by the shore of a sombre and hopeless ocean" (LJ, 173). Jim's "hopeless ocean" transposes into the "courtesy bay" that separates Gatsby from Daisy, that distance of dark water with the green light burning on the Buchanan dock before which Gatsby—with arms outstretched as though in prayer—appears in Nick's first glimpse of him and again in Nick's final recollection. Gatsby seeks his destiny across that stretch of water, and Lord Jim faces his destiny across the creek at Patusan—Jim confronting Brown at the hour of high tide. Jim cannot escape the past, and Gatsby cannot repeat it.

Jim, says Marlow, "appeared to me symbolic." What Jim symbolizes is the same as for Gatsby: the power of dream and illusion. Fitzgerald's romantic idealism *and* satiric detachment are patterned upon the characteristic Conradian ironic combination employed in the creation of Jim, Nostromo, and Kurtz. Deluded idealists! "The mind of man," as Marlow reports it in "Heart of Darkness," "is capable of anything—because everything is in it, all the past as well as all the future" (HD, 540). Conrad's dictum fits Gatsby, and Fitzgerald's romantic dogma fits equally Gatsby and Lord Jim: "No amount of fire or freshness can challenge what a man can store up in his ghostly heart" (GG, 116). At the core of *The Great Gatsby* is Conrad's paradox: the reality of dream. Stein's famous metaphor in *Lord Jim* poses the enigma of life: to be or to become. To be is to submit to the destructive element, the sea of struggling mankind. It is "the sea with its labouring waves for ever rising, sinking, and vanishing to rise again—the very image of struggling mankind . . . soaring towards the sunshine . . . like life itself" (LJ, 243). That is Marlow's metaphor, and it serves as the corollary to Stein's: "The way is to the destructive element submit yourself, and with the exertions of your hands and feet in the water make the deep, deep sea keep you up. So if you ask me—how to be?" But man cannot exist without his illusions, those aspirations by which he soars into the unknown, and that way too is destructive. "A man that is born falls into a dream like a man who falls into the sea. If he tries to climb into the air . . . he drowns." Stein's butterfly finds a heap of dirt and sits on it; "but man he will never on his heap of mud keep still" (LJ, 214, 215). That heap of mud is the destructive element, life as it is—the colorless routine existence of our submission to the established order of things, undisturbed by any flights or quests. Now that way of life is what Jim's dad advocates in the last letter Jim gets from the old man back home. Back home is a place of peace and of faith in the conventions by which the world is conveniently regulated. Stein advocates the same thing: submit!

Like Jim, Gatsby does not submit. Like Jim, Gatsby transcends reality and time. Gatsby shares the myth attributes of Jim as Icarus, Jim going about "in sunshine hugging his secret," gazing "hungrily into the unattainable," and tumbling "from a height he could never scale again" (LJ, 198, 19, 112). On his journey into Patusan Jim singes his "wings." He gets his back blistered by the sun and he experiences "fits of giddiness." He has an uncommon habit of leaping and of taking falls; and in *The Great Gatsby*, everyone hovers on the edge of an abyss ready for a fall. In *Lord Jim* Jim leaps over the stockade "like a bird," and the earth as he races from his prison "seemed fairly to fly backwards under his feet." Perched on the heights, he appears in one of Marlow's characteristic visions of him with "the incandescent ball of the sun above his head; the empty sky and the empty ocean all a-quiver; simmering together in the heat as far as the eye could reach" (LJ, 253, 167). To the natives at Patusan Lord Jim "appeared like a creature not only of another kind but of another essence." Had the natives not seen him coming up by canoe "they might have thought he had descended upon them from the clouds" (LJ, 229). At Gatsby's July party Owl Eyes has a wreck, and after a ghostly pause an apparition of a man ("a pale, dangling individual") steps out of the wrecked coupé to stare at the "amputated wheel—he stared at it for a moment, and then looked upward as though he suspected that it had dropped from the sky" (GG, 67). Brown accuses Lord Jim of having wings so as not to touch the dirty earth; Marlow accuses Lord Jim of being a romantic and repeats Stein's words: "In the destructive element immerse! . . . to follow the dream, and again to follow the dream—and so—always. . . ." That was the way (LJ, 334, 214). (We are as perplexed as Marlow as to what Stein means, for Stein fails to unriddle the enigma of his metaphor.) Conrad concludes his novel with the image of Stein gesturing vaguely at his butterflies in regret for dreams unpursued. As Fitzgerald puts it, there are the winged and the wingless.

In Gatsby's "incorruptible dream" and "unutterable visions"—the very epithets are Conrad's—Fitzgerald's hero wears the look of Nostromo and Lord Jim. All three are dream-deluded romantics. Inconceivable is Marlow's word for Jim, and Gatsby is in the same sense "inconceivable." Isolated and lonely, both Jim and Gatsby suffer bad names and are pursued by calumny; both are betrayed, and both are crucified—"Jim was to be murdered mainly on religious grounds, I believe" (LJ, 310). Gatsby's life divides into two parts, and Jim's life similarly divides into two parts: first his leap from the pilgrim ship, and secondly his leap into Patusan. Marlow defines not only Jim's plight but Gatsby's: Jim "was overwhelmed by the inexplicable; he was overwhelmed by his own personality—the gift of that destiny which he had done the best to master" (LJ, 341). The Conradian attributes of the legendary Gatsby—namely the night-day, moon-sun attributes of his divided selfhood—bear striking resemblances to Jim's duality: "He appealed to all sides at once—to the side turned perpetually to the light of day, and to that side of us which, like the other hemisphere of the moon, exists stealthily in perpetual darkness, with only a fearful ashy light falling at times on the edge. He swayed me. I own to it, I own up" (LJ, 93). In comparison with Marlow's devotion to Jim, Nick is noncommital; his admission of Gatsby's greatness is an enforced admission. Too sophisticated to show any emotion, Nick exhibits no such spontaneity as Marlow shows in his fascination for the enigmatic Jim. Nick's inherited "provincial squeamishness" sets him off from Marlow; and Nick's mind, though quite as perplexed as Marlow's, lacks Marlow's range and points of curiosity. In his inveterate curiosity Marlow reminds us of the village gossip, and in his habitual indecision he suggests an old woman sitting metaphorically on the fence. But he penetrates the mask of Kurtz and the soul of Jim, whereas Nick Carraway presents Gatsby only from the outside.   (1955)

NOTES

1. *The Far Side of Paradise* (Boston, 1951), p. 170. In taking the line that Fitzgerald was hardly aware of his literary sources Mr. Mizener conveniently forgets to make any mention of Petronius Arbiter's *The Satyricon*. It is difficult to believe that Fitzgerald was not consciously aware of his sources inasmuch as Gatsby is patterned upon Trimalchio. (See the opening sentence of Chapter VII of *The Great Gatsby* where Gatsby is identified as Trimalchio.) For points of parallelisms see Paul MacKendrick's *"The Great Gatsby* and Trimalchio," *Classical Journal*, 45 (April 1950), pp. 307-314.

2. Quoted by Mizener in *The Far Side of Paradise*, in the notes to Chapter IX, p. 336. This book is hereafter coded as FSP. Page references to *The Great Gatsby* are to the first edition: Scribner's, 1925. (The reprint edition by Grosset & Dunlap, n.d., has the same pagination.) For Conrad's "Heart of Darkness" I have used *The Portable Conrad*, edited by M. D. Zabel (New York, 1947). For *Lord Jim* I have used the Dent edition, first published in 1900. (Pagination is the same in the Modern Library edition of *Lord Jim*, 1931.) For *The Great Gatsby* I have used the abbreviation GG; for "Heart of Darkness"—HD; for *Lord Jim*—LJ.

3. Fitzgerald told Maxwell Perkins in 1940 that he read Spengler "the same summer I was writing 'The Great Gatsby,' and I don't think I ever quite recovered from him. (FSP, p. 336.) Perkins wrote Fitzgerald in 1926: "I'm almost afraid to tell you about a book that I think incredibly interesting—Spengler's 'Decline of the West'—for you'll tell me it's 'old stuff' and that you read it two years ago—for it was published eight years ago in Germany, and probably six, in France, and has been a long time translating into English." *Editor to Author: The Letters of Maxwell Perkins*, edited by John Hall Wheelock (New York, 1950), p. 47.

In "The Waste Land of F. Scott Fitzgerald," Mr. John W. Bicknell comments briefly on some points of parallelism between Gatsby and Lord Jim and Kurtz, and he notes an analogy between Conrad's Marlow and Fitzgerald's Nick Carraway, in *Virginia Quarterly Review*, 30 (Autumn 1954), 562.

Professor Dan Piper, whose book-length study of Scott Fitzgerald will appear in 1960, wrote me (September 4, 1956) that my "Conrad and *The Great Gatsby*" eliminated the need for his writing on the same topic. "I have paid particular attention to Fitzgerald's many references to Conrad among his manuscript papers. And while, from them, a more elaborate study could be put together concerning Conrad's influence, I doubt very much if the results of all that work would modify appreciably the fair and penetrating conclusions you reached in your independent study."

4. Everything in *The Great Gatsby* is reported ambiguously; the facts resist reduction to simple certitude. They lend themselves readily therefore to misreadings. The evidence for my reading of the Ella Kaye affair is based on what Nick reports, namely that James Gatz inherited from Dan Cody a legacy of twenty-five thousand dollars. "He didn't get it. He never understood the legal device that was used against him, but what remained of the millions went intact to Ella Kaye. He was left with his singularly appropriate education. . . ." (GG, 121.)

5. Conrad in his preface to Thomas Beer's *Stephen Crane*, 1923, p. 3.

By The Dawn's Early Light *Tender Is the Night*

I never blame failure—there are too many complicated situations in life—but I am absolutely merciless toward lack of effort.
                                        —THE CRACK-UP (1945)

(1)

*To turn the calendar at June and find December
On the next leaf. . . .*

THE SCHIZOPHRENIC NICOLE secretly runs off through the carnival crowds, and secretly Dick Diver pursues her: "her yellow dress twisting through the crowd, an ochre stitch along the edge of reality and unreality"; but he's forgotten his children; "then he *wheeled* and ran back to them, drawing them this way and that by their arms, his eyes jumping from booth to booth." He leaves them with a "young woman behind a white lottery wheel," and darts off to find Nicole, "but he had lost her; he *circled* the merry-go-round, keeping up with it till he realized he was running beside it, staring always at the same horse" (205).[1] Dick's running round in a circle epitomizes his life's progress, ending where he began, never getting ahead of himself, never rising. "The dualism in his views of her— that of the husband, that of the psychiatrist—was increasingly paralyzing his faculties" (204). Her split self is duplicated in his own, and the division between them is symbolized by two carnival wheels: the merry-go-round and the ferris wheel—that's where he finds her.

Dick Diver finds her "in what was momentarily the top boat of the wheel and, as it descended, he saw that she was laughing hilariously" (206). While she soars, Dick Diver, as though ashamed to identify himself with Nicole in her plight, withdraws into the crowd of common carnival spectators, whereas he always wanted to stand out from the mob.

When they first met, he saw her as "a carnival to watch" (41); well, here she is as carnival-to-watch, while the crowd smiles at her "in sympathetic idiocy" (206). The Divers revolve in opposite circles, wheel in diverse directions; but as wheels their identities nevertheless overlap. The vertical ferris wheel is fit symbol for the rising and falling mental cycle of Nicole, for one who transcends reality and returns to it from the heights. And the horizontal wheel that Dick circles is likewise fit symbol for Doctor Diver's plight: never rising but rather, like the prancing wooden horse, finding himself on the same spot—with the same horse, with the same problem. The problem is twofold: a mental patient susceptible to outbreaks of hysteria, and a man whose life progresses only in a circle. What is said of his patients in ego-therapy applies also to Doctor Diver: "their sighs only marked the beginning of another ceaseless round of ratiocination, not in a line as with normal people but *in the same circle*. Round, round, and round. Around forever. But the bright colors of the stuffs they worked with gave strangers a momentary illusion that all was well, as in a kindergarten" (198). One part of Dick Diver's double selfhood is the trained front of arranged attitude and fine manners: "My politeness is a trick of the heart" (176). He, too, presents the air of all is well, as in a kindergarten; all is happy, as in a carnival. "A part of Dick's mind was made up of the tawdry souvenirs of his boyhood" (212).

Of his father it was said "with smug finality in the gilded age: 'Very much the gentleman, but not much get-up-and-go about him'" (221). Like father, like son, with the difference that his father, a clergyman, was a moral guide. (One recalls Lord Jim's father, also a clergyman, with his code of simple truths and his faith in the virtues of conformity. In Conrad's *Lord Jim.*) As Dick and Nicole change places, Nicole coming finally to analyze her husband as though he—not she—were the mental patient, so there is a reversal of roles between Dick and Rosemary: She calls him "youngster" (171), and again four years later when he visits her in her Rome hotel (227). Rosemary has in the interim prostituted herself, and in a different sense so has Dick. " 'Are you actually a virgin?' 'No-o-o!' she sang. 'I've slept with six hundred and forty men—if that's the answer you want.' 'It's none of my business.' 'Do you want me for a case in psychology?' " (229). Do you want me, that is, as another Nicole? As Rosemary "lowered the lights for love," she remarks: "You have the longest eyelashes," to which Dick responds: "We are now back at the Junior Prom. Among those present are Miss Rosemary Hoyt, the eyelash fancier—" (228). The moonstruck Doctor Diver, as though clocked back to his Junior Prom days, regards Rosemary's face: "there was eternal moonlight in it." The difference is that his affair with Rosemary is Dick's first, whereas her affairs—at twenty-two—number—by the hundreds (all of them "abortive"). "She wanted to be taken and was, and what had begun with a childish infatuation on a beach was accomplished at last" (231). Dick's "childish infatuation" of four years ago ends in adultery.

Compared with the experienced Rosemary, Dick *is* Youngster Dick. As for *The Grandeur that was Rome,* the motion-picture Rosemary stars in ("They say it's the first thing I've had sex appeal in"), Dick Diver doesn't face up to the grandeur that was Dick Diver; he ends disintegrated, defeated, and is last seen (as in a motion-picture shot) in diminishing perspective. He descends from the big city to the little village, from Buffalo to Hornell; and in between he moved to Batavia, then Lockport, and then Geneva, New York. Always admired by the ladies, he "always had a big stack of papers on his desk that were known to be an important treatise on some medical subject, almost in process of completion. He was considered to have fine manners and once made a good speech at a public health meeting on the subject of drugs; but he became entangled with a girl who worked in *a grocery store,* and he was also involved in a lawsuit about some medical question; so he left Lockport" (334). This final chapter of *Tender Is the Night* presents Dick Diver in the camera's eye almost vanishing over the horizon. Diver dived not at all. He's a hollywoodized rerun of the story of a boy serialized as Dick Rover; like the Rover boys, Dick Diver never got beyond boyhood. His identity links with Baby Warren as Baby Dick. After marrying Tom Barban, Nicole kept in touch with Dick and liked to think that "his career was biding its time, again like Grant's in Galena" (334). Thus the narrative returns in its ending to its beginning, for the "hero" of Fitzgerald's "biography" is described at the start "like Grant, lolling in *his general store* in Galena . . . ready to be called to an intricate destiny" (6). Notice the clever connection: Grant's general store and the grocery store in Lockport (quoted above, 334), Dick lolling there in an affair with a grocery clerk. And the mention of those unpublished medical studies at the end of Dick's career also returns us to the beginning of the novel.

It begins with a hero in the role of bogus soldier ("I put on my uniform and I felt very bogus about it"), and it ends with a hero as true soldier, Tom Barban. It's on Rosemary's eighteenth birthday that Dick announces he might abandon "what you call my 'scientific treatise' " (123); he ends as bogus healer of the sick. "Doctor Diver's profession of sorting the broken shells of another sort of egg had given him a dread of breakage" (193). His own shell or front consists of good manners, a tender darkness camouflaging the light, the inner truth. "Good manners are an admission that everybody is so tender that they have to be handled with gloves" (193). Tender is the night: "In the dark cave of the taxi, fragrant with the perfume Rosemary had bought with Nicole, she came close again, clinging to him. He kissed her without enjoying it" (125). Rosemary is thus confused with Nicole (by the perfume). Again, by the parallelism of father Warren possessing his daughter, and father Diver corrupting a virgin ("chilled by the innocence of her kiss"). To possess her would be like violating a child: " 'Such a lovely child,' he said gravely" (124). "Take me," says Rosemary; to which Doctor Diver (half in innocence) asks: "Take you where?" Sitting beside her bed, he placates her whim as though he were administering to a clinical patient: " 'Good night, child. This is a damn shame. Let's drop it out of *the picture.*' He gave her two lines of hospital patter to go to sleep on" (127). He calls her "child," and she later calls him youngster; whereby their roles become thus reversed. Reference to "the picture"—"Let's drop it out of the picture"—means in effect that they are acting as in a motion-picture, Rosemary recast with Dick as her Leading Man in *Daddy's Girl.* From bed to beach Doctor Diver exploits Bedside Manners, and Rosemary likewise plays the studied rôle. In egging Dick on to possess her and in weeping when he declines, "she knew too that it was one of the greatest rôles, and she flung herself into it more passionately" (126). Like Dick, she surrenders to empty forms, to the formula of clichés and platitudes, and like Nicole, she confounds reality with unreality in that life is to Rosemary just another motion-picture scenario. Like Nicole, she is *"Daddy's Girl"* (the title of the motion picture she stars in). She is Daddy Dick's girl. Mock scenes pattern the book:

> But Dick closed the subject with the somewhat tart discussion of actors: 'The strongest guard is placed at the gateway to nothing,' he said. 'Maybe because the condition of emptiness is too shameful to be divulged' (131).

What Dick says of actors applies also to himself, for Doctor Dick with his bedside manner is also an "actor"—placing at the gateway to nothing guard, mask, or front. Actress Rosemary, after Dick kisses her goodnight, "got up and went to the mirror, where she began brushing her hair, sniffling a little. One hundred and fifty strokes Rosemary gave it, as usual, then a hundred and fifty more. She brushed it until her arm ached, then she changed arms and went on brushing" (127). Her beauty is as studied as is her "passion." Her "prettiness never seemed exactly her own but rather an acquirement, like her French" (128). She'd like Dick to appear in her movies as her "leading man," and that possibility is the only possibility for Dick to appear as Leading Man. "I've arranged a test for Dick" (a screen test); the untested Dick begs off. They've been watching a rerun of *Daddy's Girl,* that part of the film showing Rosemary and her parent "united at the last in a father complex so apparent that Dick winced for all psychologists at the vicious sentimentality" (131). We recall Nicole's father complex. By crossed identity everyone shares relationships with another.

Daddy Dick is accused of raping a girl child. It happened a few miles outside of Rome: "A native of Frascati had raped and slain a five-year-old child and was to be brought in that morning—the crowd had assumed it was Dick" (252). " 'I want to make a speech,' Dick cried. 'I want to explain to these people how I raped a five-year-old girl. Maybe I did—' " Of course he didn't, but the accusation serves a thematic purpose; we recall that Nicole's ferris wheel hysteria was brought on by the accusation that her husband had kissed a fifteen-year-old girl, her mother's letter accusing him of having seduced her daughter. "This is absurd," Dick argues. "This is a letter from a mental patient." To which Nicole replies: "I was a mental patient" (203). After the ferris wheel incident, she accuses him: "Don't you think I saw that girl look at you—that little dark girl. Oh, this is farcical—a child, not more than fifteen. Don't you think I saw?" (206). That little *dark* girl suggests their own daughter *Topsy*. Thus by implication it is as though Doctor Diver had seduced his own daughter. Again the parallel with Nicole and her father (named Warren to suggest his rabbit-like misbehavior): "What do I care whether Topsy 'adores' me or not? I'm not bringing her up to be my wife" (276).

What *Tender Is the Night* exploits is the overlapping relationship of the worlds of reality and unreality, sanity and insanity, lightness and darkness; by cross identification of the one with the other Fitzgerald fashions the "Humpty Dumpty" fall of our Age of Confusion. Doctor Dick's professional work "became confused with Nicole's problems; in addition, her income had increased so fast of late that it seemed to belittle his work" (183). "Naturally, Nicole, wanting to own him, *wanting him to stand still forever*, encouraged any slackness on his part. . . . He stayed in the big room a long time, listening to the buzz of the electric clock, *listening to time*" (183). Not being able to play on the piano a tune whose words might remind Nicole of his flirtations with Rosemary,

> 'Just picture you upon my knee
> With tea for two and two for tea
> And me for you and you for me——'

it makes Dick feel like a trapped man, no longer free.

"We own you, and you'll admit it sooner or later. It is absurd to keep up the pretense of independence" (Baby Warren's unsaid words, 193). But it is Dick who has ruined Dick. He rationalizes: "I didn't disgrace myself at the height of my career and hide away on the Riviera. I'm just not practising" (124). He practises water stunts on the Riviera, doing his "lifting trick" on the aquaplane: but what he could accomplish with ease two years ago he no longer can perform—he's not in practice. He falls off the board three times: "He could not rise." When Nicole saw Dick "floating exhausted and expressionless, alone with the water and the sky, her panic changed suddenly to contempt" (303). Whereas at the start Nicole was in the power of Doctor Diver, she being his patient, at the end Dick Diver is in the power of Nicole. As we have seen, it is the double wheels—merry-go-round and ferris—of the carnival scene (Book IV, Chapter III) that contrive this reversal of situation. Now at the end, on the Riviera with Nicole and Rosemary, subsequent to his adulterous affair with Rosemary, Dick Diver almost drowns. As for his "lifting trick," he admits: "I couldn't have lifted a paper doll that time." The paper doll he once lifted is, as it were, Rosemary. "Did you hear I'd gone into a process of deterioration?" Rosemary says she'd heard that he had changed. " 'And

I'm glad to see with my own eyes it isn't true.' 'It is true,' Dick answered. . . . The change came a long way back—but at first it didn't show. The manner remains intact for some time after the morale cracks" (Book V, Ch. VII, 304). In his smugness Dick Diver is brother to Nick Carraway of *The Great Gatsby*.

Psychiatrist Diver shares kinship with his mental charges in the Zürich clinic. Its two houses, the Eglantine and the Beeches, "houses for those sunk into eternal darkness, were screened by little copses from the main building, camouflaged strongpoints" (197-198). Here, too, is crossed identity. Eglantine (*i.e.*, honeysuckle), albeit it's the men's building, bears crossed identity with Nicole's garden, and Beeches, the women's building, suggests identity with Dick's beach. " 'Nicole's garden,' said Dick. 'She won't let it alone—she nags it all the time, worries about its diseases. Any day now I expect to have her come down with Powdery Mildew or Fly Speck, or Late Blight" (85). Late Blight is a pun on Nicole's Early Blight: her love for her father. Father Warren confesses the awful story to Doctor Dohmler: "We were just like lovers—and then all at once we were lovers— and ten minutes after it happened I could have shot myself—except I guess I'm such a God-damned degenerate I didn't have the nerve to do it" (18-19).

Another degenerate is Dick Diver. He has wasted himself in a carnival-like life: "The reaction came when he realized the waste and extravagance involved. He sometimes looked back with awe at the carnivals of affection he had given, as a general might gaze upon a massacre he had ordered to satisfy an impersonal blood lust" (84). "Lucky Dick" hasn't the luck to have encountered misfortune at the start: " 'The best I can wish you, my child,' so said the Fairy Blackstick in Thackeray's *The Rose and the Ring*, 'is a little misfortune' " (5). Dick's success comes too early, and his bad luck too late—that's *the* Late Blight. Nicole's situation provides the obverse. *Tender Is the Night* is constructed, like James's *The Ambassadors*, by an hour-glass situation: Nicole and Dick Diver change places.

All's "Humpty Dumpty"—Dick ends as broken shell.

" 'You ruined me, did you?' he inquired blandly. 'Then we're both ruined. So—' " Dick threatens to leap overboard with Nicole from Golding's yacht, the Margin (292). " 'So I'm ruined, am I?' he inquired pleasantly. 'I didn't mean that. But you used to want to create things—now you seem to want to smash them up.' " The change in Dick, Nicole admits, is perhaps her fault—"I've ruined you" (286). At the beginning, when she is in the clinic under Dick's treatment, Dick remarks to Franz: "After all I'm only a sort of stuffed figure in her life" (21). At the end Dick becomes just that. "Grown up, and that is a terribly hard thing to do. It is much easier to *skip it and go from one childhood to another*." So Fitzgerald wrote in his Notebooks (in *The Crack-Up*, edited by Edmund Wilson, p. 126). Well, Dick Diver skips it—he never dives. He falls. He almost falls in his threatened or feigned suicide dive from the *Margin*, at which moment he's at the margin. The fallen Diver collapses into a drunken sleep, "belching now and then contentedly into the soft warm darkness" (293). He's imaged thus as Baby Dick.

(2)

"Do you mind if I pull down the curtain?"
"Please do. It's too light in here."

The split selfhood of Doctor Diver is spelled out, unwittingly, by Rosemary's comparison of him with the two Englishmen "whom Abe [North] addressed conscientiously as 'Major Hengist and Mr. Horsa'" (138), but she concluded that there was no comparison. However, there is comparison of Dick as *Horsa*; for just after his kissing her and declaring he loves her, Rosemary rides on top of thousands of carrots in a market wagon with "a splendidly dressed oil Indian named George T. *Horse*-protection" through Paris "in the false dawn." The connection is that she identifies herself with "a huge *horse*-chestnut tree in full bloom bound for the Champs-Elysées, strapped now into a long truck and simply shaking with laughter—like a lovely person in an undignified position yet confident none the less of being lovely. Looking at it with fascination Rosemary identified herself with it, and laughed cheerfully with it, and everything all at once seemed gorgeous" (141). By this phallic symbol her affair with Doctor Diver is imaginatively consummated. We recall the "pneumatic rubber horse" (74) on the beach that is Dick's beach, where Rosemary fell in love with Dick on first seeing him there as "the man in the jockey cap" (66). He warned her about the sun: "It's not good to get too burned right away"—Nicole was "burned" as a child. As Nicole of Villa Diana figures as Diana, goddess of the moon, to Dick Diver as the sun, so Rosemary figuring as "a young mustang" (177) overlaps in identity with Diana Nicole; horses (I am told) are sacred to the moon goddess. Nicole seemed to Dick "like all the lost youth in the world" (25). Rosemary in *Daddy's Girl* is imaged as *"embodying all the immaturity of the race,* cutting a new cardboard paper doll to pass before its empty harlot's mind" (130). To Rosemary—because Dick is the sun—the Villa Diana "was the centre of the world" (86). Dick, moving as the sun, clips "a square of sunlight off Rosemary's shoulder" (73). Nicole in the crack-up scene, where she attempts suicide by driving the car over the hill (a tree stops the car and saves the family), wears a yellow dress. At the beginning she wore a "cream-colored dress . . . and her very blonde hair dazzled Dick" (25). By her golden hair Nicole shares the attributes of Sun God Dick. *As both women attach to Dick as sun, both also attach to Dick as horse:* By his jockey cap we know him as horse rider, so to speak, and he is identified as horse, a stationary horse, in the merry-go-round scene. Mustang Rosemary links with Horse Trader Nicole: Nicole's grandfather was a "horse-trader" (35), and she trades Horsey Dick for Tom Barban. Nicole, Huntress Diana, discards that role on committing herself to Tom: "no longer was she a huntress of corralled game" (318), the corralled game being Mustang Rosemary and Horsey Dick. Elizabeth Warren—she shortens her name to "Beth" and goes by the nickname "Baby"—reminds Dick of "other women with flower-like mouths *grooved for bits*" (42). She has a Horse Mouth. As for Horsey Nicole, Dick sees her at the start as "a promising colt" (33).

In the incipient period of their tangled affections Dick forgot Nicole, his clinical patient, and flirted with a telephone girl "red lipped like a poster, and known obscenely in the messes as 'The Switchboard' " (14). Miss Switchboard tours Europe "in a desperate roundup of the men she had known in her never-to-be-equalled holiday" (38); the roundup includes every Tom, Dick, and Harry. Nicole switches Tom (Tom Barban) for Dick: Their emotions passed through "her divided self as through a bad telephone connection" (327). Like Nicole, Rosemary "was not yet unified." "Dick saw her with an inevitable sense of disappointment. . . . her body calculated to a millimeter to suggest a bud yet guarantee a flower" (167). Rosemary (emblem of fidelity) doubles with Nicole as flower. At the funicular a sign forbids picking the flowers: "*Défense de cueillir les fleurs*. Though one must not pick flowers on the way up, the blossoms trailed in as they passed—Dorothy Perkins roses dragged patiently through each compartment, slowly waggling with the motion of the funicular, letting go at the last to swing back to their rosy cluster" (40). Nor should Doctor Diver pluck Nicole *on the way up*. Hence his fall. "I can remember how I stood waiting for you in the garden—holding all myself in my arms like a basket of flowers" (48). Nicole, the plucked flower, links with Rosemary, who on the train to Cannes "was sure she could lean from the window and pull flowers with her hand" (70). In Nicole's reverie concluding Chapter I of Book II she confounds herself with Dick and with Lanier, their son: "Sometimes I am Doctor Dohmler and one time I may even be an aspect of you, Tommy Barban. . . . Everything is all right— if I can finish translating this damn recipe for chicken à la Maryland into French" (57). Her reverie ends on "Rosemary who?"—the next scene depicts Gausse's Hôtel des Étrangers, where Rosemary and her mother check in for a three-day visit. *Rosemary,* a fragrant shrub, is used in cookery; hence the connection between "this damn recipe" and "Rosemary who?"

The Divers, "the two Divers," have also in common with Rosemary the fact that she has done diving stunts in her motion picture: "I had to dive and dive and dive all morning" (73). Rosemary and Nicole once lived on the same street in opposite buildings (129). In the Café des Alliées Dick reveals to Rosemary's mother his love for her daughter, and at the end of the narrative Tom in the same Café des Alliées declares his love for Nicole (327). Tom is Life; Dick is Death and Darkness: "I'm the Black Death. . . . I don't seem to bring people happiness any more" (237). As death and life are allies, it is fitting that their final meeting occurs in the Café des Alliées, where Dick—an alien in that he speaks a foreign language—

orders "Blackenwite." Black and white are the figures of Tom and Nicole—
"a man and a woman, black and white and metallic against the sky"—in
the final beach scene. Dick doesn't get the scotch he asked for and settles
for "Johnny Walkair"—Dick Diver as Johnny Walk*air*. " 'Your wife does
not love you,' said Tom suddenly. 'She loves me' " (327). Previous to
this scene, just after Dick's threatened suicide-pact on the *Margin*, the two
men are upstairs at Villa Diana while Nicole in the garden reflects on the
situation, wanting "the situation to remain *in suspension* as the two men
tossed her from one mind to another"—like "a ball" (295).

   That situation "in suspension" recalls the funicular scene at the beginning of the narrative (Book I, Chapter VIII): one mountain-climbing
car—emptied of water in its hydraulic chamber—ascends as its complementary car, having taken on water in its hydraulic chamber, descends
and pulls the lightened car up by gravity. In the ascending car are Nicole
and Doctor Diver—both on their way up, she spiritually and he pro-
fessionally. The history of the promising psychiatrist and of his former
mental patient climbing out of the valley to the "top of the sunshine" is
symbolically epitomized by the relationship of the complementary cars:
Nicole's car ascends while conversely Dick's car drops. The two-car
relationship spells out their reversal of situation. "When the funicular
came to rest those new to it stirred *in suspension* between the blues of two
heavens. It was merely for a mysterious exchange between the conductor
of the car going up and the conductor of the car coming down." At the
carnival crack-up scene, just before Nicole attempts suicide, she cries:
" 'Help me, help me, Dick!' A wave of agony went over him." She is
imaged in his mind as "suspended from him" (207). The motif of suspension and of falls is recurrent throughout the novel. Dick takes his
bicycle with him on the up-going funicular in order to coast down the
Alps (41); once he weds Warren Wealth he coasts downhill forever.

   In Zürich, "home of the toy and the funicular, the merry-go-round and
the thin chime," "life was a perpendicular starting off to a postcard
heaven" (7). Dick, while at the University of Zürich "had felt like a toymaker," and he marvels at the ingenuity of the funicular—a huge hydraulic
toy, as it were. Dick's toy-made world confounds him. If the cable breaks,
life is no perpendicular to a postcard heaven. The incalculable element is
the cable, and Dick is "the incalculable element" (43). "I can see it would
be a terrible thing for Switzerland if a cable broke," says an occupant of
the funicular. When Diver takes his dive he's "Johnny *Walk* [*on*] *air*."
At the start the Divers signed communications "Dicole" (166), like a
*cable*gram code.

   The lightened car ascends as the burdened car descends; while they
complement each other, they move in opposite directions. The parallelism
is provided by the merry-go-round and ferris wheels. Division between
Nicole and Dick is again symbolized by the partition dividing them at the
barber shop: "Dick and Nicole were accustomed to go together to the
barber, and have haircuts and shampoos in adjoining rooms." The ritual—

"to be shorn and washed"—is maimed by Tom Barban's intrusion; he's come to persuade Dick that Nicole wants a divorce. In the Café des Alliées, then, Dick sits "with his face half-shaved matching her hair half-washed" (329). Also her hair is half-cut. Each selfhood is incomplete. "I'm half in love with her," Dick admitted to Doctor Dohmler when Nicole was under his care at the clinic. "What!" snorts Franz. "And devote half your life to being doctor and nurse and all—never!" (31) "I've sort of been father and mother both to her," says Warren of his daughter to Doctor Dohmler (15). Rosemary is half in love with Dick and half in love with Brady: "I fell in love with him (Of Course I Do Love Dick Best but you know what I mean)." Says Mother Speers of her motion. picture daughter: "economically you're a boy, not a girl" (98). "You've suffered," says Doctor Diver to his special patient, "but many women suffered before they mistook themselves for men" (200). On the Divers' beach Dick "inspired a commotion by appearing in a moment clad in transparent black lace drawers"—"lined with flesh-colored cloth." McKisco contemptuously calls it a pansy's trick—"then turning quickly to Mr. Dumphry and Mr. Campion he added, 'Oh, I beg your pardon' " (77). In quarrelling with Dick, Rosemary feels "as if I'd quarrelled with Mother" (237). Mary North, whose former husband—beaten to death in a New York City speakeasy—crawled home to the Racquet Club to die (216), marries an Asian ("not quite light enough to travel in a pullman south of the Mason-Dixon"); North weds South. And the West visits the East when the princely household of the Divers descends upon the princely household of Contessa di Minghetti, lately Mary North (277). Mary Minghetti and Lady Caroline dress in the costume of French sailors and get arrested in Antibes. It's as though they were lesbians: " 'It was merely a lark,' said Lady Caroline with scorn. 'We were pretending to be sailors on leave, and we picked up two silly girls. They got the wind up and made a rotten scene in a lodging house.' Dick nodded gravely . . . like a priest in the confessional" (322). Her confession is a metaphoric comment on Dick's bogus role as priest, and their dressing like men has its inverse parallel in Dick's dressing like a woman. The police chief asks for their *cartes d'identité,* but they have none—they have no identity.

Identity Unknown is wittily instanced again in the murdered man at the Paris boat-train: "The man she shot was an Englishman—they had an awful time finding out who, because she shot him through his identification card" (146). Everyone's identification is shot to pieces: lost, confounded, or mixed. Maimed rituals and scenes of confusion are the dominant leitmotif in *Tender Is the Night*—as also in *The Great Gatsby* and in *The Sun Also Rises.* The sister of a soldier killed in the World War can't find her brother's grave: " 'It had another name on it. I been lookin' for it since two o'clock, and there's so many graves.' 'Then if I were you I'd just lay it on any grave without looking at the name,' Dick advised her" (119). Abe North desecrates the battlefield by imitating the real thing: " 'I'm going to bomb out this trench.' His head popped over the embank-

ment. 'You're dead—don't you know the rules? That was a grenade.' "
Dick apologizes to Rosemary: "I couldn't kid here," but his sentimentalism
is as insincere as Abe's mock-heroics: "Why, this was a love battle—there
was a century of middle-class love spent here. This was the last love
battle." His insincerity on the Battlefield of Love is paralleled by Abe's
mockery of the real thing. They tease the Tennessee girl who came across
the ocean to lay a memorial on her brother's grave, and she with the same
insincerity forgets what she came for and enjoys herself—"even began
flirtations of tropical eyerollings and pawings, with Dick and Abe. They
teased her gently." The self-contradictions of everyone in the novel seem
mocked by the song played obligingly by the orchestra at Amiens: "Yes,
we have no bananas" (120).

Scenes of mock-heroic—parodies of the real thing—pattern the book.
Geneva seen from the funicular is the Center of the World, but at the
center is confusion: "On the centre of the lake . . . lay the true centre
of the Western World. Upon it floated *swans like boats* and *boats like
swans,* both lost in the nothingness of the heartless beauty" (40). The
center of the world is rendered as schizophrenic, with the parallel in Villa
Diana as "centre of the world" and Nicole—all the world's lost youth.[2]
" 'I am here as a symbol of something. I thought perhaps you would know
what it was.' 'You are sick' he said mechanically" (201). His special
patient, an anonymity, is symbol (I presume) of the split selfhood charac-
terizing our sick world, sick and confused by loss of traditional religious
values.

The theme of our loss of faith in religious values and our transference of
faith in science is exemplified in Doctor Diver as mock Christ figure:

Rosemary greets Dick and sees him "as something fixed and godlike"
(167). "She was stricken. She touched him, feeling the smooth cloth of his
dark coat like a chasuble. She seemed about to fall on her knees—from
that position she delivered her last shot. 'I think you're the most wonderful
person I ever met—except my mother' " (95). *Tender Is the Night* is patterned by bathos. "I want to die violently," he had told her, "instead of
fading out sentimentally—that's why I gave this party" (95). He fades
out sentimentally, as befits one whose life consists of All Fool's Day parties.
In France everyone thinks he's Napoleon, whereas in Italy everyone
"thinks he's Christ"—including tin-Christ Dick. Rome, equating with his
rotten past (*i.e., The Grandeur that was Rome*), "was the end of his
dream of Rosemary" (239). Frenchmen thinking they are Napoleon and
Italians thinking they are Christ, both are "schizophrenic"—and so is
Dick himself. Mary Minghetti as a fallen woman figures as Mary Mag-
dallen to Dick as Christ, a fallen Christ (Chapter XII, Book V). The
Fallen Son, Doctor Diver, is cross identified with the fallen son who is
Dick's patient at the clinic, a kleptomaniac and an alcoholic, when Doctor
Diver is accused of having liquor on his breath (271). Father Diver, so
his son thinks, "had betrayed him" (282). At the start of his studies for
psychiatry at Johns Hopkins University, Dick had been "unstayed by the

irony of the gigantic Christ in the entrance hall" (7). Scientist Diver, who ends in a dive into obscure depths, substitutes for Christ; but rather as toy-Christ and "toymaker."

The Fallen Son disgraces himself in Rome, the Papal City: "he felt a vast criminal irresponsibility." He resolves to redeem himself: "he had bizarre feelings of what the new self would be. The matter had about it the impersonal quality of an act of God" (251). (The same godlike attribute characterizes Gatsby in *The Great Gatsby*.) Nicole's father takes up his bed and walks out of the clinic—it's as though Christ Dick had miraculously cured him (268). And simultaneously the Spaniard from Chile begs Doctor Diver to save his alcoholic son; he kneels at Christ Dick's feet: "Can't you cure my only son? I believe in you—you can take him with you, cure him" (265). What actor roles Doctor Diver assumes: mock-Christ and Savior, Fallen Son, Father Dick and Mother Dick, carnival impressario, and clown. He scorns Doctor Schwartz "with his saint's face and his infinite patience in straddling two worlds," but what he says of Schwartz applies to himself, for both are masters at weaving into their professional stock-in-trade sophistries "to the infinite confusion of all values" (210-211). Confusion of values blueprints the novel.

Science as represented by Doctor Diver is the bogus messiah: "I'm trying to save myself," Doctor Dick confesses to Nicole at the end (319). They change places with Nicole attempting to save him. "He raised his right hand and with a papal cross he blessed the beach from the high terrace" (333), a mock priest in blasphemy. "She had come to hate his world with its delicate jokes and politeness, forgetting that for many years it was the only world open to her. Let him look at it—his beach, perverted now to the tastes of the tasteless" (299). "She hated the beach, resented the places where she had played planet to Dick's sun" (307). Like Barban, she belongs to the land, whereas Rosemary associates with the sea and Dick Diver attaches to the in-between beach. Nicole in her garden addresses some rabbits as though addressing her husband: "Hey, Rabbit—hey you! Is it nice—hey? Or does it sound very peculiar to you?" Is it peculiar, that is, that I— Rabbit Warren—should have a lover? And the rabbit she addresses, "after an experience of practically nothing else *and* cabbage leaves, agreed after a few tentative shiftings of the nose" (295).[3] Immediately following this exchange Nicole overhears her gardeners, two men who possessed the same woman: "I laid her down here," says the one; "I took her behind the vines there," says the second who is called a clown. He has a rake, and as Dick is always raking the beach ("*Our* beach that Dick made out of a pebble pile") Clown Dick gets thus cross-identified. Clown Dick possessed two women, Nicole and Rosemary; Nicole—elsewhere described as buying up in wholesale lots underwear and jewels "not a bit like a high-class courtesan"—is possessed by two men, Dick and Tom.

(3)

"Mac thinks a Marxian is somebody who went to St. Mark's school"

As in *The Great Gatsby* Fitzgerald exploits in *Tender is the Night* the leitmotif of doubleness (a variant of the dominant motif of confused identity): Monte Carlo doubles as Hollywood, and the pink step-ins of a French girl double as a flag in rivalry with the Star Spangled Banner. Like "the blur of Mentone," all borderlines get blurred. And identities likewise. Fitzgerald pairs one person with another, fashioning the central theme of split selfhood by the trick of doubleness. There are two ways of the clock: For Dick "time stood still and then every few years accelerated in a rush, like the quick rewind of a film, but for Nicole the years slipped away by clock and calendar and birthday, with the added poignancy of her perishable beauty" (196). It is Dick's clock that is, as it were, schizophrenic. Nicole has two faces, one being the "face of her illness." Chicago, home of the Warrens, has two sides: "a North Side and a South Side and they're very much separated" (45); even Chicago is schizophrenic. So is the clinic of Braun on the Zugersee with its two partners, Franz and Dick Diver. As there are two funicular cars, one going up simultaneously as the second goes down, so there are two battlefields: the battlefield near Amiens and the "battlefield" of the mentally ill at the clinic. "I'm sharing the fate of the women of my time who challenged men to battle," says Dick's special patient at Zugersee. "To your vast surprise it was just like all battles," Doctor Diver responds (200). Another battle is Dick's "battle" against himself, one half of Doctor Diver as curer of the ill and the other half as lover of the ill: This scientist-priest *loves* his special patient: "he went out to her unreservedly, *almost sexually*. He wanted to gather her up in his arms, *as he so often had Nicole,* and cherish even her mistakes, so deeply were they part of her." Hypocrite Dick "stooped and kissed her forehead. 'We must all try to be good,' he said" (201). In mental clinics there are no social seasons such as exist on the Riviera; Rosemary arrives at the Riviera in the off season, "in the lull between the gaiety of last winter and next winter, while up north the true world thundered by" (70). In season and off season the Riviera is not unlike a mental clinic, mad when in season and removed from the true world in interim periods. Time on the Riviera is confounded: on the sunlit beach a woman "in full evening dress, obviously a relic of the previous evening, for a tiara still clung to her head and a discouraged orchid expired from her shoulder," spreads the rumor that Abe North kidnapped a waiter last night in order to saw him in two (61).

This joke is picked up during the party which concludes the Riviera season; Abe North, a rotten musician, plays his musical saw:

"The poor man," Nicole exclaimed. "Why did you want to saw him in two?"

"*Na*turally I wanted to see what was inside. Wouldn't you like to know what was inside a waiter?"

Well, Dick Diver in biding his time is a "waiter." What's inside?

"Old menus," suggested Nicole with a short laugh. "Pieces of broken china and tips and pencil stubs."
"Exactly—but the thing was to prove it scientifically. And of course doing it with that musical saw would have eliminated any sordidness."
"Did you intend to play the saw while you performed the operation?" Tommy inquired (89).

This musical saw of the waiter cut in two provides another variant on the theme of the novel: our split personality and the emptiness within. Nicole "cures" Tom Barban with some special camphor rub—"Dick believes in it." Just then Dick enters: "Believes in what?" (296). The answer is rather zero. It is the same with Barban as his identity is confounded with Dick's by the fact that he's wearing Dick's clothes.

Pagan Barban woos and wins the pagan goddess: "I am Pallas Athene carved reverently on the front of a galley. The waters are lapping in the public toilets and the agate green foliage of spray changes and complains about the stern" (55). She rationalizes that her affair with Tom Barban might have a therapeutic value. When they enter the shore hotel for their love-tryst, they encounter an argument between an American and the desk-clerk about the rate of exchange, an incident having moral overtones in that the rate of exchange for the lovers is adultery. Tom fills out the police blanks—his real, hers false. Nicole has no identity: "You are all new like a baby," says Tom when upstairs. But her rebirth is mocked by the scene occurring outside their hotel window: two women in rocking chairs on the balcony below noisily dispute this or that. "They're here on an economical holiday, and all the American navy and all the whores in Europe couldn't spoil it" (315). What's spoiled is their love-tryst; Nicole puts on her clothes ("they clung together for a moment before dressing"), and that's that. The lovers also are on an "economical holiday" inasmuch as their affair occurs when the Riviera is off-season. Pandemonium startles the coast when the battleship in port sounds a recall, a recall of the sailors who've been whoring it on the Riviera. "Or-ACK—BOOM-M-m-m!"—sounds the battleship's recall from the Battlefield of Love. What follows is an ironic commentary on the Barban-Nicole love-tryst. Two young girls "barbaric" enter the Barban hotel-room and from their balcony shout to their sailor-friends down on the battleship, but amidst the confusion their identity is lost. "By, Charlie! Charlie, look *up!*" But Charlie isn't looking *up* (neither is Barban). "One of the girls hoisted her skirt suddenly, pulled and ripped at her pink step-ins, and tore them to a sizable flag; then, screaming 'Ben, Ben!' she waved it wildly. As Tommy and Nicole left the room it still fluttered against the blue sky. Oh, say can you see the tender color of remembered flesh?—while at the stern of the battleship rose in rivalry the Star Spangled Banner" (315-316). Here, as in the mock battle-field scene (Book III, Chapter I), the real thing is parodied by a false imitation: The Star Spangled Banner rises from the stern of the ship, and the mock flag is hoisted from the stern of the barbaric girl. The civic loyalties of the true thing get confounded thus, prostituted by their mock identity. (The linked example is Dick's wearing flesh-colored panties, wearing woman's underwear as a joke.) So, then, everyone in *Tender Is hte Night* prostitutes himself. Even Tom Barban is suspect inasmuch as he has worn the uniforms of eight countries, changed his allegiance many times. Pink step-ins substitute for the Star Spangled Banner, and spangled are the multiple love affairs in *Tender Is the Night*.

It's sprinkled with spangles, sparkling things, and structurally this novel as poem by its multiple and almost inexhaustible linked analogies fashions "the exquisite inner mechanics" that Fitzgerald found in Keats' "Ode on a Grecian Urn." The same is true of *The Great Gatsby*. "I think you are right," Edmund Wilson wrote Gertrude Stein in 1942 about Scott Fitz-gerald, "that he had the constructive gift that Hemingway doesn't have at all—& I feel sure that some of his work will last" (in *The Flowers of Friendship*). One might reply to Stein and Wilson:

> Oh, say can't you see by the dawn's early light
> How Hemingway's *Sun* is Fitzgerald's *Night?*

For they have the same constructive groundplan as *The Great Gatsby*, all three novels having been made from the same blueprint.   (1960)

NOTES

1. Page references are to the text in *Three Novels of F. Scott Fitzgerald*, edited by Malcolm Cowley (Scribner's, 1953).
2. Nicole as all the world's lost youth figures as young America raped and troubled by her guilty past.
3. When Franz greets Dick at the start of the book, he remarks on Dick's un-aging American face: "You are still a carrot top" (p. 8).

ERNEST HEMINGWAY

The Sun Also Rises—But No Bells Ring

—breathe dead hippo, so to speak, and not be contaminated.
—"Heart of Darkness"

(1)

WE READERS submit to Jake's persuasive voice and end duped into taking for granted that Hemingway's narrator is the spokesman and moral exemplar of the code of the expatriate clan. Edmund Wilson in *The Wound and the Bow* opines: "The young American who tells the story is the only character who keeps up standards of conduct," a myth which remains the still prevailing misreading of the novel. The same applies to Carlos Baker's notion: "The moral norm of the book is a healthy and almost boyish innocence of spirit, and it is carried by Jake Barnes, Bill Gorton and Pedro Romero. Against this norm, in the antithesis of the novel, is ranged the sick abnormal vanity of the Ashley-Campbell-Cohn triangle." But how can the Moral Norm of the novel have its exemplars in Jake, Bill, and Romero when all three default on the code they presume to represent? When Brett remarks, "You wouldn't behave badly," Jake admits: "I'd be as big an ass as Cohn," but in quoting this passage Edmund Wilson lops off Jake's admission, an omission by which Jake is saved. Baker's inaccurate reading of the novel misses the whole thing—in all its counterpointed details. Hemingway's narrator seemingly represents "the true moral norm of the book," but he appears as such only to the prejudiced reader, prejudiced by the bias of the narrator's authoritative voice. The narrator's intention is one thing, and we are caught up in it, in his point-of-view; but resist the narrator's bias, and you read his narrative anew, from the opposite point-of-view.

The Sun Also Rises declares, by my reading, a reversed intention, the obverse being in contradiction of the narrator's biased point-of-view. Read the novel from Cohn's point-of-view, and you end obversely in bias against Jake Barnes and his sophomoric code and his friends who damn Cohn by it. Reversal of intention: that Hemingway consciously schemed it so is evidenced by the fact that his narrator is honest enough to include in his story the self-incriminating testimony of witnesses against him, namely Bill Gorton, Robert Cohn, and Jake Barnes himself. Jake confesses his defections from the code he seemingly exemplifies and from his role as historian of the pretenders to it.

The scene which is crucial to my reading of the reversal of roles occurs at Burguete in Chapter XII; Jake is supplanted in his role as spokesman for the social code of the clan by Bill Gorton. "The Bells are Ringing for Me and my Gal," sings Bill Gorton. He is mocking Jacob, the maimed priest for whom no wedding bells will ever ring. "Oh, Give them Irony and Give them Pity. . . . Just a little irony. Just a little pity. . . ." Pity attaches to Robert Cohn, while irony signifies the social code of that witty tribe whose leader and mock Father Confessor is Jacob, the *Herald* reporter with Biblical name. But now the roles are switched as Bill Gorton dictates the rules of the game. He thereby performs the role of questioner, replacing Jake in his usual role of spokesman and exemplar of the rules of the game:

> 'Ask her if she's got any jam,' Bill said. 'Be ironical with her.'
> 'Have you got any jam?'
> 'That's not ironical. I wish I could talk Spanish.'
> The coffee was good and we drank it out of big bowls. The girl brought in a glass dish of raspberry jam.
> 'Thank you.'
> 'Hey! that's not the way,' Bill said. 'Say something ironical, make a crack about Primo de Rivera.'
> 'I could ask her what kind of a jam they think they've gotten into in the Riff.'
> 'Poor,' said Bill. 'Very poor. You can't do it. That's all. *You don't understand irony. You have no pity.* Say something pitiful.'
> 'Robert Cohn.'
> 'Not so bad. That's better. Now why is Cohn pitiful? Be ironic.'

But Jake begs off replying to Bill's riddle. That Bill is giving Jake the Raspberry is plain enough—by the kind of jam he's eating. Under camouflage of spoofing and pun, Bill is criticizing Jake, who thus takes the place of Cohn. The cross-identity between Jake and Cohn is here replaced by that of Bill and Jake.

Bill knows how to be ironical. "Coffee is good for you," says Bill. "It's the caffeine in it. Caffeine, we are here." He addresses *caffeine:* "It's the caffeine in it. Caffeine, we are here." (Lafayette, we are here, said General Pershing.) Bill addresses caffeine as though addressing a woman: "Caffeine puts a man on *her* horse and a woman in his grave." *Caffeine* as woman transposes into Kathleen, if I may pun. Kathleen puts a man on her horse, but she'll never put Jake on *her* horse because he isn't "a man."[1] Bill's riddle is a criticism of Jake, a nasty dig at the sexless "lover."

> 'You're an expatriate. You've lost touch with the soil. You get precious. Fake European standards have ruined you. You drink yourself to death. You become obsessed by sex. You spend all your time talking, not working. You're an expatriate, see? You hang around cafés.'
> 'It sounds like a swell life,' I said. 'When do I work?'
> 'You don't work. One group claims women support you. Another group claims you're impotent.'
> 'No,' I said. 'I just had an accident.'
> 'Never mention that,' Bill said. 'That's the sort of thing that can't be spoken of. That's what you ought to work up into a mystery [*i.e.,* a mystery befitting the role of tribal king or god, the role of Jake as leader of Expatriate Gentiles]. *Like Henry's bicycle.*'
> He had been going splendidly, but he stopped. I was afraid he thought

he had hurt me with that crack about my being impotent. I wanted to start him again.

'It wasn't a bicycle,' I said. 'He was riding horseback.'

Here comes another riddle:

'I heard it was a tricycle.'
'Well,' I said. 'A plane is sort of like a tricycle. The *joystick* works the same way.'
'But *you* don't pedal it.'

As in *Huckleberry Finn*, it is trick for trick in *The Sun Also Rises*. So far, Bill has the better of Jake as double-talker; but Jake now tosses back the joke to the joker. "No," I said. "I guess *you* don't pedal it." If he means this personally of Bill, the implication is that Bill is also sexless or that he shies from romantic pursuits. Edna is his girl friend, but there is no evidence that he makes a conquest of Edna, that he is sexually promiscuous, or that he has the passionate nature of Cohn. Perhaps, then, it is true that Bill doesn't "pedal it." To pedal it is approved by the prescribed code, but Bill takes no pride in that code. He defaults; but yet he, better than Jake, exemplifies the clan code. Knowing that Jake betrays the code, the very code Jake lives by, Bill ridicules Jake in sardonic parody of what Jake and Jake's code represent. He exposes him as a defaulter. He knows what's what; not Jake. He recognizes that the rules of the game are sophomoric, devoid of any sustaining values. He is spokesman of the Critique of the Code.

As for Henry's bicycle, the likely referent is Henry James, who travelled the English countryside at Rye by bike. The accident James suffered in his youth, by which he was exempted from service in the Civil War, is vulgarly misconstrued here. James was not injured in the loins. (The vulgarized legend has prevailed until rather recently.) Nor was Henry James effeminate—he pedalled a bicycle, not a tricycle. "I think he's a good writer, too," Bill said. The "good writer" is not identified, but as we know from *The Green Hills of Africa*: "The good writers are Henry James, Stephen Crane, and Mark Twain."

Bill adds: "And you're a hell of a good guy. Anybody ever tell you you were a good guy?" At this Jake makes a confession: "I'm not a good guy." (He is no good as lover, he's a false friend, and he's a false exemplar of the code.) Again, Jake's role is reversed; for his role is as priest to whom others make confession. The spoofing ends with Bill calling Jake: "You bum!" (XII).

(2)

As Nick Carraway has doubts about Gatsby, so Jake Barnes mistrusts Robert Cohn: "I mistrust all frank and simple people, especially when their stories hold together, and I always had a suspicion that perhaps

Robert Cohn had never been middleweight boxing champion, and that perhaps a horse had stepped on his face . . . but I finally had somebody verify the story from Spider Kelly" (I). Now in *The Great Gatsby* Nick slyly admits: "I am the only honest person I've known," whereby Hemingway's narrator in saying "I mistrust all frank and simple people" is criticizing Fitzgerald's narrator.

Cohn is frank and simple, whereas Jake is deceptive and complicated. He knows that Cohn's nose was not flattened by a horse, but by the jest he gains in his score against Cohn. The jest is juxtaposed with the truth, the verified fact; but the truth thereby is camouflaged, subsumed by the joke, pun, or riddle. As Nick Carraway criticizes Jordan while simultaneously making love to her, so Jake never praises Cohn without also damning him. The opening statement of *The Sun Also Rises*—"Robert Cohn was once middleweight boxing champion of Princeton"—is juxtaposed with Jake's discrediting simultaneously what he seemingly has praised: "Do not think that I am very much impressed by that as a boxing title, but it meant a lot to Cohn." But that is not true; it no longer means anything to Cohn; *he* never mentions it. "I never met any one of his class [at Princeton] who remembered him. They did not even remember that he was middleweight boxing champion." *Only* Jake remembers it. Cohn's novel, says Jake, wasn't really as bad as the critics said, but Jake immediately retracts his praise by adding: "although it was a very poor novel." He wonders "where Cohn got that incapacity to enjoy Paris" (VI), and he advises Cohn to stay in Paris: "This is the good town" (II). But when he advises Georgette, who hates Paris, he contradicts himself in advising her to go somewhere else. Jake, the maimed lover, seemingly loves Brett while simultaneously confessing: "To hell with Brett. To hell with you, Lady Ashley. . . . I suppose she only wanted what she couldn't have" (IV). But it is Jake himself who wants what he can't have.

Says Cohn: " 'You're really about the best friend I have, Jake.' God help you, I thought" (V). The true friend is Cohn, not Jake. The true lover is Cohn; not Mike, not Brett, not Jake. When Cohn admits that he has fallen in love with Brett, Judas Jake slanders her: "She's a drunk." Cohn insists that Lady Ashley is a lady. Perhaps this is because Cohn is literally near-sighted. "There's a certain quality about her, a certain fineness. She seems absolutely fine and straight." Coarse and crooked she is— not the lady Cohn mistakenly thinks she is, but Cohn is a gentleman. He defends her. "I don't believe she would marry anybody she didn't love." "Well," says Jake, "she's done it twice" (V). Jake has said the same thing about Cohn: "I am sure he had never been in love in his life" (II). But it is Jake who has never been in love in his life. Characteristically, what Jake says of his friends applies also to himself. Jake's portrait of Cohn reflects himself; it tells us as much about Jake as about Cohn.

On Jake's own admission, we cannot accept his portrait of Cohn with any certitude: "Somehow I feel that *I have not shown Robert Cohn clearly*" (VI). "He was a nice boy, a friendly boy, and very shy. *and it made him bitter"* (I). But it is Jake who is bitter. "As he had been thinking for months about leaving his wife and had not done it because *it would be too cruel to deprive her of himself,* her departure was a very healthful shock" (I). But that perverts the truth. Cohn did not leave his wife; she left him. Our nasty-tongued narrator slants it. Jake Barnes, New York *Herald* journalist, is not a trustworthy reporter. "He was not in love yet but he realized that he was an attractive quality to women, and that the fact of a woman caring for him and wanting to live with him was not simply *a divine miracle.* This changed him so that he was not so pleasant to have around" (II). But it is Jake who is not an attractive quality to women; marriage for Jake is possible only by divine miracle. And it is Jake and Mike with their nasty tongues who are not pleasant to have around. Jake, bitter about his own status as sexual outcast, castigates the outcast Cohn for his nonconformity.

Cohn does not realize that his pretended friend hates him, nor does he suspect the reason for it; nor can he understand why Brett betrays him. He wants to marry her. "Poor devil!" says Brett, partly in pity and partly in irony, when Jake remarks that Cohn cannot keep away from her. The prejudiced narrator admits: "I was enjoying Cohn's nervousness. . . . It was lousy to enjoy it, but I felt lousy. Cohn had a wonderful quality of bringing out the worst in anybody" (XVI). When Brett and Mike send a telegram from San Sebastian, Jake falsifies the message in order to rib Cohn: "Send their regards to you." He admits:

> Why I felt that impulse to devil him I do not know. Of course I do know. I was blind, unforgivingly jealous of what had happened to him. The fact that I took it as a matter of course did not alter that any. I certainly did hate him. I do not think I ever really hated him until he had that little spell of superiority at lunch—that and when he went through all that barbering (X).

After her affair with Cohn at San Sebastian, Brett says to Jake: "I thought it would be good for him"—*that* is her brand of cruelty to Cohn. She feels superior to him. Jake responds: "You might take up social service." Says Brett: "Don't be nasty" (IX). Cohn is never nasty-tongued. But Jake, even when praising Cohn as a good tennis-player and fair sport ("He was not angry at being beaten"), injects his characteristic sneer: "He was nice to watch on the tennis-court, he had a good body, and he kept it in shape; he handled his cards at bridge; and *he had a funny sort of undergraduate quality about him. If* he were in a crowd nothing he said stood out" (VI). He begins in praise of Cohn and then he retracts. "I do not believe he thought much about clothes"—that tells us that clothes and the equivalent in smart speech as the masking thing represent the prerequisites of the sophomoric fraternal code to which Cohn remains outcast. It is the prep-school code that has "a funny sort of undergraduate quality," rather than Cohn himself.

"He had a nice, boyish sort of cheerfulness," Jake admits, a cheerfulness "that had never been trained out of him, and *I probably have not brought it out*" (VI). "I never joke people," admonishes the Count (VII). But to joke your friends is the thing to do, and they all insult Cohn because he does not participate in their social game of irony. "But here was Cohn taking it all. Here it was, all going on right before me, and I did not even feel an impulse to try and stop it. And this was friendly joking to what went on later" (VI). Even of Jake's wound they joke: "what's happened to me is supposed to be funny." Cohn, like the Count, never jokes his friends. "You've got to take that back," Cohn threatens Jake on his insulting Brett; to which Jake retorts: "Oh, cut out the prep-school stuff" (V). But what is *his* code if not prep-school stuff? Gentleman Cohn does not say anything that stands out in a crowd because his standards are those of the gentleman. "He can be damn nice," Jake admits. "I know it. That's the terrible part," Bill Gorton concedes (X). The terrible part is that he confounds the code. "The funny thing is he's nice, too. I like him," says Bill. "But he is just awful." Cohn is awful because he is always merely nice. Niceness is discredited because it declares a weakness, an exposed flaw in the mask of mock sophistication which Jake and his friends subscribe to. The criterion is irony, and Cohn never once speaks ironically.

Hence Cohn is unique. The word "bullfight" is unique, for "There is no Spanish word for bull-fight"; nor is there any Spanish word for *Cohn*. Jake receives Cohn's telegram in Spanish: "Vengo Jueves Cohn." How translate *that?* "What does the word *Cohn* mean?" Bill jokingly asks Jake (XIII). That is very funny, but the significance is that Cohn is as unique as his name is untranslatable. Jake sneers at Cohn's telegram: " 'What a lousy telegram,' I said. 'He could send ten words for the same price. "I come Thursday." That gives you a lot of dope, doesn't it?' 'It gives you all the dope [says Bill] that's of interest to Cohn.' " They criticize Cohn for being "snooty" in sending his too brief wire, but then they send Cohn a reply which is equally snooty—brief, it is one word briefer than Cohn's telegram. It reads: "Arriving tonight." "That's enough," says Jake (XIII). They exonerate themselves of infractions of the code they themselves commit. But they do not permit Cohn the same privilege. Cohn doesn't jest with Brett; instead he "just looked at her" (XIII). That is precisely what Romero does on first seeing Brett. They criticize Cohn for staring Brett down, but they exempt Romero from condemnation.

In both *The Sun Also Rises* and *The Great Gatsby* the narrators default on the standards by which they measure and judge others. Duplicity characterizes both narrators. "That was it. Send a girl off with one man. Introduce her to another to go off with him. Now go and bring her back. And sign the wire with love" (XIX). Here is Jake the priest in the rôle of Jake the pimp. We recall Nick Carraway writing his girl out in the West and signing his letter "with love," while at the same time he is courting Jordan. Moral ambivalence defines both narrators. "*I have a nasty tongue,*" so Hemingway's narrator confesses (V). He reports that Cohn "had married on the rebound from the rotten time he had in college, and Frances took him on the rebound from his discovery that he had not been everything to his first wife" (I). Maybe not, but he had been true to her, and he also had been true to Frances. So much Jake admits in saying that "for four years his horizon had been absolutely limited to his wife. For three years . . . he had never seen beyond Frances." So, then, the very fact of Cohn's fidelity is made to count against him—it limited his horizon! But surely Cohn's fidelity exonerates him and condemns Jake's own limited horizon. Unlike Joker Jake, Cohn is serious about life and tries to face realities. When Brett reads Romero's palm and prophesies "I think he'll live a long time," Romero answers boastfully: "I'm never going to die" (XVI). Cohn, on the contrary, recognizes the brevity of life: "I can't stand it to think my life is going so fast and I'm not really living it." Nor is any one properly living it among the Jake clan—not *really* living it. Jake answers: "Nobody ever lives their lives all the way up except bull-fighters" (II). It is an excuse for himself not trying to live it, in time-now. Bill bets that Brett and Mike will arrive at Pamplona on time that night, and Jake responds: "You've got a rotten chance. They've never been on time anywhere" (XII). Cohn, on the contrary, is always on time. Speaking of Zizi, the Count says: "You know, I think that boy's got a future. But personally I don't want him around" (VII). "Jake's the same way," says Brett. The parallel is with Cohn, whom nobody wants around. Candidates for the Future are not wanted; Jake doesn't want anyone with a future around because he himself has none. If anyone in *The Sun Also Rises* has possibilities for the future, it is Cohn.

"Because they were against Belmonte the public were for Romero" (XVIII); that duplicates Cohn's plight. They are against Cohn for the reason that he exemplifies a social standard in opposition to their own code. Cohn, by my reading, exemplifies Christian decency, courtly love, humanitarianism, gentlemanly courtesy, warmth of heart, and thoughtfulness for others. He is constantly asking Jake for pardon, for forgiveness: "I wish you'd forgive me that" (XV). But Mike persists in taunting him because Cohn had said he'd find the bullfight boring. "Let up on that, Mike. I said I was sorry I said it." But they won't forgive Cohn, who asks to be forgiven. They insult him, but they won't permit Mike to be "insulted": "They can't insult Mike," Bill said. "Damned English swine come here and insult Mike and try and spoil the fiesta" (XVII). Bill calls Mike a swell fellow: " 'Who cares if he is a damn bankrupt?' His voice broke." Bill's maudlin sentiment is wasted on Mike, the heel and moral bankrupt. Bill calls the Englishmen dirty swine; "I'm going to clean them out." The drunken Bill plays momentarily the role of Hercules cleaning out the stables. Cohn demands that Jake tell him where Brett has gone off to, and damns Jake the priest as Jake the pimp: "I'll make you tell me'—he stepped forward—'you damned pimp' " (XVII). Cohn knocks down first Jake and then Mike, whereupon Edna (Bill's girl, whom Mike picked up when Brett went off with Romero) says: "I'd like to have seen

Bill knocked down, too. I've always wanted to see Bill knocked down. He's so big" (XVII). Like Mike and Jake and Romero, Bill has a snooty air of superiority. They all get knocked down, excepting Bill and Cohn. "Take me away from here," Edna cries, "you bankrupts" (XVII). Only Cohn escapes her condemnation.

Contra Carlos Baker's notion of "the moral vacuum in Cohn," Cohn stands out as exemplar of the Christian virtues. That *moral vacuum* is located—by my reading—in Jake, in Brett, and in Mike; also in Romero. "Montoya could forgive anything of a bull-fighter who had afición." " 'I feel sorry about Cohn,' Bill said. 'He had an awful time.' 'Oh, to hell with Cohn,' I said" (XVIII). Montoya forgave Jake "all my friends" (XIII), and Cohn practices the same saving grace. But Jake, unlike Montoya, does not forgive. "Forgive you, hell." Cohn then pleads:

'I just couldn't stand it about Brett. I've been through hell, Jake. It's been simply hell. When I met her down here Brett treated me as though I were a perfect stranger. I just couldn't stand it. We lived together at San Sebastian. I suppose you know it. I can't stand it any more' (XVII).

Jake turns away to go to the bathroom; he turns on the taps, but "the water would not run." No water flows, signifying that he has not earned the rites of purification. He has forgiven Cohn verbally, as it were, but not out of heart.

Hemingway's narrator obscures the true nature of Robert Cohn. Given to outspoken sentiment, Cohn is friendly and generous, not petty and mean, nor nasty-tongued. Asked by Jake, "Do you know any dirt?" (dirt to use in his gossip column in the New York *Herald*), Cohn replies: "No" (II). Cohn has a clean mind and, unlike Jake and Jake's clan, he is incapable of slander. It is Jake who has a dirty mind: "I have a rotten habit of picturing the bedroom scenes of my friends" (II).

The standard Hemingway reading has it that Pedro Romero is the "only completely admirable character in *The Sun Also Rises*," and the latest version—Kenneth Kinnamon in *Texas Studies*, I (Spring 1959)—also adds that the moral stature of Romero is pointed up in the Brett-Cohn-Romero rivalry: "The rivalry culminates in a fist fight in which Cohn, although the physical victor, suffers complete moral defeat." This squares with Baker's version: Brett rejects Cohn because "he is unmanly," and Cohn "leaves Pamplona under the cloud of his own ruination" (pp. 92, 86). Perhaps I am like Cohn, near-sighted; but I fail to see Cohn's defeat as a moral defeat. It is *before* the fist-fight occurs that Cohn gives up Brett; not afterward, and not because of it. He told Jake: "I'm going away in the morning" (XVII). Nor is there anything unmanly about Cohn. "He is the most normal character in the book," as Arthur L. Scott argues in the only article I know of "In Defense of Robert Cohn" (*College English:* March 1957). Romero did not ruin Cohn; that is merely Mike's report. As Scott points out, "it is a grave mistake either to condemn Cohn as one 'of the damned' (Delmore Schwartz) or to deride him as 'a shallow sentimentalist' (Theodore Bardacke) or 'an importunate romantic oaf' (W. M. Frohock). It is the mistake of adopting uncritically the prejudices of the book's characters. A worse mistake would be difficult." *Contra* Carlos Baker, Cohn and Romero "actually have more in common with each other than any of the other characters. Cohn is obviously out of place amid all this frenetic joy-seeking. So is Romero." Both are outsiders. Etc. Romero, whom Cohn has knocked down again and again (he "massacred the poor, bloody bull-fighter"), staggers over to Cohn and asks to be hit again (so Mike reports it). " 'So you won't hit me?' 'No,' said Cohn. *'I'd be ashamed to.'* So the bull-fighter fellow hit him just as hard as he could in the face, and then sat down on the floor. He couldn't get up, Brett said. Cohn wanted to pick him up and carry him to bed" (XVII). Cohn's "I'd be ashamed to" stamps Cohn as the gentleman. "Then Cohn leaned down to shake hands with the bull-fighter fellow. No hard feelings, you know. All for forgiveness. And the bull-fighter chap hit him in the face again." Nevertheless, Romero is exonerated by the standard Hemingway Reader. Hemingway's public has been brain-washed by the Hemingway Code.[2]

(3)

The story narrated by Jake Barnes is the story of Robert Cohn, the betrayed tin Christ. Everyone in *The Sun Also Rises* regards himself as a little tin Christ—the exceptions are the Count and Montoya *and* Cohn. They crucify Cohn as though he were one. They hang a wreath of twisted garlics around his neck while he sleeps on some wine-casks: " 'Let him sleep,' the man whispered. *'He's all right'* " (XV). "What a lot we've drunk," says Cohn on waking up from his nap; to which Brett replies: "you mean what a lot *we've* drunk. You went to sleep." Just previously she had said that Cohn "passed out," and Mike in Spanish asked: "Where is the drunken comrade?" Cohn is not the drunken comrade that Mike calls him, nor has he passed out, as Brett claims. Their calumny is refuted by Jake's report: "Mike was a bad drunk. Brett was a good drunk. Bill was a good drunk. *Cohn was never drunk*" (XIV).

They blaspheme him. When Mike demands of Cohn "Eat those garlics" (XV), it is as though Cohn were Christ—Cohn crucified by Judas Mike. When Cohn awakes, it is as though Christ Cohn were resurrected from the dead: "I must have been sleeping," said Cohn. "Oh, not at all," said Brett. "You were only dead," said Bill. "What time is it?" Cohn asks. "It's tomorrow. You've been asleep two days." (It is in fact the same Sunday night of the opening day of the fiesta.) Their joke is a mockery of the San Fermin festival, a religious festival; Christ Cohn is dead and now is reborn.

Says Judas Jake: "I'm not sorry for him. I hate him, myself." Says Brett: "I hate him, too. . . . I hate his damned suffering" (XVI). "Go away, for God's sake. Take that sad Jewish face away." So Mike speaks of Cohn as though Cohn were Christ. "I do not know how people could say such terrible things to Robert Cohn," says Jake, who himself contributes a majority share in the general condemnation of Cohn. "There are people to whom you could not say insulting things. They give you a feeling that the world would be destroyed, would actually be destroyed before your eyes, if you said certain things. But here was Cohn taking it all" (VII). Judas Mike appeals to Jake to justify his rudeness: "Don't you think I'm right?" He almost weeps: "I love that woman." But notice that a moment later he flirts with Bill's girl, Edna: "You're a lovely thing. *Have* we met?" (XVI). And Brett asks Jake whether he still loves her while simultaneously telling him she's "a goner" for love of Romero, albeit she is Mike's fiancée. The only faithful lover is Cohn, and that explains his "suffering." When he moves to sit down beside Brett, she tells him: "For God's sake, go off somewhere. Can't you see Jake and I want to talk?" He apologizes, saying he didn't notice it and adding as an excuse: "I thought I'd sit here because I felt a little tight" (XVI). He wants to sit next to Brett, but he fibs to mask the truth. "Was I rude enough to him?" Brett asks Jake. They all appeal to Jake for judgments. Cohn's "behaved very badly," in that he keeps following Brett around; but she admits she knows how he feels: "He can't believe it didn't mean anything." Cohn takes seriously his love for that bitch.

"That Cohn gets me," says Bill. "He's got this Jewish superiority so strong that he thinks the only emotion he'll get out of the fight [bull-fight] will be being bored" (XV). But it is Jake, rather than Cohn, whose air of superiority damns him. "You *are* superior," says Brett to Jake on his deserting her to talk bull with Romero (XVI). Thus again they change places. It goes unnoticed by the casual reader that Jake exhibits airs of superiority or that Cohn exemplifies moral superiority. Bill calls it "Jewish superiority," but the one equates with the other. "I liked to see him [Mike] hurt Cohn. I wished he would not do it, though, because afterward it made me disgusted at myself. That was a morality; things that made you disgusted afterward. No, that must be immorality" (XIV). Well, then, on his own admission the narrator of *The Sun Also Rises* is morally confused. The superstition that Jake is "the only character who keeps up standards of conduct" is readily refuted by a close scrutiny of the narrative. The only moral standard Jake claims is "Just exchange of values" (XIV). Jake derives his philosophy from Bill Gorton, who remarked as they passed a taxidermist's shop: "Simple exchange of values. You give them money. They give you a stuffed dog" (VIII). Or, as a writer, you give them a stuffed book. "Going to have that horsecab stuffed for you for Christmas. Going to give all my friends stuffed animals. I'm a nature-writer." Jake and his friends are all stuffed animals. Jake jokes at Bill's expense: "He's a taxidermist."

Harvey Stone tells a Mencken joke against a Jew named Hoffenheimer —"he's a garter snapper." "That's not bad," says Jake (VI). But who best fits the joke? It is Jake himself who is the "garter snapper." Not Cohn —at love he is *aficionado*. Cohn, as Mike admits, "Wanted to make an honest woman of her [Brett], I imagine" (XVII). But Brett's a kept woman who can't be kept; neither can she be reformed.

Lady Brett Ashley has no sense of values *and* she has no sense of time: "I looked at the clock. It was half-past four. 'Had no idea what hour it was,' Brett said" (IV). She insults the Count: "You haven't any values. You're dead, that's all." But it is just the obverse, and the Count rightly replies: "No, my dear. You are not right. I'm not dead at all." (VII). It is Brett who has no values. "I misjudged you," says Harvey Stone to Robert Cohn. "You're not a moron. You're only a case of *arrested* development" (VI). But it is just the obverse, and we know by his very name that *Stone* is a case of arrested development. Arrested development is imaged likewise by the Paris statues: in the statue of the inventor of the semaphore "engaged in doing same" (VI), in the statue of "two men in flowing robes" (VIII), and in the statue of Marshal Ney "in his top-boots, gesturing with his sword among the green new horse-chestnut leaves" (IV). These statues represent time frozen in stone, the negation of life in flux, while the newly leaved chestnuts are a phallic emblem in mockery of Jake Barnes, the sexless lover.

Another example of Arrested Development, again in mockery of Jake's plight, occurs in the scene at Burguete where Jake, while waiting for Bill Gorton to return from fishing, kills time by reading a book. It is a book by A. E. W. Mason (the novelist friend of Henry James and Stephen Crane), "a wonderful story about a man who had been frozen in the Alps and then fallen into a glacier and disappeared, and his bride was going to wait twenty-four years exactly for his body to come out on the moraine, while her true love waited too, and they were still waiting when Bill came up" (XII). The lover frozen in time has its parallel in Jake Barnes, the lover incapacitated for living life in its flux. His predicament is about the same, except that unlike the glacier-lovers Jake's beloved Brett is *not* waiting for Jake to thaw out. Jake and Brett are cases of Arrested Development. Jake's quest—"All I wanted to know was how to live it"— recalls Lambert Strether's quest in Henry James's *The Ambassadors*. The Jamesian theme—"how to live it"—is inverted in *The Sun Also Rises* and in *The Great Gatsby*, for here Strether's "empty present" is rendered as the corrupted present. They recreate, to use Conrad's phrase, "holes in space and time." How *not* to live it is exemplified by everyone in *The Great Gatsby*, notably by Gatsby himself. The theme of the Rotten Present—hinted at in *The Great Gatsby* by the jazz-piece "In the meantime / In between time / Ain't we got fun?"—is echoed by Hemingway's drummer shouting: "You can't two-time————." Brett two-times Michael in her affair with Cohn, and also in her affair with Romero; Cohn is two-timed in his love for Brett and also in his friendship with Jake Barnes. The Conradian theme of betrayal links both *The Great Gatsby* and *The Sun Also Rises*.

Everything in *The Sun Also Rises* is rotten. Hemingway told Fitzgerald that *The Sun Also Rises* was "a hell of a sad story," whose only instruction was "how people go to hell" (Quoted from Baker, p. 81). "Isn't it rotten?" Brett admits to Jake. "There isn't any use my telling you I love you" (VII). As though she had just read Eliot's *Waste Land,* Brett says: "My nerves are rotten" (XVI). She is a rotten lover; she never writes Mike any letters and she reveals Cohn's love letters. Mike is a rotten lover, and so is Jake. "You are a rotten dancer, Jake" (VII). He thinks to himself: "Well, it was a rotten way to be wounded and flying on a joke front like the Italian" (IV). A rotten drinker (as is also Brett), he gets "a rotten headache" (IV). "I was such a rotten Catholic," Jake admits. A rotten Catholic is a case of Arrested Development.

That *Jake is a rotten sport* is hinted at by his reading while drunk Turgenev's *A Sportsman's Sketches.* His nights are, like Gatsby's, loveless; he dreads the night and, like Gatsby, awaits the sun also rising. "What a lot of bilge I could think up at night. What rot, I could hear Brett say it. What rot!" (XIV). "I have a rotten habit of picturing the bedroom scenes of my friends" (II). Zizi, whom the Count supports, is a "rotten painter," and Jake and Mike are rotten writers; "I'm ashamed of being a writer," Bill Gorton admits (XVI). Asked how his writing is going, Cohn answers: "Rotten" (V). Is it not that everything is rotten because of the rotten morality of their time?

In both *The Great Gatsby* and *The Sun Also Rises* moral confusion equates with temporal confusion. When Jake Barnes is with the harlot Georgette, "The cab passed the New York *Herald* Bureau with the window full of clocks. 'What are all the clocks for?' she asked. 'They show the hour all over America.' 'Don't kid me' " (III). Those *Herald* clocks, by which Georgette is confounded, are contradictory; they represent time as confused.

So, then, escape from Time. San Sebastian offers a world removed from time and realities, a sense of renewed life by escape from it. So it was for Cohn in his San Sebastian tryst with Brett, and also for Jake and Bill during their fishing trip in the mountains. When their gloriously happy drunken time ends for Harris, at the news that Jake and Bill must depart, Harris says: "What a rotten business. . . . What rotten luck for me" (XIII). Good times end in rotten times, and as in *Farewell to Arms* there is no sanctuary. In the Burguete mountains Jake's reading "a week-old Spanish newspaper" is, in effect, as though he had gained a week, and arriving at San Sebastian: "Spain had not changed to summertime, so I was early. I set my watch again. *I had recovered an hour by coming to San Sebastian.*" He escapes to the sea: "The water was buoyant and cold. It felt as though you could never sink" (XIX). But the quietude of this idyllic scene—Jake floating on the raft—is disrupted by Brett's telegram begging him to return to Madrid ("AM RATHER IN TROUBLE BRETT"); whereby he is forced to return to the Brett world of discord and confusion, to face again the rotten times.

And he ends where he began—at dead end. "The North Station in Madrid is the end of the line. All trains finish there. They don't go on anywhere." The sterile Brett and the impotent Jake have reached the end of *their* line, a dead spot in their journeying; and it was the same at the very start of the novel: when Jake saw a string of barges on the Seine "towed empty down the current"—down the current of life, with the empty barges as symbolic of Jake's life. Brett had just then deserted him; so he reflects as his taxi passes the Paris statue of the inventor of the semaphore. Hemingway juxtaposes the statue with the river (life in flux). Semaphores regulate traffic so as to prevent wrecks, and social codes act as invisible semaphores in our routine life. Thinking of Brett and noticing the semaphore statue, Jake remarks: "The Boulevard Raspail always made dull riding. It was like a certain stretch on the P.L.M. between Fontainebleau and Montereau that always made me feel bored and dead and dull. I suppose it is some association of ideas that makes those dead places in a journey" (VI). In *The Great Gatsby* "dead places in a journey" include that stretch between West Egg and New York City where the motor-road joins the railroad "so as to shrink away from a certain desolate area of land"—the valley of ashes.

As time and morality are rendered confused, so too are identities. Cohn wakes from a dream and hears Brett's voice. "Half asleep I had been sure it was Georgette. I don't know why" (IV). The answer is that they share identity. Brett is identified as defiled womanhood by the rhyming of her name with Georgette, the harlot, and with Lett, the homosexual. And also by her boyish haircut and mannish felt hat. Because her hair is brushed back like a boy's, Romero is ashamed of Brett: "He wanted me to grow my hair out. Me, with long hair. I'd look so like hell. . . . He said it would make me more womanly" (XIX). Brett's former husband, a sailor, "made Brett sleep on the floor" (XVII), where presumably they copulated—like swine. Cohn calls Brett "Circe," says Mike. "He claims she turns men into swine" (XIII). "Don't be an ass," says Brett of Mike, who in turn calls Cohn an ass. He says the same of Bill: "I say, Bill is an ass" (XVI). But it is notably Mike who deserves that epithet. He behaves like "a swine." Brett belongs in the same category: "I say, Brett, you are a lovely piece" (VIII). " 'Everybody behaves badly,' I said. 'Give them the proper chance.' 'You wouldn't behave badly,' Brett looked at me." To which Jake Barnes admits: "I'd be as big an ass as Cohn" (XIII). Thus as in *The Great Gatsby*, identities overlap.

The Palace Hotel Bar substitutes for a church with Brett making confession to Jake-as-priest: "You know it makes one feel rather good deciding not to be a bitch. . . . It's sort of what we have instead of God." But it was not Brett who ruined Romero, for Romero has already been despoiled by two women prior to his affair with Brett, and therefore Brett has not earned even the privilege of Not Being a Bitch.

> 'Some people have God,' I said. 'Quite a lot.'
> 'He never worked very well with me.'
> 'Should we have another martini?' (XIX)

God does not work very well with Jake either, and he'd rather drink than think about it. Substitute for God, then, a martini! *Crossed-identity confounds everything in the novel:* hotel as church, and hotel as brothel. " 'We have got the loveliest hotel,' Mike said. 'I think it's a brothel!' " (III). Vienna is identified with Paris (VIII). Vienna is the city of betrayal: a Negro prize-fighter "betrayed" a rotten contract by knocking out a white boy, and you can't do that in Vienna; wherefore Paris— personified by Brett—is also the city of betrayal. The Paris night-club where Jake dances with Brett has the ironical name "the Bal restaurant,"[3] as though this place were the temple of the ancient Semitic sun-god of fertility—Baal, a false idol. At the religious festival of San Fermin "Some dancers formed a circle around Brett and started to dance. . . . Brett wanted to dance but they did not want her to. They wanted her as an image to dance around." In the circle also are Jake and Bill; they are all three false idols. The dancers hang a wreath of garlics around her neck, and later Cohn wakes from his nap on the wine-casks to find a wreath of "twisted garlics" (XV). Thus every person interlinks with another. The scene of the dancers links with the bull-fight scene; for when Romero has triumphed, some boys dance "around the bull" (XVIII).

Jake spoofs Mrs. Braddocks by introducing the harlot as his financée, Mademoiselle Georgette Leblanc. Mrs. Braddocks, while Georgette with her mouthful of rotten teeth "smiled that wonderful smile," asks: "Are you related to Georgette Leblanc, the singer?" "Not at all," says Georgette. "My name is Hobin." It is as though she had read *The Great Gatsby*, between whose covers exist more examples of confused identities than in any other novel excepting *The Sun Also Rises*. " 'But Mr. Barnes introduced you as Mademoiselle Georgette Leblanc. Surely he did,' insisted Mrs. Braddocks. . . . 'He's a fool,' Georgette said" (III). When Jake asks for Lady Ashley at the Hotel Montana, the maid does not know her by name. "Is there an Englishwoman here?" To which the sullen maid responds: " Muy buenos. [*sic*] Yes, there is a female English." The maid returns to say that "the female English wanted to see the male English now, at once" (XIX). Their anonymity associates with the theme of fragmented selfhoods. It is the same in *The Great Gatsby*. "You got the most class of anybody I ever seen," says the Count in his maimed English; but Brett is incomplete, a fragmented personality —as is indicated by the Count's criticism of her: "You never finish your sentences at all" (VII). "Is she really Lady something or other?" asks Bill of Jake. "Oh, yes. In the stud book and everything" (VIII).

Nobody has self-entity. Not even Romero does; on the occasion of his first bull he imitates Belmonte's style, or so the crowd thinks: "They thought Romero was afraid. . . . They preferred Belmonte's imitation of himself or Marcial's imitation of Belmonte" (VIII). As in *The Great Gatsby*, everyone—including even the Count—is maimed physically or defaults spiritually. Cohn with his flattened Jewish nose recalls Wolfsheim's tragic nose (in *Gatsby*); "a flat-nosed Jew whistling the rosary."

Mike Campbell has an injured nose, likewise. Romero bears a triangular scar, Belmonte is sick with a fistula, Georgette is ill with the disease of her trade, and Jake is afflicted with a wound in the loins.

As in *The Great Gatsby,* spoofing and puns and riddles comprise the witty ironic tone of *The Sun Also Rises.* As Gatsby's first name—Jay—rhymes with the last names of the two women who betray him (Fay and Kaye), so Hemingway's Harvey Stone rhymes with Cohn, "drink" with "don't think," Mike with *Kike* Cohn. The Jews Brett borrows money from "are not really Jews. We just call them Jews. They're Scotsmen, I believe" (XIX). Mike, the Scotsman, obversely links thus with Cohn —"that kike!" Jake has insomnia and is haunted; Bill's motto is "Never be daunted." Cohn is bored, and the steers are gored. Mike wouldn't read Cohn's letters to Brett. "Damned noble of you," says Jake (XIII). Noble translates into No Bull. Jake, Mike, and Bill talk "bull," and the bull-fighters kill the bull. "The bulls are my best friends," says Romero. "You kill your friends?" asks Brett. "Always," Romero replies. "So they don't kill me" (XIII). The same applies to the relationship of Jake and Mike to Robert Cohn; they "kill" their friend. When Jake at Burguete opens his daily mail, he finds two letters and two bull-fight newspapers. "One was orange. The other yellow. They would both have the same news, so whichever I read first would spoil the other" (IV). It is the same with the persons of the novel as with the two newspapers, for each person spoils the other's selfhood.

"Almost any exhibition of complete self-sufficiency," says Nick Carraway, "draws a stunned tribute from me." That is because there is no one in *The Great Gatsby* who exemplifies self-sufficiency. It is the same in *The Sun Also Rises:* crossed identity and things-by-pairs, *because* nothing has self-entity. Crossed identity links thus with the theme of moral and temporal confusion, and the fragmented personalities manifest the fragmented morality of the age. It was this theme that Fitzgerald evoked in *The Great Gatsby,* deriving it from Eliot's *Waste Land.*

Things-by-pairs characterizes both novels. Of the two sets of "lovers," Cohn and Frances are each divorced; Brett and Mike await divorce-papers. Brett marries men she does not love: "She's done it twice." Romero has known two women prior to Brett, and Cohn has known two women prior to Brett (his wife and Frances, his mistress). "Robert Cohn had two friends, Braddocks and myself. Braddocks was his literary friend. I was his tennis friend" (I). Cohn is tennis *and* boxing champion; Jake reads two authors, Mason and Turgenev. There are two garlic wreaths; the Count has two scars; etc. More important are the thematic pairings. As though comparing his own face with Cohn's, Bill Gorton remarks on looking into the mirror: "My God! . . . isn't it an awful face?" (X). As Bill links thus to Cohn, so Cohn links also to Romero: Cohn, says Romero, "looks like Villalta"—the bullfighter. They all share some attribute of Cohn's identity, although they are all enemies of him; masking as friends—notably Jake. Cohn is mockingly referred to as

Moses when Jake notices Cohn staring intently at Brett: "He looked a great deal as his compatriot must have looked when he saw the promised land" (III). Jake is paired with Cohn, for Jake also plays the role of Moses: as historian of his expatriate clan and as the law-giver and leader of the Gentiles in Exodus from their Native Land. As Nick Carraway is mistakenly identified with Gatsby, so Hemingway's narrator is crossed in identity with Cohn: "I put on a coat of Cohn's and went out on the balcony" (XV). The surface reason for Jake's hatred of Cohn is envy that Cohn has possessed Brett, but the real reason stems from the sub-conscious recognition—rendered implicitly by his sharing Cohn's coat, for instance—that he, the outcast Jacob, shares identity with the outcast Robert Cohn and that in hating Cohn he is in effect expressing his own self-hatred.

That Jake shares identity with his antagonist, what does that spell out but the fact of a reversal of intention in *The Sun Also Rises*. How can Jake be represented by Hemingway critics as superior to Cohn if Jake is identi-fied with Cohn? They thus switch places, and thereby I fashion my up-side-down reading of the novel: Read it from Jake's side and he is right; read it from Cohn's side and he is right. But once you read it from Cohn's point of view, Jake is all wrong. Jake rebels against and disbelieves in that other side of his selfhood which Cohn represents. They are, as it were, the conflicting double selfhood of their creator—one side of Hemingway criticizing the other. Did Hemingway consciously intend to trick the reader? The answer is Yes *if* by internal evidence my reading supports it. As for external evidence, the Fitzgeralds saw a good deal of Hemingway in Paris in the summer of 1925: *The Great Gatsby* had been published in April, and Hemingway started writing *The Sun Also Rises* on July 21, on his 26th birthday, in Valencia, completing the first draft on September 6 in Paris. (This data is furnished by Carlos Baker, except for the refer-ence to *The Great Gatsby*. Neither Baker nor any other Hemingway critic has detected any connection.) "I knew nothing about writing a novel when I started it [*The Sun Also Rises*], but in rewriting it I learned much." (Quoted from Charles Poore in *The Hemingway Reader*, 1953.) It's just possible that Hemingway learned how to write *The Sun Also Rises* from Fitzgerald's *The Great Gatsby*.

"All modern American literature," Hemingway claims in *The Green Hills of Africa*, "comes from one book by Mark Twain called *Huckleberry Finn*." But this neglects Henry James, who derived from Twain not at all, and Stephen Crane, in whose work Twain's influence was rather a minor strand. Hemingway perhaps means by "all modern American literature" solely Hemingway. But this neglects F. Scott Fitzgerald. "Which author had Hemingway imitated when he wrote *The Sun Also Rises*?" asked Carlos Baker (in *Hemingway The Writer as Artist*, 1952). "Fitzgerald in *This Side of Paradise* or Michael Arlen in *The Green Hat*?" The answer is (I think) rather Fitzgerald in *The Great Gatsby*.

(4)

The morally confused narrator betrays Montoya's trust: At the start Montoya smiles at Jake "as though bull-fighting were a very special secret between the two of us" (XIII), but at the end "Montoya did not come near us." Jake is no more *aficionado* than the corrupted bicycle-riders he confronts at the hotel in San Sebastian: "They had raced among themselves so often that it did not make much difference who won. Especially in a foreign country. The money could be arranged" (XIX). Their Money Morality is the same as Jake's: "Just exchange of values." The bicycle-racers provide an analogy with Jake at a time when he does not want to be reminded of himself. He has come to San Sebastian to cleanse himself of his messy, rotten time, and in the sea he undergoes purification—like Huck Finn on the Mississippi. The boy and girl he watches on the raft are Innocence personified. The boy does not notice that the girl has undone her bathing-suit to brown her back in the sun, but Jake notices it. This idyllic scene is thematically juxtaposed with the hotel scene of the bicyclists; the dirty-jokers, the rotten sports. They default on their code shamelessly (even on the night before the race they drink); and Jake likewise defaults on his. In the ritual of fishing Jake the Fisher King defaults. It is a maimed ritual, as is also the bull-fight—in that ritual Romero defaults on the sacred code of bull-fighters. *Contra* Baker's notion that the moral norm is represented in the scenes of Jake and Bill at Burguete and of Romero at Pamplona, the fact is that both scenes are maimed by the defaulting of Jake in the first instance and of Romero in the second. Fisher King Jake fishes for trout by sinker and worms, and whereas Bill Gorton, playing the game according to code, casts with fly and wades downstream, Jake fishes right at the dam. He does not *feel* the first trout strike. Bill is the good sport; Jake is the rotten sport. Bill fishes for the sport of the thing ("If they won't take a fly I'll just flick it around"), whereas Jake aims to catch his trout in the shortest possible time. And by hook or crook. After catching his trout, he kills time by reading a book while waiting for Bill to return. He defaults also in not waiting till Bill returns before drinking the wine he ought to share (XII).

The Fisher King legend—the same that T. S. Eliot had refashioned in *The Waste Land*—"tells how the king was wounded in loins and how he lay wasting in his bed while his whole kingdom became unfruitful; there was thunder but no rain; the rivers dried up, the flocks had no increase, and the women bore no children" (quoted from Malcolm Cowley's Introduction to *The Portable Hemingway*, 1944).[4] Frazer's *The Golden Bough* illuminates *The Sun Also Rises* more importantly than Eliot's *The Waste Land*. Baker opines that Hemingway "early devised and subsequently developed a mythologizing tendency of his own which does not depend on antecedent literatures, learned footnotes, or the recognition of spot passages," and he adds that Hemingway's esthetic opinions "carried him away from the literary kind of myth adaptation" (pp. 87, 88); but the fact is that Frazer's *The Golden Bough* is the well-spring source of Hemingway's mythologizing tendency in *The Sun Also Rises*. Any well-informed reading of the novel owes homage to *The Golden Bough*. It is loaded with "spot passages" and "learned footnotes" from Frazer, and—*contra* Baker—it exploits "the literary kind of myth adaptation."

"In Greenland a woman in child-bed and for some time after delivery is supposed to possess the power of laying a storm. She has only to go out of doors, fill her mouth with air, and coming back into the house blow it out again." As the Greenlander thinks he can make the wind to blow or be still, so Jake Barnes simulates faith and prays for a still wind when Romero performs in the bull-ring—the wind is bad for him. ("Greenlanders believe that a king or god can be killed by a wind," says Frazer.) Brett remarks as she and Jake leave the chapel: "The praying has not been much of a success." She gets nervous inside any church. As Jake knows from *Huckleberry Finn*: "You Can't Pray a Lie." Like Huck, Brett complains: " 'I've never gotten anything I prayed for. Have you?' 'Oh, yes,' 'Oh, rot,' said Brett. 'Maybe it works for some people, though' " (XVIII). She says: "I'm damned bad for a religious atmosphere," and adds: "I've the wrong type of face." Jake also has the wrong type of face: "You don't look very religious, Jake." "I'm pretty religious," Jake replies, having in mind his Biblical namesake. "Oh, rot," said Brett (XVIII). He goes to church a couple of times, once with Brett, but it is an empty ritual. "She said she wanted to hear me go to confession, but I told her that not only was it impossible but it was not as interesting as it sounded, and, besides it would be in a language she did not know" (XIV). Immediately on leaving the church Brett has her fortune told, the sacred ritual being juxtaposed here with one of primitive magic.

The true priest is Montoya, whose Hotel Montoya serves as the temple for King Romero. The life of certain kings, says *The Golden Bough*, "is trammelled by the observance of certain restrictions or taboos. Thus he may not sleep in any house but his own official residence, which is called the 'annointed house' with reference to the ceremony of annointing him at inauguration." Romero sleeps in Montoya's "annointed house," but he desecrates it by not observing the taboos. He drinks, smokes, speaks a foreign tongue, and goes to bed with Brett. "It would be very bad, a torero who speaks English. . . . Bull-fighters are not like that" (XVI). Huntsmen and fishermen of primitive societies "were likewise required to abstain from any commerce with their women for the like period, this last condition being considered indispensable to their success. A chief who failed to catch a whale had been known to attribute his failure to a breach of chastity on the part of his men." Although Romero transgresses the taboos of his sect, he nevertheless succeeds in the bull-fighting. The savage Timmes of Sierra Leone reserve to themselves the right of beating the king on the eve of his coronation; "and they avail themselves of this con-stitutional privilege with such hearty goodwill that sometimes the un-

happy monarch does not long survive his elevation to the throne." Romero
is beaten up, as it were, on "the eve of his coronation." Ceremonies of
haircutting, rituals and taboos of drinking and bathing and fishing—they
are all recreated in *The Sun Also Rises* from *The Golden Bough,* a parallelism which has not been noticed (so far as I know). The reign of the
maimed king and mock-priest, Jacob, is—in Frazer's terms—"the reign of
the lame king." *That* is why the world of *The Sun Also Rises* is "rotten."

Only Jake, only he would say: "To hell with people." That admission
makes him the social outcast and links him, though on other grounds,
with Cohn and Romero. And *only* Jake denies his own identity: "Don't
call me Jake" (XVII). Excepting Montoya and the Count, the only true
gentleman is Robert Cohn and he alone is worth saving—and for that very
reason. Henry Seidel Canby's notion that "there is, frankly, only one
character indubitably worth saving, and that is Jake" ought to be dismissed without mention except that his notion has been widely circulated
as the introduction to the Modern Library edition of *The Sun Also Rises.*
Cohn needs to be "saved" because he has been damned by all Hemingway
critics, 1926-1957. Brett's final admonition to Jake is: "Jake, don't get
drunk." And their last words express sentiments that Cohn, incapable of
sarcasm, would never utter. " 'Oh, Jake,' Brett said, 'we could have had such
a damned good time together. . . .' 'Yes,' I said, 'isn't it pretty to think so?' "

" 'You've got a hell of a biblical name, Jake,' says Brett (III)." "You
ought to dream," says Bill to Jacob. But no visions come to Jacob. Cohn
has a bad dream, Bill has a good dream, and Frances Clyne has a "vision."
"I know the real reason why Robert won't marry me, Jake. It's just come
to me. They've sent it to me in a vision in the Café Select. Isn't it mystic?
Some day they'll put a tablet up. Like at Lourdes." It's a rotten vision, and
that it is false is hinted at by the fact that Jake in disgust abruptly leaves
her. Her mock vision is that Cohn has "always wanted to have a mistress,
and if he doesn't marry me, why then he's had one" (VI). But Frances herself supplies the real reason why Cohn won't marry her when unwittingly
she reveals the truth: "I always thought we'd have children. . . . I never
liked children much, but I don't want to think I'll never have them." What
Cohn recognizes is that marriage with Frances Clyne would end as another
rotten marriage. The mystic vision should have come to her at the start of
her affair with Cohn two years before. "When I made you get rid of your
little secretary on the magazine I ought to have known you'd get rid of me
the same way." But she had *then* no vision, and as for *now* by her own
admission Cohn is cleared of the calumny she spreads against him: "It's
my own fault, all right. Perfectly my own fault." Her admission goes unnoticed, and as we readers see Cohn's case only from the point of view of
Jake and his friends as the butt of their calumny and cruel jokes, now
frequently registered at Jake's instigation or now again with his silent
approval, we assent to their distorted appraisal.

They all detest Jew Cohn, the unwanted outcast. "I never heard him
make one remark that would, in any way, detach him from other people"

(VI). Detached from Jake's clan—*that* is Cohn's plight. If any remark by Cohn would detach him from Jake and his friends, it is his admission: "I'm not interested in bull-fighters. That's an abnormal life" (II). Cohn's values stand as the obverse of Jake's. Cohn's critique of the Narrator's Point-of-View provides the novel with its aesthetic antithesis. Montoya and the Count serve the same purpose. Cohn's criticism of Jake and his sophomoric code is subtilized, whereas Bill Gorton's ridicule of Spokesman Jake is Out There On the Page.

In the bull-fight Romero waits for the bull to charge and then "without taking a step forward, he became one with the bull" (XVIII). As Romero is identified with the bull, so in another sense is Cohn. As Cohn is a boxer, so the bull knows how to use his horns—"He's got a left and a right just like a boxer," says Jake of the charging bull. A bull becomes dangerous only when detached from the herd. Says Bill: "Don't you ever detach me from the herd, Mike." Cohn, the detached bull, knocks down Jake and Romero. Mike is steer to Bill Gorton as bull, in the above allegory, and Jake is steer to the bull Cohn, detached from the herd. As steers are castrated, so is Jake. Jake speaks of Bill as though he were a steer: " 'Of course, if *you* went in there you'd probably detach one of them from the herd, and he'd be dangerous.' 'That's too complicated,' Bill said." As Bill's role changes from bull to steer, so bull Cohn figures also as steer Cohn: When a steer is gored, "None of the bulls came near him, and he did not attempt to join the herd." Cohn as steer is gored. Mike identifies Cohn as steer: "I would have thought you'd loved being a steer, Robert." "What do you mean, Mike?" "They lead such a quiet life. They never say anything and they're always hanging around so." Bull Mike gores steer Cohn: "You came down to San Sebastian where you weren't wanted, and followed Brett around *like a bloody steer*." Bill in role of steer leads Bull Cohn away from the herd as though to protect him from Bull Mike: "Shut up, Michael. Try and show a little breeding." Whereupon Mike, as though denying any kinship with the bulls, says: "Breeding be damned. Who has any breeding, anyway, except the bulls" (XIII). Both Cohn and Romero's first bulls have impaired vision, and the identification of Cohn as bull is further indicated by the implied significance of Mike's remark. Translate it thus: "Who has any breeding, anyway, except Robert Cohn." He alone is pedigreed.

Here, then, is a paradigm of switched identities (each person's identity —now as bull and now as steer—crossed with another's). The parallelism is the switched identities of the narrator—Jake Barnes as spokesman for the codified clan defaulting on his own code *and* being subjected to a critique of his own code by his friend Bill Gorton, whereby Bill usurps Jake's "identity" and confounds it.   (1959)

NOTES

1. The equation of horse and woman has precedent in *Henry IV, I* (Act II, Scene III): "What is it carries you away?" asks Lady Percy. Hotspur answers:

"Why, my horse, my love, my horse." He addresses Kate as "my love," but he is playing ironically on "my love" as it attaches both to Kate and to "my horse." "Why, my horse" *who is my love,* "my love, my horse." My love is my horse, my roan is my throne, etc.

2. "The ironic gap between expectation and fulfillment, pretense and fact, intention and action, the message sent and the message received, the way things are thought or ought to be and the way things are—this has been Hemingway's great theme from the beginning; and it has called for an ironic method to do it artistic justice. All of his work thus far published deserves study with special attention to this method." E. M. Halliday in *American Literature,* XXVIII (1956). Halliday traces briefly Hemingway's ironic method in *A Farewell to Arms* and *For Whom the Bell Tolls,* but oddly enough he skips *The Sun Also Rises.* However, I should add that his essay is mainly concerned to point out inaccuracies in Baker's reading of *A Farewell to Arms.*

3. Ironical, by my reading, though other readers may prefer the literal rendering of *Bal* as dance, simply that. However, the ironical reading gets supporting evidence by the parallel mockery of the Palace Hotel bar serving as church, the Café Select providing Frances her "vision," and the San Fermin dance mentioned above linking with "the Bal restaurant" as temple.

4. "It is this instinct for legends, for sacraments, for rituals, for symbols appealing to buried hopes and fears that helps to explain the power of Hemingway's work and his vast superiority over his imitators" (p. xxii). Hemingway's debt to *The Waste Land* is studied in "Sunrise out of *The Waste Land,*" *Tulane Studies in English,* IX (1959), by Richard P. Adams, whose offprint reached me while correcting galley on *The Houses That James Built* (1960). I see now that other critics, as well as Adams, have made a connection between *The Sun Also Rises* and *The Great Gatsby,* namely the connection of the influence of *The Waste Land* on both novels.

A New Reading of "The Snows of Kilimanjaro"

When in doubt, it seems, when in fear, when taken by surprise, when lost in bush or desert and without a guide, the human, the animal, heart prescribes a circle. It turns on itself as the earth does and seeks refuge in the movement of the stars.
—Laurens Van Der Post: VENTURE TO THE INTERIOR (1951)

WHAT HAS NOT BEEN NOTICED about "The Snows of Kilimanjaro" is how it is designed. Scenes of external reality alternate with juxtaposed scenes of internal monologue, reminiscences of Harry's past life that Harry failed to utilize as writer. These cutbacks—they are set into italics—are not dreams, but rather they are recollected reality; the point is that they relate thematically. They are not irresponsible reminiscences. They are relevant in that they elicit, albeit obliquely, one motif or another relating to the plight of the protagonist. The narrative progression moves now forward in present reality and now backward to recollected reality.

The story is about an artist—or potential artist—who died spiritually the day he traded his integrity for security, and here he is dying now with a gangrenous leg whose stink has symbolic import. You begin to stink when you sell yourself out. Then is when moral gangrene sets in; after that, well, life becomes painless. "The marvellous thing is that it's painless," says Harry about his gangrenous leg. "That's how you knew when it starts."[1] His gangrenous leg is token symbol of his moral gangrene as creative writer. Obversely put, writing is a struggle, an act of labor and pain. Stephen Crane had the same theory: *"The Red Badge of Courage . . . was an effort born of pain—despair, almost; and I believe that this made it a better piece of literature than it otherwise would have been. It seems a pity that art should be a child of pain, and yet I think it is."*[2] But Harry never exerted himself, never tried because he feared he might fail; instead of using his talent he traded on it. He blames the rich bitch Helen ("You rich bitch. That's poetry. I'm full of poetry now. Rot and poetry. Rotten poetry"), but he admits: "He had destroyed his talent himself. Why should he blame this woman because she kept him well? He had destroyed his talent by not using it, by betrayals of himself . . ." (593). Harry's dying now of gangrene counterpoints with Harry's dying of spiritual gangrene years ago. He kept from thinking, "and it was all marvellous"—marvellous because painless. His painless death implies his painless life. Ironically, while dying he can't help *not* to keep from thinking. That he recollects his fragmented past, experiences he failed to recreate into formed literary works, that he recollects all that he has missed out on as potential artist, evokes the ironical poignancy of Harry's situation. What's painful about his present plight is just *that*. "Now he would never write the things that he had saved to write until he knew enough to write them well. Well, he would not have to fail at trying to write them either" (587).

Like Kurtz in Conrad's "Heart of Darkness," Harry incriminates himself as failure. By his own self-admission Harry has sold Conscience short. So, too, does Doctor Diver in *Tender is the Night:* "My politeness is a trick of the heart." It is the characteristic Hemingway division and conflict between internal code or conscience and an external and meretricious code of manners or social front, a division and conflict exploited notably in *Huckleberry Finn.* One exemplar of integrity or conscience is Francis Macomber in Hemingway's "The Short Happy Life of Francis Macomber." Whereas at the start Macomber is presented in mock triumph, at the end he attains a moral triumph; the story is thus plotted with a reversal of the initial situation. "Francis Macomber had, half an hour before, been carried to his tent from the edge of the camp in triumph on the arms and shoulders of the cook, the personal boys, the skinner and the porters. The gun-bearers [however] had taken no part in the demonstration." Reversal of situation is obtained by the Conradian device of a wrenched chronology, the opening scene relocated so as to begin the story on the note of mock triumph. Because Macomber has defaulted in the lion hunt, he has lost face; the gun-bearers shun the false demonstration. The story begins with Macomber asking: "Will you have a lime juice or lemon squash?" The guide Robert Wilson says: "I'll have a gimlet," rejecting thus Macomber's kind of drink. " 'I'll have a gimlet too. I need something,' Macomber's wife said. 'I suppose it's the thing to do,' Macomber agreed. 'Tell him to make three gimlets.' " Mrs. Macomber, ashamed of her husband, drinks Wilson's kind of drink; and Macomber, ashamed of himself, follows likewise the leader. But when Wilson later defaults on the hunter's code by chasing in the automobile the buffalo they hunt, he loses face; this reversal is spelled out by Macomber: "Now she [Margot] has something on you." The story began with Macomber in the power of Wilson and Mrs. Macomber; it ends with Wilson and Mrs. Macomber in the power of Macomber—he triumphs morally over them. As in "The Short Happy Life of Francis Macomber," reversal of situation defines the structure of *The Portrait of a Lady, The Ambassadors, The Return of the Native,* "The Bride Comes to Yellow Sky," and *Tender is the Night.*

"The Snows of Kilimanjaro" is constructed very differently, the various parts being related not logically but psychologically:

> *That was one story he had saved to write. He knew at least twenty good stories from out there and he had never written one. Why?*
>> 'You tell them why,' he said.
>> 'Why what, dear?'
>> 'Why nothing.'

The narrative shifts from recollections, from the mind of Harry, back to reality; here the transposition is clearly managed by the linked "Why?" Harry's memoried experiences furnish a kind of scrapbook of images which Harry had intended to recast into stories; they are all fragments, disjointed episodes, not yet organized into dramatic wholes because Harry never converted them into works of art. They are the unformed life he failed to form. Harry has not organized them, but Hemingway has.

While their sequence is seemingly haphazard, these internal monologues progress toward the climactic and final image of Williamson who was hit by a German bomb as he crawled through the trench's protective wire, *"with a flare lighting him up and his bowels spilled out into the wire, so when they brought him in, alive, they had to cut him loose. Shoot me, Harry. For Christ sake shoot me."* It is as though Williamson's plea were Harry's own death-wish, and almost immediately subsequent to this image of death-by-agony Harry himself dies—in contrast to Williamson, however, Harry does not die in agony. When "the weight went from his chest" (606), Harry dies in his sleep. "It was morning and had been morning for some time and he heard the plane." Harry at the moment of his dying dreams that Compton comes to take him away by plane. "It was difficult getting him in, but once in he lay back in the leather seat, and the leg was stuck straight out to one side of the seat where Compton sat." All of this dream episode is set in Roman type so as to distinguish it from the italicized passages of Harry's recollections of the past; they are not dreams. The transition from reality to dream is as adroitly managed here as in Bierce's "An Occurrence at Owl Creek Bridge," Hemingway's device deriving from

Bierce's famous story. In both stories the ending returns us to that point in the narrative where the death-dream began. Harry's wife, awakened by an hyena's almost human crying sound, discovers by flashlight in the dark tent that Harry's leg hangs down alongside his cot. "The dressings had all come down and she could not look at it." Harry does not answer her cry, "and she could not hear him breathing" (609). Dream and reality—point-present-reality as distinguished from recollected reality—are rendered as blending almost unnoticeably one with the other, the projected leg in Harry's death-dream connecting with the projected leg in Harry's cot. Harry has no last name, and his wife is named only once, *only* in his dream: "Helen had taken Compton aside and was speaking to him" (607). She's not exactly Helen of Troy, but she links with Helen of Troy inasmuch as loving her—Harry's way of loving her—is destructive: "That's the good destruction" (595). The Elizabethan meaning of *to love* in its double sense of *to love* is *to die* is exploited also in *A Farewell to Arms*.

Caroline Gordon in the textbook anthology *The House of Fiction* (1950) opines that Hemingway "has made no provision for the climax of his symbolic action. Our attention is not called to the snow-covered peaks of Kilimanjaro until the end of the story; as a result we do not feel that sense of recognition and inevitability which help to make a *katharsis*." At the end of Harry's dream, during which the perspective is from the airplane with images evoking a sense of Harry's belated nostalgic love for life, "all he could see, as wide as all the world, great, high, and unbelievably white in the sun, was the square top of Kilimanjaro. And then he knew that that was where he was going" (608). But he isn't going there, not at all; because he has not earned admission to the heights, admission to "the House of God," as the western summit of Kilimanjaro is called.

> *Kilimanjaro is a snow covered mountain 19,710 feet high, and it is said to be the highest mountain in Africa. Its western summit is called the Masai 'Ngàje Ngài,' the House of God. Close to the western summit there is the dried and frozen carcass of a leopard. No one has explained what the leopard was seeking at that altitude.*

The story opens with this italicized passage, which I presume is one of Harry's recollections since all his other recollections are likewise italicized passages. So, then, the symbol is not "something the writer has tacked on" (*contra* Caroline Gordon); but rather it is an integral part of the story. "He uses the snow-covered mountain of Kilimanjaro as the symbol of death, but the symbolism . . . is not part of the action and therefore does not operate as a controlling image. . . ." She damns the story as a magnificent failure, whereas I see it as a magnificent success.

Harry's "vision" of Kilimanjaro in his death-dream returns us at the end to the opening passage and shapes the whole in circular form. Immediately following that italicized image of the Kilimanjaro summit, which in effect is a riddle to be unriddled, Harry says: "The marvellous thing is that it is painless." But it wasn't painless for that leopard to ascend the summit, an ascent which Harry never attempted; he has attained an immortality which Harry never earned. The symbol is far more than simply a symbol of death. That leopard exceeded the nature and aspirations of his kind: *"No one has explained what the leopard was seeking at that altitude."* Well, he wasn't seeking immortality, being only a dumb beast; but he got just that in attaining the heights, admission to "the House of God."

In contrast to the noble leopard is the hyena which Harry imagines as death. Death "like a hyena"—but now suddenly shapeless, crouches and weighs down on his chest. " 'You've got a hell of a breath,' he told it. 'You stinking bastard' " (606). In addressing the stinking hyena Harry is addressing himself; Hyena Harry—a cowardly and carnivorous beast. Or he is addressing himself as vulture, since he imagines death also as a bird. " 'Love is a dunghill,' said Harry. 'And I'm the cock that gets on it to crow.' 'If you have to go away,' she said, 'is it absolutely necessary to kill off everything you leave behind? I mean do you have to take away every-thing? Do you have to kill your horse, and your wife and burn your saddle and your armour?' 'Yes,' he said. 'Your damned money was my armour. My Swift and my Armour' " (590). She is his Armour, a pun on his *Amour*. Not Helen of Troy, but rather Helen of Swift & Armour, the Chicago slaughter house; and as for Harry, he's Slaughter House Harry, as it were, slaughtering not only his wife but his "horse."

In the second Internal Monologue or stream of consciousness interlude (588-590) Harry remembers an old man looking at the snow falling in the mountains of Bulgaria. Nansen's Secretary asks him *"if it were snow and the old man looking at it and saying, No, that's not snow. It's not snow and them all saying, It's not snow we were mistaken. But it was snow all right and he sent them on into it when he evolved exchange of populations. And it was snow they trampled along in until they died that winter"* (588-589). It is an incident depicting flight, retreat, betrayal; hence it mirrors Harry's own plight—Harry in flight from himself, Harry betraying himself. Like Nansen's Secretary, Harry betrays his trust.

Death by snow sums up that memoried image, but it is the snow that saves the deserter in the episode immediately subsequent: *"the deserter came with his feet bloody in the snow. He said the police were right behind him and they gave him woolen socks and held the gendarmes talking until the tracks had drifted over."* Here again is flight, and in both actions snow is deceptive.

Next comes an image of skiers on snow *"as smooth to see as cake frosting and as light as powder and he remembered the noiseless rush the speed made as you dropped down like a bird."* But "the snow was so bright it hurt your eyes"; so again snow is deceptive. And again the action is of flight.

Next comes the story of Herr Lent who lost at card-playing *"Everything, the skischule money and all the season's profit and then his capital."* It occurs in a snow-blizzard, when they were snow-bound a week in the Madlener-haus, and Harry *"thought of all the time in his life he had spent gambling."* Harry, too, has gambled on life and lost.

The fifth recollected experience evokes again the motif of betrayal. *"But he had never written a line of that, nor of the cold, bright Christmas day with the mountains showing across the plain that Gardner had flown across the lines to bomb the Austrian officers' leave train, machine-gunning them as they scattered and ran."* He broke faith during the Christmas truce. When he returned to his own men, somebody said: *"You bloody murderous bastard."* Here again snow, though not mentioned, is implied; thus again the motifs of snow and death, snow and betrayal. Also, here again is an action of flight. The final two scenes are again reminiscences of skiing, of snow—"the fast-slipping rush of running powder-snow on crust" —as life. Thus Harry figures in these reminiscences as all these things: the betrayer, the deserter, the skier, the gambler, the murdering betrayer of code. And snow, figuring in all these scenes, associates with the title of the story and the snow-covered Kilimanjaro with its leopard as mock commentary on Harry's plight. He's no leopard transcending reality; Harry's merely the common bestial man devoid of transcendent virtues.

"The Snows of Kilimanjaro," says our biased critic, "lacks tonal and symbolic unity," but a close reading disproves that claim. "Its three planes of action, the man's intercourse with his wife, his communings with his soul, and the background of Enveloping Action, the mysterious Dark Continent, are never integrated." Well, let us examine what's what.

As the image of the leopard on Kilimanjaro's summit is integrated with the various incidents in the above recollections of Harry, so is it integrated with what Harry recollects in the subsequent italicized passage, Internal Monologue 3 (597-599). It is again counterpointed against Harry as betrayer. Harry as two-timer writes the woman he loves that he cannot bear life without her, and her letter in reply is discovered by his wife: " '*Who is that letter from, dear?' and that was the end of the beginning of that."* Even that same night he wrote her from the Club he went out and picked up a girl and took her out to supper, but he two-timed her: *"left her for a hot Armenian slut, that swung her belly against him so it almost scalded. He took her away from a British gunner subaltern after a row."* Another incident he remembers has to do with artillery firing into its own troops, a metaphor of Harry destroying himself.

The fourth section of italicized reminiscences (600-603) presents in contrast the happy Paris life when *"he had written the start of all he was to do. There never was another part of Paris that he loved like that,"* etc. He hadn't yet sold himself out to the rich; but he never got around to writing about the Paris he loved, nor in fact about any of the rest of his experiences.

Internal Monologue 5 (603-604) follows close upon the previous recollection, and the final one of Williamson follows almost immediately. Their frequency increases towards the end of the narrative when Harry approaches death. Now he recalls the murder of an old man by a half-wit boy, whom Harry betrays. He gets the boy to aid him in packing the old man's body *("frozen in the corral, and the dogs had eaten part of him")* onto a sled, *"and the two of you took it out over the road on skis, and sixty miles down to town to turn the boy over. He having no idea that he would be arrested. Thinking he had done his duty and that you were his friend and he would be rewarded. . . . That was one story he had saved to write. Why?"* Why Nothing sums up Harry. (Why Nothing sums up Dick Diver in *Tender is the Night,* who likewise sold himself out to the rich.) Harry remembers "poor Julian and his romantic awe of them and how he had started a story once that began, " 'The very rich are different from you and me.' And how some one had said to Julian, Yes, they have more money. But that was not humorous to Julian. He thought they were a special glamorous race and when he found they weren't it wrecked him just as much as any other thing that wrecked him" (604).[3]

The fifth monologue spells out Harry as betrayer and links thus with the second and third italicized recollections. Again, it is a scene of death in snow and thus links with the second internal monologue. All six sections of italicized recollections present a death scene and link thus with the plight of the protagonist. Again, actions of betrayal are recurrent—in monologues number 2, 3, 4, and 5. To say that "Our attention is not called to the snow-covered peaks of Kilimanjaro until the end of the story" is to ignore these multiple interrelationships of recollected scenes with their recurrent motifs of death, deception, betrayal, and flight. The final death-dream is itself a scene of flight, flight from the Dark Continent to the House of God. The leopard made it there, but not Harry. To say that the leopard symbolism "is not part of the action and therefore does not operate as a controlling image" is to ignore the whole substance of Harry's recollected incidents; they furnish obliquely linked analogies with Harry himself and thematically they are counterpointed against the opening image of the leopard dead in the snows of Kilimanjaro's summit. Man betrays man; only the leopard is true. That opening image of the miraculous leopard operates, by my reading, as controlling and focal symbol. Don't underrate Hemingway! (1960)

NOTES

1. Page 585 in *The Hemingway Reader,* edited by Charles Poore (1953). This statement by Harry opens the story.

2. In *Stephen Crane: Letters,* edited by R. W. Stallman and Lillian Gilkes (1960).

3. In the original version Hemingway used the name of his friend F. Scott Fitzgerald, changing it to Julian when Fitzgerald protested. Julian's story is Fitzgerald's "The Rich Boy." See Arthur Mizener's *The Far Side of Paradise* (1951), pp. 270–271.

WILLIAM FAULKNER

A Cryptogram: *As I Lay Dying*

"I am here as a symbol of something. I thought perhaps you would know what it was."
—F. Scott Fitzgerald: TENDER IS THE NIGHT.

"THE STRIKING FEATURE OF MODERN ART," said Thomas Mann, "is that it has ceased to recognize the categories of tragic and comic, or the dramatic classifications, tragedy and comedy. It sees life as tragi-comedy, with the result that the grotesque is its most genuine style—to the extent, indeed, that to-day that is the only guise in which the sublime may appear." I quote here from his essay on Conrad's *The Secret Agent* (in *Past Masters, and other papers,* 1933), but what Mann says of Conrad's *The Secret Agent* applies even more aptly to the fictional works of Faulkner. The grotesque, says Mann, is the genuine anti-bourgeois style. Well, that is Faulkner's style precisely. Whereas in Conrad it occurs solely in *The Secret Agent,* the comic-grotesque characterizes the main body of Faulkner's works, notably in *As I Lay Dying.* Faulkner is the exemplar par excellence of the comic-grotesque. To define it by example: The coffin of Ma Bundren is "bored clean full of holes and Cash's new auger broke off in the last one. When they had taken the lid off her they found that two of them had bored on into her face." (Vardaman, the young boy, drilled those holes so that his mother could *see* out of her coffin.) They cover her face with a veil of mosquito bar "so the auger holes in her face wouldn't show."[1]

The literal-minded Cash lists his reasons for making Ma's coffin "on the bevel" (Cash Chapter 18, 397). "There is more surface for the nails to grip," and on the bevel "There is twice the gripping-surface to each seam." "In a house people are upright two-thirds of the time. So the seams and joints are made up-and-down. Because the stress is up-and-down." Whereas "In a bed where people lie down all the time, the joints and seams are made sideways, because *the stress is sideways.*" (So it was for Addie; Anse wore her out.) In a coffin "The animal magnestism of a dead body makes the stress come slanting, so the seams and joints of a coffin are made on the bevel." Why? Because then "The water will have to seep into it on a slant. Water moves easiest up and down or straight across." The thematic point here is that water is the dangerous force—it is life, the restless flow. Hence Ma Bundren dies in a rainstorm, because with her death *life begins.* Anse is proud that the river's on the rise; "how high the water was, and I be durn if he didn't act like he was proud of it, *like he had made the river rise himself"* (417). As hypocrite Whitfield declares, they are the "waters of Thy mighty wrath."

They want her to die so that they can get into town. Her death and the prospect of getting to Jefferson provides them all release from Holdfast

Bundren, the negation of life and the begetter of it. Darl says to Dewey Dell: " 'You want her to die so you can get to town: is that it?' She wouldn't say what we both knew" (Darl Chapter 10, 365). Anse, born on that mountain-top, has not been to town in twelve years. "And how his mother ever got up there to bear him, he being his mother's son," says Doctor Peabody (367). Peabody's name belies his obesity. He's so fat he has to be pulleyed up the mountain by rope. "You picked out a fine time to get me out here and bring up a storm" (369).

Why don't they bury her at New Hope? Anse's "folks buries at New Hope, too, not three miles away. But it's just like him to marry a woman born a day's hard ride away and have her die on him" (Tull Chapter 8, 357). Anse hasn't the face of a lucky man. He's luckless in not having married a woman willing to be buried in the nearest cemetery. Faulkner's humor *is* comic-grotesque. " 'Refusing to let her lie in the same earth with those Bundrens.' 'But she wanted to go [to the Jefferson cemetery],' Mr. Tull said. 'It was her own wish to lie among her own people' " (Cora Chapter 6, 353). As she denied her husband when living (except to manifest herself in offspring she didn't want), so when dying she denies him again: she insists on returning to the dead past. She made Anse promise to bury her at Jefferson. My aloneness, she says, "had never been violated until Cash came. Not even by Anse in the nights. . . . Then I found that I had Darl. At first I would not believe it. Then I believed that I would kill Anse. It was as though he had tricked me, hidden within a word [*i.e.*, "love"] like within a paper screen and struck me in the back through it. But then I realized that I had been tricked by words older than Anse or love, and that the same word had tricked Anse too, and that my revenge would be that he would never know I was taking revenge" (464). She rejects New Hope, Anse's family cemetery, because she knows that—like Anse—the New Hope Cemetery masks the realities in mere words. New Hope for Addie lies in ending where her life began.

New Hope for Anse begins when his wife dies: " 'God's will be done,' he says. 'Now I can get them teeth' "—and start life anew. With new teeth Anse can begin to get a new bite on life, and by gum he does—he returns from Jefferson with Mrs. Bundren No. 2, "a kind of duck-shaped woman all dressed up" (531). "He got them teeth. . . . It made him look a foot taller. . ." (531). Anse is reborn in the sense of beginning a new life once Ma is buried. As the neighborhood gossips prophesy, with Ma dead they can all get married—Anse, Cash, Jewel, Darl. But Darl goes mad, Cash loses his leg, and Dewey Dell while pregnant is violated. I think Faulkner's philosophy is summed up in Cash's literal-minded profundity that "It ain't on a balance." Ma's coffin "ain't on a balance" when the river upsets it, and the water itself "ain't on a balance" (442). Nothing is "on a balance" —neither the river (life) nor the coffin (death); life and death remain inexplicable. Darl, who isn't on a balance, lives in a house that isn't on a balance: "Tilting a little down the hill, as our house does, a breeze draws through the hall all the time, upslanting" (Darl Chapter 5, 351). Cash is on a balance—he's *on the bevel.*

"I have tried to live right in the sight of God and man," says Cora (Mrs. Tull), "for the honour and comfort of my Christian husband and the love and respect of my Christian children. So that when I lay me down in the consciousness of my duty and reward I will be surrounded by loving faces, carrying the farewell kiss of each of my loved ones into my reward. Not like Addie Bundren dying alone, hiding her pride and her broken heart. Glad to go. Lying there with her head propped up so she could watch Cash building the coffin, having to watch him so he would not skimp on it, like as not. . . ." "Glad to go." So says the self-righteous Cora (in Cora Chapter 6, 353-354).

"She's a-going," Anse Bundren says. "Her mind is set on it" (357). Her mind was set on it after her last childbirth, after that she has always signified "as I lay dying." *Glad to go.* "I could just remember how my father used to say that the reason for living was to get ready to stay dead a long time" (461). *She hates life.* "I would hate my father for ever having planted me. I would look forward to the times when they [her students] faulted, so I could whip them" (461). She wants to "get ready to stay dead." Says Darl: "It takes two people to make you, and one people to die. That's how the world is going to end" (Darl Chapter 10).

Her whole life is funneled into her dying days, and she sees her dying days from beyond time. As one reader puts it, "The whole book occurs, in short, as she looks on, as she dies in the minds of each of the bereaved; she is the central eye which sees those diverse minds as accomplishing the fact, which sees the separate moments of accomplishment as simultaneous" (*Hopkins Review:* Summer 1951). What happens is told from multiple points of view, Faulkner always circling back upon the point-present event, and consequently the narrative progression is in slow time. Neither chronology nor logic links the tableaux.

In his Preface to *The Awkward Age* Henry James diagrammed his technique of the point of view: "in the neat figure of a circle consisting of a number of small rounds disposed at equal distances about a central object." In *As I Lay Dying* the central object is Addie, Faulkner employing James's method. The small rounds are lamps throwing light on the situation. In *The Portrait of a Lady* Isabel's friends illuminate the central object, Isabel herself; and in *As I Lay Dying* Addie's family and friends serve the same purpose for the central subject. One difference is that Faulkner's lamps are segregated: each chapter being a monologue by one of the reflectors. Olga Westland suggests that these Faulknerian lamps "operate on four different levels: action, words, conscious thought, and the unconscious. Moreover each of these levels has its own particular blending of observation, association, reflection, and emotion. Certain of the characters are limited to only one of these levels. . . . The different levels of consciousness are rendered by Faulkner through variations of style rising from the dialect of actual speech to the intricate imagery and poetic rhythms of the unconscious" (In *Perspective:* Autumn 1950).[2]

Faulkner's technique of circling back upon the given event, as in a motion-picture re-run, is imaged in what Tull says of Anse: "But even when we were on the bridge Anse kept on looking back, like he thought maybe, once he was outen the wagon, the whole thing would kind of blow up and he would find himself back yonder in the field again and her laying up there in the house, waiting to die *and it to do all over again*" (Tull Chapter 31, 435).

The device of the time-shift, as Edward Crankshaw points out in his *Joseph Conrad: Some Aspects of the Art of the Novel* (1936), "is an aid not only to the presentation of the novelist's subject in its proper light and so getting the last ounce out of the subject, but also to getting the last ounce out of every word and sentence, every paragraph and episode, by multiplying their duties." What was the matter with the Novel, and the British novel in particular, Ford Madox Ford declared:

> was that it went straight forward, whereas in your gradual making acquaintanceship with your fellows you never do go straight forward. You meet an English gentleman at your golf club. He is beefy, full of health, the model of a boy from an English Public School of the finest type. You discover gradually that he is hopelessly neurasthenic, dishonest in matters of small change, but unexpectedly self-sacrificing, a dreadful liar but a most painfully careful student of lepidoptera and, finally, from the public prints, a bigamist who was once, under another name, hammered on the Stock Exchange. . . . Still, there he is, a beefy, full-fed fellow, model of an English Public School product. To get such a man in fiction you could not begin at the beginning and work his life chronologically to the end. You must first get him in with a strong impression, and then work backwards and forwards over his past. . . . That theory at least we [Ford and Conrad] gradually evolved.

Faulkner's method in *As I Lay Dying* is the Conrad-Ford broken method of narration "With straightforward chronological narration," as Crankshaw says, "each paragraph, save by accident or luck, is doing one thing and one thing only; each paragraph, each sentence, each incident recorded. There are no overtones; there is no diffused radiance. In the normal chronological narrative, beginning at the beginning and ending at the end, the beginning and the end in time, the contribution of each sentence to the total effect is no more than its own face value. Each sentence is no more than a statement of the fact expressed by it. This is a waste of space and it makes for thinness of texture, no matter how complex and decorated the individual sentences may be." Crankshaw spells out what Aldous Huxley termed "the musicalization of fiction": "the novelist's equivalent of the fugue in which the subject, or subjects, are with the listener from beginning to end, and where the interest derives from the pattern made by the changing juxtaposition of the subjects, themselves thoroughly explored and turned inside out. That defines not only Conrad's "Heart of Darkness,"[3] but also Faulkner's *As I Lay Dying*. Their effect is fugue-like.

Faulkner learned from Conrad to dislocate chronology, and he is as fond of circles as Conrad is in *The Secret Agent*. *A Wheel is the emblem of Ma's life as a circle:* "the road lies like a spoke of which Addie Bundren is the rim" (413). That is the "red road" to New Hope, which turns off at right angles from the road to Jefferson they travel. The Jefferson road is outside her circle, whereas the "unscarred" road to New Hope figures as the spoke to Ma's rim. The scarred road of time is outside her circle of timelessness, her wheel of eternity: "time . . . outside the circle" (464).

Jewel's horse is described as "a big pinwheel" (433). " 'Jewel's mother is a horse,' Darl said" (Vardaman Chapter 23, 409). Here again Addie thus figures as a wheel. Crossed identity—a trick used recurrently throughout *As I Lay Dying*—is imaged in Jewel on horseback: "his body in mid-air shaped to the horse" (346). Horse and Jewel are one—"Save for Jewel's legs they are like two figures carved for a tableau savage in the sun" (345). " 'Eat,' he says [to his horse]. 'Get the goddamn stuff out of sight while you got a chance, you pussel-gutted bastard. You sweet son of a bitch,' he says" (Darl Chapter 3, 346). In addressing the horse as "sweet son of a bitch," Jewel is addressing himself, that bastard. At Samson's place Jewel sleeps with his horse—commits incest, by implication ("Jewel's mother is a horse," 406). Jewel equates with horse, and horse equates with wheel; Jewel thus—like his mother, who figures both as horse and as fish—belongs to the circle that transcends time. But I find Faulkner's logic confounded in that he identifies Anse as horse also: "Looking like a uncurried horse dressed up" (424). But Anse does not belong to the circle transcending time.[4] Faulkner—by my logic—also has erred in the misidentification of river as horse—the river "lathering, like a driven horse" (439). For the river represents the turbulent flux of life: "Only it kind of lived. One part of you knowed it was just water, the same thing that had been running under this same bridge for a long time, yet when them logs would come spewing up outen it, you were not surprised, like they was a part of water, of the waiting and the threat" (436). As the logs are identified with the water, so the trees beside the bridge—and by implication the bridge itself—are identified with time: they sway "back and forth slow like on a big clock" (436). Tull's bridge *tolls* as the bridge of time. It is at once the bridge to the past (to the cemetery) and the bridge to the future (to the city). Call it a clock-bridge, and the link is with Ma's clock-shaped coffin. Thus the coffin is *a bridge* to the past *and* to the future.

Time's roadway—"the Lord puts roads for travelling"—is cursed by Anse Bundren because it brings bad luck to his door: "A-laying there, right up to my door, where every bad luck that comes and goes is bound to find it" (Anse Chapter 9, 362). When the Lord "aims for something to be always a-moving, He makes it long ways, like a road or a house or a wagon, but when He aims for something to stay put, He makes it up-and-down, like a tree or a man. And so he never aimed for folks to live on a road, because which gets there first, I says, the road or the house? Did you ever know Him to set a road down by a house?" (Anse Chapter 9,

362) The land used to lay "up-and-down ways" until the new road "come and switched the land around longways"—then the godless times began. The road ruined Ma, and the road ruined Dewey Dell. It brought her Lafe from town to impregnate her: "I don't see why he didn't stay in town. We are country people not as good as town people" (381). Ma was "well and hale as ere a woman ever were, except for that road" (363). When the land "laid up-and-down ways," Darl was all right then, but Darl changed too when "the road come and switched the land around longways and *his eyes still full of the land,* that they begun to threaten me out of him, trying to short-hand me with the law." The road ruined Cash too—and Anse Bundren, because he had to pay taxes. Cash took to carpentry "when if it hadn't been no road come there, he wouldn't a got them ["carpenter notions"]; falling off of churches," etc. Darl on the restless road to Jefferson, Darl on the road of time—"he went crazy in our wagon" (525). *"The land runs out of Darl's eyes; they swim to pin-points"* (422). The land thus is equated with the sands of time; Darl's hourglass empties during the journey down the restless road of time. That road is too much for him.

They all suffer hell in getting Addie Bundren in her coffin transported across the flooded river. " 'Well, it'll take the Lord to get her over that river now,' Peabody says. 'Anse can't do it.' 'And I reckon He will,' Quick says. 'He's took care of Anse a long time, now.' 'It's a fact,' Littlejohn says. 'Too long to quit now,' Armstid says. 'I reckon He's like everybody else around here,' Uncle Billy says. 'He's done it so long now He can't quit' " (402). God's fallen into the habit of taking care of that worthless ass, Anse; so too have his neighbors. Says Doctor Peabody to Cash, whose leg is gangrened by the concrete casted onto his broken leg: " 'Concrete,' I said. 'God Amighty, why didn't Anse carry you to the nearest sawmill and stick your leg in the saw? That would have cured it. Then you all could have stuck his head into the saw and cured a whole family . . .' " (Peabody Chapter 52, 516). Who is to blame?—the roadway that ruined them all (as Anse claims), or Anse himself? Faulkner's answer in *As I Lay Dying* is Cassius': The fault "is not in our stars,/But in ourselves, that we are underlings." Fatalism, however, dominates the philosophy of the book's characters, expressed from multiple points of view. *"A fellow wouldn't mind seeing it* [cotton and corn] *washed up if he could just turn on the rain himself. Who is that man can do that? . . . Ay. The Lord made it to grow. It's Hisn to wash up if He sees fitten so"* (403). Well, Addie does just that—she turns on the rain when she dies. Meanwhile she rises from her death-bed to inspect Cash's coffin—the Cash Box which registers her death. Addie *adds* to life by her death. Addie addresses us from the coffin, and Cora addresses Addie as though Addie were still alive. Addie Chapter 38 is located between Cora Chapter 37 and Whitfield Chapter 39. Why? Miss Westland spells it out brilliantly: "Cora Tull and Whitfield react to the family in ethical terms, in words and phrases. Anything done during the death and burial is bound to be another step in Cora's self-justification and the Bundrens' eternal damnation. Addie's soliloquy, which is concerned with emphasizing the separation of words and acts, is flanked by the empty rhetoric of Cora and Whitfield." "The contrast between the two women," Roma King remarks, "is most obvious when each narrates her love affair. Addie tells in poetic language of her lover who came to her as 'the instrument ordained by God who created the sin, to sanctify the sin he had created.' Dewey Dell prosaically relates her chance seduction by a shifty character who leaves her with an unborn baby, ten dollars, and some bad advice about an abortion. Her subsequent violation by Macgowan, a soda jerk masquerading as a doctor, is a gross parody of Addie's affair with the parson."

Addie is most alive when dead. That is because *Addie is Eternity* (371). Anse remarks: "But if she don't last until you get back . . . She will be disappointed" (348). *She is spoken of as dead when still alive, and when dead she is regarded as still alive:* Cash and pa and Vernon and Peabody raise the coffin carefully: "lifeless, yet they move with hushed precautionary words to one another, speaking of it as though, complete, it now slumbered lightly *alive, waiting to come awake*" (395). " 'She's counted on it,' pa says. 'She'll want to start right away. I know her. I promised her I'd keep the team here and ready, and she's counting on it' " (349). When dead she is still counting on it. The others are counting on her to die, each one looking forward to her death as a release of unfulfilled desires that she held them back from fulfilling. But dead she is still alive: at each stroke of the saw "her face seems to wake a little into an expression of listening and of waiting, as though she were counting the strokes" (374). She's counting on going to the cemetery in her own wagon: "She'll rest easier for *knowing* it's a good one, and private. She was ever a private woman" (350). Everyone has faith that she'll hold up time. "She'll hold on till everything's ready, *till her own good time*" (350). Once dead, however, she wants to hasten time: "with that family burying-ground in Jefferson and *them of her blood waiting for her there,* she'll be impatient. I promised my word [says Anse] me and the boys would get there quick as mules could walk it, so she could rest quiet" (350).

The dead wait for her—that cemetery is quite alive!

If the doctor told her "the time was nigh, she wouldn't wait. I know her. Wagon or no wagon, she wouldn't wait. Then she'd be upset, and I wouldn't upset her for *the living world*" (350). The living world was dead to Addie after her lastborn. Rid me of life as life has ridden me—that sums up Bundren's Burden. Addie is glad to go.

In her coffin she stirs and speaks to Vardaman and Darl:

> "She's talking to God," Darl says. "She is calling on Him to help her."
> "What does she want Him to do?" I say.
> "She wants Him to hide her away from the sight of man," Darl says.
> "Why does she want to hide her away from the sight of man, Darl?"
> "So she can lay down her life," Darl says.
> (Vardaman Chapter 47, 495)

They hear her "turn over on her side," and Vardaman declares: "She's looking at me through the wood"—through the wood coffin. "How can she see through the wood, Darl?" (496). Darl never answers that one. But if Addie can manipulate time, holdfast its course to suit her will, she can as well perform other supernatural acts and commune with the living—even as her ancestors in the Jefferson cemetery communed with Addie before she died.

Ashamed of being alive, she's ashamed of being dead: "She wants Him to hide her away from the sight of man." The dead fish Vardaman brought home slid from his hands, flopped down "gap-mouthed, goggle-eyed, hiding into the dust *like it was ashamed of being dead,* like it was in a hurry to get back hid again" (Tull Chapter 8, 359). That fish signifies Ma Bundren; it figures as the emblem of her divinity. She is identified with the fish thus: "You seen it laying there," says Vardaman to the Tulls. "Cash is fixing to nail *her* [Ma] up, and *it* [the fish] was a-laying right there on the ground. You seen it. You seen the mark in the dirt" (Tull Chapter 16, 388). Cora Tull says she can't get anything out of the boy "except about a fish. . . . It's a judgment on them. I see the hand of the Lord upon this boy for Anse Bundren's judgment and warning" (389). She speaks with Bible in hand. "But my mother is a fish," says Vardaman. "Vernon seen it. He was there" (409).[5]

Addie figures as a circle of isolation, aloneness, and timelessness: "My aloneness had been violated and then made whole again by the violation: time, Anse, love, what you will, *outside the circle*" (464). The circle opens when they cohabit: "you and me ain't nigh done chapping yet, with just two" (464). Her first two offspring are Cash and Darl, both now between twenty-eight and thirty-one. Jewel, born in sin, approaches twenty years of age. Dewey Dell is seventeen, and Vardaman eight. By his name Jewel, who has no recognized father, contradicts his illegitimacy and challenges conventional morality. To be Born-in-Sin is a word substituting for the actual experience of birth. So time or reality—the event and its history—subsist in our configurations of the event through our abstractions about it, in our words. "I would think how *words* go straight up in a thin line," Addie muses, "and how terribly *doing* goes along the earth, clinging to it, so that after a while the two lines are too far apart for the same person to straddle from one to the other . . ." (465). Addiction to words characterizes Anse, Cora Tull, and Whitfield. Addiction to words characterizes those who live in time—*outside* the timeless circle. Darl, who loses touch with reality in madness, transcends time and belongs thus *within* Ma's circle, the wheel transcending time's reality (or reality as time). So too does Jewel, albeit he is the exemplar of deed versus word. Cora misinterprets Jewel:

> But you'd think from the way she talked that she [Addie] knew more about sin and salvation than the Lord God Himself. . . . When the only sin she ever committed was being partial to Jewel that never loved her

and was its own punishment, in preference to Darl that was touched by God Himself and considered queer by us mortals and that did love her. I said, "There is your sin. And your punishment too. Jewel is your punishment. But where is your salvation?"

The answer is Jewel—he is *Jewel* because he is *not* a Bundren (not a burden). It's not Ma's only sin in being partial to Jewel; her true sin—Cora doesn't know about it—was in Ma's being partial to Whitfield, in thus betraying Anse. If Darl is "touched by God Himself and considered queer by us mortals," then by equation God is—like Darl—irrational "and considered queer by us mortals." As for Jewel, "He is my cross and he will be my salvation. He will save me from the water and from the fire" (460). And Jewel redeems his mother's prophecy—he saves her from the river and from the burning barn. Jewel *is* her Savior, Christ the Redeemer. "He is my cross and he will be my salvation" is misinterpreted by Cora to refer to God. "Then I realized that she did not mean God. I realized that out of the vanity of her heart she had spoken sacrilege." Addie's identification of Jewel with Christ is more than Cora can bear: "I begged her to kneel and open her heart," etc. But Addie "just sat there, lost in her vanity and her pride, that had closed her heart to God *and set that selfish mortal boy in His place*" (Cash Chapter 36, 461).

As a schoolteacher Addie learned the futility of words, as well as the futility of violence. She whips her students: "When the switch fell I could feel it upon my flesh . . . and I would think with each blow of the switch: Now you are aware of me! Now I am something in your secret and selfish life, who have marked your blood with my own for ever and ever" (461-462). As Jack Gordon Goellner summarizes it (in *Perspective:* Spring 1954): "But the violence was not the answer, the lonely nights were still unbearable. . . . Not until she 'had' Cash, when the entity of her being was irrevocably divided and given two separate existences, and her aloneness violated by a presence of herself outside herself, did she realize the hopelessness of complete identity with other human beings. . . . Betrayed a second time by Anse's word, 'love,' and forced to submit to a second violation of her aloneness in a separation of another part of her being into Darl, she tried to protect herself in hatred. Her acquired understanding of the insignificance of words prevailed however. 'But then I realized that I had been tricked by words older than Anse or love, and that the same word had tricked Anse, too . . .' " (464).

Although she could never again accept Anse, because he clung still to words and did not perceive with her their ineffectuality, she nevertheless stayed with him. This was her forgiveness. "I did not even ask him for what he could have given me: not Anse. That was my duty to him, to not ask that, and that duty I fulfilled. I would be I; I would let him be the shape and echo of his word" (465). This is what she means when she says that Anse was dead. Dewey Dell says of her pa: "He looks like right after the maul hits the steer and it no longer alive and don't know yet that it's dead" (381). "And then he died," says Addie of her husband. "He did

not know he was dead" (466). Alive, he is dead because "the only burden Anse Bundren's ever had is himself" (390). That is Bundren's *burden.*
He dare not sweat lest he die; but *not* to sweat is *not* to live. Anse "puts
his shoes on, stomping into them, like he does everything like he is hop-
ing all the time he really can't do it and can quit trying" (359).

Neither Addie nor Anse has any living relative; they have no relation
to the past except to the dead past:

> Later he told me, "I ain't got no people. So that won't be no worry
> to you. I don't reckon you can say the same."
> "No. I have people. In Jefferson."
> His face fell a little. . . . "I know how town folks are, but maybe when
> they talk to me. . . ."
> "They might listen," I said. "But they'll be hard to talk to." He was
> watching my face. "They're in the cemetery."
> "But your living kin," he said. "They'll be different."
> "Will they?" I said. "I don't know. I never had any other kind" (463).

So she took Anse and had her firstborn —"I knew that living was terrible
and that this was the answer to it" (463).

What distinguishes Addie is her attribute of not-time. She cohabited
with Whitfield, the hypocrite preacher of God; her sin, in her sense, was
with God himself. Whitfield "was the instrument ordained by God who
created the sin, to sanctify that sin He had created. While I waited for
him in the woods, waiting for him before he saw me, I would think of
him as dressed in sin. I would think of him as thinking of me as dressed
also in sin, he the more beautiful since the garment which he had ex-
changed for sin was sanctified" (466). Sin and love are "the high dead
words in time," and Addie lives in a timeless world except on occasions of
creation and birth "in order to shape and coerce the terrible blood to the
forlorn echo of the dead word" (467, 466). "He has wore her out at
last," says Doctor Peabody of Anse. "And I said a damn good thing and
at first I would not go because there might be something I could do and
I would have to haul her back, by God" (Peabody Chapter 11, 366).
However, it was Addie who picked her own time to die, in a storm. *Her
coffin is time boarded up:* "And Cash like sawing the long hot sad yellow days up into planks and nailing them to something" (355). Her
capacity for living in two worlds is suggested thus: "But for me it was
not over. I mean, over in the sense of beginning and ending, because
to me there was no beginning nor ending then" (Addie Chapter 38, 467).
Her timelessness is suggested also by the fact that her coffin is "clock-
shape." She carries therein, as it were, "the living world."

"They had laid her in it reversed. Cash made it clock-shape, like this

with every joint and seam bevelled and scrubbed with the plane, tight
as a drum and neat as a sewing basket, and they had laid her in it head to

foot so it wouldn't crush her dress. It was her wedding dress and it had a flare-out bottom, and they had laid her head to foot in it so the dress could not spread out . . ." (400). After lying in the coffin several days, waiting for Jewel and Darl to bring from home a new wheel for the wagon that is to carry the coffin to Jefferson cemetery, Addie delivers her monologue (Addie Chapter 38), saying that "The shape of my body where I used to be a virgin is in the shape of a   and I couldn't think *Anse,* couldn't remember *Anse*" (465). That blank space is Faulkner's cryptogram, which to unriddle it spells out the word *pear.* The shape of her body where she used to be a virgin is in the shape of a pear, the same shape as her clock-shaped coffin. The identity of the one with the other explains why she remembers that fact. She remembers her pear-shaped womb while inside her pear-shaped coffin.[6] Birth and death are thus equated, and obversely death and birth; for her position in the pear-shaped coffin is head first—the same position of a child in the womb. By laying her in the womb-like coffin reversed, so as not to crush her wedding dress, they've prepared her Ready To Be Born Again. She represents time in the figure of eternity—creation, death and creation. For ever and ever the cycle, as is symbolized by the circular progress of her own life. She ends where she began.   (1959)

NOTES

1. In Modern Library edition, pp. 390, 400-401. Chapters are not numbered in the Faulkner text. These are Tull Chapter 16 and Vardaman Chapter 19.

2. My reading of Faulkner criticism on *As I Lay Dying* was limited to a half-dozen journals at the time of writing this essay in first-draft while at the University of Strasbourg, 1958-59, where I taught *As I Lay Dying*—it was on the prescribed graduate school reading-list for French students of American literature. Up to 1958 very little had been written on this novel, and so far as I could ascertain while at Strasbourg no critic had anticipated my reading of the novel's time-theme.

3. "It was like another art altogether," Conrad writes about "Heart of Darkness." "That sombre theme had to be given a sinister resonance, a tonality of its own, a continued vibration that, I hoped, would hang in the air and dwell on the ear after the last note had been struck." Preface to *Youth* (1902), in *Conrad's Prefaces,* ed. Edward Garnett (1937), p. 73.

4. Perhaps Faulkner intends to suggest that everyone partakes of the attribute of Eternity?

The *horse* and the *fish* symbols (Ma figures both as horse and as fish) occur in many mythologies, as Roma King, Jr. observes: "The horse generally denotes the subhuman, the animal state of man's nature, his virility, his instinctive passions. As a means of locomotion, the horse represents the surge of passion that carries man away; as a beast of burden it is related to the mother archetype. The fish, too, is traditionally a symbol of life. It represents the woman, the mother, the primitive sources of life; as a phallic symbol it indicates fertility and life renewal; in Christian symbolism, it stands for Christ and for the life-giving Sacraments, Holy Baptism and Holy Communion."

"The two symbols, traditionally related, Faulkner employs for his own purposes. He associates the horse with that part of Addie which, belonging to her lover (Whitfield), produces Jewel; the fish, with that part which, belonging to Anse, gives birth to Vardaman. The significant thing about Faulkner's fish is that it is dead. It forcefully contrasts, therefore, with the horse, with life, vitality, for certainly nothing is deader than a dead fish, than life which is no longer life." From *University of Kansas City Review:* Summer 1955.

5. "My mother is a fish" has its counterpart in "Jewel's mother is a horse." As Roma King points out, "These are both elements of the same symbol—two ways of seeing Addie, both equally important. . . . Vardaman's mother is the suffering, bleeding, dying woman, giving birth to her younger son as a token of responsibility to Anse. Jewel's mother is a horse, traditional symbol of spirit and passion. Addie is both the enduring, suffering wife, and the proud, defiant, prevailing lover; both life and death." This note amends my own reading, although I too see Addie as the eternal mother: "I think if he [Anse] were to wake and cry, I would suckle him too."

6. Dewey Dell, pregnant, speaks of *"the womb of time; the agony and the despair of spreading bones, the hard girdle in which lie the outraged entrails of events"* (Dewey Dell Chapter 29, 422). The pear-shaped coffin is at one thus with the pear-shaped "womb of time."

Faulkner sets the above passage into italics; elsewhere, occasionally, italics for a word or phase or short sentence are mine.

PART TWO

The New Critics

Erasmus did not scold his age, he assimilated it.
     —Allen Tate: review in NEW REPUBLIC (June 8, 1927)

(1)

THERE IS ONE basic theme in modern criticism: it is the *dissociation of modern sensibility*. The loss of a spiritual order and of integrity in the modern consciousness is T. S. Eliot's major premise. The issue of our glorification of the scientific vision at the expense of the aesthetic vision is the central theme in both the poetry and the criticism of the Southern poet-critics. It is this theme of spiritual disorder which the late Paul Valéry exploited; it shows through the current of the critical writings of I. A. Richards, F. R. Leavis, Yvor Winters, R. P. Blackmur, and the Southern critics. The New Critics, while differing among one another in theory or in practice, are as one through the unifying relation of this obsessive burden.

To what use does the critic put it? My purpose in this essay is to order into a synthesis the critical ideas and methods of the New Critics, and for my starting point I shall trace the ways in which this theme operates at the critical level.

One variation upon the theme is *the loss of tradition*. We lack a religious and a social tradition which would extend moral and intellectual authority to the poet. Dante and the poets of other great ages of poetry had at hand a body of ideas and a faith in them. There is no such agreement today. Never were poets more profoundly divided from the life of society than in our time. The effect upon our Experimental Generation of the loss of an antecedent discipline such as tradition provides forms the subject of Yvor Winters' *Primitivism and Decadence*. The loss has resulted in a poetry of structural confusion. The theme of Eliot's *After Strange Gods* is the limiting or crippling effect upon our literature of our dislocation from a living tradition. The effect is twofold: (1) confusion as to the boundaries of criticism, and (2) extreme individualism in viewpoints —the expression of a personal view of life, the exploitation of personality. Allen Tate, following Eliot, defines tradition as "a quality of judgment and of conduct, rooted in a concrete way of life" that we inherit from our immediate past, or, if we are makers of tradition (and it demands our constant rediscovery), the quality of life that we create and pass on to the next generation. Tradition, no less than religion itself, is formed of a structure of absolutes—points of moral and intellectual reference "implicit and emergent in experience at all times, and under certain conditions, explicit and realized." This conception of tradition is the foundation for the critical outlook of both Eliot and Tate. Eliot's conception of an immutable order is ultimately religious; like Valéry's, Tate's is ultimately aesthetic.

The theme is repeated in other terms—from Hulme to Blackmur—as *the loss of a fixed convention* providing the poet a unifying relation to his society. The modern poet, deprived of some rational structure from which he might derive discipline and authority, is under the constant necessity of either resurrecting a dead convention (Millay) or erecting a new one of his own (Yeats). A tradition or a culture manifests itself in the language, in the medium of the poet's words. It is only in terms of language, which may be defined as the embodiment of our experience in words, that a convention exists or survives. The work of a great poet is the creation of a new convention, a new order of language. A convention is simply the way in which language has been used by the poets of a preceding generation, used so powerfully that we can but carry on its major significance. The operation of this principle in Tate's criticism is best illustrated by his judgment on Edna Millay. By using the language of the preceding generation to convey an emotion peculiar to her own, and by making that language personal, Edna Millay restored life to a dead convention. This is her distinction, but it is also her limitation. She preserved, in the traditional style of the preceding decadent age, the personality of her own age—without altering either. The criticism of Tate, Brooks, and Blackmur is built upon this principle of the language: does the poet make "a genuine attempt to use in his poems the maximum resource of poetic language consonant with his particular talent"?

A third thematic variation is the loss of an objective system of truths imbedded in a homogeneous society—*the loss of belief* in religion and in myth. Eliot claims that what Blake's genius required and lacked "was a framework of accepted and traditional ideas which would have prevented him from indulging in a philosophy of his own, and concentrated his attention on the problems of the poet. . . . The concentration resulting from a framework of mythology and theology and philosophy is one of the reasons why Dante is a classic, and Blake only a poet of genius." Eliot's theme informs Tate's standard for judging such poets as Robinson, MacLeish, and Cummings. Because they had no systematic philosophy or external framework of ideas to sustain them, they substituted their own personality as the core of experience and meaning. MacLeish lacked what Milton had, namely "an objective convention that absorbed every implication of his personal feeling." Lacking an epos or myth, E. A. Robinson had to repeat himself, the same ground again and again, writing a poem that would not be written. On Cummings the criticisms of Tate and of John Peale Bishop came to the same point: Cummings' poetry is an image of his unique personality. In ages which suffer the loss of religion there is chaos and violence expressed, and that is what Eliot's *The Waste Land* means. It means "that men who have lost both the higher myth of religion and the lower myth of historical dramatization have lost the forms of human action; it means that they are no longer capable . . . of forming a dramatic conception of human nature. . . ." In place of the dramatization of the soul, as we find it in Emily Dickinson's poetry, we get from a contemporary poet like MacLeish the dramatization (in *Conquistador*) of personality against an historical setting.

Another form the theme takes is *the loss of a world order,* a world order which can be assimilated to the poetic vision. Shakespeare had such a world order in his medieval pattern of life, and Emily Dickinson had one in her New England Puritan Christianity. Without moral and intellectual standards the poet has no means for measuring and testing his personal experience. Our age lacks what Shelley called the "fixed point of reference" for the poet's sensibility. The assumption—a fallacy common to contemporary poets[1]—that order or adequate form can be created simply by the poet's act of self-expression, by his imitation of the world disorder in what Winters has labeled Expressive or Imitative Form—fails the poet as a solution for the problem of poetic structure. For Winters, Tate, F. R. Leavis, John Crowe Ransom, or R. P. Blackmur—a poem for these critics must have a rational structure, a core of meaning, a scheme of objective reference which orders and gives meaning to the poet's emotions.[2] "Shelley, at his best and worst, offers the emotion in itself, unattached, in the void" (Leavis in *Revaluation*). In MacLeish's *Conquistador* a mechanism of personal sensation is substituted for theme or meaning; the personality attached to Cummings' *Viva* is the only meaning in Cummings' poems; the coherence of *The Bridge* is merely the coherence of the tone or poet's attitude. Tate sets down Crane's career as "a vindication of Eliot's major premise—that the integrity of the individual consciousness has broken down." The failure of *The Bridge,* by virtue of its structural disorder, is symptomatic of the failure of modern poetry generally. Tate's analysis of Crane's poetry extends beyond the poems to the outer area of disorder and cross-purposes in the contemporary milieu. Tate relates the world disorder to the poetic one. Likewise, in examining other poets (Eliot, Pound, Emily Dickinson, Bishop), he scrutinizes both the conscious intention of the poet, the intention which is framed within the poem, and the unconscious intention—the cultural mind of the poet's world order as it is expressed in the poetry.

Intellectual chaos has been the background of American poetry and criticism during this period. The problem confronting a poet is to transfer to the poetic process a unified point of view synthesized out of the social and intellectual climate; but in our world today the complexity of these relations is not readily resolvable into a unity. "The modern can never avoid the suspicion," Samuel Hoare observes, "that whatever attitude he takes up is only a partial expression of himself and a partial activity. And he has no scale of values which would justify him in concluding that this part is the most important, that this activity is the fundamental activity. Without this, great poetry is impossible." It is a commonplace of criticism, I repeat, that our present-day world is in radical disintegration and that the artist is severed from a living relation to society. Both W. H. Auden and Stephen Spender have explored this theme in their critical writings, Auden pointing out that when there is no organized dogma within society the artist becomes self-consciously didactic. As D. S. Savage says (in *The Personal Principle*), "The modern artist cannot take his values from contemporary society, because that society lacks all coherent standards and values. This it is which explains the artist's isolation from society. In his isolation he is forced to depend upon what values he can find within himself, and this makes a 'classical' art impossible."

The critics tell us that ours is an age of intellectual chaos and spiritual disunity, and yet, despite the prevailing disjuncture between artist and society, it is an age of great poetry. The dilemma of the modern poet, according to Tate, has its counterpart in the disfranchised intellect of the critic. (Blackmur singles out Yvor Winters as a conspicuous example.) It is claimed that the dissociation of sensibility—a theory which has echoed throughout criticism since it first appeared in Eliot's definition of the Metaphysical poets—transposes into the split mind of the critic. And yet it is an age of great criticism. Order, system, and (notwithstanding all the cross-currents of disagreement) unity toolmark the total achievement of the critics of our time.

(2)

Criticism is the positing and criticizing of dogmas, and its quest is standards of judgment and value. Though Tate disclaims the act of the systematic literary critic, his criticism nevertheless is systematic as an aesthetic theory and as a synthesis of dogmas. The critical ideas do not conflict with each other, as they do in Herbert Read's criticism, but form a coherent system of principles. The system is unified by a single point of view. The point of view, which is that of T. E. Hulme, derives from Bergson. There is a radical division between the realm of faith and the realm of reason; between, on the one hand, the intuitive and qualitative, and, on the other hand, the intellectual and quantitative. It was Hulme's thesis that our spiritual disunity is the result of our failure to recognize the division which exists between the Religious Attitude, which postulates absolute values by which man is judged as limited and imperfect, and the Humanist Attitude, which regards man as fundamentally good and life as the source and measure of all values. Hulme designated the confusion of these two orders as the essence of Romanticism. "The view which regards man as a well, a reservoir, full of possibilities, I call the romantic; the one which regards him as a very finite and fixed creature, I call the classical." Hulme's identification of humanism with romanticism and of the religious attitude with classicism is followed by Eliot, and likewise by Tate.

Classicism means the discrimination between reason and faith; and romanticism, the confusion of reason and faith. This confusion, Eliot complains, has been the background of the modern consciousness since the Renaissance. But as Read remarks, our age "is not clearly either a romantic or a classical age, nor are the categories of a romantic or a classical tradition applicable to it." More significant and fundamental is the dichotomy between art and science. This post-Renaissance dichotomy, which replaces the Renaissance antinomy between faith and reason, represents an opposition between qualitative knowledge (art) and quantitative knowledge (science). The modern problem, as John Middleton Murry sees it, is to reach a synthesis between these two orders of knowledge. He maintains that not until a new synthesis is posed will any work of art of the first magnitude be possible again. In advocating the medieval synthesis as projected into the Thomist system, Murry suggests that "the Classicism of the Middle Ages can serve us only as a symbol, not as a pattern, of a new synthesis" ("Towards a Synthesis," *Criterion:* May, 1927). Tate sums up our modern dilemma through the same perspective and in similar terms. In the decay of Protestantism is to be found the chief clue to our understanding of English literature. Tate's opposition to the modern positivist procedure, the reduction of all knowledge to the quantitative kind, has the same foundation as Murry's opposition to the scientific materialism of our time.

Both Eliot and Tate have thoroughly orientated themselves in Hulme's *Speculations.* As his critics have observed, Hulme's dicta, in the same or in different settings, appear throughout Eliot's writings. They show up also in Tate's. In Hulme is grounded, for instance, Tate's objection to Emerson's conception of man. (It was Emerson's conception which dissipated all tragic possibilities in that culture for dramatizing the human soul, as Robert Penn Warren points out.) Hulme might have phrased this accounting for the great wastes in Emily Dickinson and Walt Whitman:

> The great bulk of the verse of each appears to have been written on the sustaining pretense that everything was always possible. To see boundless good on the horizon, to see it without the limiting discipline of the conviction of evil, is in poetry as in politics the great stultifier of action. . . . With no criterion of achievement without there could be no criterion of completion within.
>
> (R. P. Blackmur in *The Expense of Greatness*)

Hulme defined the mood and perspective of our age; and this is his importance, almost exclusively. He is important not because he was an original thinker, but because of his influence upon those who have dominated and largely directed the course of contemporary criticism. Tate is a disciple of Hulme in his campaign against scientism, romanticism, and humanism ("the belief that the only values that matter are human values"). Tate accepts as necessary a system of religion because it provides standards by which man can measure his own imperfections. ("The religious unity of intellect and emotion, of reason and instinct, is the sole technique for the realization of values.")

The affinity between the Southern critics and Hulme lies in their common claim that our present disunity has been created by the confusion of two categories: the aesthetic vision, which is concerned with quality, and the scientific vision, which is concerned with quantity. The disunity of the modern mind is the single theme of Tate's *Reason in Madness*. It is the scientism of our age that has forced out the religious attitude and reduced the spiritual realm to irrelevant emotion, under the illusion that all experience can be ordered scientifically. It is the decline of organized religion that has given rise to utilitarian theories of art. Dewey's theory of the integrating power of art attributes to art all the psychological virtues of a religion. Under the formula that all art is action, he identifies art and religion and science as "satisfying the same fundamental needs." Tate, of course, rejects this equation. In "The Aesthetic Emotion as Useful" (in *This Quarter:* Dec., 1932), he exposes the fallacy of the pragmatic aesthetic. Both Tate, in *Reason in Madness,* and Ransom, in *The New Criticism,* attack victoriously the positivists' position and thereby perform for modern criticism, as one of their critics acknowledges, an invaluable service. In line with an aesthetician like Eliseo Vivas, the Southern critics regard the aesthetic and the practical as opposites. Contrary to Dewey's pragmatic aesthetic, art is neither another kind of religion nor another kind of science. Poetry is poetry and not science or religion.

The canon of the Southern critics is based upon a division of art and science into two independent, objective, and equally valid categories of experience. Science and poetry are the opposite poles of truth; art and religion, though both are the vehicles of qualitative experience, are not identical. It was Arnold's faith that poetry, since religion had yielded to science, could take over the work of religion. (Though the facts of science had undermined religion, they could still support poetry!) Arnold's viewpoint has its contemporary version in I. A. Richards' *Science and Poetry*. Richards here endorsed Arnold's dictum that what is valuable in religion is its aesthetic aspects. Tate's analysis of Arnold shows his position as giving the case for poetry away to the scientist. Arnold's poetics turns poetry into a "descriptive science or experience at that level, touched with emotion." Tate and Ransom attempt to solve anew Arnold's problem. They attempt to place poetry on an equal footing with science. They do so by claiming that poetry is primarily of the intellect and that poetry is "an independent form of knowledge, a kind of cognition equal to the knowledge of the sciences at least, perhaps superior." They claim for art those cognitive ingredients which the early Richards, by his former positivist position, discredited. The knowledge which poetry gives us is a special kind of knowledge and not, as Richards once persuaded us to think, merely an inferior kind of science. Richards misunderstood the aesthetic emotion and equated poetry with life, so Montgomery Belgion declared in his critique, "What Is Criticism?" (*Criterion:* Oct., 1930). The later Richards of *Coleridge on Imagination* (1934), however, has repudiated his former utilitarian theory of art, and with his present definition of poetry—"Poetry is the completest mode of utterance"—Tate acknowledged an essential agreement. (Paul Valéry and T. Sturge Moore have expressed similar insights.) As Tate frames it, "the high forms of literature offer us the only

complete, and thus the most responsible, versions of our experience."
The arts "give us a sort of cognition at least equally valid with that of the
scientific method."

Ransom's theory of poetry as knowledge is fundamentally the same
as Tate's. Science and poetry present two different descriptions of the
world. Science presents an abstract description, poetry attempts a total
description of the object. Poetry's representation of the world is an al-
ternative to that pictured by science. The abstract structures of science
sacrifice "the body and substance of the world." Poetry, by virtue of its
concrete particulars, restores "The World's Body." (The difference be-
tweeen art and science is marked out in similar terms by Ramon Fernandez: art qualifies, individualizes; whereas science schematizes, collects
relations.) "The local, the immediate, and the concrete are the take-off
of poetry," Tate remarks (in *Poetry:* May, 1932). The problem of the
poet is essentially a problem of aesthetics: what shall the poet "imitate"
and to what end? "Art arises in particulars, and it arrives at order at the
point of impact between the new particulars and whatever recognized experience the poet has been able to acquire" (*New Republic:* Aug. 2, 1933).
Ransom, practising his imitation theory of knowledge upon a poem by
Hardy, observes that Hardy's language "is not content with the concepts,
but is constantly stopping to insert or to attach the particularity which is
involved in images; a procedure which might be called the imaginative
realization of the concepts. A genuine poetic energy will work with both
these dimensions at once." (*Southern Review:* Summer, 1940). Translated into Tate's terms, the two dimensions embodied in a poem are "extension" and "intension," and the meaning of a poem is its "tension" of
these two extremes of language. A good poem achieves a unity of fusion
between abstraction and concretion. Idea and image are in tension. On
the term *tension* Tate has built his entire aesthetic. (This key word is to
Tate's criticism what the term *paradox* is to Brooks's critical theory.)

For Tate, as for Schopenhauer, art aims at nothing outside itself. This
formalist creed has brought against the Southern critics the charge of
art for art's sake, but their principle of art for art's sake must be interpreted very differently from the aestheticism of the Nineties. Rightly
understood, the principle has tremendous implications. Tate's position
again squares with John Middleton Murry's: "Art is autonomous, and to be
pursued for its own sake, precisely because it comprehends the whole of
human life; because it has reference to a more perfect human morality
than any other activity of man." Tate's stand puts him at odds with any
critical program which inflicts upon art the values of science, or of metaphysics, or of social philosophy. He repudiates, for instance, the program
of Edmund Wilson for an art-science. Wilson's view is that art and science,
as they come to apply themselves more directly to life, may yet arrive
"at a way of thinking, a technique of dealing with our perceptions,
which will make art and science one." Wilson's optimism is based on
Whitehead's idea that the poetic and the scientific impulses, being radically

different, must unite harmoniously in a compromise. This proposal of a compromise is at the heart of Wilson's rejection of the Symbolists (in his *Axel's Castle*). His optimism has kinship with Wordsworth's faith, as Edwin Muir interprets it, that as soon as the world of science becomes somehow as "familiar" as the primitive world of religious myth, our cultural integrity and our literature will be restored. "This belief ignores the hopeless breach between the abstractionism of science and the object itself, for which the abstraction stands and to which it is the business of the poet to return" (Tate in *The Nation:* Nov. 17, 1926).

(3)

We have discussed the relation of the New Criticism to the spirit of the age, we have traced the central and unifying theme upon which the New Criticism is based, and we have defined the leading dogmas and critical attitudes which have influenced and formed the canons of the New Critics. The most important American critics who have organized our critical attitudes are Eliot, Tate and Ransom, Winters, and Kenneth Burke. Burke is the Aristotle of our criticism, the Aristotle who constructs vast systems. Of all our critics no one has done more towards revolutionizing our reading of a poem than Cleanth Brooks, and no critic has been of greater practical influence. While Brooks and Warren have brought the New Criticism into the universities, it is Tate and Ransom who have furnished it with systematic aesthetic studies. Their critical ideas constitute a single doctrine, their critical positions being basically identical. True, Ransom is the *point de repère* of American letters, as Donald A. Stauffer says; but Tate stakes out the issues more resolutely, and without Ransom's ironic detachment. As the spokesman for the Southern school of poet-critics, he has the greatest eye for the facts of the times and he is downright and persuasive in declaring them. It is this which accounts for my placing of Tate at the center of this present perspective. In these critical cross-currents there are violent disagreements, but, as Ransom remarks, any one of the New Critics shows the influence of the others, and the total effort amounts to a sort of collaboration.

Tate's critical writings constitute a campaign against all schools of critics who judge art for its pragmatic values. Art proves nothing: "it creates the totality of experience in its quality; and it has no useful relation to the ordinary forms of action" (*Reactionary Essays*). According to Tate's theory of art, art springs from the irresistible need of the mind for an absolute experience, one which cannot be adequately satisfied in ordinary experience. The only coherent reality that we can experience is in art, for it is here alone that the disparate elements of our experience attain coherence and form. Art apprehends and concentrates our experience within the limitations of form. The poet as maker strives toward a signification of an experience, emotion, or idea, until it becomes, within the dimensions of the poem, "absolute." Poetry is the fusion of "an intensely felt ordinary experience, an intense moral situation, into an intensely realized art." The great poems are absolute: there is nothing beyond the poem. Tate offers the critic no formula for recognizing this quality of absolutism. Ransom follows Tate's doctrine here in his insistence that "Good critical writing is always more or less empirical in method, which means that the critic looks first and last at the poem, while he tries to determine what poetic theory will be the one to accomplish its analysis. Each poem is a new poem, and each analysis is probably the occasion of a new extension of theory in order to cope with it" ("Ubiquitous Moralists," *Kenyon Review:* Winter, 1941). In "Poetry and the Absolute," which contains the core of Tate's poetics, Tate made the same point, namely that the test of a poem must be applied *a posteriori*.[3]

> One may say that Yeats's poems, *Upon a Dying Lady*, survive the test, in any formulation. . . . He has presented a newly-created *emotion* never before felt by anyone and never to be felt creatively by anyone else; has contributed an absolute signification to an old and relative fact. It is absolute because it is unique and contains no point of relation to any other signification of that fact.

In the perfectly realized poem there is no overflow of unrealized emotion, no emotion or action in excess of the object or situation which should be the objective equivalent for that emotion. Poets must be selected by some absolute, even if it is only a provisional one. If there is any originally ulterior motive, such as Dante's moral contempt for his enemies in Hell, the ulterior motive "is absorbed and becomes implicit in form, rather than explicit and didactic." Paul Valéry has described the perfect poem by way of a simile, comparing it to "a distant sailing-vessel—inanimate but articulate, seemingly with an absolute life of its own."

Eliot's Impersonal Theory of Art, which he announced in "Tradition and the Individual Talent" and elaborated in *The Sacred Wood* (1920), is repeated in scattered instances of Tate's critical dicta. A poem is not the secretion of personal emotions. The emotion or idea embodied in a work of art is impersonal. "The more perfect the artist," Eliot declares, "the more completely separate in him will be the man who suffers and the mind which creates." Contrary to Coleridgean theory, which has led criticism out of the poem and into the mind, Tate's poetics assert that the specific poetic element is an objective feature of the poem, rather than a subjective effect. We can never determine whether a work is a work of art by establishing its subjective, or purely personal, correlatives. The critic who asserts that he is investigating poetry from the psychological approach is actually leading us away from the fact of the art-work, Tate observes.[4] His stand is poles apart from Herbert Read's "ontogenetic" criticism, as practiced on Shelley in his *In Defense of Shelley,* "which traces the origins of the work of art in the psychology of the individual and in the economic structure of society." But literary criticism (the definition is Desmond MacCarthy's) is concerned with values, not with the psychological origin of such values. The traditional critic like Tate, as distinguished from the experimental critic like Read, investigates the nature of the poem *as* poem; not the origin of the poem (Read), nor its effect upon the reader (Richards), nor its value for civilization (Dewey).

For Ransom, likewise, the business of the literary critic is exclusively with an aesthetic criticism. Aesthetic values are anchored within the poem; it is solely the aesthetic structure, the internal organization of the poem, that gives any poem its value. Its value as a poem does not lie in its relation to the mind of the author. In "The Objective Basis of Criticism" (*Western Review:* Summer, 1948), Eliseo Vivas defines an aesthetic structure to be one "which successfully excludes the irrelevant values and controls vigorously the values and meanings it communicates." A work of art, I contend, contains but a single intention, and all the seemingly disparate and conflicting elements which are enclosed within the dimensions of the work accrete around and function towards that one intended end. As for Tate and Eliot, a work of art has a life of its own. True, the ultimate question concerning a work is out of how deep a life does it spring? But the critical question which determines whether it is a work of art is: has it a life of its own? "The life of art is in its form" (Bishop). The difference between art and its germinal event is absolute. The expression of those elements which give art its aesthetic identity and its absolute quality, Roger Fry states in his *Vision and Design,* is never identical with the expression of these elements in actual life. Though Fry limits his discussion to the field of the plastic arts, the concept is open to more general application. Consideration of poetry bears this out. In poetry, life and art can in no way be made equivalent because the emotions or experience which poetry offers are not the actual emotions or experience which everyday life presents, they are specifically aesthetic emotions. (Fry defines the aesthetic experience to be the apprehension of the purely formal relations of a work of art.) This distinction between life and art is also made by Belgion in criticizing Richards' supposition, in *Practical Criticism* that there is no gap between the two realms. Not only is the aesthetic emotion different from the emotion we should have if we experienced the poem's subject in actual life, but it can be produced without having originated in life at all. And Tate attests to this fact in his Preface to his *Selected Poems:* ". . . that, as a poet, I have never had any [original] experience, and that, as a poet, my concern is the experience that I hope the reader will have in reading the poem." We as readers, T. Sturge Moore comments in his study of Valéry, come to poetry not to know what poets feel; "we read poems because they are wholes, composed of harmonized words and meanings which inter-echo symphonically."

To analyze and elucidate the formed meaning of a poem or novel is the prime job of the critic; but criticism must also make judgments as well as analyses, and therefore criticism cannot stand apart from theory. For technical criticism we look to Brooks, Blackmur, or Empson; for theoretical formulations of the nature of poetry, to Burke, Ransom, Tate,

Winters, or Richards. Ransom, like Burke, is a philosophical critic. As critic his prime interest is in the metaphysics of aesthetics; it is only incidentally that he is committed to the technical criticism of poetry. As in *The World's Body,* he begins with aesthetics as the starting point for a philosophical defense of poetry. He gives us a poetics, and the core of it lies in his principle that the differentium of poetry is a metaphysical or ontological one. Poetry is ontology. Poetry, Charles Maurras similarly points out in his Preface to *Musique Intérieure,* is ontology, "for poetry strives . . . towards the roots of the knowledge of Being." Ransom transposes the problem of being, which is for him the basic problem in aesthetics, to the plane of the imaginative content of literature and art. He examines the "ontology" of a work and makes a metaphysical or aesthetic judgment of it. In the principle that the intellect is the foundation of poetry and that the criterion of judgment is a qualitative one, Ransom and Tate are Aristotelian. To quote Tate, Ransom "has explored possibilities of an Aristotelian criticism of the poetic disorder of our time." He has attempted to establish poetic truth as objective. A poem is a self-enclosed world which "recovers for us the world of solid substance." Its status is "objective," even as the criticism which is a criticism of that poetic structure is objective. Poetry is one way of knowing the world. The knowledge obtainable from poetry is unique. It is radically or ontologically distinct from the prose or scientific formulation. In any scientific formulation objects exist not as solid objects but as points in a structural pattern which controls them. The thought pattern controls and subordinates them to the realization of a thesis. Now in a poem what is analogous to the prose or scientific formulation is its logical structure-meaning. The structure of a poem is its prose argument (the universal); but a poem has not only this determinate meaning, which attaches to the structure, but it has a texture-meaning as well. The texture is the context of indeterminate and heterogeneous details (the concrete). These many-valued texture-meanings are significant since they function in the total meaning of the poem, but they are logically irrelevant to the structure-meaning alone. (This tissue of concrete irrelevance is more valuable for its own sake than for its contribution to the prose argument of the poem.) "A poetic discourse embodies within itself . . . a prose discourse. I think this is a law of poetry. . . . No prose argument, no poem. The prose argument is the poem's 'structure'; and then 'texture' suggests itself for the name of the ubiquitous and unstructural detail" ("The Inorganic Muses").

The flaw in much of modern poetry, and for Ransom this is the flaw in *The Waste Land,* is that it is all texture and no structure. "Poetic texture without logical structure is not the right strategy." The differentium of poetry is this texture-structure order of objectivity. And the critic's job is to examine and define this texture-structure formulation in individual poems under his scrutiny. To do this, Ransom insists, requires an aesthetician's understanding of what a poem generally "is." "The thing that makes a lyrical poem supreme over other literary forms, and indeed the epitome and standard of literary forms, is its range of content; or, what is the same thing, its density" ("Mr. Empson's Muddles"). It is by the content or subject matter that Ransom differentiates a poetry from a poetry—on the basis of the ontology of the poem, "the reality of its being." In *God Without Thunder,* he poses the view that though poetry and religion are agents of the irrational, they nevertheless yield a greater reality than science does. "Art is radically not science." What distinguishes a poetic discourse from a scientific one is the degree of irrelevant and indeterminate concreteness, the texture.[5]

Permanent poetry, Eliot holds, is a fusion of these two poles of the mind: emotion and thought. For Tate it is a fusion of concretion and abstraction, image and idea, or (to substitute Ransom's dichotomy) texture and structure. Tate reframes Eliot's view: poetry does not give us "an emotional experience," nor "an intellectual experience"; it gives us a poetic experience. In commenting on Wallace Stevens' *Ideas of Order,* Blackmur defines the poetic experience from a parallel viewpoint. Ideas are abstractions, but they are also things seen. "It is the function of poetry . . . to experience ideas of the first kind with the eyes of the second kind, and to make of the experience of both a harmony and an order: a harmonium" (In *The Expense of Greatness*). In all great poetry there is a clash of opposite elements issuing in a tension between abstraction and sensation. In Donne and in Emily Dickinson, "There is no thought as such at all; nor is there feeling; there is that unique focus of experience which is at once neither and both." Emily Dickinson's abstractions are not visible separately from her sensuous illuminations of them; idea and image are in tension. Like Donne, "she *perceives abstraction and thinks sensation*" (Tate in *Reactionary Essays*). The genuine poem embodies both the emotion (or thought) *and* the situation which provokes it. Tate regards Hardy's abstractions as beyond the range of his feelings, since Hardy "rarely shows us the experience that ought to justify them, that would give them substance, visibility, meaning" ("Hardy's Philosophic Metaphors"). He judges Crane and Cummings by the same criterion. (It is the criterion of the Objective Correlative.) Winters' formula that poetry is technique for dealing with irreducible emotion, which Tate attacks in "Confusion and Poetry" (*Sewanee Review:* Apr., 1930), conceals a contemporary version of the romantic dogma that poetry is emotion.[6] Emotion is not the exclusive subject matter of poetry. As Auden says, "abstractions are empty and their expression devoid of a poetic value." And the poet's emotions, these too have no value in themselves. In his Preface to Valéry's *le serpent,* Eliot states the point: "Not our feelings, but the pattern which we make of our feelings is the centre of value."

The New Critics have found their standards for great poetry in the seventeenth century Metaphysicals. Using Richards' viewpoint, Brooks defines metaphysical poetry as a poetry of synthesis and claims for it the highest order. It is a poetry which joins widely divergent and conflicting elements in imagery that is functional rather than decorative, and it achieves thus the desired union of emotion and thought. In Donne's poems the comparisons are not illustrations attached to a statement, as they are in Arnold's. In Donne "The comparison *is* the poem in a structural sense." The poetry of synthesis as defined by Richards is synonymous with the poetry of the imagination as defined by Tate (in contradistinction to the poetry of the will—allegory or propaganda art). A poetry of the will, as distinct from a poetry of the imagination, ignores the whole vision of an experience for some special moral, or political, or social interest; the meaning is forced and the total context of the human predicament oversimplified or unexplored. Such didactic poetry is "one-sided"; it is therefore inferior both as a poetic discourse and as a prose or scientific one ("Three Types of Poetry"). "Platonic poetry" is Tate's and Ransom's descriptive term for this didactic poetry which brings poetry into competition with science, falsifying their relationship. Unlike the Metaphysical poet, the Platonic poet discourses in terms of things, "but on the understanding that they are translatable at every point into ideas"; or he elaborates ideas as such, "but in proceeding introduces for ornament some physical properties." Platonic poetry deals with ideas, Physical poetry deals with concrete things. For Ransom, all genuine poetry is a phase of Physical poetry ("A Note on Ontology").

Brooks's *Modern Poetry and the Tradition* (1939) is a critical synthesis of this modern revolution in our conception of poetry. The revolution, in sum, has consisted chiefly in a return to the Metaphysicals and hence in a repudiation of their heretical deviators: the Augustan Neo-Classicists, who regarded metaphor as a decoration of poetic thought-content; and the nineteenth century Romantics, who discredited irony or wit (the essential ingredient of metaphysical poetry) and regarded poetry as an elevated way of expressing elevated beliefs. Milton and Shelley have been the two main points of attack in this revised perspective of the poetic tradition. We have witnessed the thorough repudiation of Shelley (by Leavis, Tate, and Eliot), and the dislodgment of Milton— for which Eliot was wholly responsible. We have paid homage to Dryden, especially to Dryden the critic, with Eliot and Mark Van Doren as the chief instigators of his ascendant reputation. Pope, placed by Leavis and Brooks in the Metaphysical line (in *Revaluation* and in *The Well Wrought Urn*), has finally come into his own again. But it is Donne who has dominated our poetic and critical climate. While the New Criticism begins with Eliot's *Sacred Wood*, it had its taking-off in Hulme's pronouncement that the Romantic convention had reached a point of exhaustion and that, of immediate necessity, it was now the moment for a new convention or technique to replace the dead one. For the new convention, modern poetry drew upon the school of Donne and, along with it, the school of the French Symbolists—both schools representing radical departures from the common poetic tradition. The New Criticism was created out of this new convention—to explain it and to make it accessible.

(4)

We have outlined some of the prevaling critical theories of art and the nature of poetry, and we have traced the critical interchanges of principles and methods among the New Critics. What remains to be sketched in are some redefinitions of the nature and function of criticism.

The sole purpose of criticism is to enlighten the reader, to instruct the reader, to create the *proper* reader. The critic prepares the reader to appreciate the ascendant artists of his time by defining for him standards of taste and examples of taste in operation. The chief end of criticism is to elucidate the relation of the poet, or the reader, to the poem. All critical writings can be classified under one or more parts of this three-part poet-to-poem-to-reader relationship. All of Richards' criticism, for instance, fits into this framework. This schematic idea is epitomized in his theory of poetry as communication: a poem is an organization of experience, a resolution and "balancing of impulses," and the reader gets the same harmony or "ordering of the mind" as the poet originally experienced. Though neither Brooks nor Tate fully assents to Richards' theory of poetry as communication, Brooks holds similarly that we, as the poet's readers, in a process akin to the poet's exploration of his material, "refabricate from his symbols . . . a total experience somewhat similar, if we possess imagination, to the total experience of the poet himself." Eliot's idea of the Objective Correlative suggests a parallel correlation: the objects or chain of images in a poem, if it is the objective correlative of the poet's original emotion about it, immediately evokes in the spectator the same emotion.

The poet-poem-reader relationship is again illustrated by the Problem of Belief: the question whether it is necessary for the reader to share the poet's beliefs in order to enjoy fully his poetry. The problem of the poem as related to the poet's, or the reader's, beliefs is resolved by Eliot thus: "When the doctrine, theory, belief, or 'view of life' presented in a poem is one which the mind of the reader can accept as coherent, mature, and founded on the facts of experience, it interposes no obstacle to the reader's enjoyment. . . ." With this interpretation, which Eliot makes in *The Use of Poetry* (1933), all later critics concur. The question of the specific merit of a poetic statement as truth or falsehood does not arise when the beliefs of the poet are ordered into an intrinsic whole. It is on this ground that Tate rejects Shelley's poetry, not because Shelley's ideas are immature but because his statements are not an integral part of a genuine poem. As Eliot notes: "Both in creation and enjoyment much always enters which is, from the point of view of 'art,' irrelevant." One irrelevance is the truth or falsity of the belief expressed in the poem *as* poem. It was a mistake for the young Richards to think that what, in the way of acceptance, is demanded of a poem is the poet's own beliefs. All of Spender's best poems convey single emotions, but, as Tate says (in

New Verse: May, 1933), "these *single emotions* are created, in the sense that a table or chair is created; they are not believed."

Belief, as applied to the arts, is a sociological category. To assign objective status to the content of a poem apart from its form is to reduce the poem's meaning to its original state, and this is to locate it in the historical process. Within terms of this affirmation the critic is testing poetic subject matter by its correlation with the world it represents—the correlations being either historical, psychological, ethical, or economic. This doctrine of relevance is false. The only relevance the New Critics subscribe to is the relevance which subject-ideas have to each other within the formed meaning of the work itself. Poetry, as Blackmur affirms (in *The Double Agent*), "is life at the remove of form and meaning"; criticism has to do with "the terms and modes" by which this remove was made, that is, with the relation between content and form. A work of art is autonomous. It has a life of its own, and it is limited by its own technique and intention. The New Critics isolate the meaning of a poem only in terms of form.

Their critical practice is consistent with their critical theory. Contrary to Jacques Barzun, Tate does not repudiate the validity of textual exegesis (his own explication of his *Ode to the Confederate Dead* is proof enough). A paraphrase is not the work itself; a paraphrase defines only the poem's structural plan. It is the inferior poem alone that can be replaced by a statement; to paraphrase such a poem is to reduce it to something like its originally unrealized condition. The aesthetic whole, however, resists practical formulation. Tate's whole point is that there is no substitute for the poem itself. The poem "is its own knower, neither poet nor reader knowing anything that the poem says apart from the words of the poem." Brooks and Ransom take of course the same stand.[7]

In the manner of Empson, Blackmur, or Brooks, who are our most expert technical critics, the critic lets the reader in on the poem's intention. He digs out the facts (and not alone the subsurface ones) and the principle governing the facts; he elucidates the poem's intention (the meaning objectified within the work, which is its form); he analyzes the texture-structure strategy of the poem, and he makes comparative judgments about its technical practice. Such judgments are not abstractions. These critics make analyses and judgments that are informed by a body of principles, but their approach is empirical. The Southern critics and the critics of the *Scrutiny* school are Aristotelian in their method: they analyze the aesthetic object in and for itself. H. A. Mason, in his defense of "F. R. Leavis and 'Scrutiny' " (in *The Critic:* Autumn, 1947), points out that the reader of Leavis' criticism "tends to forget the critic entirely and fails to note that in the process he has appropriated a good number of Mr. Leavis' judgments as his own." The point holds similarly for Empson and for Blackmur. "As there is no Leavisian doctrine or philosophy, there is nothing to seize on in his criticism but the example of first-hand valuation and there is no interference in the triangular inter-

play between reader, author and critic." The standards of these critics are
aesthetic ones, and this sets them apart from other critics whose standards
are sociological (Auden), historical (Wilson), psychological (Burke),
or ethical (Winter).[8]

The critical writings of Tate and Leavis show a close kinship in their
sources, their aims and critical attitudes, and particularly in their conception of the critic's function. Leavis is at one with Tate's rejection of
critical relativity, with his dogma of authority in absolute standards which
allow the reader no choice in point of view or taste, and with his contention for the values of a tradition as imperative. The critic, directly or by
implication, deals with a tradition. He deals with tradition in terms of
representative poets (and with individual poets in terms of representative
samples of their work). The poet's objective is the same as the critic's.
The poet probes the deficiencies of a tradition. As Tate explains, the
poet, in the true sense of Arnold's dictum that poetry is a "criticism of
life," criticizes his tradition "either as such, or indirectly by comparing
it with something that is about to replace it . . . he *discerns* its real elements and thus establishes its value, by putting it to the test of experience"
(*Reactionary Essays*). Always the business of criticism, Leavis states in
his Introduction to *Towards Standards,* is "to define, help form, and
organize the contemporary sensibility [the traditional mind which lives in
the present or not at all], and to make conscious the 'standards' in it."

Both Tate and Leavis derive their critical position from Eliot. They
have crystalized and expanded germinal ideas planted in *The Sacred
Wood*. As Leavis makes clear in *Education and the University* (1943),
he opposes, however, Eliot's doctrinal approach.[9] Both critics reject
Richards' theory of art and, for the past two decades, they have vigorously
assaulted his pseudo-scientific, pseudo-psychological, and semasiological
approach. It was only in the early Richards that Leavis felt points of
agreement, his *Practical Criticism* providing incitement towards Leavis'
program for instructing public taste and reforming literary education, for
which he pioneered in *Mass Civilization and Minority Culture* (1930)
and in *How to Teach Reading* (1933). Like Brooks, Leavis insists upon
the importance of critical study in the university education of general
intelligence, and, like Ransom, he sets strict boundaries to the conception
and practice of literary criticism, contending that it "should be controlled
by a strict conception of its special nature and methods." Literary criticism
"should be the best possible training for intelligence—for free, unspecial-
ized, general intelligence, which there has never at any time been enough
of, and which we are peculiarly in need of to-day."

In comparison with Tate, Leavis has more scholarship to buttress his
criticism, and, in comparison with Brooks, he has a somewhat wider
range. It is Johnson whom Tate and Leavis resemble, for their criticism
is a dogmatic and rational criticism. Tate's prose is savage in tone. Where
Leavis defends the fort, Tate pursues the enemy. Brooks's debt is chiefly
to Empson and Richards, but a striking parallelism is provided by

Leavis' work, namely between his *Revaluation* and Brooks's *The Well Wrought Urn*, and again between his *New Bearings in English Poetry* and Brooks's *Modern Poetry and the Tradition*. In the first instance their criticism is technical criticism; in the second instance it is historical rather than critical in approach. The work of Martin Turnell, the leading associate of Leavis' *Scrutiny* school, is likewise both technical and historical criticism. I mention Turnell because I think that he and Leavis and G. Wilson Knight are the most important critics in England today.

Our age is indeed an age of criticism. The structure of critical ideas and the practical criticism that British critics—Leavis, Turnell, Empson, Read—and American critics—Ransom, Tate, Brooks, Warren, Blackmur, Winters—have contrived upon the foundations of Eliot and Richards constitute an achievement in criticism which has not been equaled in any previous period of our literary history.   (1947)

NOTES

1. Pointed out by Winters in discussing MacLeish's poetry, and by Blackmur on Sandburg's.

2. For Cleanth Brooks a poem finds its main unity in its tone rather than in its rational structure; "the logical unity does not organize the poem." In *The Well Wrought Urn* he writes: "I question whether the parts of any poem ever attain any tighter connections than the 'psychological' or that the coherence, even of the metaphysical poets, is not ultimately a coherence of attitude." Compare Ransom's views in *The World's Body*, pp. 270-303.

3. This important essay is one of Tate's earliest (*Sewanee Review:* Jan., 1926). The core of Ransom's poetics is found in "Criticism as Pure Speculation" (1941).

4. In his review of Ramon Fernandez' *Messages* (*New Republic:* Aug. 17, 1927), and by way of stating his agreement with Fernandez' critical approach.

5. I agree with Stauffer that Ransom's theory goes too far in the separation of texture and structure. "What a poem needs is not the irrelevant word but the relevant word, whether it is expected or unexpected" (*Sewanee Review:* Summer 1948). The parallel to Ransom's doctrine of Logical Irrelevance is Eliot's doctrine of the Third Dimension, which Eliot made in his critique of Ben Jonson in *The Sacred Wood*.

6. Compare Burke's theory that a work of art is a psychological machine deliberately designed to arouse emotions.

7. See Brooks's chapter "The Heresy of the Paraphrase" in *The Well Wrought Urn* (1947). (Yvor Winters' position furnishes "the most respectable example of the paraphrastic heresy.")

8. In "experimental" critics like Kenneth Burke and Edmund Wilson the aesthetic interests are subordinated to psychological and sociological interests. Their concern is primarily with the nonresident values of a work of art, whereas the Southern and *Scrutiny* critics are concerned almost exclusively with the resident values—the purely formal and aesthetic ones. They attend to the properties of poetry as a fine art. Richards, to the contrary, protests against this isolation of the aesthetic values and argues for the integration of literary and nonliterary disciplines. Auden agrees with this program for the interdependence of ethics, politics, science, and aesthetics. The main difference between them is that Richards finds his standards for judging a work in psychology, Auden finds his in sociology. Auden's claim that aesthetic canons are not absolute is

diametrically opposite to Tate's or Ransom's, namely that the "artificial" division between art and life is necessary and worth preserving. Of all critics, Ransom sets the strictest boundaries to criticism. The traditional critic, as distinguished from the experimental critic, aims to clarify the center of criticism rather than expand its scope and borders. (The distinction between "traditional" and "experimental" critics is made by Eliot in *Experiment in Criticism.*)

9. "The debt I recognize is to Eliot's best criticism (*Sacred Wood*),—exemplifying purity of interest ('when you are considering poetry you must consider it as poetry and not as another thing') and the *application,* relevantly, of *intelligence* to poetry. But he left me to work out (a tip or two coming from Middleton Murry) the analytic method" (Leavis in a letter to the author).

Fiction and Its Critics

All this is precise yet symbolic. . . .

—Conrad: UNDER WESTERN EYES

(1)

SHORTLY AFTER THE APPEARANCE of R. P. Warren's critical study of *Lord Jim* (in *Sewanee Review:* 1948), I wrote that at the moment there is much that portends a Conrad boom. That it was in the making then seemed possible, but it did not materialize until another decade. Critics in those days concerned themselves almost exclusively with the criticism of poetry. The shift to the criticism of fiction did not begin until the mid-forties, and that accounts for the lag in Conrad criticism. It is only recently, within the present decade, that Conrad's works have begun to be revaluated; subjected to scrutiny *now,* they emerge thus in new light. In Douglas Hewitt's *Joseph Conrad: A Reassessment* (London, 1952) there isn't a single reference to an American Conrad critic, but the fact is that— excepting Crankshaw, Leavis, and Miss Bradbrook—Conrad's critical readers were all American critics. Beginning with J. W. Beach (1932), they included M. D. Zabel (1941, 1942, 1945, 1947), Albert J. Guerard (1947), R. P. Warren (1948), Walter Wright (in *Romance and Tragedy in Joseph Conrad,* 1949); I shall add that I, too, pioneered (1948, 1949). Criticism of Fiction Critics were a decade ago rather scarce; what they were reading *then* was Melville, or Henry James, or Kafka—but Conrad not at all. "Of Conrad little is heard," E. K. Brown complained in 1945. But "I believe that before thirty years have passed, the world of his imagination will fascinate the general reader as surely as it did twenty years ago; and that the close critical examination of his work, which has barely begun, will take a large place in the interpretation of fiction" (In *Yale Review:* 1945). His prophecy is fulfilled (and anticipated) in *The Art of Joseph Conrad: A Critical Symposium,* which I edited for Michigan State University Press (1960).

Every complex novel, Guerard reminds us, becomes a different one on later readings. *Lord Jim* is "an art novel, a novelist's novel, a critic's novel—perhaps the first important one in England after *Tristram Shandy*. This means that it becomes a different novel if read very attentively; or, becomes a different novel when read a second or third time." An interpretation which is the result of years of familiarity with the given work frequently strikes the casual reader as "irresponsible," whereas what's irresponsible is in fact the casual reader. (As Guerard remarks, many professional critics are casual readers.)[1]

What should we read of Conrad? "Everything," said Paul Claudel, whereupon André Gide studied the English language in order to read Conrad's works. "He was the only one of my elders," Gide wrote, "that I loved and knew."

Conrad's rank amongst the greatest authors of fiction, both in the novel and in the short story, is today everywhere acknowledged. (The best short summary of Conrad's achievement that I know of is Guerard's article in *The Reporter* for March 21, 1957.)

(2)

According to a critic of Conrad in the *Hudson Review* a few years ago, good fiction is nothing more than "a genuine story." In his view, the proper use of language in fiction excludes the poetic. Conrad is at his best at the literal narrative level; minus myth, minus symbol, minus the whole texture of Conrad's reflexive use of language. This critic does not like symbolism, but then neither does he like Conrad.

"As for myth and symbol," says he, "each has furnished its adherents with a career"; apparently his own career promises to be furnished by literal-minded readings of plots and characters. But even when he finds in Conrad a genuine story (such as "The Secret Sharer") he doesn't like it. He settles on two works as Conrad's best: "Typhoon" and *The Nigger of the "Narcissus."* His choice of *The Nigger* confounds his own platform.

But, finally, not even *The Nigger* is exempted from his wholesale denigration of Conrad's works. Three years after his *Hudson Review* attack he recants on his appraisal of *The Nigger*, in "The Artist's Conscience and *The Nigger of the 'Narcissus'*" (in *Nineteenth Century Fiction:* March 1957). He now grants Conrad success only in "Typhoon." Conrad's detractor remained unidentified in my *Kenyon Review* essay, "Fiction and Its Critics," but in a subsequent *Kenyon Review* he issued an announcement: "My article is entitled 'Conrad and the Terms of Modern Criticism.' It appeared in the Autumn 1954 issue of the *Hudson Review*, and I wrote it." The author of this mud-slinging article is M. Mudrick.[2]

He attacks Conrad for being "the poet in fiction" and claims that Conrad makes symbol and myth business all too clear: "destructively clear, for by the time we have given our energy to relating such coarse, obvious and super-abundant clues at the neatly systematic clinical level proper to them—the interest of myth reduced to the interest of murder 'mystery'— we have lost interest and faith in the narrative itself." On the contrary, what's lost I think is interest and faith in this critic as a reader of Conrad. His very phrases give him away: "bargain-basement fatalism," and "popular-priced psychoanalysis." Rather, what's shown here, it seems to me, is how to vulgarize criticism. He accuses Conrad of "catch-all symbolism" and of dishonesty of spirit: "he will without scruple betray his entertaining narrative and his rather unsubtly contrasted characters at the appeal of any portentous image or generalization or symbolic gesture, often wholly impertinent. . . ." As for "The Secret Sharer," it's all too obvious to require any critical scrutiny: "Who could fail to predict every item of the depth psychology paraphernalia that will tidily turn up? And who could possibly miss, on the most inattentive first reading, Conrad's oversimplified, imposed mythical structure, symbol to character in the crudest one-to-one relationship, nailed to the flesh of the narrative in almost every sentence?"

Though the symbolic interpretation of Conrad has Conrad's own sanction, our critic, with his flat-headed insistence that Plot and Character constitute Everything There Is To Say About A Novel, claims that "Conrad might have done better, clinically as well as artistically, if he had been describable by his critical partisans not as a poet in fiction, but as a man who merely tells a tale." Though he doesn't care much for "The Secret Sharer," while admitting it's "a genuine story," he believes it possible to "save" the story by virtue of its being "grounded in the details of life at sea—Conrad's only element, in spite of his angry disclaimers. . . ."

" 'Youth' has been called a fine sea-story. Is it? Well, I won't bore you with a discussion of fundamentals. But surely those stories of mine where the sea enters can be looked at from another angle." Our *Hudson Review* critic sees Conrad straight, not from any angle. He proposes to return us to the simple literal-minded reading that Conrad endured from his contemporary critics, including Curle and McFee.[3] Wipe out all criticism since then. Don't mention Conrad's reflexive use of the poetic properties of words; don't mention symbols, don't mention myths, don't mention Conrad except for such genuine sea-tales as he produced in "Typhoon" and *The Nigger!* In *The Nigger,* as Conrad points out in *Life and Letters,* (II, 324), the problem that faces the men in the "Narcissus" "is not a problem of the sea." Barely one-tenth of his work is "sea-stuff," Conrad tried to persuade the literal-minded Richard Curle; "and even of that, the bulk, that is *Nigger* and *Mirror,* has a very special purpose which I emphasize myself in my Prefaces. . . . I do wish that all those ships of mine were given a rest, but I'm afraid that when the Americans get hold of them they will never, never, never get a rest" (II, 316-317).

As Ford Madox Ford (in *Portraits from Life*) said, Conrad "never

tired of protesting that he was not a writer about the sea; he detested
the sea as a man detests a cast-off mistress, and with the hatred of a small
man who has had, on freezing nights of gales, to wrestle immense yards
and dripping cordage; his passion became to live out of sight of the sea
and all its memories; he never tired of repeating Christina Rossetti's last
written words: 'A little while and we shall be, / Please God, where there
is no more sea.' " "Most of our reviewers," Conrad complained, "seem
absolutely unable to understand in a book anything but facts and the
most elementary qualities of rendering." Sir Sydney Colvin, for instance,
declined to review *The Shadow Line* because he had no first-hand
knowledge of the Gulf of Siam.

While admitting the validity of the conception of the artist as conscious
craftsman, our *Hudson Review* critic rejects it strategically on the grounds
that though "useful" it is also, "in certain constructed over-confident uses
that have been made of it, *dangerous;* and these uses, moreover, seem to
possess an irresistible appeal for critics who have uncritically adopted the
terminology of modern criticism." It is dangerous because the faith of the
critic that every part of the literary work contributes to the whole leads
him to read out of the work more than is warranted by the literal level of
plot and character alone. "Having frequently cheapened the valuable terms
they have helped make current, many of our critics, especially in the
literal-minded second generation of modern criticism, have proceeded to
cheapen the crucially valid notion of the artist as craftsman." But who
is more literal-minded than the critic who ridicules extra-literal readings
of works, and who but himself cheapens the conception of the artist as
craftsman by his denigration of Conrad?

In "Fiction and the Criticism of Fiction," published in *Kenyon Review*
(Spring 1956), Philip Rahv repeats the theme of the *Hudson Review*
critic: the infection of the prose-sense by the poetic. Extending it into an
attack on critics whose readings elucidate a novel's tissue of particulars as
hidden clues to symbols and myths, and on critics who contend that all
artistic writing has for its essential activity "style" and "technique," P.
Rahv uses as examples of the latter kinds of critic Ransom and Schorer;
and of the former, myself. The crux of his position is that language used
in fiction does not play the same role as language used in poetry.

Rahv aligns himself with the more moderate of the Russian Formalists,
Victor Zhirmunsky, who contends that "a novel and a lyric poem are not
to be equated as works of verbal art because the relation in them between
theme and composition is quite different." Against the extreme wing of the
Russian Formalists, who were inclined "to over-react to the undeniable
fact that fiction is made up of words, just like poetry," Rahv protests
against the superstition of the word: "Normatively the language of the
novel does not possess the autonomous value that it has in poetry. It only
intermittently lends itself to that verbal play characteristic of poetic
speech. . . ." "The norms of the novel cannot accommodate a declaration

by the smaller unit, the word, the phrase, the sentence or the paragraph."
Against this position, however, I take the standpoint of Conrad whose
credo was, "Give me the right word and the right accent and I will
move the world," and of Henry James whose novels not only "accommodate" but exploit the smaller unit of word or phrase, and not "intermittently" but at every brushstroke. In *The Portrait of a Lady,* for instance,
every brushstroke functions. It's the same in *To the Lighthouse;* but
Rahv dismisses the works of Virginia Woolf as belonging to what the
Russians call "ornamental prose fiction," and in the same category I presume he would locate Conrad, Henry James, and Joyce. Ornamental
prose-fiction "keeps the reader's attention fixed on the small detail: the
words, their sounds, their rhythm." Well, I should think that's where
any artist-in-words would want his reader's attention fixed, on the words
and their arrangement by which they attain their meaning and import.
Rahv and the Russians, on the contrary, disparage stylization as irrelevant
to the novel. If the novelist, says Rahv, is *also* a fine stylist, that is something thrown into the bargain. If he is *also* an artist, that too is thrown
into the bargain.

Rahv quotes with approval D. S. Mirsky's superstition that "Ornamental
prose has a decided tendency to escape the control of the larger unit
[*i.e.,* character and plot, I presume], to destroy the wholeness of the
work," and he also quotes with approval E. R. Curtius' "fine critical
passage comparing Balzac and Flaubert": *"The artificial linking of artistry
and the novel,* for which Flaubert is responsible . . . leads to a blind
alley." Curtius, with his admission that "It is evident that Balzac cannot
be weighed in the scale of Flaubert's art-ideal," and D. S. Mirsky and
V. Zhirmunsky, and finally Christopher Caudwell—all of these critics
whom Rahv uses in buttressing his own theory of fiction commit the same
fallacy as Rahv himself: it is the fallacy of dividing everything into left
and right, black and white. They exhibit the same obsession for dichotomies as Rahv himself, who divides American literature into two types—
"Paleface and Redskin."

In support of his notion of the autonomy of poetic language Rahv
quotes Suzanne Langer on the nature and scope of the lyric poem, a
viewpoint which I think is readily assailable as a misconception, whereas
for Rahv what she is saying "is so self-evident as to be hardly more than
a truism." Mrs. Langer considers the lyric poem the one literary genre
most directly dependent on verbal means, and this is because its motif
is usually nothing more than "a thought, a vision, a mood, or a poignant
emotion. . . . The lyric poet uses every quality of language because he
has neither plot nor fictitious characters, nor, usually any intellectual
argument to give his poem continuity." But plot and fictitious characters
inhabit the poem no less than the novel (*e.g.,* "Edward," Keats' "La Belle
Dame Sans Merci," Browning's "My Last Duchess," or Eliot's "Sweeney
Among the Nightingales"); nor is the lyric poem exclusively mere mood
or emotion. Nor is the lyric poem "of all literary genres the one most

directly dependent on verbal means," for in contradiction the example is a Shakespeare play or the novel insofar as it attains to literary art (*viz., To the Lighthouse*).[4]

No one literary art-form usurps priority in exploitation of verbal means. I contend that the play, the novel, and the poem use the same language and that, while they differ in form and scope and technique, they use the same language for different ends or effects according to the scope and technique their form affords. In their use of verbal means they differ mainly in the degree of compression and intensity, the counterpointing of word or phrase being more intensified in the poem than in the novel not because the poem eschews plot and character, but rather because its formed meaning is, by comparison with the novel, restricted in scope.

Until I am persuaded otherwise, it is right that the poetic should infect the prosaic and, conversely, that the prosaic should infect the poetic. *Contra* Rahv and the Russians, I see no iron curtain between poem and novel linguistically. Nor is the novel different from the poem in the relation between theme and composition, *contra* Rahv and the Russians. The fundamentals of any work of art consist, in sum, of these basic principles: (a) if a thing is given, then it will be given again; (b) if a thing is given, then its obverse will also be given. And again and again. The richer work incorporates both strands, each strand counterpointed against the other. It is by these principles of repetition and contrast that the novel, insofar as it attains to literary art, achieves design. The novel, no less than the poem, exploits the reflexive use of language, style, and technique.

"For the poet the major problem is always style, which it seldom is for the novelist. If you look into the working notebooks of two novelists so vastly different as James and Dostoevsky you are struck by the fact that verbal stylization is never among the difficulties they wrestle with." Rahv may be making a point, but it strikes me as neither here nor there. In the *Notebooks* James wrestles not with style but with plot, sequence of scene, problems of point-of-view. Rahv says that the language in which these things are to be embodied is taken more or less for granted. But it's the same for the poet; he too sets down in his notebook not notes about the diction and syntax of the poem he plans to write, because these things he wrestles with during the process of composition, but rather notes on plot-situations and germinal themes for future poems, for without these things as seed nothing can sprout. It's after he has composed the poem that Hopkins writes Bridges to explain his use of language, and it's after he has written *The Ambassadors* that James, in his Preface to that novel, defines the problem of style which engaged him *during* its composition: "To project imaginatively, for my hero, a relation that has nothing to do with the matter (the matter of my subject) but has everything to do with the manner (the manner of my presentation of the same) and yet to treat it, at close quarters and for fully economic expression's possible sake . . .—to do that sort of thing and yet muddle nothing may easily become, as one goes, a signally attaching proposition; even though it all remains but part and parcel, I hasten to recognize, of the merely general and related question of expressional curiosity and expressional decency." Again: "Since, however, all art is *expression,* and is thereby vividness, one was to find the door open here [in the final scene of the novel] to any amount of delightful dissimulation." It's during the process of composition that the artist wrestles with language; in his notebooks he tinkers with plots, but that fact does not permit the inference that an artist like James took language for granted. In his Prefaces he returns again and again to the stylistic problems he faced in recasting his scenarios into final form. "The consistent, the sustained, preserved *tone* of 'The Tragic Muse,' its constant and doubtless rather fine-drawn truth to its particular sought pitch and accent, are, critically speaking, its principal merit—the inner harmony that I perhaps presumptuously permit myself to compare to an unevaporated scent."

This unevaporated and sustained Jamesian "scent" distinguishes his kind of novel from that of Dostoevsky, whose works translate into the English more faithfully than the works of James could possibly translate into the Russian by virtue of the fact that James is a "stylist" and Dostoevsky is not. Dostoevsky's style is all "velocity; once it has yielded him that it has yielded nearly everything that his dramatic structure requires of it." "But in itself, if we set out to examine it in small units," as Rahv admits, "it is not rewarding." Dostoevsky wrote rapidly, but even if he had not been under pressure what he would have spent himself in revising, given more time, was plot rather than style. It's not that Dostoevsky, given more time (to quote Rahv), "would apply himself to improving his diction and sentence-structure." James, in his review of Trollope's *Can You Forgive Her?* (the review should have been titled "Can You Forgive Him?"), takes Trollope to task for "writing so rapidly; but as in much rapid writing we are often made to regret the absence of that sober second thought which may curtail an extravagance . . . so in Mr. Trollope we perpetually miss that sustained action of the imagination, that creative movement which . . . would intensify and animate his first conception." In his essay on Trollope, James scores him for having no style, and no art and no theory about it. " 'Judge me in the lump,' we can imagine the author saying; 'I have only undertaken to entertain the British public. I don't pretend that each of my novels is an organic whole.' Trollope had no time to give his tales a classic roundness. . . ." (In *The Art of Fiction,* edited by Morris Roberts, 1948.) In one of his reviews of Trollope (in *Notes and Reviews,* 1921), James remarked that the book is a stupid book—"Mr. Trollope is a good observer; but he is literally nothing else. . . . All his incidents are, if we may so express it, *empirical.* He has seen and heard every act and every speech that appears in his pages. That minds like his should exist, and exist in plenty, is neither to be wondered at nor to be deplored; but that such a mind as his should devote itself to writing novels, and that these novels should be successful, appears to us an extraordinary fact." As Roberts says: "The literal and the formless are much the same thing in a work of art. About the value of style James had no more doubt than Flaubert himself. 'There is no complete creation without style,' he says, 'any more than there is complete music without sound.' " James's kinship was of course with Turgenev, the stylist, and Flaubert, whose days were spent in search of the right word. "To write an admirable page—and his idea of what constituted an admirable page was transcendent—seemed to him something to live for." So James speaks of Flaubert in his essay on Turgenev, whom he called the novelists' novelist. Turgenev is the novelist as poet; the finest thing in him is "the effect, for the commonest truth, of an exquisite envelope of poetry." The novels of Tolstoy and Dostoevsky, because James considered them deficient in composition and meaning or theme, he dismissed as "fluid puddings."

"No one could desire more than he [Turgenev] that art should be art; always, ever, incorruptibly, art." James's tribute applied equally to himself. His collected Prefaces (in *The Art of the Novel,* edited by R. P. Blackmur, 1941) consltute, as James wrote Howells, "a sort of comprehensive manual or *vade-mecum* for aspirants in our arduous profession." They are a "plea for Criticism, for Discrimination, for Appreciation on other than infantile lines." I find it hard to figure why F. R. Leavis dismisses James's Prefaces as peripheral when in fact they provide a poetics, as well as a manual for aspiring novelists. It seems to me that they provide furthermore a manual for certain critics. It is one of the great merits of Turgenev, says James, that his work "deals death to the perpetual assumption that subject and style are—aesthetically speaking or in the living work—different and separable things." (Roberts, p. xiii.)

Rahv sees eye-to-eye with Anthony Trollope, of whom James, by the way, reports in his *Notebooks* an amusing account: "I heard some time ago, that Anthony Trollope had a theory that a boy might be brought up to be a novelist as to any other trade. He brought up—or attempted to bring up—his own son on this principle, and the young man became a sheep-farmer, in Australia."

Expanding on this germinal situation, James projected it into a potential short story (a decade later it became "Grenville Fane") ending with the literary child grown now to manhood; in the final glimpse of him, "the intended novelist has embraced some extremely prosaic situation. . . ." An extremely prosaic situation is what Rahv has embraced. "All that we can legitimately ask of a novelist in the matter of language," says Rahv, "is that it be appropriate to the matter at hand." Now I grant that "What is said must not stand in a contradictory relation to the way it is said," but I know of no novel worth our attention which commits this contradiction. "A Dostoevskyean story cannot be appropriately told in the style, say, of Dreiser, as that style is too cumbersome and the pace too slow." But the very notion of substituting the style of one work for the style of another is preposterous. It's as preposterous as to suggest transposing a character of Dreiser's say, Sister Carrie, into the *Brothers Karamazov*. What we term the characters of a novel are composed of verbal arrangements, not of flesh-and-blood. Being composed of words, they function (as Bonamy Dobrée puts it) as the part-symbols out of which the whole is constructed. They exist only in relationship to each other and to the whole of which they are the component parts. It is inconceivable, therefore, that they could possibly exist in any world other than their own, and likewise that they could exist by any verbal arrangement other than their author's own. Because a novel is the product of language, a novel depends for its very life upon the word.

Rahv, on the contrary, contends that the novelist takes for granted his verbal means since he uses language at its literal or dictionary level only; hence he is exempt from the poet's quest to find the right word. Since the novel has for its primary aim the representation of experience, namely plot and character at the literal level, the novel demands no more of the writer than that he use words adequately—*i.e.,* literally. In Proust "the dust of reality is mixed with magic sand," but says Rahv: "It is pointless, however, to ask of a novelist whose themes do not require such an intensive stylistic effort that he captivate us through language when he is quite capable of captivating us through other means." But whom does he captivate? The uncritical literal-minded reader; only he is captivated by plot and character alone since for him, as for Rahv, language is supererogatory to what the novel is obviously all about, namely the representation of experience. Here, then, is "the Norm of the Novel." The test of a novel's belonging to the Norm is whether or not it is translatable; it translates into another language "with but minor loss to the integrity of the text," whereas novels not belonging to the Norm fail by this test. Henry James is not as translatable as Dostoevsky; neither are Hawthorne, Melville, Flaubert, Conrad, Proust, Turgenev and Chekhov. Therefore they are not as great as Dostoevsky, or Tolstoy, or Stendhal. The translatableness of an author is the test of his greatness, and by this test you know that his works belong to the Norm of the Novel. Rahv's absurd canon puts *Moby Dick* into dry dock, and along with it the works of Hawthorne, Flaubert, Conrad, Proust—all stylists, technicians, artists.

In "The Understanding of Fiction" (*Kenyon Review:* Spring 1950), which essay Rahv attacks, Ransom remarked that the author of *War and Peace* "does not possess fully the technical advantages of a style. For concentration he substitutes repetition. . . ." Tolstoy meant to have nothing to do with literary tricks; consequently, as the range of our reading widens, or rather deepens, we resist him increasingly because he presents scenes and characters "artlessly and wastefully." Thackeray in *The Newcomes,* Dumas in *The Three Musketeers,* and Tolstoy in *War and Peace* substitute life for composition. But what, asks Henry James, "do such large loose baggy monsters, with their queer elements of the accidental and the arbitrary, artistically *mean?* We have heard it maintained, we will remember, that such things are 'superior to art'; but we understand least of all what *that* may mean, and we look in vain for the artist, the divine explanatory genius, who will come to our aid and tell us. There is life and life, and as waste is only life sacrificed and thereby prevented from 'counting,' I delight in a deep-breathing economy and an organic form." (Preface to *The Tragic Muse.*)

"Let us beware of regarding technique as some sort of gimmick which it takes a certain amount of intelligence to master, after which the writer is at liberty to 'create' to the top of his bent." (I quote here Rahv.) While admitting that Thomas Wolfe could do nothing more than spill his subject rather than express it, he defends him because of his sensibility, which is to say that he is capable of captivating us through other means than technique. Antecedent to technique is sensibility; "the sensibility of Wolfe is not something he could alter." Rahv, in argument with Schorer's "Technique as Discovery," concludes that "technique is not nearly enough." But (to turn Rahv's coin over) let us beware of sensibility minus technique, quite as much as of technique minus sensibility. Wolfe exploited his untutored sensibility, a gimmick which takes no intelligence to exploit, and he exploited it to the top of his bent. Wolfe, on his own admission, was no artist.[5] The prose of Dreiser, it seems to me, provides us a model of How Not To Write. As Ransom remarks: "We might go a long way towards defining the fiction which we call 'naturalistic' by calling it the fiction of the author who has no style; or at least does not develop one at the conscious literary level." Rahv's position—insofar as anything resembling a coherent position can be pieced together from the scattered dicta of his writings—would embrace Dreiser and James T. Farrell. For Farrell's ambitions, as Mark Schorer says, the style of the newspaper and the lens of the documentary camera would be quite adequate; "in sheer clumsiness of style no living writer exceeds him, for his prose is asked to perform no service beyond communcation of the most rudimentary kind of fact." (In *Critiques and Essays on Modern Fiction, 1952.*)

What is Rahv's theory of the novel? Neither in his *Kenyon Review* attack on the New Criticism of fiction nor in *Image and Idea*, does Rahv formulate *his* position. Faced with his quotations, I conclude that Rahv's position squares with that of the Russians he quotes from, Zhirmunsky and Mirsky, and that he likewise exempts the novel from the claims of language, style, technique, artistry. Intermittently, however, Rahv seemingly concedes these attributes of the novel as legitimate attributes; his next step is to shadowbox them. He's contradictory and elusive as to what precisely he himself stands for. But you know him by his quotations. In "Notes on the Decline of Naturalism" (in *Image and Idea*), to cite one instance of shifting his ground, he praises Dos Passos' *U.S.A.* as "one of the very few naturalist novels in which there is a controlled use of language, in which a major effect is produced by *the interplay between story and style.*" In the *Kenyon Review*, on the contrary, he takes the radical and (I think) untenable standpoint of denying any relevant interplay between narrative and style, style and artistry being not only irrelevant but detrimental to the novel. For the Norms of the Novel "the word stylist, or even the word *writer,* and the word *novelist* are not really synonymous." He deduces this notion from the equally presumptive premise that the fictive world of Stendhal captivates us in spite of the fact that his stylistic gifts, as Rahv admits, are unimpressive. I think Valéry is right in his criticism of Stendhal's "negligence, the wilful negligence, the contempt for all the formal qualities of style."

Rahv is consistent only in his bias for dichotomies and in his predilection for contradictions. In the space of a single essay he admits technique as a necessary ingredient in the novelist's craft, while on the other hand by agreeing with Curtius versus artistry in the novel, he denies and belittles its importance. Antecedent to technique is sensibility or vision, and vision he identifies with style. But if this were so, then it should follow that novelists possessing vision possess also style. Rahv, on the contrary, is opposed to novelists who are stylists. (He is as contradictory as the *New York Times* critic who recently argued thus: "The great symbolical novels would be great without their symbolism"). Rahv sacrifices logical consistency for the strategic purpose of assaulting the New Critics of fiction, on the rise since 1949 when Rahv's *Image and Idea* saw print. He remarked there, in his essay on Naturalism, that the altogether free and open character of the medium prevents the novel "from developing such distinctly technical controls as poetry has acquired." Not taking his hint, the New Critics in fiction have proceeded to erect ingenious interpretations on the mistaken theory that the novel uses the same devices of language and technique as the poem. But says Rahv, "it is simply not the case that what goes for a microscopic unit such as the lyric poem goes equally well for the macroscopic compositions of the writer of narrative prose." Rahv aims to undermine the validity and achievement of close textual analysis of fiction; his strategy for doing so is by dislocating language and style and technique *from* the novel.

Rahv suggests that a prosaic of the novel might be formulated on the theory that Christopher Caudwell worked out in *Illusion and Reality.* In Caudwell's formulation of the novel, Rahv asserts with finality, "we get at last to the root of the matter." Rahv, to pin him down, derives his position—his theory of a dichotomy between poetic language and fictional —from Caudwell's theory that the "poetic word is the logos, the word-made-flesh . . . whereas the novel's word is the sign, the reference, the conversationally pointing gesture." Caudwell's theory includes also the following absurdities, all of which Rahv embraces. Novels, according to Caudwell, "are not composed of words." Does Rahv really assent to this preposterous superstition? Yet elsewhere in this *Kenyon Review* essay he speaks of "the undeniable fact that fiction is made up of words, just like poetry." Either Rahv is naive enough not to recognize his own contradictions, which might explain why he never attempts to reconcile them, or he is arrogant enough to override them. In either case, he is as muddle-headed as critics can get. Novels are not composed of words, says Caudwell. They are composed of *real* people! "They are composed of scenes, actions, *stuff*, and people, just as plays are." The hero of a novel is "a real concrete individual." "A 'jewelled' style is a disadvantage to the novel because it distracts the eye from things and people to the words. . . ." In poetry "the affective associations are organized by the structure of the language, while in the novel they are organized by the structure of the outer reality portrayed." Thus for Rahv, as for Caudwell, the novel—minus language and style and technique—is nothing but a fictionalized copy of reality: "a mirror carried along a roadway," as Stendhal defined it.

Rahv contends that "the representation of experience, which is the primary asset of the novel," is not a mere appearance; the novel posits "no split between appearance and reality." Rahv quotes Henry James in support of his theory of realism: truth of detail and "solidity of specification" James considered the supreme virtues of the novel; "if these be there, they owe their effect to the success with which the author has produced the illusion of life." Now it is true that James demanded realism, an air of reality; but he also demanded technique, style, language exploited to the utmost of its resources, the poetic imagination, and above all form. They are the very attributes that Rahv exempts as irrelevant to the Norms of the Novel. Yet by implication, he would have it that James belongs to his own Caudwellian camp. Rahv's theory of the novel is enough to make James bristle with abhorrence. James did not equate the imagined reality of the novel with reality, nor art with life. Nor did he consider "illusion of reality" the criterion of the novel's aesthetic worth. Of Balzac he complained that the artist is smothered by the historian; the novel is neither a mirror nor a slice of life. "It is art that *makes* life . . . and I know of no substitute whatever for the force and beauty of its process." (*Letters of Henry James*, 1920, II, 490.) "Form alone *takes,* and holds and preserves, substance—saves it from the welter of helpless verbiage that we swim in as in a sea of tasteless tepid pudding. . . ." James is here castigating Tolstoy and Dostoevsky for their lack of composition (letter to Hugh Walpole, II, 237). In his Preface to *The American* he criticized that novel as "an affront to verisimilitude," but even so he concluded that the novel creates a world of its own and should be judged thus rather than by any other test: "the content and 'importance' of a work of art are in fine wholly dependent on its *being* one; outside of which *all prate of its representative character,* its meaning and its bearing, its morality and humanity, are an impudent thing."

On Rahv's theory that the primary asset of the novel is its representation of experience, criticism—on that assumption—would deal then with assessing the identity or correspondence between reality and the novel's illusion of reality, or else it would deal with the significance of the illusion as a symbol of humanity. I shall answer this much under two heads: (1) Fidelity to life (as I've elsewhere argued it) does not establish any work as work of art. The criterion of absolute correspondence between the characters, events, and effects of art with those of reality constitutes, I contend, a critical fallacy. Realism taken as plastic or graphic verisimilitude, critically considered, is plainly irrelevant. Mere degree of illusion provides no basis for critical assessment, as for one thing it cannot be tested. Crane, having written *The Red Badge of Courage* prior to any experience of warfare, sought out a battlefield to test his picture—"I have found it as I imagined it," he told Conrad. But it's not every author or critic who has a battlefield handy for testing the truth of the picture, a test which Middleton Murry aptly dubs the "pictorial heresy." Suppose that Crane had found the real thing *not* to be as he'd imagined it; what difference would that make in the evaluation of *The Red Badge* as a literary work of art? *The Red Badge,* as Hemingway said, "is all as much of one piece as a great poem is." In the Preface to *The Aspern Papers* James observes that Jeffrey Aspern's only link with reality lies in the atmosphere, "in the tone of the picture wrought around him," which is itself an "artistic hokus-pokus," as unreal as the character himself, but which on that very account helps the illusion and makes the whole plausible. The point is that no question of reality is involved, but only a question as to the completeness of illusion." (Quoted from Morris Roberts' *Henry James's Criticism,* 1929.)

Other than Schorer's "Technique as Discovery," the only essay I know of that recapitulates the Jamesian theory of the novel is C. H. Rickword's "A Note on Fiction"; though ostensibly nothing more than a review of Elizabeth Drew's *Modern Novel,* Rickword's essay provides in germinal form an aesthetics of the novel. [It first appeared in the *Calendar of Modern Letters* (1925-27), where I "discovered" it two decades ago; subsequently it saw print in this country in *Forms of Modern Fiction,* 1948, edited by W. Van O'Connor.] Rickword, disputing the common assumption that the novelist's primary creation is of character, considers character as the part symbol of the whole, created by the poetic property of words, character being the product of plot, which is itself "structurally a product of language, eloquence." A Character "is merely the term by which the reader alludes to the pseudo-objective image he composes of his responses to an author's verbal arrangements." The new novelist, said Rickword in 1926, tends to rely for his effects "not on set pieces of character drawing, but directly on the poetic properties of words. The idea of a character's consciousness is created in the reader by the exploitation of the emotive powers of language. . . ." Character and plot are fictitious, character being an emergent quality of the narrative; neither character nor plot is "an active element in the whole work in the way that melody and harmony are elements in a piece of music." As for the novel's illusion of reality, "novelists who can do nothing else are able to perform the trick with ease, since 'nothing is easier than to create for oneself the idea of a human being, a figure, and a character, from glimpses and anecdotes.' Nor does depth of illusion matter: Raskolnikov is 'deeper' than Tom Jones, in the sense that more of his interior is directly exposed, but he is a figure of different not greater significance."

(2) As for the significance of the illusion as a symbol of humanity, that much any critic can readily spot without possessing any more literary insight than the common reader. While Rahv admits that novels abound in symbolic devices, he protests against the prevailing obsession with symbolization that now "afflicts our literary life and that passes itself off as a strict concern with aesthetic form. . . . But when we speak of the symbolic import of a novel what we have in mind is nothing more mysterious than its overplus of meaning, its suggestiveness over and above its tissue of particulars, the actual representation of which it is comprised; and that is scarcely the same thing as treating these particulars as 'clues' which it is the ingenious critic's task to follow up for hidden or buried meanings that are assumed to be the 'real point' of the text under examination." Critics of Rahv's literal-minded school, including not only the Russians but also the *Hudson Review* critic whose reading of "The Secret Sharer" reduces the whole thing to A Simple Tale too obvious to warrant critical scrutiny, condemn analytical critics whose close-textual readings are disposed (to quote Rahv) to purge the novel of its particulars of scene, figures, and action; "to purge them, that is to say, of their gross immediacy and direct empirical expressiveness." Rahv's addiction to dichotomies is here again evinced by his contention that analytical critics scrutinize the particulars of the novel's texture to the exclusion of its particulars of plot and character, but what critic other than Rahv himself commits the very sin of omission which he protests against? For who but Rahv himself purges the novel of texture, style, language, technique, artistry?—only the late Christopher Caudwell, and Rahv's Russian colleagues, and our *Hudson Review* critic. The late C. H. Rickword anticipated all of them in his formulation of the novel as possessing for its basic unity a poetic quality. The organic is the province of criticism—not solely the particulars of plot and character, nor on the other hand solely the particulars of texture, but rather the one in relationship to the other. What the novel is really all about resides in its tissue of particulars, and it is only by examining and elucidating these minute particulars and their more or less concealed relationship that the critic can establish grounds for convincing us that what the literary work is really all about differs considerably from what other critics read as merely its over-all symbolic import. Obviously, a right apprehension of the whole thing depends upon a right apprehension of its elements, its tissue of particulars, each of which provides clues to the figure-in-the-carpet by which the whole is designed. To read *The Secret Agent* without apprehending the significance of all its particulars is to misread Conrad's novel as nothing more than "A Simple Tale."

The more penetrating the scrutiny the more likely it is that what significance emerges will differ radically from the novel's over-all symbolic import. Nor will this new reading seem convincing to readers who, like Rahv, neglect to explore the literary text with the same painstaking inquiry as the critic himself performed. They dismiss his interpretation as "absurd" because their own fixed idea about the given work is superficial, as superficial as, for instance, the interpretations of *The Red Badge* by

Crane's contemporary reviewers. Rahv's literary platform is Realism, same as theirs, and his reading of *The Red Badge* is pitched at their level—it's a war novel, that and nothing more, and in realism Crane outdid them all, etc. For Rahv it's "actually 'about' what it seems to be, war, and its impact on human beings moved by pride, bravado, fear, anxiety and sudden panic." Crane's reviewers said the same thing, and some of them went one step further to define the novel's symbolic import: "The youth's mind is a battleground too." It's a parable, said *The Critic,* of the inner battle which every man must fight. The young soldier, said *The Bookman,* "may be either an individual or man universal; the battle may be either the Battle of the Wilderness or the Battle of Life." My reading sees Crane using realistic details symbolically; Crane is not a photographic realist; he struck out in new directions. Symbolism does not deny realism, rather it extends it. I remain as convinced now as I was when I first became interested in Crane over a decade ago that symbols exist in his fiction (though as I have pointed out the greater number of his works are nonsymbolic) and that the existence of symbols in his works can be verified, although the interpretation of them may vary from reader to reader. They exist in *The Red Badge*—despite Rahv's literal-minded reading of it as nothing more than a war novel, "chiefly noted for the advance it marks in the onset of realism on the American literary scene." That is the standard formula, but I am convinced that Crane is not a realist, in either *The Red Badge* or *Maggie,* and for the reasons and evidence I advanced in my *Crane: Omnibus* (1952). *Maggie* has so far been read only as the exemplar of Sociological Realism, as a pioneer study of the demi-world of the big city, as a document in literary Naturalism. The label Naturalism tells us nothing about the work *as* work of art. That is what can be determined only by critical scrutiny of the interrelationships forming the whole.

The significance or meaning of a literary work is not likely to be found on its surface; wherefore criticism, as I see it, probes subsurface obliquities, concealed relationships.

> In this light (of criticism springing from deep sources) "one sees the critic as the real helper of the artist, a torch-bearing outrider, the interpreter, the brother. . . . For there is something sacrificial in his function, inasmuch as he offers himself as a general touchstone. To lend himself, to project himself and steep himself, to feel and feel till he understands, and to understand so well that he can say, to have perception at the pitch of passion and expression as embracing as the air, to be infinitely curious and incorrigibly patient . . . these are fine chances for an active mind, chances to add the idea of independent beauty to the conception of success" (Henry James in *The Review:* May 1891).

To approach a work critically requires analysis of it, and to analyze requires what Henry James called "the acuter vision." Rahv's objections to ingenious critics who treat the novel's tissue of particulars as so many clues to hidden meanings seem to me nonsense, as is also his restriction of symbolic readings simply to the novel's general symbolic import. Also his notion that exhaustive or ingenious interpretations makes the text itself dispensable; "it ceases to be of use once you have extracted the symbols it contains." I regard the critic not in Rahv's figure of him as a kind of dentist extracting symbols, but rather as a detective unriddling the ambiguous, the enigmatic, the cryptographic.

Let the critic push analysis to the point where it becomes creative. *Contra* P. Rahv and his companion critic M. Mudrick of the *Hudson Review,* the critic's job is not simply to point out a genuine story and extract its plot and characters and test their verisimilitude to reality; rather it is to probe the work beyond its literal level for what it signifies both as a whole and as an interrelationship of all its parts. As Northrop Frye remarks, "the literal level of meaning, though it takes precedence over all other meanings, lies outside the province of criticism. Understanding a verbal structure literally is the incommunicable act of total apprehension which precedes criticism" (In *Kenyon Review:* Spring 1950). I think this principle needs to be qualified by certain exceptions, such as Henry James whose literal level in his richest works is itself ambiguous.

(3)

I did not know about Rahv's *Kenyon Review* attack on me until I read about it much later in an editorial taking issue with his essay and making some remarks in my defense: "If Mr. Stallman's discovery of symbols in Crane and Conrad went too far for the sensibility of Mr. Rahv, Stallman is still probably nearer the truth about these two authors than Mr. Rahv who, by implication, seems to be saying that there is little or no symbolism" (in *Western Review:* Summer, 1956). He wants to argue that if Crane's *Red Badge* is symbolic, "it is in the patent sense in which all good art, in so far as it opens out to the world at large . . . can be said to be symbolic. But to attribute a symbolic character to Crane's novel in this universal sense has nothing whatever to do with Mr. Stallman's idea of symbolism, an idea indistinguishable from the 'fallacy of misplaced concreteness,' systematically applied to works of literature." If Rahv will look into my Crane *Omnibus* he will find that I have not neglected to discuss the symbolic import of *The Red Badge;* I have also discussed the literal reading of *The Red Badge* as plainly a war novel. Rahv has based his attack on an early Crane essay of mine which appeared in *Critiques and Essays on Modern Fiction,* without having taken the trouble to look into *Stephen Crane: An Omnibus,* which appeared later that same year (1952).

He accuses me of erecting my interpretation of *The Red Badge* solely on the basis of a single image, but the fact is that he himself dismisses my interpretation on the basis of a single image (*i.e.,* the red sun "pasted in the sky like a wafer"). On the basis of a single image extracted from my interpretation of Conrad's "The Secret Sharer," he dismisses my reading of Conrad. And on the basis of a single image separated from the context of Crane's "The Open Boat," he dismisses my interpretation of Crane.

He quotes nothing of my reading of Conard's "The Secret Sharer" but a single passage in which I suggested a diagram for the story. By some coincidence it is the same passage that the *Hudson Review* critic had quoted. But I had already expunged this passage from subsequent reprintings of my essay, over a decade ago. It appeared originally in *Forms of Modern Fiction;* it does not appear in the text of *Art of Modern Fiction,* nor in the periodical publication of my essay in *Accent* for Spring of 1949.

He indicts my interpretation of *The Red Badge* because of the way I interpreted "The red sun was pasted in the sky like a wafer." He contends that in the first edition of Crane's novel the word "wafer" was preceded by the word "fierce." What this tells me is that Rahv has not looked at the reconstructed texts of *The Red Badge* as presented from the original manuscripts in my Crane *Omnibus.* The hard fact is that the word "fierce" preceded the word "wafer" in the shortened newspaper version (1894), but this is not the first edition of *The Red Badge.* The word "fierce" was expunged from the first edition (1895) and did not appear in any subsequent American edition until the *Omnibus,* where it is given in brackets as follows: "The [fierce *cancelled*] red sun was pasted in the sky like a fierce wafer." Scholarship is the prerequisite of the critic; able critics check on their facts.

"The absurdity of Mr. Stallman's reading of Crane becomes all too apparent," says Rahv, "when you look up the text to check on his quotations." "Moreover, in the first edition of the novel 'wafer' was preceded by 'fierce,' a modifier hardly suggestive of the Christian communion." Crane's notorious metaphor, notorious inasmuch as it has been ridiculed or praised by a dozen critics before my own appearance on the scene, is used at a crucial point in the narrative, the death of Jim Conklin, and it is used with symbolic intent—the wafer of the Mass. Rahv argues that the word "fierce" is proof against my reading, by which the novel "is transmogrified into a religious allegory."[6]

Apparently Crane thought first of the red sun as "fierce," and then added the same epithet to "wafer" so as to give "wafer" the same attribute. A wafer is conceivably fierce when it is emblematic of the dying God. Red connotes the red wine of the sacrament—the white wafer which was to have been the flesh has been saturated by the red of Christ's blood. And I might mention that Isaac Rosenfeld wrote in his review of the Crane *Omnibus* which appeared in the pages of this journal: "Mr. Stallman remarks of this simile, 'I do not think it can be doubted that Crane intended to suggest here the sacrificial death celebrated in the Communion.' I, for one, do not doubt it, and even if the statement about Crane's *intention* can never be verified, one cannot deny that the line in question functions in this manner."

Rahv also quotes and comments on a passage from my *Critiques* essay on Crane: "In 'The Open Boat' the paradox of 'cold, comfortable sea-water' [is] an image which calls to mind the poetry of W. B. Yeats with its fusion of contradictory emotions. This single image evokes the sensation of the whole experience of the men in the boat. . . . What is readily recognizable in this paradox of 'cold, comfortable sea-water' is that irony of opposites which constituted the personality of the man who wrote it." Rahv thinks this represents a "wholesale disgorgement of shibboleths lifted from contemporary poetry-criticism"; he seems to me not only absurd in his turn but arrogant. I am accused of having made this image paradoxical by sequestering it from its context in Crane's story; "but in point of fact within the context of the story the juxtaposition of 'cold' and 'comfortable' cannot strike us as paradoxical but rather as wholly natural." On the contrary, I think it must be read as paradoxical if you do not sequester it from its context. For this image shares with other images in "The Open Boat" a mockery of the plight of the men in their God-forsaken dinghy. Does the imagery throughout the story carry an ironic intent? I think it does, and I believe that I can prove it.

Rahv's literal reading ignores the over-all play of Crane's ironic point-of-view through which this image must be read. Establish this relationship and you cannot fail to see that the image of "cold, comfortable sea-water" represents that contradiction of emotions or paradox which I've ascribed to it. The fact that the image is thus intended can be proven by establishing the ironic intent of the word "comfortable" as used elsewhere in the story. The men in the boat are mocked by the gulls sitting on the sea near patches of seaweed: "The birds sat *comfortably* in groups, and *they were envied* by some in the dinghy, for the wrath of the sea was no more to them than it was to a covey of prairie chickens a thousand miles inland." The men envy the gulls for being comfortable; hence their own plight, obversely, is uncomfortable and the sea-water in the boat is cold-comfortable therefore in the ironic sense. One of the gulls tries to alight upon the captain's head: "His black eyes were *wistfully* fixed upon the captain's head." The epithet "wistfully" transfers to the captain, for it is he and not the gull who is in fact thinking wistfully. The gull has no reason to think wistfully as he is already comfortably situated.

Again, Crane writes with irony: "It is almost certain that if the boat had capsized he would have tumbled *comfortably* out upon the ocean as if he felt sure that it was a great soft mattress." I don't see how it can be doubted that "comfortably" is here used ironically, and as in this instance so likewise in the above companion-images—notably in "cold, comfortable sea-water." What is meant, Mr. Rahv, is just the opposite of what is stated. Obviously, the ocean is anything but "a great soft mattress"; actually, were the men tumbled into the ocean they'd find its cold water "sad" and "tragic."

Rahv contends that "the water *in* the boat feels 'comfortable' as against the waves beating *at* the boat," that the water-in-the-boat "seems positively domesticated. Hence the adjective 'comfortable'." I shall answer this notion under two heads: (a) In what sense can the water at the bottom of the boat be considered more comfortable than the water outside? And (b) in what sense is it "domesticated"?

(a) Whereas the oiler, "a wily surfman," is the spokesman for the hard cruel facts and is the only realist in the group, the others are given to illusions. Even the hurt captain and the cynical correspondent are given to illusions. It is the correspondent who imagines the water-in-the-boat as comfortable (or, to be precise, as cold-comfortable). That he so imagines it is an ironic illusion, this one being patterned by all the other ironic illusions. No sooner is the correspondent spelled by Billie than he falls asleep, and he falls asleep not comfortably but "despite the fact that his teeth played all the popular airs." What Mr. Rahv, is *comfortable* about that?

Only to the gulls, Mr. Rahv, is the January sea-water (icy literally both in the boat and outside it) comfortable *naturally*.

(b) The cold boat-water seems to the correspondent "domesticated" not "positively" but rather ironically. You will notice that the men are given to domestic thoughts and that these domestic images mock their plight quite as much as do the comfortable gulls. The men are mocked also by the indifferent shore with its windmill turning its back upon their plight. Things viewed by the men at sea are viewed as though they were men on land. Thus the cold-comfortable sea-water image is patterned by the same ironic outlook as is everything else in the story, by the contrast between what is and what seems. Land images impinge upon their situation at sea; the waves seem like a mountain-cat, each crest seems but a hillside ("Viewed from a balcony"), seagulls remind them of a covey of prairie chickens a thousand miles inland, and their dinghy seems like a wild colt ridden by circus-men. They are so "comfortable" in the cramped and cold dinghy that even the icy sea-water seems "domesticated," but of course not literally so. Thus the ocean is said to be their mattress, two lights on the sea look like "the furniture of the world," and their grotesque domicile is even furnished with a stove, but of course not literally so. The cook "seemed almost stove-like." The stove-like shape of the cook provides the frozen correspondent a semblance of warmth and domesticity.

Non-literal readers will recognize the above items as metaphors having a grotesque ironic intent. Huddling against the stove-like shape of the cook provides the correspondent the only warmth that the icy boat-water affords; namely (1) on the literal level, a semblance of bodily warmth from huddling against the cook's cork lifebelt, and (2) on the spiritual level the warmth of brotherhood. While literally the boat-water is as cold as the ocean outside the boat, what makes the boat-water seem cold-comfortable is that brotherhood which their plight has effected in an otherwise uncomfortable dinghy. It is "comfortable" only in this spiritual sense, but even this is ironic; for their brotherhood is earned through the bitter experience of their plight. It is furthermore ironic because of the fact that the men in the boat cannot comprehend the full meaning of that brotherhood, the reality of it, until they are safe on land. And again it is ironic that even on land their comfort and their brotherhood are spoiled by grief at the loss of the oiler.

He alone held no illusions. And perhaps that is why he, the wily surf-man, meets his death on the surf. Or, as your literal reader will likely prefer, it is because Higgins, the original for Crane's oiler, met his death precisely in this way. (1957)

NOTES

1. In his *Conrad the Novelist* (1958). My review of his Conrad study in *Sewanee Review* (Winter 1959), "Conrad Criticism Today," forms part of my Introduction to *The Art of Joseph Conrad,* from which I have drawn the opening paragraphs of the present essay. "Fiction and Its Critics" restores portions which were expunged from *Kenyon Review* (Spring 1957).

2. In a deft demolition of Mudrick's notions about *The Nigger of the "Narcissus,"* Ian Watt in *Nineteenth Century Fiction* (March 1958) wrote: "But we must not overlook the fact that Mudrick, who cast himself as the spectral Mr. Jones interrupting the feast celebrating Conrad's victory over the critics, is also possessed of a marked cannibalistic trait. . . . In his earlier essay on Conrad, Stallman's reading of 'The Secret Sharer' was his main target; but he now finds *The Nigger of the 'Narcissus'* subject to the same general charge: a heavy overemphasis on 'catch-all' and 'claptrap' symbolism which only a naive predisposition for that sort of thing could possibly render acceptable." "It's a crackerjack," Stephen Crane wrote Hamlin Garland of Conrad's *The Nigger.* It takes a cracker-barrel critic to see it as anything else.

3. As Thomas Mann asserts, it is "a limitation of Conrad's fame to speak of him only as a writer of sea-tales." (In *A Critical Symposium,* p. 228) Conrad "disliked being labeled a novelist of the sea. He wrote of the sea, as perhaps no one, not even Herman Melville, has written; but dominant in all his writing of the sea is the note of struggle and escape. His hero is not the sea, but man in conflict with that cruel and treacherous element. Ships he loved, but the sea—no." John Galsworthy in *Two Essays on Conrad* (Privately Printed, Freelands, 1930, pp. 46-47).

4. Rahv's readers are misled into assuming that Mrs. Langer supports his literal-minded position, whereas she in fact takes just the opposite standpoint: "prose fiction is exactly as high and pure a creation as lyric poetry, or as drama . . . the prose writer chooses his words as precisely as the verse writer, and spins out his apparently casual lines just as carefully. A name or a turn of phrase may be the means of creating a setting or a situation at one stroke." In *Feeling and Form* (1933), p. 297.

5. "One can understand why William Faulkner, in that famous interview at a Southern university, said that he 'rated Wolfe first' among his contemporaries. He was expressing the admiration of one hard-working 'writin' man' for another. We all fail, said Faulkner, but Wolfe 'made the best failure because he tried hardest to say the most.' It seems ungracious, in the face of that tribute, to worry the matter further, but worry it we must. The criticism of literature, if it is to be of any value at all, demands the application of critical standards. . . . Wolfe was not an artist but a suffering soul with a gift of gab." I am quoting here from "The Colossus of Asheville," London *Times Literary Supplement,* September 26, 1958. The reviewer adds:

"We are asked to consider Wolfe as a novelist, and an important one at that. The answer is that we cannot. . . . In Europe the Dreisers and the Wolfs would have been sat upon as writers in the early stages and they would either have learnt how to write or turned their undoubtedly great talents to some other field. However, the American system, tolerant as no other, let them through, and so they struggled in a branch of literature which they never really mastered. This, in a sense, is the American literary story all through, and the result is the most eccentric, the most half-baked, and at times, the most genuine, the most moving and the most felicitous writing of modern times. But simply because America presents us with such phenomena we cannot let standards of judgment go by the board. We can hardly say of Wolfe, as the *Literary History of the United States* says of Dreiser, 'Forgetful of the integrity and power of [his] whole work, many critics have been distracted into a condemnation of his style.' Distracted, indeed. Do we really need to say it? 'Le style, c'est l'homme même.' If it is literature we are discussing, then certain criteria apply, as who should know better than a nation which has bred a Hawthorne, a James and a Faulkner." Or a Stephen Crane, I would add; or a Scott Fitzgerald, or a Hemingway? Etc.

6. In a new edition of *The Red Badge* (Harper's Classics, published January 1957), Daniel G. Hoffman echoes, buttresses, and extends my interpretation. Mr. Hoffman's reading of Crane's novel stands in agreement with my theory that Jim Conklin, with his tall spectral bearing, his wounded side and bloody hand, and the very initials of his name, is intended to represent Jesus Christ, that the religious symbolism radiates outward from Conklin, and that the religious symbols reach their climax in the famous metaphor which makes a sacrament of the death of the Son: "The red sun was pasted in the sky like a wafer." Hoffman adds that *The Red Badge*, "then, is an apocalyptic novel in which war is not so much the subject as the source of the governing metaphors." He adds: "But why should Crane choose war as the occasion of the Second Coming (a choice which Faulkner, in *A Fable,* has recently repeated)? Because in war man must most clearly endure the chastisements of the God who is as unmerciful as He is just. . . . This vengeful and merciless God is the Lord preached by Crane's mother's family, evangelical Methodists from the western frontier of New York State. From his kindly father, on the other hand, Crane learned of the redemptory Divine Grace offered through Christ to all men." In sum, Crane brings together the martial and religious strains in his own family heritage.

BIBLIOGRAPHICAL NOTE

I

"The Houses That James Built—*The Portrait of a Lady"* was read in much shortened form on the Program in Criticism at the University of Texas (1957) and at the Instituto Universitario Orientale of Naples and at the Università degli Studi of Bologna (1958). Also at the Universities of Lausanne, Geneva, Bern, and at the Anglo-Swiss Club of St. Gall and at the Swiss-American Society of Basle, Switzerland (1959). Also at the Universities of Ljubjlana and Zagreb, Yugoslavia (1959). The essay was published in shortened form in *Texas Quarterly,* Vol. I, No. 4 (Winter 1958-59), with an errata note in the following issue. The present essay includes unpublished portions.

" 'The Sacred Rage': The Time-Theme in *The Ambassadors"* was published in *Modern Fiction Studies:* Henry James Special Number: Spring 1957. A much condensed version appears as afterword in my edition of

The Ambassadors (New American Library, February 1960). The present essay is recast with new materials.

"A Note on the Text of *The Ambassadors*" is drawn from my Note in the New American Library edition of *The Ambassadors* (1960), which text reproduces the Methuen 1903 text for the first time. The present Note is an expanded version.

"Hardy's Hour-Glass Novel" was published in *Sewanee Review:* Spring 1947.

"Crane's *Maggie in Review*" appears here for the first time.

"Crane's *Maggie:* A Reassessment" was published in *Modern Fiction Studies:* Stephen Crane Special Number: Autumn 1959. The original short version appeared in *New Republic* for September 19, 1955: "Stephen Crane's Primrose Path."

The Red Badge of Courage essay draws from *Stephen Crane: An Omnibus,* edited, with Introductions and Notes, by R. W. Stallman (Knopf 1952, Heinemann 1954). "Notes Toward an Analysis of *The Red Badge of Courage*" was first published in my Introduction to the Modern Library edition of *The Red Badge of Courage* (Random House, 1951). It was reprinted—virtually unchanged but with added commentaries—in "Stephan Crane: A Revaluation," in *Critiques and Essays on Modern Fiction, 1920-1951,* edited by John Aldridge (Ronald Press, 1952), and again in *Stephen Crane: An Omnibus* (1952), again with added commentaries. The original Modern Library Introduction was reprinted in *The Red Badge of Courage: Text and Criticism,* edited by Richard Lettis and others (Harcourt, Brace, 1960).

"Crane's Short Stories" draws from the Introductions in *Omnibus.*

"Time and *The Secret Agent*" was read in shortened form on the Program in Criticism at the University of Texas and at the University of Missouri (1957); also at Connecticut College (1958). My interpretation was first made in 1951 in my graduate seminar on modern fiction, and in subsequent seminars various first drafts of my essay were mimeographed and distributed to my students. The key idea (I find now) is given in William York Tindall's *The Literary Symbol* (1955): "the attempt on the Greenwich observatory, which marks our time, becomes an attempt on time, space, and navigation." I did not come upon this Tindall insight until 1959, when I obtained the paperback edition of *The Literary Symbol* (Indiana University Press, 1958). My essay was published in *Texas Studies in Literature and Language,* Vol. I, No. 1 (Spring 1959); it is reprinted here from *The Art of Joseph Conrad: A Critical Symposium,* edited by R. W. Stallman (Michigan State University Press, 1960).

"Gatsby and the Hole in Time—*The Great Gatsby*" was first published in *Modern Fiction Studies,* Vol. I, No. 4 (November 1955).

"Conrad and *The Great Gatsby*" was first published in *Twentieth Century Literature,* Vol. I, No. 1 (Spring 1955).

"By the Dawn's Early Light *Tender is the Night*" is published here for the first time.

"The Sun Also Rises—But No Bells Ring" was read in shortened form as a program lecture for the exhibit "Les Années Vingt/Les Écrivains Américains à Paris et Leurs Amis/1920-1930"—at Centre Culturel Américain, Paris (April 1959). It was also read at the Universities of Ljubljana and Zagreb, Yugoslavia (May 1959). It is published here for the first time.

"A New Reading of 'The Snows of Kilimanjaro' " is published here for the first time.

"A Cryptogram: *As I Lay Dying*" is published here for the first time.

II

"The New Critics" was first published in *A Southern Vanguard*, edited by Allen Tate (Prentice-Hall, 1947). In revised form it was reprinted in *Critiques and Essays in Criticism: 1920-1948*, edited by R. W. Stallman, (Ronald Press, 1949).

"Fiction and Its Critics" was first published in *Kenyon Review:* Spring 1957. The present essay includes unpublished portions, expunged from *Kenyon Review*.

"Some Rooms From The Houses That James Built"—reconstructed from my essay "The Houses That James Built—*The Portrait of a Lady*—appeared in Peter Buitenhuis' edition of Twentieth Century Interpretations of *The Portrait of a Lady* (1968).

"The Sacred Rage: The Time-Theme in *The Ambassadors*" was reprinted —in somewhat shortened form—in *Aspects of Time*, ed. by C. A. Patrides (Manchester, England; Toronto, Canada, 1976).

Related to my studies of Henry James's novels are two notes: "Time and the Unnamed Article in *The Ambassadors*," *Modern Language Notes*, 72 (1957) 27-32. And "Time and Mrs. Newsome's Blue Message: A Reply to Leon Edel," *Modern Language Notes*, 76 (1961), 20-23.

Related to my essay on *The Portrait of a Lady*, but not reprinted in *The Houses That James Built* is an article concerned with the identity of Gilbert Osmond. It reproduces in photograph the oil painting of Henry Brewster, the original for Henry James's Gilbert Osmond. "Who Was Gilbert Osmond?" was published in *Modern Fiction Studies*, 4 (1958), 127-135.

My essay on *The Portrait of a Lady* was reprinted as Preface to the Limited Editions Club Edition of *The Portrait of a Lady* (1967).

"Hardy's Hour-Glass Novel" (1947) was reprinted in *The Return of the Native*, ed. by James Gindin (Norton Critical Edition, 1969), pp. 469-475.

"Crane's *Maggie* in Review," first published in *The Houses That James Built And Other Literary Studies* (1961), was reprinted in *Studies in Maggie and George's Mother*, ed. by Stanley Wertheim (1970), pp. 14-24. In the same *Studies*, pp. 118-120, is my Note on *George's Mother* (1952).

"Crane's *Maggie:* A Reassessment" (1959) was reprinted first in *The Houses* and then in *Maggie: Text and Context*, ed. by Maurice Bassan (1966), pp. 368-391.

"Stephen Crane: A Revaluation," first published in *Critiques and Essays on Modern Fiction: 1920-1951*, ed. by John Aldridge (1952) and in my *Stephen Crane: An Omnibus* (1952), was reprinted in *The Red Badge of Courage, An Authoritative Text/Backgrounds and Sources/Criticism*, ed. by Bradley, Beatty, and Long (Norton Critical Edition, 1962); pp. 195-205 in Second Edition (1976).

My Introduction to the Modern Library Edition of *The Red Badge of Courage* (1951), which became a much extended version in "Stephen Crane: A Revaluation" in *Critiques* and in *Omnibus* (1952), was reprinted —translated into the Greek—for an edition of Crane's war novel in Athens (1956). It appeared in an undated edition of *The Red Badge of Courage* in Thailand (1952 ?). It was translated into the German for a German edition in Frankfurt (1971). *La Insignia Roja del Valor Y Otros Relatos*, which reprinted my *Omnibus* reading of Crane, translated by Miguel Ehrlich, was published in Buenos Aires (1967).

The Modern Library Introduction was reprinted in *The Red Badge of Courage: Text and Criticism*, ed. by Richard Lettis and others (Harcourt,

1960). My "Notes Toward an Analysis of *The Red Badge of Courage*" (a portion of my 1951 Introduction to that book, (Modern Library Edition) was reprinted in *Adventures in American Literature,* ed. by James Early (1968). This essay was translated into the Indian language and published in an unnamed magazine sponsored by the U. S. Information Agency in India.

My notes on "The Blue Hotel," recast from the Crane *Omnibus,* appear in *The Houses* (under "Crane's Short Stories") and were reprinted in *Stephen Crane: The Blue Hotel,* ed. by Joseph Katz (1969), pp. 482-483.

"Note on the Texts of *Maggie* and *The Red Badge of Courage*" appeared in *Stephen Crane: The Red Badge of Courage and Other Stories* (London, Oxford University Press, The World's Classics, 1960; paperback 1969). Its Introduction by V. S. Pritchett, pp. vii-xiii, although a very short note, is richly rewarding.

"Time and *The Secret Agent*" was reprinted from *The Houses That James Built* (1961) in *Joseph Conrad: A Collection of Criticism,* ed. by Frederick R. Karl (1975), pp. 59-81.

In *Conradiana,* 6 (Spring 1974) I published "Checklist of Some Studies of Conrad's *The Secret Agent* Since 1960," and then in *Conradiana,* 6 (Summer 1974) I published in essay form a variant version: "Studies of Conrad's *The Secret Agent* Since 1960."

Not reprinted in *The Houses,* but related to the above Conradiana, is "Conrad and The Secret Sharer," reprinted from *Accent* (1949) in my edited collection, *The Art of Joseph Conrad* (1960) and in Bruce Harkness's *Joseph Conrad's The Secret Sharer, and the Critics* (1961).

****

Here I wish to express my gratitude to the University of Connecticut Research Foundation for grants aiding me in research costs and recently for grants aiding the publication costs of reissuing in paperback *Stephen Crane: A Biography* (Braziller, 1968, 1973) and *The Houses That James Built* (1961, 1977).